Worlds of Color

THE OXFORD W. E. B. DU BOIS

Henry Louis Gates, Jr., Editor

The Suppression of the African Slave-Trade to the United States of America: 1638–1870
    Introduction: Saidiya Hartman

The Philadelphia Negro: A Social Study
    Introduction: Lawrence Bobo

The Souls of Black Folk
    Introduction: Arnold Rampersad

John Brown
    Introduction: Paul Finkelman

Africa, Its Geography, People and Products
Africa—Its Place in Modern History
    Introductions: Emmanuel Akyeampong

Black Reconstruction in America
    Introduction: David Levering Lewis

Black Folk: Then and Now
    Introduction: Wilson J. Moses

Dusk of Dawn
    Introduction: Kwame Anthony Appiah

The World and Africa
Color and Democracy: Colonies and Peace
    Introductions: Mahmood Mamdani and *Gerald Horne*

In Battle for Peace: The Story of My Eighty-third Birthday
    Introduction: Manning Marable

The Black Flame Trilogy: Book One
The Ordeal of Mansart
    Introduction: Brent Edwards
    Afterword: Mark Sanders

The Black Flame Trilogy: Book Two
Mansart Builds a School
   Introduction: Brent Edwards
   Afterword: Mark Sanders

The Black Flame Trilogy: Book Three
Worlds of Color
   Introduction: Brent Edwards
   Afterword: Mark Sanders

Autobiography of W. E. B. Du Bois
   Introduction: Werner Sollors

The Quest of the Silver Fleece
   Introduction: William L. Andrews

The Negro
   Introduction: John K. Thornton

Darkwater: Voices from Within the Veil
   Introduction: Evelyn Brooks Higginbotham

Gift of Black Folk: The Negroes in the Making of America
   Introduction: Glenda Carpio

Dark Princess: A Romance
   Introduction: Homi K. Bhabha

The Black Flame Trilogy: Book Three
WORLDS OF COLOR

W. E. B. Du Bois

Series Editor, Henry Louis Gates, Jr.

Introduction by Brent Edwards

Afterword by Mark Sanders

OXFORD
UNIVERSITY PRESS

For Cornel West

OXFORD
UNIVERSITY PRESS

Oxford University Press, Inc., publishes works that further
Oxford University's objective of excellence in research,
scholarship, and education.

Oxford   New York
Auckland   Cape Town   Dar es Salaam   Hong Kong   Karachi
Kuala Lumpur   Madrid   Melbourne   Mexico City   Nairobi
New Delhi   Shanghai   Taipei   Toronto

With offices in
Argentina   Austria   Brazil   Chile   Czech Republic   France   Greece
Guatemala   Hungary   Italy   Japan   Poland   Portugal   Singapore
South Korea   Switzerland   Thailand   Turkey   Ukraine   Vietnam

Copyright © 2007 by Oxford University Press

Published by Oxford University Press, Inc.
198 Madison Avenue, New York, NY 10016
www.oup.com

Oxford is a registered trademark of Oxford University Press

All rights reserved. No part of this publication may be reproduced,
stored in a retrieval system, or transmitted, in any form or by any means,
electronic, mechanical, photocopying, recording, or otherwise,
without the prior permission of Oxford University Press.

Library of Congress Cataloging-in-Publication Data is available.

ISBN: 978-0-19-938726-7

TO ARTHUR EDWARD McFARLANE II

My Great Grandson

Contents

SERIES INTRODUCTION: THE BLACK LETTERS ON THE SIGN ... xi

INTRODUCTION ... xxv

    I. THE AMERICAN NEGRO'S WORLD ... 1

    II. THE COLOR OF ENGLAND ... 12

    III. THE COLOR OF EUROPE ... 21

    IV. THE COLOR OF ASIA ... 38

    V. COLOR IN THE WEST INDIES ... 44

    VI. THE CONFERENCE ... 52

    VII. THE SOUTHERN WORKER ... 61

    VIII. THE FREE NORTH ... 68

    IX. THE ITINERANT PREACHER ... 86

    X. BISHOP WILSON ... 97

    XI. AGAIN WORLD WAR ... 108

    XII. BLACK AMERICA FIGHTS AGAIN ... 124

    XIII. ROOSEVELT DIES ... 134

    XIV. THE NATIONS UNITE ... 144

    XV. THE ATTACK ON MANSART ... 158

XVI. THE DISMISSAL OF JEAN DU BIGNON	170
XVII. ADELBERT MANSART AND JACKIE CARMICHAEL	186
XVIII. BACK TO AFRICA	198
XIX. THE SANCTUARY OF MARRIAGE	209
XX. DEATH	223
AFTERWORD	241
WILLIAM EDWARD BURGHARDT DU BOIS: A CHRONOLOGY	257
SELECTED BIBLIOGRAPHY	265

The Black Letters on the Sign: W. E. B. Du Bois and the Canon

"... the slave master had a direct interest in discrediting the personality of those he held as property. Every man who had a thousand dollars so invested had a thousand reasons for painting the black man as fit only for slavery. Having made him the companion of horses and mules, he naturally sought to justify himself by assuming that the negro was not much better than a mule. The holders of twenty hundred million dollars' worth of property in human chattels procured the means of influencing press, pulpit, and politician, and through these instrumentalities they belittled our virtues and magnified our vices, and have made us odious in the eyes of the world. Slavery had the power at one time to make and unmake Presidents, to construe the law, and dictate the policy, set the fashion in national manners and customs, interpret the Bible, and control the church; and, naturally enough, the old masters set themselves up as much too high as they set the manhood of the negro too low. Out of the depths of slavery has come this prejudice and this color line. It is broad enough and black enough to explain all the malign influences which assail the newly emancipated millions to-day. . . . The office of color in the color line is a very plain and subordinate one. It simply advertises the objects of oppression, insult, and persecution. It is not the maddening liquor, but the black letters on the sign telling the world where it may be had . . . Slavery, stupidity, servility, poverty, dependence, are undesirable conditions. When these shall cease to be coupled with color, there will be no color line drawn."

—Frederick Douglass, "The Color Line," 1881.

William Edward Burghardt Du Bois (1868–1963) was the most prolific and, arguably, the most influential African American writer of his generation. The novelist and poet James Weldon Johnson (1871–1938) once noted the no single work had informed the shape of the African American literary tradition, except perhaps *Uncle Tom's Cabin*, than had Du Bois's seminal collection of essays *The Souls of Black Folk* (1903). While trained as a sociologist at Berlin and as a historian at Harvard, Du Bois was fearless in the face of genre—even when some of the genres that he sought to embrace did not fully embrace him in return. Du Bois published twenty-two single-author works, twenty-one in his lifetime (his *Autobiography*, edited by his friend and literary executor, Herbert Aptheker, would not be published until

1968). A selection of his greatest works, *An ABC of Color: Selections from over a Half Century of the Writings of W. E. B. Du Bois*, appeared in 1963, the year he died. And while these books reflect a wide variety of genres—including three widely heralded and magisterial books of essays published in 1903, 1920, and 1940 (*The Souls of Black Folk*, *Darkwater: Voices from within the Veil*, and *Dusk of Dawn: An Essay toward an Autobiography of a Race Concept*), one biography, five novels, a pioneering sociological study of a black community, five books devoted to the history of Africa, three historical studies of African American people, among others—Du Bois was, in the end, an essayist, an essayist of the first order, one of the masters of that protean form that so attracted Du Bois's only true antecedent, Frederick Douglass (1818–1895) as well as Du Bois's heir in the history of the form, James Baldwin (1924–1987). (Baldwin, like Du Bois, would turn repeatedly to fiction, only to render the form as an essay.)

Du Bois, clearly, saw himself as a man of action, but a man of action who luxuriated within a verdant and fecund tropical rainforest of words. It is not Du Bois's intoxication with words that marks his place in the history of great black public intellectuals—persons of letters for whom words are a vehicle for political action and their own participation in political movements. After all, one need only recall Du Bois's predecessor, Frederick Douglass, or another of his disciples, Martin Luther King Jr. for models in the African American tradition of leaders for whom acting and speaking were so inextricably intertwined as to be virtually coterminous; no, the novelty of Du Bois's place in the black tradition is that he wrote himself to a power, rather than spoke himself to power. Both Douglass and King, for all their considerable literary talents, will be remembered always for the power of their oratory, a breathtaking power exhibited by both. Du Bois, on the other hand, was not a great orator; he wrote like he talked, and he talked like an extraordinarily well-educated late Anglo-American Victorian, just as James Weldon Johnson did; no deep "black" stentorian resonances are to be found in the public speaking voices of either of these two marvelous writers. Booker T. Washington (1856–1915) spoke in a similar public voice.

First and last, W. E. B. Du Bois was a writer, a writer deeply concerned and involved with politics, just as James Baldwin was; as much as they loved to write, Douglass and King were orators, figures fundamentally endowed with a genius for the spoken word. Even Du Bois's colleague, William Ferris, commented upon this anomaly in Du Bois's place in the tradition, at a time (1913) when he had published only five books: "Du Bois," Ferris wrote, "is one of the few men in history who was hurled on the throne of leadership by the dynamic force of the written word. He is one of the few writers who leaped to the front as a leader and became the head of a popular movement through impressing his personality upon men by means of a book" ("The African Abroad," 1913). Despite the fact that Du Bois by this time had published his Harvard doctoral dissertation in history, *The Suppression of the African Slave-Trade* (1896), his sociological study, *The Philadelphia Negro* (1899), *The Souls of Black Folk* (1903), the sole biography that he would publish, *John Brown* (1909), and his first of five novels, *The Quest of the Silver Fleece* (1911), Ferris attributed Du Bois's catapult to leadership to one book and one book alone, *The Souls of Black Folk*. Indeed, it is probably true that had Du Bois published this book alone, his place in the canon of African American literature would have been secure, if perhaps not as fascinating!

The Souls of Black Folk, in other words, is the one book that Du Bois wrote which most of us have read in its entirety. It is through *The Souls of Black Folk* that we center Du Bois's place in the literary canon; it is through *Souls* that we structure the arc of his seven decade career as a man of letters. There are many good reasons for the centrality of this magical book to Du Bois's literary career, but it is also the case that the other works that comprise Du Bois's canon deserve fresh attention as a whole. And it is for this reason that my colleagues and I have embarked upon this project with Oxford University Press to reprint Du Bois's single-authored texts, and make them available to a new generation of readers in a uniform edition. The only other attempt to do so—Herbert Aptheker's pioneering edition of Du Bois's complete works, published in 1973—is, unfortunately, long out of print.

The Souls of Black Folk is such a brilliant work that it merits all of the attention that it has been given in the century since it was published. In April 1903, a thirty-five-year-old scholar and budding political activist published a 265 page book subtitled "Essays and Sketches," consisting of thirteen essays and one short story, addressing a wide range of topics, including the story of the freed slaves during Reconstruction, the political ascendancy of Booker T. Washington, the sublimity of the spirituals, the death of Du Bois's only son Burghardt, and lynching. Hailed as a classic even by his contemporaries, the book has been republished in no fewer than 120 editions since 1903. In fact, it is something of a rite of passage for younger scholars and writers to publish their take on Du Bois's book in new editions aimed at the book's considerable classroom market.

Despite its fragmentary structure, the book's disparate parts contribute to the sense of a whole, like movements in a symphony. Each chapter is pointedly "bicultural," prefaced by both an excerpt from a white poet and a bar of what Du Bois names "The Sorrow Songs" ("some echo of haunting melody from the only American music which welled up from black souls in the dark past.") Du Bois's subject was, in no small part, the largely unarticulated beliefs and practices of American Negroes, who were impatient to burst out of the cotton fields and take their rightful place as Americans. As he saw it, African American culture in 1903 was at once vibrant and disjointed, rooted in an almost medieval agrarian past and yet fiercely restive. Born in the chaos of slavery, the culture had begun to generate a richly variegated body of plots, stories, melodies, and rhythms. In *The Souls of Black Folk*, Du Bois peered closely at the culture of his kind, and saw the face of black America. Actually, he saw two faces. "One ever feels his two-ness—an American, a Negro," Du Bois wrote. "Two souls, two thoughts, two unreconciled strivings; two warring ideals in one dark body, whose dogged strength alone keeps it from being torn asunder." He described this condition as "double consciousness," and his emphasis on a fractured psyche made *Souls* a harbinger of the modernist movement that would begin to flower a decade or so later in Europe and in America.

Scholars, including Arnold Rampersad, Werner Sollors, Dickson Bruce, and David Levering Lewis, have debated the origins of Du Bois's use of the concept of "double consciousness," but what's clear is that its roots are multiple, which is appropriate enough, just as it is clear that the source of one of Du Bois's other signal metaphors—"the problem of the twentieth-century is the problem of the color line"—came to him directly from Frederick Douglass's essay of that title. Du Bois had studied in Berlin during a Hegel revival, and Hegel, famously, had written on the relationship between master and bondsman, whereby each defines himself through the recognition of the other. But the concept comes up, too, in Emerson, who wrote in 1842 of the split between our reflective self, which wanders through the realm of ideas, and the active self, which dwells in the here and how, a tension that recurs throughout the Du Bois oeuvre: "The worst feature of this double consciousness is that the two lives, of the understanding and of the soul, which we lead, really show very little relation to each other."

Even closer to hand was the term's appearance in late-nineteenth-century psychology. The French psychologist, Alfred Binet, writing in his 1896 book, *On Double Consciousness*, discusses what he calls "bipartititon," or "the duplication of consciousness": "Each of the consciousnesses occupies a more narrow and more limited field than if there existed one single consciousness containing all the ideas of the subject." William James, who taught Du Bois at Harvard, talked about a "second personality" that characterized "the hypnotic trance." When Du Bois transposed this concept from the realm of the psyche to the social predicament of the American Negro, he did not leave it unchanged. But he shared with the psychologists the notion that double consciousness was essentially an affliction. "This American world," he complained, yields the Negro "no true self-consciousness, but only lets him see himself through the revelation of the other world. It is a peculiar sensation, this double-consciousness, this sense of always looking at one's self through the eyes of others, of measuring one's soul by the tape of a world that looks on in amused contempt and pity." Sadly, "the double life every American Negro must live, as a Negro and as an American," leads inevitably to "a painful self-consciousness, an almost morbid sense of personality and a moral hesitancy which is fatal to self-confidence." The result is "a double life, with double thoughts, double duties and double social classes," and worse, "double words and double ideas," which "tempt the mind to pretense or revolt, hypocrisy or to radicalism." Accordingly, Du Bois wanted to make the American Negro whole; and he believed that only desegregation and full equality could make this psychic integration possible.

And yet for subsequent generations of writers, what Du Bois cast as a problem was taken to be the defining condition of modernity itself. The diagnosis, one might say, outlasted the disease. Although Du Bois would publish twenty-two books, and thousands of essays and reviews, no work of his has done more to shape an African American literary history than *The Souls of Black Folk*, and no metaphor in this intricately layered book has proved more enduring than that of double consciousness, including Du Bois's other powerfully resonating metaphors, that of "the veil" that separates black America from white America, and his poignant revision of Frederick Douglass's metaphor of "the color line," which Du Bois employed in that oft-repeated sentence, "The problem of the twentieth-century is the problem of the color line"—certainly his most prophetic utterance of many.

Like all powerful metaphors, Du Bois's metaphor of double consciousness came to have a life of its own. For Carl Jung, who visited the United States in the heyday of the "separate but equal" doctrine, the shocking thing wasn't that black culture was not equal, the shocking thing was that is was not separate! "The naïve European," Jung wrote, "thinks of America as a white nation. It is not wholly white, if you please; it is partly colored," and this explained, Jung continued, "the slightly Negroid mannerisms of the American." "Since the Negro lives within your cities and even within your houses," Jung continued, "he also lives within your skin, subconsciously." It wasn't just that the Negro was an American, as Du Bois would note, again and again, but that the American was, inevitably and inescapably, a Negro. The bondsman and the slave find their identity in each other's gaze: "two-ness" wasn't just a black thing any longer. As James Baldwin would put it, "Each of us, helplessly and forever, contains the other—male in female, female in male, white in black, black in white."

Today, talk about the fragmentation of culture and consciousness is a commonplace. We know all about the vigorous intermixing of black culture and white, high culture and low—from the Jazz Age freneticism of what the scholar Ann Douglass calls "mongrel Manhattan" to Hip Hop's hegemony over American youth in the late-twentieth and early-twenty-first centuries. Du Bois yearned to make the American Negro one, and lamented that he was two. Today, the ideal of wholeness has largely been retired. And cultural multiplicity is no longer seen as the problem, but as a solution—a solution to the confines of identity itself. Double consciousness, once a disorder, is now the cure. Indeed, the only complaint we moderns have is that Du Bois was too cautious in his accounting. He'd conjured "two souls, two thoughts two unreconciled strivings." Just two, Dr. Du Bois, we are forced to ask today? Keep counting.

And, in a manner of speaking, Du Bois did keep counting, throughout the twenty two books that comprise the formal canon of his most cogent thinking. The hallmark of Du Bois's literary career is that he coined the metaphors of double-consciousness and the veil—reappropriating Frederick Douglass's seminal definition of the semi-permeable barrier that separates and defines black-white racial relations in America as "the color line"—to define the place of the African American within modernity. The paradox of his career, however, is that the older Du Bois became, the more deeply he immersed himself in the struggle for Pan-Africanism and decolonization against the European colonial powers, and an emergent postcolonial "African" or "Pan-Negro" social and political identity—culminating in his own life in his assumption of Ghanaian citizenship in 1963. And the "blacker" that his stand against colonialism became, the less "black," in a very real sense, his analysis of what he famously called "The Negro Problem" simultaneously became. The more "African" Du Bois became, in other words, the more cosmopolitan his analysis of the root causes of anti-black and -brown and -yellow racism and colonialism became, seeing the status of the American Negro as part and parcel of a larger problem of international economic domination, precisely in the same way that Frederick Douglass rightly saw the construction of the American color line as a function of, and a metaphor for, deeper, structural, economic relations—"not the maddening liquor, but the black letters on the sign telling the world where it may be had," as Douglass so thoughtfully put it. The Negro's being-in-the-world, we might say, became ever more complex for Du Bois the older he grew, especially as the Cold War heated up and the anti-colonial movement took root throughout Africa and the Third World.

Ironically, Du Bois himself foretold this trajectory in a letter he wrote in 1896, reflecting on the import of his years as a graduate student at Friedrich Wilhelm University in Berlin: "Of the greatest importance was the opportunity which my *Wanderjahre* [wander years] in Europe gave of looking at the world as a man and not simply from a narrow racial and provincial outlook." How does the greatest black intellectual in the twentieth century—"America's most conspicuously educated Negro," as Werner Sollors puts it in his introduction to Du Bois's *Autobiography* in this series—make the rhetorical turn from defining the Negro American as a metaphor for modernity, at the turn of the century, to defining the Negro—at mid-century—as a metonym of a much larger historical pattern of social deviance and social dominance that had long been central to the fabric of world order, to the fabric of European and American domination of such a vast portion of the world of color? If, in other words, the Negro is America's metaphor for Du Bois in 1903, how does America's history of black-white relations become the metaphor of a nefarious pattern of economic exploitation and dominance by the end of Du Bois's life, in 1963? Make no mistake about it: either through hubris or an uncanny degree of empathy, or a mixture of both, throughout his life, W. E. B. Du Bois saw his most naked and public ambitions as well as his most private and intimate anxieties as representative of those of his countrymen, the American Negro people. Nevertheless, as he grew older, the closer he approached the end of his life, Du Bois saw the American Negro as a metaphor for class relations within the wider world order.

In order to help a new generation of readers to understand the arc of this trajectory in Du Bois's thinking, and because such a large part of this major thinker's oeuvre remains unread, Oxford University Press and I decided to publish in a uniform edition the twenty-one books that make up Du Bois's canon and invited a group of scholars to reconsider their importance as works of literature, history, sociology, and political philosophy. With the publication of this series, Du Bois's books are once again in print, with new introductions that analyze the shape of his career as a writer, scholar, and activist.

Reading the canon of Du Bois's work in chronological order, a certain allegorical pattern emerges, as Saidiya Hartman suggests in her introduction to *The Suppression of the African Slave-Trade*. Du Bois certainly responded immediately and directly to large historical events through fierce and biting essays that spoke adamantly and passionately to the occasion. But he also used the themes of his books to speak to the larger import of those events in sometimes highly mediated ways. His first book, for example, proffers as its thesis, as Hartman puts it, a certain paradox: "the slave trade flourished under the guise of its suppression," functioning legally for twenty years following the Compromise of the Federal Convention of 1787 and "illegally for another half century." Moreover, Du Bois tackles this topic at precisely the point in American history when Jim Crow segregation is becoming formalized through American law in the 1890s, culminating in 1896 (the year of the publication of his first book) with the infamous *Plessy v. Ferguson* "separate but equal" decision of the Supreme Court—exactly twenty years following the end of Reconstruction. Three years later, as Lawrence Bobo shows, Du Bois publishes *The Philadelphia Negro* in part to detail the effects of the "separate but equal" doctrine on the black community.

Similarly, Du Bois's biography of John Brown appeared in the same year as a pioneering band of blacks and whites joined together to form the National Association for the Advancement of Colored People (NAACP), the organization that would plot the demise of legal segregation through what would come to be called the Civil Rights Movement, culminating in its victory over de jure segregation in the Supreme Court's *Brown v. Board of Education* decision, which effectively reversed the *Plessy* decision, and in the Civil Rights Act of 1964 and the Voting Rights Act of 1965. John Brown, for Du Bois, would remain the emblem of this movement.

Likewise, Du Bois's first novel, *The Quest of the Silver Fleece*, published just two years following his biography of John Brown, served as a subtle critique both of an unreflective assimilationist ideology of the early NAACP through its advocacy of "a black-owned farming cooperative in the heart of the deep South," as William Andrews puts it, just as it surely serves as a critique of Booker T. Washington's apparently radical notion that economic development for the newly freed slaves could very well insure political equality in a manner both irresistible and inevitable, an argument, mind you, frequently made today under vastly different circumstances about the role of capitalism in Du Bois's beloved Communist China.

Du Bois registers his critique of the primitivism of the Harlem Renaissance in *The Gift of Black Folk*, as Glenda Carpio cogently argues, by walking "a tightrope between a patriotic embrace of an America in which African American culture has become an inextricable part and an exhortation of the rebellion and struggle out of which that culture arose." In response to the voyeurism and faddishness of Renaissance Harlem, Du Bois harshly reminds us that culture is a form of labor, too, a commodity infinitely exploitable, and that the size of America's unprecedented middle class can be traced directly to its slave past: "It was black labor that established the modern world commerce which began first as a commerce in the bodies of the slaves themselves and was the primary cause of the prosperity of the first great commercial cities of our day"—cities such as New York, the heart of the cultural movement that some black intellectuals passionately argued could very well augur the end of racial segregation throughout American society, or at least segregation between equal classes across the color line.

Paul Finkelman, in his introduction to *John Brown*, quotes the book's first line: "The mystic spell of Africa is and ever was over all America." If that is true, it was also most certainly the case for Du Bois himself, as John Thornton, Emmanuel Akyeampong, Wilson J. Moses, and Mahmood Mamdani show us in their introductions to five books that Du Bois published about Africa, in 1915, 1930, 1939, and 1947. Africa, too, was a recurring metaphor in the Duboisian canon, serving variously as an allegory of the intellectual potential of persons of African descent; as John K. Thornton puts it, "What counted was that African history had movement and Africans were seen as historical actors and not simply as stolid recipients of foreign techniques and knowledge," carefully "integrating ancient Egypt into *The Negro* as part of that race's history, without having to go to the extreme measure of asserting that somehow the Egyptians were biologically identical to Africans from further south or west." The history of African civilization, in other words, was Du Bois's ultimate argument for the equality of Americans white and black.

Similarly, establishing his scholarly mastery of the literature of African history also served Du Bois well against ideological rivals such as Marcus Garvey, who attacked Du Bois for being "too assimilated," and "not black enough." Du Bois's various studies of African history also served as a collective text for the revolutions being formulated in the forties and fifties by Pan-African nationalists such as Kwame Nkrumah and Jomo Kenyatta, who would lead their nations to independence against the European colonial powers. Du Bois was writing for them, first as an exemplar of the American Negro, the supposed vanguard of the African peoples, and later, and more humbly, as a follower of the African's lead. As Wilson J. Moses notes, Du Bois once wrote that "American Negroes of former generations had always calculated that when Africa was ready for freedom, American Negroes would be ready to lead them. But the event was quite opposite." In fact, writing in 1925 in an essay entitled "Worlds of Color," an important essay reprinted as "The Negro Mind Reaches Out" in Alain Locke's germinal anthology *The New Negro* (as Brent Staples points out in his introduction to Du Bois's fifth novel, *Worlds of Color*, published just two years before he died), Du Bois had declared that "led by American Negroes, the Negroes of the world are reaching out hands toward each other to know, to sympathize, to inquire." And, indeed, Du Bois himself confessed at his ninety-first birthday celebration in Beijing, as Moses notes, that "once I thought of you Africans as children, whom we educated Afro-Americans would lead to liberty. I was wrong." Nevertheless, Du Bois's various books on Africa, as well as his role as an early theorist and organizer of the several Pan-African Congresses between 1900 and 1945, increasingly underscored his role throughout the first half of the century as the father of Pan-Africanism, precisely as his presence and authority within such civil rights organizations as the NAACP began to wane.

Du Bois's ultimate allegory, however, is to be found in *The Black Flame Trilogy*, the three novels that Du Bois published just before repatriating to Ghana, in 1957, 1959, and 1961. The trilogy is the ultimate allegory in Du Bois's canon because, as Brent Edwards shows us in his introductions to the novels, it is a fictional representation of the trajectory of Du Bois's career, complete with several characters who stand for aspects of Du Bois's personality and professional life, including Sebastian Doyle, who "not only studied the Negro problem, he embodied the Negro problem. It was bone of his bone and flesh of his flesh. It made his world and filled his thought," as well as Professor James Burghardt, trained as a historian at Yale and who taught, as Du Bois had, at Atlanta University, and who believed that "the Negro problem must no longer be regarded emotionally. It must be faced scientifically and solved by long, accurate and intense investigation. Moreover, it was not one problem, but a series of problems interrelated with the social problems of the world. He laid down a program of study covering a hundred years."

But even more important than these allegorical representations of himself, or early, emerging versions of himself, Du Bois used *The Black Flame* novels to underscore the economic foundation of anti-black racism. As Edwards notes, "The real villain," for Du Bois, "is not an individual Southern aristocrat or racist white laborer, but instead capitalism itself, especially in the corporate form that has dominated the economic and social landscape of the world for more than a century," which underscores Du Bois's ideological transformations from an integrationist of sorts to an emergent mode of African American, first, and then Pan-Africanist cultural nationalism, through socialism, landing squarely in the embrace of the Communist Party just two years before his death.

Despite this evolution in ideology, Mansart, Du Bois's protagonist in the triology, ends his series of intellectual transformations precisely where Du Bois himself began as he embarked upon his career as a professor just a year after receiving his Harvard PhD in 1895. In language strikingly familiar to his statement that the time he spent in Berlin enabled him to look "at the world as a man and not simply from a narrow racial and provincial outlook," Du Bois tells us in the final volume of the trilogy that Mansart "began to have a conception of the world as one unified dwelling place. He was escaping from his racial provincialism. He began to think of himself as part of humanity and not simply as an American Negro over against a white world." For all of his ideological permutations and combinations, in other words, W. E. B. Du Bois—formidable and intimidating ideologue and ferocious foe of racism and colonialism—quite probably never veered very far from the path that he charted for himself as a student, when he fell so deeply in love with the written word that he found himself, inevitably and inescapably, drawn into a life-long love affair with language, an affair of the heart to which he remained faithful throughout an eighty-year career as a student and scholar, from the time he entered Fisk University in 1885 to his death as the Editor of "The Encyclopedia Africana" in 1963. And now, with the publication of the Oxford W. E. B. Du Bois, a new generation of readers can experience his passion for words, Du Bois's love of language purely for its own sake, as well as a conduit for advocacy and debate about the topic that consumed him his entire professional life, the freedom and the dignity of the Negro.

✦ ✦ ✦

The first volume in the series is Du Bois's revised dissertation, and his first publication, entitled *The Suppression of the African Slave-Trade to the United States of America*. A model of contemporary historiography that favored empiricism over universal proclamation, *Suppression* reveals the government's slow movement toward abolition as what the literary scholar Saidiya Hartman calls in her introduction "a litany of failures, missed opportunities, and belated acts," in which a market sensibility took precedence over moral outrage, the combination of which led to the continuation of the Atlantic slave trade to the United States until it was no longer economically beneficial.

Lawrence D. Bobo, one of the foremost urban sociologists working today, argues in his introduction to *The Philadelphia Negro: A Social Study* (1899), that Du Bois was not only an innovative historian, as Hartman properly identifies him, but also a groundbreaking social scientist whose study of Philadelphia displays "the most rigorous and sophisticated social science of its era by employing a systematic community social survey method." Although it was well reviewed at its publication—which coincided with the advent of the field of urban sociology—*The Philadelphia Negro* did not become the subject of significant scholarly attention until the 1940s, and has become, since then, a model for the study of black communities.

The distinguished scholar of black literature and culture, Arnold Rampersad, calls *The Souls of Black Folk* "possibly the most important book ever penned by a black American"—an assertion with which I heartily agree. A composite of various essays, subjects, and tones, *Souls* is both very much of its time, and timeless. It contributed to the American lexicon two terms that have been crucial for more than a century in understanding the African American experience: the "color line" and "double consciousness." For Rampersad, that we have learned so much about both issues since Du Bois first wrote, but have not made either irrelevant to our twenty-first century experience is, in a real way, our scholarly blessing and burden.

Abandoning the scholarly and empirical prowess so vividly on display in *Suppression* and *Philadelphia Negro*, Du Bois meant his biography of John Brown to be not a work of scholarship but rather one "about activism, social consciousness, and the politics of race," argues the legal historian Paul Finkelman in his introduction to *John Brown* (1909). The only biography in Du Bois's vast oeuvre, the book grew out of his participation in the Niagara Movement's meeting at Harpers Ferry in 1906 (an event the centenary of which I had the good fortune to celebrate), and—with the myth of John Brown taking precedence at times over the facts of his life—marks Du Bois's transition from professional academic to full-time activist.

There was not a genre that Du Bois did not attempt in his long career as a writer. After the John Brown biography, Du Bois turned to the novel. In his introduction to *The Quest of the Silver Fleece* (1911), Du Bois's first novel, the literary historian William Andrews looks beyond the Victorian diction and sometimes purple prose to see a work that is the "most noteworthy Great *African American* Novel of its time." *Quest* is a "Southern problem" novel writ large on a national and even mythic canvas, and one that is ultimately radical in its endorsement of strong black womanhood, equality and comradeship between the sexes, and, in Du Bois's words, "a bold regeneration of the land," which for Andrews means a hitherto-unheard-of proposed economic alliance between poor blacks and poor whites in the rural South.

Moving from a national to an international canvas, Du Bois published *The Negro* (1915), more than half of which is devoted to African history. In this way, John K. Thornton argues in his introduction, Du Bois firmly grounded for an educated lay readership the history of African Americans in the history of Africa. Drawing on the emergent disciplines of anthropology and linguistics and including, even sketchily, accounts of what would now be called Diaspora communities in the Caribbean and Latin America, *The Negro* is important in that it presents, in Thornton's words, "African history [as having] movement and Africans . . . as historical actors and not simply as stolid recipients of foreign techniques and knowledge."

Dismissed by some critics and lauded by others as the "militant sequel" to *The Souls of Black Folk*, *Darkwater: Voices from Within the Veil* (1920) appeared in a world radically transformed by the ravages of World War I. In addition to these international upheavals, and to the "crossing and re-crossing" of the color line engendered by the war, the historian Evelyn Brooks Higginbotham tells us in her magisterial introduction to this volume that blacks at home in the U.S. faced major changes and relocations. The Great Migration was in full swing when Du Bois wrote *Darkwater*, and the change in the center of black life is reflected in the change of scene to the North, a far, urban cry from the rural setting of most of *Souls*. If *Souls* saw the American landscape in black and white, Higginbotham finds that *Darkwater* is like chiaroscuro, the painting technique developed by artists of the Italian Renaissance: "Du Bois, like these Renaissance painters, moves beyond the contouring line of the two-dimensional and introduces depth and volume through his representation of color—through his contrast and shading of white and various darker peoples." Higginbotham goes on to say that "Du Bois continually undermines the fixedness of racial boundaries and subverts the visual coherence of racial identities to an extent that cannot be accidental." The Du Bois who emerges in *Darkwater* is increasingly a citizen of the world, whose gaze may be fixed on his native land but whose understanding of that land is inextricably bound to the larger world around him.

The Gift of Black Folk (1924) had an odd genesis as part of the Knights of Columbus's series on "Racial Contributions to the United States." In her introduction, Glenda Carpio notes that Du Bois's celebration of black accomplishments did not turn away from the bitter history of slavery that spawned them: these were not gifts always rendered freely, Carpio points out. Though less substantial than many of his other works, and primarily a catalog of black accomplishments across different fields, *Gift* is notable for the complex ways Du Bois links African American contributions in the arenas of labor, war, church and social life, fraternal organizations, and especially the arts, by both women and men, to the bitter history of slavery.

Homi Bhabha sees *The Dark Princess* (1928) as another odd work, a "Bollywood-style Bildungsroman," in which the race-man Mathew Towns teams with Kautilya, the "dark Princess of the Tibetan Kingdom of Bwodpur," to combat international colonialism in the struggle for global emancipation. But in this somewhat messy novel, which renders the international scenes with a Zolaesque precision, Bhabha detects a serious philosophical purpose: to elaborate on the "rule of juxtaposition" (first defined in *Darkwater*), which "creat[es] an enforced intimacy, an antagonistic proximity, that defines the color-line as it runs across the uncivil society of the nation."

Du Bois moved from the esoteric exercise of *The Dark Princess* to a more accessible form for his next publications, *Africa, Its Geography, People and Products*, and

Africa—Its Place in Modern History (1930). Published as Blue Books for the educated lay reader by E. Haldeman-Julius of Girard, Kansas, the two volumes are, for the African historian and African Emmanuel Akyeampong, remarkably useful and trenchant. The first volume is a relatively straightforward analysis of Africa's geography, climate, and environment, and the impact these physical factors have had on the development of African civilization. The second volume, which seeks "to place the continent at the very center of ancient and modern history," is more polemical, with economics cited as the central motivating factor behind modern colonialism and the slave trade.

The anger that was evident in the second of the two Blue Books came to full flower in *Black Reconstruction* (1935), a sweeping corrective to contemporary histories of the Reconstruction era, which (white) historians had shaped with the view of blacks as inadequate to the task of capitalizing on the freedom that emancipation had given them, and black history as "separate, unequal, and irrelevant," in the words of Du Bois's Pulitzer Prize-winning biographer, David Levering Lewis. Inspired by *The Gift of Black Folk* and from Du Bois's own withdrawal of his article on the Negro in the *Encyclopedia Britannica*, which demanded an excision of "a paragraph on the positive Reconstruction role of black people," *Black Reconstruction* provided original interpretations of black labor's relation to industrial wealth and, most radically, of the *agency* of black people in determining their lives after the Civil War. In his introduction, Lewis contends, rightly, that the books marks a progression in Du Bois's thought, from his early faith in academic knowledge and empiricism as a cure-all for the nation's problems, to the "more effective strategy of militant journalism informed by uncompromising principles and vital social science."

Wilson J. Moses presents *Black Folk Then and Now* (1939) as a midway point between *The Negro* (1915) and *The World and Africa* (1946). While all three volumes sought to address the entire span of black history, the special mandate of *Black Folk* was to "correct the omissions, misinterpretations, and deliberate lies that [Du Bois] detected in previous depictions of the Negro's past." In this volume, he went back to the original Herodotus and provided his own translation, which led him to affirm, with other black writers, that the Egyptians were, indeed, black (a conclusion he had resisted earlier in his career). But even in this work, with such evidence of his intellectual background on display, Du Bois is less interested in intellectual history than in social history. Even as he tracks developments in the United States, the Caribbean, Latin America, Du Bois neglects the Pan-African movement and his own involvement in it.

Du Bois's autobiography, on the other hand, shows a man far more interested in writing about his intellectual journey than his personal or social life. The philosopher Anthony Appiah, in his subtle introduction to *Dusk of Dawn*, tells us that Du Bois was famous for nothing so much as his accomplishments as an intellectual and a writer; his institutional affiliations (with the NAACP, with the Pan-African Congress) were fleeting, and his internal contradictions were vexing (he was both a committed Socialist and a committed elitist). The aim of this account, like so much of Du Bois's other work, was to address the problem of the color line, and he presents his distinguished, singular life as emblematic of that problem, and himself as hopeful for its solution.

At the time he rejoined the NAACP to oversee its global programming in 1944, Du Bois was prepared to dedicate himself completely to the abolition of colonialism, which he saw as the driving force behind all global conflicts. What was remarkable about his anti-colonialism was, as Gerald Horne rightly points out in his introduction to *Color and Democracy* (1946), Du Bois's inclusion of Asia, and particularly Japan, in the discussion. As fertile ground for colonial enterprises, Asia yielded still more evidence of the "inviolate link between color and democracy."

Color continued to preoccupy Du Bois, and in *The World and Africa*, he attempted to correct the ways in which color (black) had affected history. Mahmood Mamdani tells us in his introduction that Du Bois's motivation in writing this somewhat hasty volume was to tell the story of "those left out of recorded history" and to challenge, in effect, "an entire tradition of history-writing ... modern European historiography." Du Bois was aware that this was just a beginning to a much larger project, to connect the history of Europe that dominated the academic discipline of history to events and progress in the world at large, including Africa.

In Battle for Peace: The Story of My 83rd Birthday features an embattled Du Bois enduring prosecution by (and eventually winning acquittal from) the federal government whose indictment of him as an unregistered agent for the Soviet Union was, according to Manning Marable, a trumped-up means by which to discredit the great black leader and frighten his fellow supporters of international peace into silence. It worked, at least in part: while Du Bois drew support from many international associations, the NAACP essentially abandoned him. Ten years later, in 1961, Du Bois would permanently leave the United States for Ghana.

Brent Hayes Edwards in his introduction calls the *Black Flame* trilogy of novels Du Bois's most neglected work. Written in the last few years of life, *The Ordeal of Mansart* (1957), *Mansart Builds a School* (1959), and *Worlds of Color* (1961) follow the life of Manuel Mansart from his birth in 1876 (the last year of Reconstruction) to his death in 1956, a period which spans his rise from a noted but provincial Southern educator to a self-educating citizen of the world of color. With its alternating apocalyptic and utopian tone, its depiction of real historical figures and events, and its thoughtful "animation of economic history and especially labor history," the *Black Flame* trilogy offers, according to Edwards, "the clearest articulation of Du Bois's perspective at the end of his life, and his reflections on an unparalleled career that had stretched from Reconstruction through the Cold War."

Du Bois was a largely marginalized figure in the last decade of his life, and his work published at that time, most notably the *Black Flame* trilogy, went into the critical and cultural abyss. Mark Sanders suggests that the "invisibility" of the trilogy, then and now, can be explained by an evolution in literary "taste" in the 1950s, wrought by new trends in literary criticism and magazine culture, the emergence of the Civil Rights Movement, and Du Bois's own development. Even if we have rejected in many real ways the ethos of the 1950s, for Sanders, our prescriptions for taste still owe a great deal to that decade.

Werner Sollors finds "four major narrative strains" in the posthumously published *Autobiography of W. E. B. Du Bois* (1968): the personal (including "startling" sexual revelations from the famously staid Du Bois); the academic, editorial, and organizational, in which his work is fully explored, and the political is always personal even while science and reason are held to be the solution to the race problem; the Communist, first as interested onlooker and then as Party member; and the elderly, in which an old man takes stock of contemporary youth culture with something of a jaundiced eye. Sollors suggests that far from being disjointed, the various strands of the *Autobiography* are united by Du Bois's ongoing quest for recognition. I would argue that there is nothing pathetic in this quest; it is simply the desire for respect from the society (black and white) that Du Bois spent his long life trying to understand.

Henry Louis Gates, Jr.
Cambridge, Massachusetts
December 7, 2006

Introduction

Brent Hayes Edwards, Rutgers University

In April 1925, W. E. B. Du Bois published an essay called "Worlds of Color" in the policy journal *Foreign Affairs*. A few months later he gave a revised version of the piece (retitled "The Negro Mind Reaches Out") to the philosopher Alain Locke for inclusion in *The New Negro*, Locke's indispensable anthology of Harlem Renaissance literature. Du Bois's contribution stands out in the collection not only for its attention to the sphere of politics but also for its explicit internationalism. The essay counsels that to understand the state of the world in the wake of World War I, we must direct our attention to the colonies of Africa and Asia, "the periphery of the vast circle, where unseen and inarticulate, the determining factors are at work." Such a "wide perspective" forces us to recognize that "empire is the heavy hand of capital abroad." Linking domestic economic expansion to colonialism and trade in a single "field of inquiry," Du Bois strives to imagine a response to empire from the "shadows," in the form of the nascent nationalist and labor movements of the global South. For him, African American intellectuals are crucial catalysts in this organization of the "darker peoples of the world": "Led by American Negroes, the Negroes of the world are reaching out hands toward each other to know, to sympathize, to inquire."

More than three decades later, Du Bois recycled the essay's original title and geopolitical sweep for the third novel in *The Black Flame* trilogy. Published by Masses and Mainstream in April 1961, *Worlds of Color* opens when Manuel Mansart is sixty years old, a successful and established college president who finds himself compelled by a series of cataclysmic events to consider the wider world. Already in the second volume of the trilogy, *Mansart Builds a School* (1959), the educator is beginning to expand his horizons in order "to get some broad grasp of the world about him at this time. He took the *Crisis* and read each word each month." Now the task seems all the more pressing; as we read on the first page of *Worlds of Color*, "the First World War, the Depression and the New Deal had shaken Mansart to the depths of his being. All the old certainties were gone—all that neat little world with its good God, bad men and hovering angels."

In the spring of 1936, Mansart attends a conference of the presidents of the Negro land-grant colleges in the south. The fictional scene parallels an initiative spearheaded by Du Bois himself. In April 1941, with funding from the Carnegie

Foundation, Du Bois convened the First Phylon Conference of black educators, where he proposed a concentrated effort to agitate for an increased share of federal funding for black southern colleges with the goal of producing a collaborative series of sociological studies of black life in each state. In *Worlds of Color*, it is decided that Mansart will direct a similar project; at the same time, the educators come to the conclusion that Mansart should take a sabbatical and travel around the world, because "his education has been narrow" and he has little or no understanding of labor on a broader scale, or of the "problem of colonies in the world."

Du Bois was unable to complete the land-grant studies since he was forced to retire from Atlanta University in 1944, just after the project had been approved. He considered his ouster from Atlanta, and the lost opportunity to pursue the land-grant initiative (which collapsed without his support), to be a "catastrophe." Thus the first third of *Worlds of Color*—in which Mansart travels through England, France, Switzerland, Germany, Russia, China, and Japan, slowly gaining a sense of global politics—can be read as an attempt to imagine the kind of black educator who might have been able to pursue Du Bois's collaborative work in sociology. By the end of these chapters, after much reading and long discussions about class and color with a variety of Europeans and Asians, Mansart begins to escape his "racial provincialism" and to gain "a conception of the world as one unified dwelling place."

As the fiction draws closer to Du Bois's present, it comes to be crowded with what seems to be an ever-increasing population of historical characters (including Harry Hopkins, A. Philip Randolph, Felix Eboué, Hitler, Stalin, Alger Hiss, and Du Bois's second wife, Shirley Graham) and detailed descriptions of major events (including the 1936 Olympic Games in Berlin, World War II, the 1943 riots in Detroit, the 1945 Manchester Pan-African Congress, and the United Nations Conference in San Francisco). While in Paris, Mansart meets the great Trinidadian intellectual C. L. R. James, who tells him that "the slave trade and slavery were the economic basis of the French Revolution." There is violence and intrigue, especially in chapters thirteen and fourteen, when Mansart's grandson Adelbert becomes involved with an anti-imperialist pressure group in France, the Rassemblement Africain Démocratique, and ends up departing with a fierce Vietnamese revolutionary to work in Ghana. But *Worlds of Color* is above all a love story. After Mansart's first wife dies, a romance develops between the educator and his colleague Jean Du Bignon, despite their twenty-five-year difference in age.

Given the dedication of the first two novels of *The Black Flame* to Shirley Graham (*Worlds of Color* is dedicated to Du Bois's great-grandson), the relationship between Mansart and Jean immediately calls to mind Du Bois's own 1951 marriage to Graham, a much younger woman and an important intellectual in her own right. But the parallel is a complex one, first of all because Du Bois's character and career are reflected much more clearly in Jean Du Bignon than in Manuel Mansart. It is Du Bignon who plans the land-grant study, setting out "a tentative plan for cooperative, continuous sociological investigation in each state as a scientific beginning." It is Du Bignon who is harassed by the federal authorities during the Cold War and eventually prosecuted—and acquitted, as Du Bois himself was in 1951—for the trumped-up charge of failing to register as an "agent of a foreign power." It is she who is ousted from the college in the wake of the scandal over her trial, just as Du Bois had been removed from Atlanta University. Du Bignon tells Mansart that she has written a novel—a "semi-biography" of a woman "black but in appearance white," like Jean herself—that no publisher will accept (the initial fate of *The Black Flame*), and she reads him a passage from it. Thus if *The Black Flame* is "vicarious autobiography," as the critic Arnold Rampersad has described it, then the trilogy is a curious and perhaps surprising self-portrait.

The idyllic nature of the romance in *Worlds of Color* does not alleviate the darkness of the novel's overall tone. In a sense this quality is heightened as a result of the novel's shifting, fractured form; seemingly innocuous domestic interludes or stolid historical accounts give way to fleeting nightmares and gory hallucinations. In chapter eleven Mansart is taking a train to visit his son Revels in New York when he is overcome by a terrifying vision:

> The world swept by—the dark loafers at the stations—the white girls in the factories—the burdened wagons staggering along dusty roads. Then, suddenly, with startling clearness, out there in the night he seemed to see a great green Spider nestling in Hell, weaving an impenetrable Web. It sat in a pool of blood, which had gushed down from China, flowed in from Spain and seeped through from Mississippi. The Spider seemed to be spinning out thin tendrils of American gold, linking strand to strand. To the drying, stinking mess, the Spider added clods of British dirt and moistened all with the slime of France, until the spreading Web grew wide as the Earth and high as Heaven. It was too horrible. It seemed to divide the Darkness from the Light and the White World fought the Dark World and both faced Death.

This vision is never mentioned again in the novel. But as they erupt in the narrative time and again, these kind of unintegrated moments haunt the reader, not only because they are melodramatic and "horrible" but also because they seem to run so thoroughly contrary to the trilogy's progressive historical framing. If *The Black Flame* takes up history through the "fiction of interpretation," as Du Bois describes it in the "Postscript" to *The Ordeal of Mansart* (1957), then the trilogy continually reminds us of the "mess," the morass of human evil and suffering that cannot be explained or healed by the instrumental use of reason.

Worlds of Color concludes neither with revolutionary triumph nor with personal romance but instead with hesitation, doubt, and bleak portents of the future. Like Du Bois's *Dark Princess* in 1928, *Worlds of Color* culminates with a secret internationalist gathering of the "darker peoples of the world," a conclave of African, Caribbean, and African American dignitaries, political leaders, and intellectuals who meet one night in Rockefeller Center. But rather than the messianic fervor of Du Bois's earlier novel, there is a devastating anticlimax as the group is informed by a European princess that the meeting has been convened by the forces of white corporate supremacy, "the real rulers of one world," who demand the allegiance of the African diaspora in their efforts to "crush and beat back the crazy Chinese and Russian Communists." Mansart objects vehemently but finds himself alone, and he is led "unobtrusively" from the hall as the other guests acquiesce to their hosts' demands.

The scene occurs in the final chapter, which is titled simply "Death," and the trilogy ends with Mansart's demise. Earlier, in chapter nineteen, Jean has an apocalyptic vision of the "Black Flame," which here (as in the conclusion of *Mansart Builds a School*) represents the potential of black civilization, still deferred but destined one day to take its place "between the pillars of the universe." This apotheosis is never realized. On his deathbed Mansart has two visions: a global apocalypse on the one hand, with "bombs filling the skies," and a revolutionary utopia on the other, with "the golden domes of Moscow shining on Russia's millions" and Ho Chi Minh celebrating "peace on earth" in Paris. He does not resolve them or choose between them, but dies lying back in Jean's arms. The only echo of the trilogy's title is the "dissonant flame of protest" that Mansart's daughter Sojourner plays on her violin to mark his passing.

Worlds of Color

CHAPTER I

The American Negro's World

The Black Mansarts were descended from that Tom Mansart who in 1876 was lynched in Charleston, S. C., for a crime he did not commit. His son Manuel, born the night of his father's death, was educated at Atlanta University, a colored college in Georgia, and became a teacher. He had four children—three boys and a girl. All but one had done fairly well: his eldest boy was a rich Chicago politician; his second son was a judge in New York City. His daughter was married to an ambitious young preacher. One son, literally almost beaten into crime, had been hanged.

Manuel Mansart, after teaching in the public schools of Georgia, had become president of the Colored College and developed it slowly into a good and growing institution of learning. His chief helper in this work was his assistant, Jean Du Bignon, a "white Black Girl" from New Orleans; that is, a well educated young white woman who was classed as "Colored," because she had a Negro great-grandfather.

Manuel Mansart was sixty years of age in 1936. He was beginning to feel the pall of age. Perhaps this was more mental than physical. Had he not long regarded sixty as "old" he might not have noticed the slightly retarded reflexes and the easier fatigue; but as it was, Life seemed suddenly to raise warning of its inevitable end and of things which must be done and plans which shrieked for final laying.

The First World War, the Depression and the New Deal had shaken Mansart to the depths of his being. All the old certainties were gone—all that neat little world with its good God, bad men and hovering angels. Even work and wage, wealth and poverty, money and debt became wavering concepts. What now was this thing called the "Negro Problem" at which all his life he had been working? He knew the details of a social "problem"; now he wanted to see it entire and try better to grasp it. These colored colleges, for instance, of one of which he was president; there were a score in all, one or more in each Southern state. They were called "Land Grant," because they were born of the idea of land granted by the federal government to the states for encouraging popular education. As in all efforts in the South, from the beginning they faced the Negro. First, they became a simple problem of graft—how to divert these federal funds mainly to the whites. But the silly Negroes protested, as if they had any real right to federal income!

There followed a phase of deliberate cheating: founding cheap colored schools, flimsy and scantily built, half-manned and run by black stoolpigeons owned by white grafters. Protests came from honest Southern white educators and from federal officials, and of course from Negroes. Rivalry rose with the better known private colored colleges like Fisk, Atlanta, and Talladega. Desperate effort in Washington kept inspectors or even cabinet officials from having any real power to compel the white South to treat Negro state education fairly. Under the sacred aegis of "States Rights," the cheating of Negroes flourished in education as in so many other facets of life.

At the same time a nation-wide crusade had long been growing to limit, reduce and in part eliminate the standard type of Southern Negro college, built on New England models. They began to droop, curtail and disappear. In their place the South tried to foist on the Negro, state and federally supported "Land Grant" colleges. But this program compelled the state gradually to let these institutions develop into real centers of learning.

So the "separate but equal" policy reigned, which first insured that black state colleges exist but be poorer than white state schools. Then, when states, pushed by white voters, began to make white public schools better and Land Grant colleges large and elaborate, Negro colleges necessarily became larger and better equipped. Such colleges could not be run by ignorant stoolpigeons and grafters.

A fight ensued which evolved a new type of race politician—a colored man, fairly well educated, honest in handling funds, and efficient; ambitious for the rise of his people to equal status with the whites; and yet schooled or schooling himself to ask less than he wanted; or even vehemently to deny many natural aims. Booker Washington was his prototype, but he went far beyond this beginning of manipulation of whites by blacks in the South. Often this made die-hard Southerners furious, but what could they do? A newly elected governor of Florida faced the old Tuskegee-trained head of the sick Colored State College with a blunt ukase: "No 'nigger' president is worth $5,000 a year!" The colored man said nothing but politely presented his excellent budget to the State Board appointed by the governor. Eventually the Board approved it, including the $5,000 salary!

So in North Carolina, the little brown president of the colored Agricultural and Mechanical College asked the governor for a herd of cattle. The governor exploded:

"'Niggers can't take care of cattle. They're too careless and dumb. I won't waste the state's money on such a project."

The solemn little brown man agreed. "Governor, you're absolutely right! My people know nothing about raising cattle. Of course, if they could get some training it would be a great thing for North Carolina."

They got "a little training" and before the governor left office a herd of cattle from the Colored State College won first prize at the State Fair.

It was an extraordinary game and the presidents of the colored state schools when they met each other, laughed themselves to tears at their experiences in making white morons do what they were determined not to do. But the game also had its risks and tragedies; sometimes a Negro president found himself replaced by a less scrupulous rival who bid lower for power. Sometimes an honest man inadvertently lost his own soul like one of the black presidents of a large school whose reach had extended his grasp and who explained to a critic of his servility: "You know, Sir, that is part of my 'stragedy.' "

In the background ever loomed black public opinion which flared unexpectedly in the path of many a black educational politician who proved too yielding in letting down the standards of the colored school. Then, too, among the whites was rising a type of white educator and administrator who hated lying and cheating to keep Negroes "in their places." Like old Dr. Baldwin of the white University of Georgia, they believed the Negro, let alone, would sink naturally to his inferior level. They were ashamed to join in forcing him down, especially in cases where they had to admit undeniable Negro superiority. Continually, such idealists sought to yield to Negro pressure and even offer them educational progress which they had not yet dared to demand. Sometimes such innovators succeeded. Often, they were discarded and went North in search of civilization.

It was a great game and Mansart enjoyed it. He knew many of the colored presidents. He wanted to know more. He had visited some of their schools. He wanted to visit all. So he took a trip after sixteen years' work, and visited colored schools, ending with a biennial meeting of the Colored Land Grant College presidents, in Baton Rouge, Louisiana, at Southern University in the spring of 1936.

As he sat in the beautiful and well-planned auditorium of this school whose budget for buildings this year amounted to more than a million dollars, he looked around with mounting astonishment. Huey Long, governor of Louisiana, and that fine-featured brown man yonder, had planned this thing. The brown president was northern-trained with an excellent brain. In fact, as Mansart looked he saw other types of the new Negro educator in the South who were not so much teachers as social statesmen, building a new culture on a singular bi-racial basis.

As he sat, Jean Du Bignon coached him. Jean was his private secretary and assistant. She was white but black, a woman of 36, with that slight touch of Negro blood which classed her as "colored." She was well-educated and had worked for Mansart since he became president in 1920. She had wide acquaintance with the college presidents. She said: "The small, well-dressed yellow man moving quickly and continuously among all is from West Virginia Institute and is the brains of this group. In his state he ranks among the best administrators, black or white. He thinks and knows. He has all the various intricate problems of all at his fingers' ends. He knows political Washington, too, and pulls the strings.

"His college is not conspicuously built but it has a well-trained faculty.

"He is talking now to another type of man, Gandy of Virginia. Gandy is solidly built in mind and body. He moves and speaks slowly and with dignity. The officials of his state deeply respect him and treat him with careful courtesy. On him they try no 'nigger' jokes and when he asks for some action or policy they know it is so carefully thought out and buttressed, that yielding for the most part is only a matter of time. Thence came the finely constructed, carefully located and functionally excellent buildings on his Petersburg campus, and above all a faculty of highly paid and well-educated men and women.

"The black man from North Carolina is not so well-trained as many of his colleagues and complacently admits it. But he has just won a singular battle, like many other similar bouts in the past twenty years which were slowly culminating in a major campaign of victory. Just as Negro public schools were at first invariably situated in slums and back alleys, so the great Colored Land Grant colleges were seldom located on main thoroughfares but usually hidden in woods or near swamps, on land which netted former white owners a pretty penny. But the college at Greensboro had just last year emerged on the main northern and southern highway, where the wayfaring man though a fool had to notice it. Here, too, was planted that chemical laboratory long demanded—how it happened none seemed to know—and the black president said nothing but smiled blandly."

Jean reminded Mansart at lunch that there was no representative of the poor and confused Colored Land Grant College of South Carolina. This was a Negro defeat. For years Negroes attended and even taught in the University of South Carolina along with whites. Displaced by force and fraud, with the help of the federal government, new leaders appeared and separate colored schools. The man who started higher Negro education in this state with federal aid was a typical Southern gentleman, white in color, and carrying in his veins the proudest blood of Carolina; yet Thomas Miller admitted and boasted of his Negro strain. Tillman and Blease fought him to his death, disfranchised his people and drove him into exile.

Mansart remembered him. The college he founded eventually became the playground of white and black grafters, and totters today under the displeasure and neglect of Byrnes, once Supreme Court Justice, then Secretary of State and governor. Yet in this very state the groundswell against race caste in education began, and it may yet prove, thought Mansart, that white South Carolina was too successful in fighting blacks.

The man who once headed the Negro Land Grant College in Florida sat beside Mansart at lunch. He was a strong, independent man, a graduate of Oberlin, who had just been replaced by a more compliant Negro. Young had demanded independence and expansion for this school which the state authorities, already incurring criticism for yielding too much to this "impudent darky," had refused and hoped to secure more complacency from the new appointee. But to appease the black public and answer Northern criticism from tourists, they had just given the school the largest appropriation in history. Mansart had seen the fine library and modern hospital which they were building on the campus. He smiled as Young told him of his new job in Missouri, where a Negro grafter had just died and the voting colored citizens had revolted and demanded an outstanding scholar to head the school. What was "impudent" for Florida proved attractive to Missouri.

Mansart came to know Henry Hunt of North Carolina who was just transferring from a private church school to a state institution. He was thin and tall and looked like a poor white, which led to endless complications. But Hunt was cool, honest and persistent. He was a trained administrator with but one purpose— his people's best good. He smiled at Mansart wryly. "I've got a Board of complete sons-of-bitches, but they're cheap and inexperienced whites. If I let one steal a hundred dollars, he'll vote through five thousand dollars worth of needed repairs. It's their habit of direct insult in dealing with us, that rankles. But," he added philosophically, "I can keep still in seven different languages."

Jean introduced Mansart to Trenholm of the state school at Montgomery, Alabama. He was young, alert and had degrees from two excellent Northern colleges. In his battle for a Negro college he had lost and won. Here in Alabama between the Cotton Belt and the iron and coal mines, on the very site of Booker Washington's plan for industrial training of Negroes, he was stopped in his tracks by white trade unions from teaching Negroes trades. White political power would not permit him to teach the building trades, mining, weaving or spinning nor any modern industrial techniques; so he built a teachers' college and secured as some sort of compensation adequate buildings, good equipment and an overflowing body of students. Here was another Pyrrhic battle for the superior white race. Mansart spent an hour discussing Trenholm's problems after lunch. He was fascinated by the music program of the college led by Trenholm's wife.

From Mississippi came not its Negro leaders but two teachers from a small and almost forgotten school. Alcorn had once seen a future, but when the Negroes lost political power in 1876 it was neglected and the black folk under Isaiah Montgomery began a singular experiment in race segregation as an answer to the Negro problem. They founded the Negro city of Mound Bayou, and dreamed of furthering such experiments. The enterprise was widely hailed and publicized by the white world, but Negroes were not so unanimous. They whispered: what can a black town do in a white state where the blacks have no vote? Little or nothing, the Negro leaders themselves admitted; but all the more doggedly they maintained that their federal citizenship supported by membership in the great Republican Party would eventually restore the vote to the black majority of Mississippi, and let black towns, black banks and black industry flourish unhindered in the state. They fought long and hard and lost even their vote inside the Republican Party. The representatives from Alcorn reflected this. They were well-dressed and polite but silent. What could they say?

One man who addressed the presidents in the afternoon session attracted Mansart especially. Jean knew him well, but for some undisclosed reason did not like him and did not introduce him to Mansart. Hale of Tennessee was the colored son of a man once governor of his state and related to many of the first families. This relationship was well known and he openly used it for political power. Whatever Hale demanded for his Negro school he usually got. The school rose rapidly in size, power and equipment. He built one of the best stadiums for athletes in the South. He was a ruthless dictator on his campus, allowing no one a word or act without his personal permission. Yet he worshipped education and drove his pupils, his teachers and his own children. His career brought hatred on both sides of the color line. He handled state money carelessly and lavishly, and not long after this meeting, as a result of grave financial charges, he committed suicide. Mansart could never forget his clean-cut young arrogance.

There was a man at this gathering whom Mansart did not notice, and did not realize who he was, until years after. Banks, of Texas, was tall, lanky, awkward and self-effacing. His clothes did not fit, which made him noticeable in this well-dressed group. He had come up from a country field hand to working his way through college, teaching in the public schools and at Benson's school in Kowaliga, Alabama, finally gaining the presidency of an obscure Texas colored college supported stingily by the state to ease its educational conscience and avoid the law. He worked long and quietly until he knew every Negro high school in Texas, every principal and every graduate; he knew too every white man worth knowing, and white men wanted to know him because he knew so much and so accurately what they wanted to know. He asked nothing for himself; his salary remained ridiculously small as his school grew larger. He sought no office nor gift and no one thought of offering him graft. He just wanted to know about Negroes in Texas, what they were doing and what they needed. He became the admitted race relations consultant in a state which was rapidly becoming one of the most powerful in the nation and beginning to stir the world.

He organized his isolated school as a nearly self-sufficient economic unit, with food-raising, bakery, canning outfit, electric plant, home-building by student artisans; a hospital which even whites sought; a few hand industries and larger efforts in the wind if the state did not forbid. Indeed, Prairie View, rising on the lone plain, looked like a miracle created by faith in a people by one of them. What Banks wanted was to make this a real colored state university and industrial center as well as a center of scientific knowledge of the Negro.

Then came a sudden change. Texas became the home of monopoly in oil and sulphur and manufacturer of a thousand new products. This Negro problem must not interfere with industry and must find quick, easy solution. The millionaires planned a Negro University in the wonder city of Houston which they had moved from inland to the sea and made into a great port. This university would have money, teachers and buildings and be strictly controlled by white industry. Banks would be president, naturally. He was unassuming and safe. But Banks unexpectedly demurred. He was unwilling to be president under control. He preferred to be on the Board of Trustees, with access to the eyes and ears of the rulers. But this meant no salary. Very well; he would live on his small pension. He thus became and remains the strongest member of the Board of Trustees. His was the most extraordinary of the Negro Land Grant presidents' careers.

Mansart saw the Southern and Northern attitude towards Negro education changing. The Negro was determined to have college training for his youth. If it was not furnished in the South it would be sought in the North and no dependence on luck, or ability or discrimination in marking, would avail to stop it. Negro students often excelled—not always but often in the fierce competition of the North. Even the History Department of Chicago University could not continue to deny the Ph.D. degree, by unfair marking, although it tried desperately for years, and supported a department of white Southern race philosophy. Some colleges like Ohio State were being swamped by Negro students despite every subterfuge.

There was but one answer: Negro colleges in the South or admission of Negroes to all Southern colleges. This latter was unthinkable in 1936, so Big Business in its national philanthropic cloak, planned and began to endow a select set of private Negro colleges in the South like Fisk, Atlanta, and Dillard. They headed a

"Negro College Fund" drive, much too small but advertised sufficiently to force beggars out of the field of philanthropy; and carefully supervised by Big Business. Even Hope, at the New Atlanta University, had white Florence Reed of the Rockefeller outfit planted to restrain his broader plans.

But South as well as North, the state university would eventually bear the burden of higher education. These universities must be under political control and thus Big Business would control democracy. In the South the Negro problem complicated all this. Despite the continuing push of Negro college presidents of the Land Grant group and the increasing millions already going to Negro state colleges, Negroes were still not getting half of what their proportion in the population entitled them to; if now a federal Supreme Court ever got guts enough to decree justice to Negroes; or more, if a federal administration was ever tempted by the growing Negro vote to administer federal funds equitably, the Southern Negro state college might soon equal and even overshadow the white. The South was scared.

All this was discussed in private conversation at the Baton Rouge meeting. Jean Du Bignon, through the man from West Virginia and the tall seer from Texas, laid out a tentative plan for cooperative, continuous sociological investigation in each state as a scientific beginning. It would be a controlled laboratory test on a grand scale unequalled in history. While plans for this were cooking, the president of Southern suggested in private that this study be centered at Georgia State and that preliminary to this, Mansart be encouraged to take a sabbatical in Europe to broaden his vision of the Race Problem.

"He is fine and sincere; but his education has been narrow. He simplifies the Negro Problem as one of education and ethics; he has no conception of the role of industry, the plight of the worker, and the work of the trade union. Indeed, most of our group, while running 'agricultural, mechanical and industrial colleges' really know little and do less in farming, industrial technique and production of goods. They realize this but do not know what to do about it. Again, we and Mansart know nothing of the central problem of colonies in the world."

Only a few of the presidents took much interest in this suggestion, or at most looked at it as a personal matter and perceived no overtones of the Huey Long line of thinking and doing. They did not realize how far in settling the Negro problem the role of the teacher was overshadowing the vital role of the worker. Indeed, because of the fight against Booker Washington's ideas there had grown something like enmity between teacher and laborer just when in the world labor was forging forward to its own.

On the other hand, they all agreed that Jean Du Bignon could in Mansart's absence plan and start the group study. This was rather unusual agreement on their part, for Negro men of action still harbored unconscious prejudice against women, stemming in part from the fact that family rebuilding among Negroes stressed "the woman in the home"; and partly because Negro girls were far outnumbering boys in school and thus presenting a severe problem of sex competition in earning a living.

But Jean Du Bignon was in some ways different or at least seemed so. In spite of her comeliness she was not beautiful, and her total impression was not of sex but of sense. Her conversation with a man slipped easily from arch dalliance to straight talk on his pet subject in which he soon got the impression of someone who knew as much if not more than he. Of course, Jean was careful to pick her conferees from those interested in her own fields of study, and to avoid venturing into depths which she had not plumbed. She did not try to settle problems of family relationships or prospective love adventures. She linked psychology to work rather than play, and listened when art and literature were discussed. She listened, and also commented.

This proposal of Mansart's trip intrigued her. He needed not simply rest but total spiritual change. He needed to see a world divorced from the essentially trivial and temporary question of skin color which had always been the center of his thought and action, and to realize that to mankind at most times and in most places color of skin was no more important than color of hair or length of foot. No amount of argument would ever convince Manuel Mansart of this fact. He must see and live it. For this reason he must not go as a lone traveller, buffeted by fellow American tourists with their alternation of patronage and insult to dark folk. His must be a guided tour, but guided not by the usual commercial agencies but by special arrangements. She immediately began consultation and correspondence.

Jean wracked her brains for ways to make Mansart's trip a source of enlightenment and information and not a series of slights, discomfort and loneliness. She knew by reluctant testimony and observation, what such a trip might mean to a dark stranger in Europe. Without special and personal introductions to the right persons of knowledge and delicate intuitions, the stranger would be regarded as a curiosity, a matter of pitying condescension or of isolated position. He would be avoided from courtesy, fear or distaste. If to balance this, the colored person sought letters or words of introduction, who in America would furnish them? Would Senator Baldwin or any member of his board of trustees do so? Whom would a colored American know in England to ask to undertake such a task? In France, where colored folk were less in the category of curiosities in all levels of society, a Haitian or a Martiniquan might be suitably introduced and welcomed, but a Negro from the United States would know no such friends.

Jean had known many colored friends—teachers, professional persons and others—who returned from a trip to Europe thoroughly hurt and unhappy, even if they testified to enjoying it. They had been quite naturally introduced to Americans who either ignored or insulted them. They therefore tried to avoid white Americans like the plague, but where could they turn? If they had some special place or mission, like students or artists, or officials, they would after a time find their natural level with fellow workers; but a chance visitor or tourist? Jean shuddered as she contemplated the sensitive Mansart in such a role. She wrote to some former friends of school days and certain teachers with hearts and imagination.

After some months and a few trips, she evolved a plan. She arranged personal contacts in England, France and Germany. She secured friends and persons who could find other friends of the same kind. She thus got a number of persons of understanding who knew or could learn what an American Negro experienced and yet with sufficient manners not to let this sympathy and knowledge so obtrude as to make the colored man feel like a curiosity, a museum piece or an infant. This quest was not easy. He began to get advice. A United States Senator said:

"How do you do, President Mansart; I sure am glad to see you. I hear you're taking a sabbatical? That's fine. You deserve it. Where do you plan to go?"

"I had thought of England and France, sir; and Germany. Then, I'm a bit curious about Russia."

The Senator scowled. "I wouldn't advise that. I hear it's in an awful mess: a sort of national whore-house and murder racket. Have you read what Trotsky is revealing? When thieves fall out—you know. No, don't go there; it's liable to fall to pieces any day."

"I see. But I do want to see a bit of Asia."

"Good! Then go by way of Italy and Egypt and so to India. A fine trip—I'd like it myself."

"Sounds so, sir; I'll think it over. But I am afraid it might prove too long. But thank you for the advice."

Mansart talked it over with Jean. She agreed. "You see," she said, "there's another reason; you might find that Russia is making swift headway instead of failing. In that case it would be unwise to say so when you returned. That would be difficult."

Mansart made no reply.

Mansart had been surprised by correspondence which began to drop out of nowhere. A visit to a meeting of the American Educational Association in Chicago brought an invitation to join a small party on a trip to England. It was fascinating, even when he did not realize what this companionship would save in embarrassment when seating in the ship's dining room and when placing of deck chairs harassed the steward. He gladly accepted. Then from England came an invitation from an elderly gentleman with a "Sir" before his name. He had heard of Manuel and his career—how, he did not say—and having an interest in the Negro race because his family lived long in Africa, he wondered if on his projected visit to England President Mansart would not be his guest? Details followed. Manuel was astonished and inclined to hesitate. In his experience invitations from white people to Negroes had strings attached. But Jean induced him to accept.

Next Jean started on France. After a glimpse at British aristocracy she wanted Manuel to come in contact with the French middle class; the people who worked, but lived for beauty and self-expression in a simple atmosphere. A young French writer living in London was about to return to his home in southern France. Jean found through a friend that he would be delighted to have Manuel as his guest, from whom he could learn of America from a Negro's point of view and in turn show him something of France—or rather of the world from the French point of view.

Asylum in Germany was finally obtained through the Karl Schurz Foundation. There was some hesitation, but this might prove good propaganda on both sides. China and Japan eagerly welcomed this visitor without special arrangements.

There was one matter which bothered Jean and Mansart and yet they said little about it to each other. That was the conduct of the school during his absence. Where would authority rest? Who would really be in charge? There were persons on the faculty who would be anxious to assume Mansart's power; there were other Negro officials in and out of the state who would be only too willing to step into Mansart's shoes; and above all, white trustees and merchants might see this absence as the time to work for a new distribution of authority. Against all this was the fact that the absence was to last but three months of actual school time; and above all, the machine was now running so smoothly and well, that it would take some time and work to disarrange it. Jean herself knew more of this working and was more efficiently entrenched in details than anyone else. Logically she ought to be made dean or acting dean. But sex jealously among black and white precluded even the suggestion of this. Jean came forward with an idea which was adopted: A small executive committee was to be left in charge and Jean chose it. It consisted of a white trustee who appreciated Jean's work; a colored trustee who was not personally ambitious! The third member was Jean herself.

Jean had coached Mansart for his trip in various ways. She made discreet suggestions as to his table manners; she taught him how to eat a soft-boiled egg from the shell with a spoon. She secured through the brother of a white classmate the services of a first-rate tailor in New York and had him outfitted with suits for day and dress, fine shirts, pajamas and underwear. She saw to his hats, gloves and shoes. After much complaint he finally succumbed. The trustees were only too pleased to have Mansart take a year off with full salary. All had grown to like and respect him. He left in June, 1936.

In New York, Manuel Mansart stopped to call on Max Rosenfeld, the teacher who helped his daughter Sojourner in her music and taught for a while at his college. He had some difficulty in searching him out in his poor lodging on the East Side, but Rosenfeld was extravagantly pleased to see him. He was particularly interested to know that Mansart was going to Germany and said he wanted to send a message by him.

"But you must be careful. This goes to a Jewish proprietor of a bookstore, a cousin of mine. Remember that the Jews in Germany are in bad plight just now, so give it to him secretly, and then he will tell you what is going on."

Mansart was surprised. He had never had any real conception of a Jewish problem, except of course in religion, where the problem, as far as Mansart was concerned, centered in the fact that the Jews did not believe Jesus was God. He did not think that too important. Of problems beyond this, which were racial, cultural, and economic and involved hatreds quite as bitter as in the Negro problem, Mansart was only faintly aware. There was a Jewish wholesaler in Macon against whom the white merchants tried to gang up; but Mansart persisted in giving him custom and found him shrewd and honest. On the other hand, from the parents of his students in town and country, came frequent complaints of sharp practices and even cheating on the part of small Jewish merchants in their dealing with poor laborers and tenants. There seemed some basis for these complaints. He often had wanted to make inquiries, but there was never time.

On the boat Manuel had time to catch up with long-neglected reading. He read as he sailed, a version of what had happened lately to the world. European culture in the 19th century had rested on peace between the Great Powers; a world market regulated by international trade; a gold standard for prices and free individual initiative in industry for capitalists.

For about a hundred years, 1815 to 1914, peace among the leading European powers was fairly well kept. Wars for colonial empire, on the other hand, were continuous, linking imperial Europe and eventually North America in world domination of the darker peoples of the earth. As this European consortium became increasingly tightened and perfected, three nations, Germany, Italy and Japan, frozen out of their larger profits, began more and more peremptorily to demand a share of the colonial areas.

The result was the First World War, with Germany fighting for colonies against the great colonial powers and the United States; and these allies securing the cooperation of Japan, whose price was recognition as the equal partner of dominant white European powers. This war disrupted the industrial organization on which the 19th century rested. The world markets and the gold standard ceased to function, and Russia came forward with a design to challenge free industry by planned economy for the raising of workers' income and power.

Desperate effort was made from 1918 to 1929 to restore the world market and the gold standard; and to resist Communism in Russia. It was the irony of fate that just as Western Europe was practically united to overthrow Russia by force of arms, the system of culture which had lifted the West to world dominance during the 19th century, built on conquest of India, Negro slavery in America, the Sugar Empire, and Cotton Kingdom and the Industrial Revolution, crashed in unprecedented ruin. Naturally, in what Mansart read, there were interpretations which questioned or contradicted this thesis. But this was Mansart's general conclusion as he landed in England.

CHAPTER II

The Color of England

Sir John Rivers, who had a lovely estate in Essex, was immensely intrigued by the prospect of his black visitor from America. Lady Rivers was a bit worried. After all, she had heard disturbing tales of these colored folk. But a generation removed from actual savagery, the poor things could not of course be expected to have much culture; and fine as it was theoretically to make it pleasant for a deserving black teacher, she wished that Sir John had talked the matter over with her before actually committing himself. Three weeks! Good Lord! She discussed the situation carefully with Reeves and his wife, the butler and housekeeper. Her daughter, Sylvia, who taught at St. Hilda's, decided on a vacation in France during the time of Mansart's stay; and her grandmother, the dowager, would as usual spend most of her time in her own secluded apartment.

But Manuel proved disarming and quite charming. He was not loud like most Americans. He wore good clothes and clean linen and his table manners, though often strange, were never objectionable. Sir John was quite delighted. He was about Manuel's age and thoroughly British. He was big, red and healthy; he had never been obliged to earn a living but was broadly interested in life—that is, real life among people who were fortunate enough to have something of actual value to keep them busy. Sport interested but did not overwhelm him, and politics brought one into intimate contact with many people whom he decidedly disliked. For similar reasons, he never tried any of the professions, unless his efforts at farming and horticulture could be so denominated.

But he liked human beings in the abstract and certain concrete specimens attracted him greatly. This was particularly true of Negroes, especially those who were "rising"; that is, coming "up from slavery" to full freedom and manhood. He had journeyed to London in 1900 to meet Booker Washington, who was the guest of his friend, the Duke of Sutherland. He was gratified at Washington's modesty and solid manner, although a little disappointed at his silences.

For the first time in his life Manuel began to know just what a gracious and comfortable life could be. He breakfasted at nine when all his life he had been used to starting the day's work not later than seven. The breakfast was leisurely and individual, each dropping in as he chose. It was served usually out of doors on the terrace, with flowers near and a wide sweep of velvet grass guarded by noble trees. There was music from birds, and silent contemplation and carefree conversation and quiet, perfect service.

Indeed, all life here was leisurely, with time for thought and dreams; with no apprehension of ill or thought of lack of security. Without apparent plan or effort, the time was always filled in—wandering in the flower garden or though the solemn, lovely woods with little streams and a lake; there were the dogs and horses to visit, and one could descry the world from the hill or from the ancient tower built before America was discovered. It was a beautiful and peaceful world, with thatched cottages, winding roads, flocks and pastures; and here and there in the distance, great and palatial estates.

Visitors dropped by casually during the day, all groomed and spotless, even when in apparent undress. Conversation never lagged; it was pleasant and gay with sharp but kindly thrust and counter-stroke, and sometimes interesting reminiscences and late news and comment. Then there was the library, always quiet and musty, with chairs and couches, lights and ladders and beautifully bound books in every language. There were pictures on the wall and in portfolios and periodicals from all the world.

Dinner in the great hall was a ceremony which for some time Manuel dreaded. There was the unfamiliar dress which a valet always appeared in his bedroom to arrange, despite Manuel's repeated assurance that he could dress himself. There were the stony, very respectful but all-seeing eyes of the servants—the haughty butler and the two pretty but unsmiling maids; there was the endless array of unfamiliar silver and glasses and the quick retrieving of anything dropped or misplaced. Above all, the family and guests. But these unobtrusively guided conversation, told appropriate reminiscences and distracted attention from awkward situations. After the first week Manuel found he could eat dinner and really enjoy it.

Of all the meals, Mansart liked afternoon tea best, perhaps because it was so unusual at that time of day to stop everything and enjoy pleasant gossip and delightful tid-bits in the open or by the blazing hearth, in complete relaxation. Callers would drop in, dogs came in ingratiatingly and everybody would talk or keep happy silence. Manuel determined to have afternoon tea when he returned home. Of course, he never did.

Mansart from the first was fascinated by the servants; first by their number—the butler and housekeeper, the cook and her helpers, the maids and valets, the gardeners, chauffeurs and laborers. He counted fourteen for this family of four. Then there were their duties: they seemed so sure, so expert, and yet went about with so little effort. They accepted Manuel but of course, without, in their unemotional way, showing any evidence. They sensed that he knew what work meant and sympathized with any hardship. He did things which would have occurred to no gentleman-born, and yet were in no sense ill-bred—like turning and carrying the dining-room maid's extra heavy tray; and holding the door back for the laden butler. Sometimes Manuel asked questions which no one brought up to leisure would have thought of: their hours of work and their homes, and where they went to school, and—fancy!—if they liked their job! Now and then he volunteered his own experiences, for which naturally they were too well-bred to ask but eager to hear about. They learned that he had worked with his hands and been a servant and taught school.

On the other side, Manuel's manners were not only to the servants but to the family, a matter of pleasant surprise. He was quite unconscious of this and never appeared anxious or strained; often when he made a *faux pas* he smiled and mentioned it, asking the correct way. He expressed no alarm or shame. In all this, his ten years as a college head had helped. He was used to being stared at by thousands of bright, intelligent and exploring eyes; he knew how to sit quietly and apparently unmoved while white men of wealth and power tried to insult him or draw him out or confuse him. He knew not only how to conceal his thoughts or conclusions but better, how to let his observers wonder if he had sensibilities or judgments.

Here of course most strangers were kind and sympathetic and the family almost overdid it until they realized that he was a man of thought and experience which had caked into good manners. Now and then ill-bred or careless persons appeared, like the haughty old countess who asked if any black women were chaste; or the child who rubbed Manuel's face to see if the color was fast. He answered simply that his daughter was chaste, and held his cheek still while the child rubbed hard.

His intercourse developed slowly and naturally. They were all, and especially Sir John, careful to appear not in the least way inquisitive or over-curious. They sensed that his color and race had always been so central in his life that their first duty was to make him forget. So at first the talk ran to generalities and even trivialities. The weather served its eternal duty and its contrast to Georgia made it often quite interesting; the trip across the sea; the travel by rail, the trees, birds and flowers. Then came the food, the question of interesting games, the day's news. When Manuel realized how much they were really interested in him as a human being, he began to relate little pieces of information—about his childhood; about his college and his students. He avoided the race problem as such but stressed the human side. They soon were hanging on his words. Quite naturally, Sir John began to compare experiences and was gratified to realize how alike human beings were even if they lived a thousand miles apart in distance and even further in cultural experience.

Sylvia had run down to pack for France and incidentally to appraise this wild black American. Lady Rivers asked, to keep up conversation:

"Mr. Mansart, what in England strikes you most?"

Manuel plunged: "Your idleness."

They were at tea. The flavor was rare; the scones were hot and delightful and the tea cakes unusual. The silent, efficient service saw that everyone had what they wanted just as they were aware of the need. A light rain was falling. The smooth, green lawn stretched richly to the magnificent woods.

"And don't you like it?"

"I love it, but it scares me. You see, I would not dare to rest so much while others work so hard. I suppose it is just a difference of what looks to some like duty."

"Or," said Lady Rivers, "perhaps it is only American rush and hurry which seems to us so unnecessary and even useless."

"Milady, you never picked cotton. You see, I was a child of workers. I was raised to work for what I wanted. You, if I may say so without offense—do not work."

Sylvia settled back in her chair, luxuriantly. Sir John came to the rescue.

"I realize your implied criticism, Mr. Mansart. You see, the situation is complicated and historical. To many it is hard to grasp. For instance, my grandfather pioneered in the Niger delta, traded in gold and pepper and at last in tin. He got title to valuable tin mines. He raised capital in England to develop the mines, hired natives to work them, brought in British technicians to direct this work; from the results of this, I and my family live."

Mansart was silent, but Sylvia looked at him and said smiling: "We are waiting, Mr. Mansart!"

Mansart was uncomfortable but replied, "I can see, Sir John, how your grandfather earned his income and how the natives must have been satisfied to work for him. But on my voyage over, I read a number of books which my assistant recommended. These have set me to thinking. My mind goes this way. Your grandfather's discovery of tin in Nigeria deserved reward. But not repeated reward; not continuous reward. Not extravagant reward. And reward for the discovery should go to the discoverer and not to his children. The tin belonged to Africa, not to England. After the discovery, it was certainly as much the property of the Africans as of the British. The British brought knowledge of extracting tin for use. This was of greatest importance. But this knowledge and technique was public property in Europe. Englishmen learning and using this knowledge deserved pay for their work. But not repeated and eternal pay. And this pay should go to the one who applied this skill for what he did and not to others who did nothing. And the machines and tools should be paid for, but paid for once, not continuously. Their repair should be paid for, but paid for once, not repeatedly. In other words, Sir, I can see clearly that your grandfather deserved pay for his work, for his effort in acquiring skill; for materials imported and used and their repair. But, pardon me, Sir, if I ask where do you come in? What effort are you being paid for? The black workers who served your grandfather got paid once; their descendants are being paid not for what their fathers did but for what they do now. Why this difference between the pay of the European and the African? Both should be paid for their effort—should they not?—and for nothing else."

"There comes in there, dear Mr. Mansart, something called Property."

"Is this Property the result of effort?"

"It is the result of law."

"Who makes the law?"

"It is here that the great British institution, the Family, comes in for understanding."

Sylvia stretched out her long limbs and took another cup of tea. "Daddy, do continue to tell Mr. Mansart," she said.

Sir John looked serious. "We Britishers believe in the Family—its long life, its unity, its sacrifice, its ideals. We strive to hold it together, to perpetuate it. Frankly, we do not believe in equality as you Americans profess to do. I even venture to believe you do not really, and are here precisely because you are superior, far superior to your fellow Americans, black and white. Some people are born to rule, to hold superior position, to have leisure for thought, creation and enjoyment. By selection of a ruling group the world advances and Empire spreads. Mistakes occur, to be sure; faults and even crimes crop out. But what other way has humanity yet discovered to advance but by way of aristocracy? I am first to admit that not all, not most of the subjects of the British Empire are happy or content. But I sincerely believe that most of them are getting what they deserve and as much as their natural station in life entitles them to."

Lady Rivers added: "You must admit two things, Mr. Mansart: first that our way of living is pleasant; and second, that no system of life could provide such comfort for everybody, even granted everybody would want it. Therefore, it comes down to this: on what basis shall we choose who shall have these amenities and comforts—by popular vote, by the king's grace or by the law of survival?"

"We have served well," interrupted the Dowager in her thin but high-bred voice. She had today made one of her seldom appearances. She stared at Mansart quite frankly. "We have served nobly as heroes and conquerors; as knights and earls; as warriors on land and sea, at Agincourt, Flodden Field, Oudenarde, and," she choked a bit, "on Flanders Field!"

Sir John placed his hand gently on hers and said, "But, Maman, we must not boast; the world neither knows nor cares—that is, this world that has replaced the real world." She lapsed into calm silence. Sir John continued: "We had the skill and courage; the persistence. We found the tin, bought the machinery and showed the natives how to dig it."

Manuel was a little irritated. "And you, Sir, what did you do that these mines and these miners should work for you?"

Sylvia chortled, "You inherited, dear Dad—no more, no less. That wasn't hard work!"

"If not I, someone else; and although I am all too unworthy, I and my family can have the pleasure of entertaining you, Mr. Mansart. The world's best people should have wealth and authority. You, sir, are the exception among your folk. You have position and power. You should have more, but your family has just begun the long trek. It would never do to let the mass of American Negroes have power to do as they wish."

Manuel was astonished to realize that Sir John was quite sincere. He hastened to add: "You can't realize, Sir John, by what narrow chance I had the opportunity just to live, much less to grow healthy, go to school and college and get this work. I was born, Sir, in my father's blood as he was shot to bits by a mob. My mother worked her hands to the bone to keep me in school. I cringed and crawled to keep my job as a school teacher and to head this college. And while I was doing this, thousands of black boys and girls had no chance, no opportunity and sank to hunger and crime and shameful death because God forgot them.

"Sir John, I would not for a moment set my judgment against yours. But I have an experience which gives me a point of view which you can never understand. I know a nation and a land which talks as you do about ten million people—they are wrong and I know it because I am one of those people. We are not happy. We are not content. We are not in the status which best suits us or is best for the welfare of our white neighbors. The reason is that in deciding worth and ability, we are not consulted. Others judge what we deserve and what we can do and of just what worth we are. And Sir, while I have the deepest respect for your judgment, before agreeing with you I'd like to see African labor and hear what it says."

Said Sylvia, "You needn't go to Africa. Just listen to British workers and hear what they say of our leisure and the inborn superiority of British aristocracy."

Lady Rivers said: "I am afraid, Mr. Mansart, you do not realize just what my husband has done for his world: his breadth of sympathy which arose from broad reading and hard thinking; the positions of influence he has held, not eminent but so needed; his advice and wide individual acquaintanceship with high and low, rich and poor, peer and criminal. He has been rewarded graciously, I admit, but does this patrimony quite repay all that the Rivers family have given Britain, including—the life of my son?"

Mansart hastened to say: "I assure your ladyship that Sir John richly deserves what the world gives him. I only ask, and with humility, if Africa is today in position to pay the debt, and if her bankruptcy is her fault, since surely it is not the fault of Sir John?"

Sylvia burst out: "Africa? Can even England pay? Look at London's East End."

Her Ladyship complained, "This is more of Sylvia's socialism. Why, considering our own home—what would our servants do if we did not hire them?"

Sylvia yawned and flung back, rising: "I've said it before, our butler might enter Parliament and the maids could have babies, legitimate if possible."

Sir John laughed and also arose. "I'm wondering if Mr. Mansart would not like to drive up to London tomorrow and lunch at my club?"

"Can I drop in, too?" asked Sylvia.

"Delighted, my dear."

The trip to London in Sir John's Rolls-Royce was fascinating—beautiful as they rolled through Essex, interesting as they traversed the more and more crowded parts of the city. They skirted the crowded East End and came down through Epping and Barnett and then winding through the city came to the white marble façade of the Liberal Club. It was Mansart's first experience with the club life of London; those great, quiet buildings, luxuriously furnished, where the members could rest at ease and have their meal; where they could meet friends and if necessary themselves have a room for the night. Without his club, or perhaps two or three of them, no Londoner could realize English life at its best.

Sir John naturally belonged to several clubs but his favorite on the whole was the Liberal Club because it was more catholic in its tastes and one could meet all sorts of people and yet know that they were mostly well-bred Englishmen. They talked a while with a number of acquaintances to whom Sir John introduced his black friend. Mansart was, with perhaps one exception, received with courtesy and all talked together with mutual interest.

Naturally, the matter of the Empire had to intrude and something was said about the unrest in West Africa.

"Labor in Africa," said one gentleman, "must of course be more or less compulsory. The people are not used to our steady, dependable labor."

Another interrupted. "And, of course, compulsory labor must act as a drug, keeping the people traditionally in harness like the coolies of China or of India."

"Or," said another, "if the drug does not subdue them into insensibility it may on the other hand arouse them, so that they begin to get impatient and dissatisfied."

"You are implying," said the third, "that compulsory labor in colonies leads either to apathy or to revolution."

"And that," said the fourth, "is by no means confined to colonies."

At this time, as Sylvia arrived, a part of the company joined her and her father and Mansart at luncheon. The reserved table filled slowly. Sir John occupied the center of the side facing the main dining area. He placed Mansart at his right and his daughter at his left. Beside Manuel was a prosperous merchant, plump and pleasant. Opposite the host was a vacant chair and beside it a voluble, gray-haired lady, carelessly but expensively dressed and, as Manuel was told later, of considerable wealth. At last, a tall man approached the vacant chair. He was massive in build, smooth skinned and perfectly groomed from hair to shoes, from kerchief to folded yellow gloves. His attitude was clear conscious knowledge of his rank and power, with an air of distinct deprecation of any possible assertion of these, until his eyes fell on the black face of Mansart. Involuntarily he stiffened and his evident military bearing asserted itself. Without a word he did a right-about-face and quickly stepped into the hall. Sir John stared in astonishment, but quietly turned to order the lunch served when a servant hurried up with a message; Sir John excused himself and went to the lobby. He returned shortly with profound excuses from Sir Evelyn Charteris. It seems he had carelessly forgotten a most important engagement which he must not miss. He would try to return before lunch was finished. Meantime, would the guests accept his profound apologies. He especially sent regrets to dear Mrs. Cartwright—

Mrs. Cartwright was much put out. "I had so counted on seeing Sir Evelyn today. There is a great Englishman, my friends. On such as he the Empire rests!" Sir John took up the conversation easily, but Manuel was not for a moment deceived. Here was an imperial servant who did not eat with "Niggers." Was this a mistake of Sir John's? A misunderstanding or what? It would of course be just like Sir John to forget to say, in inviting Sir Evelyn, that his American guest was black. The colloquy in the lobby had been a bit sharp: "But Sir John, I can't eat with a darkey—where would the British Empire go, if its representatives lowered themselves to the level of the hordes over whom we are supposed to rule?"

"This man is a gentleman, and the guest of my family, and I thought we were raising them, not lowering ourselves."

"But Hell, they can't be raised and if they can, they're even more dangerous and must be kicked back. But pardon me, old friend, why the devil didn't you say your American guest was black?"

"My God—"

"Well, well! Please make my excuses to the guests and especially to Elspeth."

Meantime the lunch went placidly on. The portly gentleman to Mansart's right took up the praise of Sir Evelyn.

"Fine fellow. It's such staunch representatives of our rule that build our power. Absolutely fair, carefully trained, meticulous about his duties."

"He makes our dividends certain," mused Sylvia.

"But he's absolutely honest in his dealings with the natives."

"No reason why he shouldn't be. He's well paid, has luxurious quarters and more servants than he can use. The natives will pay him a good pension when he retires at sixty and he'll come home as an honored authority on native denizens of territories. He'll see a lot. Spiffy, I call it."

Mrs. Cartwright was indignant. "Sylvia, you have long needed spanking. Sir Evelyn deals honestly with the natives."

"But do we?" insisted Sylvia. "Don't let's be hypocrites!"

"Agreed, but we did free the slaves and stop the slave trade."

"Also, we made the Negro slave trade to America a great industry which built our cities and founded trade and industry. In the eighteenth century the African slave trade was the most valuable trade in our Empire and West Indian property our most valuable property. We kept it up as long as it paid. When the slaves revolted we stopped the trade; and when they refused to be as cheap labor as we could find in Asia or Africa, we found more profitable investment for our capital there. Philanthropy and religion help, but they follow the biggest dividends. Pitt, not Wilberforce, freed the slaves."

Mrs. Cartwright retired into aristocratic silence. Manuel broke the silence by asking his neighbor a question which seemed to force itself on his tongue:

"I cannot help wondering just what this lunch costs in black miners' wages?"

The merchant stared and finally said:

"Supply and demand take care of such matters."

"British demand, African supply?"

"Naturally," said the merchant and turned to his neighbor who was expert on stock prices.

The company began to discuss labor and socialism. Mansart listened but said little, until someone turned to him.

"What, Mr. Mansart, is your attitude toward Africa? And what is the attitude of American Negroes in general?"

Mansart replied, "We really know comparatively little of Africa, but of course theoretically what we want is that Africa should be free and independent."

"Why?"

"Well, we sort of think that is the heritage of mankind."

"Of all men?"

"Yes, eventually of all men."

"If 'eventually'," said Sylvia, "lugs along a hundred years or more, I wonder if you're right. If it is a matter of beginning now and working in this generation, I agree with you."

"In a hurry as usual, Sylvia," said her father smiling. And then all arose to greet a newcomer. He was a young Englishman, tall and thin, rather carelessly dressed and very earnest in his manner. It seemed that he and Sylvia were planning to take Mansart on a journey. So after a time they left the group and the comfortable rooms of the great club with its marble façade and walked around the corner to Sylvia's little Austin. They drove away toward the east with desultory conversation and then, parking on the side, Sylvia produced a shabby old raincoat which she wanted Mansart to don. And she substituted a very disreputable hat for his new Knox.

"Please pardon us, but we're going into the slums."

The young man supplemented this by apologetically removing his tie and that of Mansart and proceeding to rumple up Mansart's clean linen. "You know, our hosts are a little sensitive when people, especially strangers, come among them and are too well dressed."

As Sylvia left them alone for a time, Manuel mentioned his stay at her home and how he had enjoyed it. The young man agreed about the family and touched the matter of the death of Sylvia's brother. "We were not exactly chummy, but I knew him well and his death was a blow to Sylvia; and yet a relief.'

Manuel looked astonished: "A relief?"

The young man relighted his pipe and continued slowly:

"Yes, he was a snob, a born aristocrat, English style. He never worked, but expected the world to work for him; correctly schooled and tailored, a captain in the Guards, aiming at a rich marriage and a peerage; a dilettante in sports and arts, an exquisite idler who leapt at war just as he murdered Big Game. He died in a gutter filled with mud and the blood of England's flower. Sylvia was stricken, for she loved her handsome brother dearly. But she was glad he did not live to be what he wanted to be."

The little car lurched over the rough East End cobblestones. Endless miles of slum streets, their dreary murk broken only by the garish invitation of brightly lighted "pubs." At one time they entered one and ordered a pint of mild and bitter. The patrons were working folk, noisily comparing notes on wins or losses in the latest football pool or placing bets on the chances of Whitechapel's heavyweight pride, Erny Hawkins, to win the title. There were the usual number of beer-sodden men cradling head on arms in despairing attempt to get away from it all.

But it was the women who for years remained in Mansart's memory. One incident stayed with Mansart all his life. It was not the main picture nor most significant. But it persisted. Among the quiet women with shawled heads were many in tawdry finery, grimy feather boas encircling their unwashed necks, heads crowned by bedraggled plumed hats. The arms of one of these tipsy tarts cradled a babe. Its hungry wails put a damper on the "gaiety" until the barman protested: "'Ere naow, 'ere naow! If you cawn't shut the brat's mouth you'll 'ave to tyke 'im out of 'here!" The Cockney wit of her obscene retort drew guffaws of laughter, and the drunken madonna dragged a filthy handkerchief from her bosom, twisted up a corner, dipped it into her gin and put it in the infant's mouth. The wails subsided into a contented gurgle.

Mansart and his companions, choking back a rising nausea, emptied their glasses and quickly sought their car.

It was well toward midnight when Mansart and Sylvia, having dropped their companion by the way, arrived at the Rivers' house in Essex. For miles they had been very silent. Indeed, Mansart never fully expressed just what he saw in the London East End and what it meant to him; but it marked an epoch in his life. For the first time he realized that white men and women in a civilized country and in the twentieth century could suffer in degradation, helplessness and crime quite as much as any Negroes whom he knew in America; and, he surmised, as much as Negroes and Asians suffered overseas. It was to him an astonishing realization.

CHAPTER III

The Color of Europe

Mansart spent about a week more in England and then one afternoon there came to the estate the young Frenchman who was to accompany him to France and be his host for several weeks. He was an interesting young man, well dressed and cultivated, speaking meticulously correct English and very polite and thoughtful. He said to Mansart and the family that he was sorry he was not going to be able to entertain his guest so graciously as he was being entertained in England. He explained that in France they had by no means recovered from the devastation of the First World War. "But," he said, "I hope to make you understand something of what France means to us and to the world."

He added, "I fear that in England you have seen the Extreme and not the Mean; the aristocracy and the slums but not the great English Middle Class. But," he added philosophically, "that makes little difference. This Middle Class gives birth to the nobility and both ape each other, so in a sense they are identical." Mansart, remembering the sturdy, satisfied and very respectable merchants and clerks he had seen, was not quite sure as to just what the typical Englishman was.

Both Sir John and Lady Rivers hastened to assure Mansart that he was going to have an unforgettable experience and that nothing in England, after all, was quite equal to what France had given civilization.

Singularly enough the matter that disturbed Mansart most on leaving Britain was the tips for the servants. He hated tipping; it stank of slavery. He did not believe in tipping and could not afford it. He took the bull—or rather the butler—by the horns and spoke to him frankly. The butler was polite and unperturbed. But he showed no enthusiasm. The housekeeper, when the message was delivered, was disgruntled: "If he's able to travel, he ought to be able to pay his way. I never did hold with niggers nohow." Some of the maids and men sneered; others giggled.

As he rolled away on his journey, his hosts remembered not only this dark and well-bred gentleman who had become their friend, but for themselves they remembered their honeymoon in Paris at the Exposition of 1900, and the walks they took across the Pont Alexandre, the new bridge which was then linking France and Russia.

After a pleasant and uneventful journey across the rough channel and then on the train between Calais and Paris, Mansart and his friend came to a month of experience which always thereafter had for Mansart the uncertain quality of a dream.

Manuel Mansart did not realize until long afterward how expertly he was guided by M. Villiers. Villiers tried to show him at once the physical Paris and its meaning, past and present. They looked out upon the city from the Eiffel Tower and saw the Seine, the Left Bank and Notre Dame. They wandered in the Bois de Boulogne, having lunch in a secluded restaurant among the trees. Coming back they paused over the Eternal Fire within the Arc de Triomphe, and they went up to Montmartre. The beautiful church looked down upon the city which they had left with the Tuilleries in the distance, the Madeleine and the Palais Royale, and with the plethora of streets, churches, public buildings, and squares.

Walking down from the white church they came through the little streets of shops, and by the Moulin Rouge until they reached the Opera and the Grand Boulevards. They stopped one day for chocolate and soft-boiled eggs at a world-renowned little restaurant, and then taking a cab rode through the Square of the Republic to the Bastille.

Here the whole thing began to take on a different significance. Mansart was at the place where the French Revolution started, where the modern world was born, and where people began to dream of the equality of human beings and their right to have a voice in government. It seemed queer and unbelievable, the history that had taken place in this now so vast square with the old prison gone and the Column of July rising alone in the center.

As they walked they talked and Villiers tried in various ways to interpret the living France:

"It is difficult to characterize a nation. Hardly any classification of its motives is all wrong; none is completely right. The only final judgment is what happens and that is difficult to see as a whole and grasp entire. Complete and accurate measurement of what men do is not attempted; it is not even envisioned as possible nor desirable.

"How then shall we characterize France? We French are Saint Joan and her peasants who birth the people, believe in God and skimp and save and push the world backwards. We are the shopkeepers climbing into gross corporations, immortal, infernal, supermen, armed to the teeth, owning all ability; controlling thought and news; maiming, murdering and driving men insane. Yet we differ from you Americans—we still have writers and artists, unbribable, unsaleable, free and helpless, looking Death straight in the face. This picture of France, Mr. Mansart, is as false as the nation itself. While we are dirty and vile amid our beauty, and love sex and say so, yet we have not yet sunk to the level of the whores of Hollywood who wallow in pools and collect autographs and wave their legs and bare their asses to the world.

"And France is Europe. For five hundred years, all Europe has fattened on the entrails of Asia and Africa and built her glory on the blood and guts of 'chinks' and 'niggers.' What a brave and mighty folk we are, and how unrivalled and unprecedented in lying and murder!"

They stopped in a small restaurant along the Seine embankment. It was filled with laborers and clerks, but Villiers found some acquaintances in the rear and they crowded around a table against the wall. Among the group Manuel was pleased to see a colored man from the West Indies. He was a M. James and was a writer. With him was a Russian and a Frenchman who could speak Russian.

"Communists," said Villiers with a smile. Manuel was interested. He had never met a Communist and was curious.

"I have hoped," he said diffidently, "that your revolution would supplement the French, which gave us Liberty, Equality, and Brotherhood...."

James flared. "You mean which tried and failed. The slave trade and slavery were the economic basis of the French Revolution. 'Sad irony of human history,' comments Jaurès. 'The fortunes created at Bordeaux, at Nantes, by the slave trade, gave to the bourgeoisie that pride which needed liberty and contributed to human emancipation.' The French revolt of 1789 gave liberty to a large group of Frenchmen, but it was the revolt of the slaves in Haiti which tried to force equality on France. But the reaction called Thermidor beat back the Terror of the rise of the French workers and crucified the house-servant Babeuf, who tried to lead them to brotherhood with black workers and brown. Thus, the French Revolution was never finished. Napoleon tried to transform it into colonial imperialism but Christophe and Dessalines balked him and the United States grabbed the spoil of Louisiana."

The Russian spoke rapidly as the Frenchman translated:

"And don't you see the Russian Revolution now comes to fulfill the French and Haitian? We take the worker to the place where the French Revolution tried to lift him and, setting him side by side with the black and colored people, bring a world brotherhood of which the most progressive white world never dreamed. Indeed, white Europe and America were headed straight toward a world war of race and color, which the Soviet Union alone will prevent."

Manuel stared at this interpretation of the Russian Revolution. He had heard the Soviet Union had made color discrimination a crime; but to him the "color line" was principally a matter of admission to street cars, trains, schools, and restaurants. Of an equality higher and broader than this, involving economic equality, he had not given much thought.

Some days later they came down to the Seine, looked at the fascinating book shops on its banks and then passing over, went to a restaurant which from its portico afforded a view of the celebrated Isle de la Cité, with the vast towers of Notre Dame in the distance. This was the center of Paris. There the first Napoleon was crowned and there stood the Palace of Justice.

They came across the Pont Neuf with the statue of Henry IV, and turning to the left saw the great palaces of the Louvre, the Arc du Carrousel, and the gardens of the Tuilleries. They looked through the Rue Royale toward the church of the Madelaine and rode up the Elysian fields through the Park of Peace, La Concorde.

It was in the Louvre itself that they spent long hours, not all at once but one and two hours at a time over a week of visiting. Mansart knew almost nothing of art. He had seen before coming abroad practically no great pictures and what he had looked upon as sculpture was rather miserable stuff. Here he could sit down quietly and look upon the Winged Victory of Samothrace and the Venus de Milo. He saw Mona Lisa, and his companion showed him many other pictures less advertised but quite as beautiful. He gained in time an idea of how the great painters of the world from Italy to Holland and France had tried to set down their conception of the beauty and meaning of the human body and its surrounding world. Later he tried to understand Matisse, Gauguin and Picasso. He emerged into a new conception of what the earth was and what man could see in its and its inhabitants.

After a week or so, they went to the Rive Gauche along the Boulevard St. Germaine and into the Boul'Mich. They spent afternoons in the beautiful gardens of Luxembourg and went down to see the loveliest of Botanical gardens. They rode by the Institute Pasteur on the Rue de Vaurigard and lived at a little hotel there for a week, a hotel characteristically parisien, with its black-gowned hostess, its omnipresent servant and its morning breakfast-in-bed of coffee and croissons. Many of these sights they visited again and again; the Bois de Boulogne, Montmartre, the garden of Tuilleries and the cemetery of Père Lachaise.

During this time they were talking together, of themselves and their world; of that fabulous America of which the young man was both so curious and so critical and wanted specifically to be coached on just what a "lynching" was. He himself was the son of a well-to-do peasant in South France, who still tilled the family farm. Indeed, there he and his friend were going to spend the last week of this trip and there they would meet his father and mother and the married sister; a sister who, by the way, he said, had married an American and who wanted to go to America. But the husband was unwilling.

M. Villiers was unmarried and had a small income from his writings. He spoke with care and thought. He sought the exact word that would express just the specific meaning that he wished to convey. Save that he wanted to express himself in writing or by some other medium, he was not sure as to what his life was going to be. He had no plans. He did not have wealth nor want it. He was fairly certain not to starve. He sought a world of taste and discrimination, without suffering and hurt, and filled with all manner of men.

They came to the farm by way of Roman France; they saw Arles and Nîmes and they walked if they did not dance across the bridge at Avignon. They glimpsed the blue Mediterranean below the hill of their farm. The parents were simple and cordial, courteously curious and full of questions. The married sister especially greeted them with joy, because of her deep sympathy with her brother and her interest in America.

She talked freely about her husband who was not at the time present. He had been in the American army in the First World War and had been brigaded with the French army. He had been wounded and had won the Croix de Guerre. But he did not want to return to America. He seemed in a way curiously prejudiced against America and this his wife could not quite understand. She asked a great many questions about America and explained that in France it was difficult since the war for a young man to get a real start. Her husband lacked the over-precise curriculum of the French schools which was so necessary to get admission to certain lines of professional work. Naturally, he also did not have the connections and acquaintances which would open ways to him.

On the other hand, he had had a good American education and it seemed to her that the place to make his way was in America. The wages were high there, the chances of work were broad. She could not understand why he would not for a moment entertain the idea of going. Of course, she knew that Negroes formed a caste in America—but an officer and a gentleman would naturally be treated as one even in the United States. She talked earnestly to Mansart about this, and Mansart himself could not understand until the husband came home. He was a brown man.

It was characteristic, on the one hand, of his French hosts that they apparently had never thought of mentioning this fact to Mansart, which was of course in his mind of the greatest importance. It explained why the young husband did not want to return to America and why he knew, although he did not try to make this clear to his wife and her family, just why he could not see a career in America. He was a thick-set man of perhaps thirty-five; solidly built with a good-looking but rather discontented countenance. His mental balance was unstable. He was as startled when he saw Mansart as Mansart was to see him.

It is always a problem for American Negroes to know just what attitude they should assume toward each other when abroad. Of course, if they are alone they come rather naturally together. But if they are in different social settings, what then? This colored man was the husband of the only daughter in a French family and he, Mansart, a Negro teacher travelling in France. Shall they treat each other as understanding friends or shall they rather ignore each other, or what path between was there? Mansart tried to be pleasant and understanding but the young colored man did not respond very eagerly. He was curt in his answers and did not try to enter into the conversation. On the whole, it was rather an unpleasant experience.

Only once did Mansart seek to get close to him. They met in the fields by accident, looking out upon the well-fed cows and the waving grain.

"Do you think of returning to America at some time?" asked Mansart.

"No," said the man shortly.

"You have not been home in some years."

"No."

"Perhaps you won't mind if I tell you that there are changes in America—we are improving in our race relations and there is a chance for a Negro to get on rather better than I have ever seen before."

"I suppose you mean to get on as a Negro? I am not a Negro. I am a Frenchman, and I am going to stay so. But I tell you what I am going to do. I am going to Africa."

Mansart was a bit astonished. "Africa? Why—that's fine! I—I'm glad you thought of it."

"Oh, I don't mean the Africa you have in mind. I'm not going down on the fever coast to work like a 'nigger.' I'm going into the French Civil Service or perhaps the military service in French West Africa. I am going to invest there what money I can get hold of. I am going to have servants and laborers and live like a gentleman. I've been down there for a while and I know how a white man can live and what he can do. And I am a white man from now on."

Mansart said nothing.

"You have been talking to John, I see," said his young host. "I'm glad. I wish you'd try to have some influence on him. I confess I don't quite understand him. I can see why he doesn't want to return to America, and perhaps he's right. I've heard of the Negro's status there. But what in God's name does he want in West Africa? It's a hellish sort of hole, hot, fever-ridden, fly-blown. Of course, he is attracted by certain aspects of colonial life. If a man can get a well-paid position and is willing to do nothing for the rest of his life except to yell at servants, well, I suppose he can make it, although how he can live without art, literature, self-expression of any sort, I don't see; and I don't myself fancy being surrounded by poor devils, ignorant, diseased and hopeless. Apparently he rather likes that sort of thing. I'm sure my sister won't."

The sister came up about this time and she began talking with Mansart.

"I can understand," she said, "how a man brought up as John must have been wants to escape the plight of ordinary people without wealth and privilege. But I cannot see why he wants to go to the opposite extreme and lord it over the unfortunate. I rather like to work among the poor and the laborers. One finds real people there, don't you think?"

"I certainly do," said Mansart. "I can't imagine working anywhere else. And I question the whole institution of thoughtless service, of obeying commands on the farm or in the house or anywhere without any chance to know and to do on one's own account. It seems to me that there is something wrong with a man to whom that is an ideal."

John came up just then and he spoke bitterly. "Of course, you can't understand. You're a white folk's 'nigger,' Mansart. You've been kicked and walked on so much that you're used to it, and you wouldn't know what to do if you had a chance to do a little kicking yourself. Well, I am going to kick. I am going to step on people who are only worth stepping on. I am not going back to America. I am going to French West Africa and there I am going to be somebody." He turned away abruptly. There were tears in his wife's eyes as she followed him.

The incident of this talk with John led to further conversation concerning Black France.

"Your country, by the way, was a considerable colored empire—seventy-five million colonials against forty million home folks," said Mansart, who had been reading.

"Yes, we have fifty million in Africa, twenty-seven million in Asia and a half million in America. Frankly, I don't like it. Some of these we have assimilated by actual migration to France; others by making them legal French citizens in their homes. But that is but a handful; less than five million I should guess. The rest are ignorant serfs to be exploited by our Big Business. Some will free themselves by revolt as they are trying to do in Indo-China and may soon in North Africa. The five millions of Madagascar may erect their private system of home exploitation; a few more will become citizens and turn into exploiters of their kin, as John plans. It's a mess, Mansart, I admit. But what is the future of the world's colonies? Can you see it? I can't."

"I don't know. They must be led. Missionaries have proven but tools of Big Business. Business benevolence differs only in degree from Business for profit. I wonder if the world will ever produce a power which will open the way for colonies really to become free?"

"What is free?"

Mansart thought. "The right to vote, to work, to go to a school...."

"No, freedom is the right to use the wealth they produce for themselves! Nothing else matters," said Villiers.

"Yes, something else—the knowledge how to use that produce for science, health and art."

"It's impossible!" said Villiers.

"Is it? If it is, civilization is impossible!"

"That may be so."

"In fact, it has been in Spain."

"Spain?" Mansart looked puzzled.

"Do not tell me that you do not know what my country, Britain and the United States have been doing—are doing to the people of Spain?"

Mansart was silent. No, he did not know. He had read something about a civil war there; and now a new leader, Franco, but...

"Germany and Italy are helping crush the Spanish republic; the United States, contrary to all its traditions is refusing arms. It is wicked. But surely you have heard of the International Brigade?"

"I never heard of it," confessed Mansart. Within he began to wonder how much of the real history of the world was being hidden from him.

After a month, a wonderful and unforgettable month, Mansart left France and through Switzerland came into Germany. It was now no longer a guided tour thoughtfully planned by careful friends. He was now on his own, face to face with white Europe. He met nothing of American indifference and antagonism, but also he met few friends. The surrounding world was curious and sometimes startled at his dark face, but he was treated with careful courtesy in hotels and restaurants and on the streets. He carried with him thoughts and memories of what he had been through, but he was unable to bring away from France as he had from England the picture of a complete civilization. France was something different from that; it was a continually developing idea; a certain attitude toward life; a way of thought and of changing ideal. It meant something when France had a dozen political parties, and England and the United States, two— or one with two names. But he was happy with the memories that he brought. He had something that he would never forget so long as he lived.

Mansart's trip to Germany was part of the plan of Americans of German descent, to bring Americans and Germans together; and after much thought it was decided that it might be well to include a Negro among the visiting Americans, so that in spite of the race propaganda in this new Germany, the Germans would realize that there were Negroes in America and that they were well-treated. The trip then was carefully planned so that Mansart should meet as little personal indignity as possible, but on the other hand there was little of the social contact which he had had in England and France. He was put on guided tours, he made visits in company with groups, and he had plenty of leisure to read.

Mansart went to Switzerland by way of Lyons and Geneva. He saw the great French manufacturing city much more quiet and settled than similar American or British towns, but skillful, tasteful, and with a certain contentment and happiness.

Then he went on to Geneva, crossed the beautiful lake of Lausanne, and came to Bern. He never forgot that sight of the Alps at Bern. He was standing on the high plaza looking up over the city to the mountains and the great white cloud formations above, and thinking how lovely it all was. And then almost by accident he raised his eyes to the skies and there above the towers, above the mountains and above the clouds, rose the startling magnificence of the high Alps with their silver peaks piercing to the top of the sky. He shuddered in ecstasy. Never before had he seen anything quite so magnificent. And he said to himself, "With all its dirt and sin and disappointment, this world is a beautiful, a very beautiful thing."

Eventually, by rail Manuel Mansart came to Munich in South Germany. He used haltingly some of the German which he had learned in school. He realized that this city was being re-built and renewed in folkways as the center of that new rising power in Germany under Adolf Hitler. It was almost by accident that he went to see the Museum of Technology. Never before had he witnessed anything like it. He saw the modern world in microcosm. It had 70,000 exhibits extending through nine miles of rooms. Merely to glimpse it Mansart spent four days walking through. There were seventy-three rooms devoted to geology, mining and metallurgy, with a complete coal mine. There were thirty rooms for transportation and twenty-one rooms for clocks, mechanics and electricity. Ten rooms exhibited sound and music, and in the rooms devoted to chemistry one could traverse four centuries in an hour. All the wood products of the world were there, and three planetariums illustrating the heavens. All this technique was the foundation of the power which Europe had directed for her world domination, and this was the explanation of the world in 1936.

Mansart realized that while he knew something of raising raw material—cotton, rice and sugar, corn, wheat and peanuts—of the intricate and long processes by which material was turned into consumer goods, he and his people knew little. He turned to his guide, an old man, white-haired and white-bearded, who spoke several languages well and clearly and had evidently been a man of status once in his life; but now beginning to break, with no light in his eyes. Mansart started to ask him some technical questions about the exhibit, and then suddenly found himself saying.

"Sir, when Germans have all this and can use it, why do they fight?"

The man stopped and stared at him, reddened and then seeing how serious Mansart was, said:

"That, sir, will take some telling, but perhaps if you will join me at lunch we can talk about it."

They went out together at noon, and Mansart suggested apologetically that the guide allow him to be the host and that they go to some well-known restaurant so that he could see something of the real life of Munich. The guide hesitated and then said,

"There is one restaurant in town which every stranger ought to see, and that is the Münchner Hofbräu. I cannot afford to go there but if you can, I will be your guest there. At one time this was the greatest restaurant in Bavaria, with the finest beer. It has lost much of its prestige and its beer is just ordinary stuff, to be exported to . . ." He started to say, "America," and then added ". . . foreigners."

"Let me tell you, young man," he proceeded, "Germany, although separated and provincial, was a great country in the 17th and 18th centuries. Its work then, its thought, its science, can never be forgotten. But politically we were in a straitjacket, so that men were asking: 'Where is the German fatherland?' We were humiliated by the French and by an Italian peasant with delusions of grandeur.

"In the 19th century we had to fight in order to form what we thought would be a self-protecting nation, one of the great three countries of the world. The Germans would think, France would feel, and let England trade. I was at one time a professor in one of our greatest universities. I saw our science, our music, our social investigations leading the world, so that those who wanted to do and know studied in Germany. Where else?

"We had to make ourselves an armed nation. And led by the great Bismarck and culminating at Sedan, we became the German Empire. But this was not the world that it used to be when we started on this path. It was a changed world. It was a world which was not built of nations unified, each with its own educated directing and laboring classes; but part of a new organization of dominant nations where the working classes were not mainly within the nations but in colonies overseas. And we Germans had no colonies and unless we got colonies we were going to fall far behind in what was a world fight.

"Even our great Bismarck did not recognize this. He did not want colonies. He wanted a unified Germany. He gave Africa to France and Britain, and ignored Asia. But he was forcibly put out of office, and into power came the men who knew that Germany must have colonies, a navy and an army to maintain its place in the world." He paused and asked:

"Do you remember the Races Congress in London, in 1911?"

"No," said Mansart. "I was teaching at the time and read about it in our magazine, the *Crisis*. But I could not attend."

"It was a great meeting," answered the guide. "It would have been epoch-making if it had not come on the threshold of world war. There were great and wise men there and they were trying to unite the world across the barriers of race. Black, yellow and white men met and conferred as equals. They would have been very influential if at that time it had not been absolutely necessary for the survival of Germany to restrain England and France in their headlong economic imperialism. I remember some of the colored men there—Indians, Chinese and Japanese—one young black social scientist from America, from a school called Wilberforce, Earl Finch. And an editor who read a poem. But Science and Poetry were not listened to. Indeed, it was one of our own greatest scientists who said at that meeting—and almost disrupted it—that Germany must arm for war! He meant that Industry and Commerce must rule civilization and not considerations of humanity, happiness and knowledge.

"Well, it was all of no use. We armed, we fought, we lost the flower of our youth, and we went down into the fires of hell. Do you realize what happened to Germany at Versailles? Do you realize the succession of blows that have prostrated this nation since? Look at me. I was once an honored man, with a small but assured income from a pension so that I could have ended my life in study and ease. I lost everything. I am now the paid servant of foreigners, from most of whom I do not meet the courtesy that you have shown me today."

And so, after eating in this great and garish restaurant with crowds of tourists and few Garmans, they went back to finish the Museum of Technology.

From Munich Mansart went north to Beyreuth. This was a tribute to his daughter, Sojourner, at home. He himself knew little of music and drama but he must not miss this opportunity to hear the great works of Richard Wagner. He found lodging on a street where once Liszt had lived and not far from Wagner's own home. The hostess was a lady of breeding who spoke English quite well. She recognized her guest's innate breeding but hesitated at his color. She was a widow, whose sole fortune was this beautiful house in the better part of the city. Here she made a living by giving board and lodging to tourists, chiefly English and American. The color prejudice of Americans was well-known and even among Germans there was being expressed a new race prejudice due to the rise of Hitler and his doctrines. Nevertheless, she yielded to the chance of free opportunity to see the old and wonderful operas and accepted Mansart's hesitating invitation to accompany him. It was different from anything that he had conceived. The opera was really a day's work. One went out to the suburbs, arriving at four in the afternoon, and sitting down to the curtain at five. Then, for three hours one looked and listened. At eight all paused an hour for dinner: elaborate courses, easy conversation, lounging. And then they went back for another two or three hours of theater. Except in the case of one English couple, the presence of Mansart excited no comment. A few stared, but on the whole the hostess enjoyed the evening.

What astonished Mansart was the picture of the German soul which this music and theater painted. He thought how among American Negroes, legend and fantasy might thus be wed to histrionic ability and imagination, to build a great dramatic tradition. The one here was magnificent. The rolling thunder of the music transported him. He did not pretend to understand it. Sometimes it was vague and voiceless, but at other times he knew what Wagner meant and what he had accomplished. Especially at that last portrayal of the Death of the Gods, the power and glory of the music gripped him. He could never forget it.

When he returned home he talked with the hostess and as she conversed with him tears came into her eyes. "See what we have lost, Mr. Mansart. Think of the nation which built this music and the genius which voiced it. It went down in awful war. But one man is holding it together, and that is Adolf Hitler. He keeps Beyreuth going, and I don't care what may be said about him. This one thing makes him to me the greatest of men. We lost, but not forever, not entirely."

From Beyreuth Mansart went to Frankfurt, and then took that unforgettable journey down the Rhine. The boats were less crowded and slower, naturally, than those coming up from Rotterdam. Nevertheless there was more time and even with Mansart's small knowledge of German one could listen to conversation and look at the people.

One afternoon they were passing mountains. They saw old castles, lovely vineyards and nestling towns. Mansart seemed vaguely to remember about one mountain and consulted his guidebook. Then he turned to a fellow-traveller and said in halting German:

"Is not this the Lorelei and is not there a song?"

The German scowled at him. *"Ja!"* he snapped, *"Das ist die Lorelei. Aber heute, kein echte Deutscher singt das lied der Juden, Heine!* (But no German sings the song of that Jew, Heine!)" And almost at the moment a group of boys and girls on vacation began to sing a song, but it was not the Lorelei.

Mansart asked no more questions. He saw the busy Ruhr, that great manufacturing district, whose work and profit united French and German capitalists even in the midst of war. And then after a hurried glimpse of Holland and Belgium—crowded, clean, well-to-do and busy, he came to the real object of this trip—Tervourien.

The beautiful building was set within a magnificent park and yet began on a false note. In its first room was the exhibit of the exploitable riches of Africa on which European culture could be built. The Belgian Congo was fourteen times the size of the mother state and from the first was regarded primarily as a profitable investment. The worst outrages of Leopold had now been curbed. Missions were at work on elementary education and laws restricting the great corporations had been enacted. But still, as Mansart could see as he wandered through the endless and beautifully arranged rooms, the chief end of the Belgian Congo today, as it was under Leopold I, was to increase the private fortunes of Belgian, and of European and American capitalists.

Mansart remembered the story of cheating and cruelty which had made the heart of Africa a colony of Europeans. He remembered particularly the flamboyant promise of Henry M. Stanley peacefully to plant "Christianity and civilization." In fact, they planted theft, murder and disease, while the people died at their hands. But here they were, the people and their products, but from the first room to the last exhibit, the emphasis was not on the people nor on their products but on the profit which the processing and sale of these products would bring; and would bring not to black men but to white.

Mansart now journeyed overland. He stopped at Eisenach near Luther's Wartburg, and at Goethe's Weimar. Then down by the great trading houses of Leipzig and the art of Dresden, up to Berlin, the capital of Germany. He was met at the station by a tall, blond-haired youth, who greeted him in excellent English and took him out to the small but neat suburban home where he was assigned to stay by the Carl Schurz Foundation. The mother was gracious and kept a typical, neat German home. She did not speak English but as time went on she and Mansart talked together with the help of her tall son. Soon her grievance and her prayer burst out. This son of hers, with all his Nordic blondness and evident talent, could get neither work, education nor a career in the Germany of that day, because as she said, "His father was a Jew!"

Mansart evidently looked astonished and puzzled, but she explained.

"With the new racial philosophy which Hitler has brought, the state helps only Germans. Others, even those half-German, can get no encouragement nor support.

"My son therefore has but one alternative, and that is to leave Germany. I especially asked to have you stop with us because I wanted to beg you to use your influence to get an opening for my son in America."

Mansart smiled wryly, and then was near to tears. It was difficult to explain to this woman how little influence he had in America and how he would be the last man on earth to be able to help this young man in finding a career. It seemed as though even to the last the woman could not quite understand.

Mansart began to see and know Berlin as a great and efficient modern city. But it was tense, filled with meetings and its streets thundered with glaring radio propaganda. It was curiously upset with what Mansart regarded as unimportant things. For instance, he went to a movie to see the fight of Joe Louis with Schmeling. The audience was in turmoil. Their championship of the German fighter was uproarious. Their race hate of the young brown contender was frightening. When Louis was knocked out the whole audience went berserk. One would have thought that St. George had slain the Dragon. Mansart could hardly understand. The scene, however, was made clearer when he visited the Olympic games held in Berlin that summer.

The setting was imposing and Mansart thrilled to witness so fine an example of human equality, as dark figures threaded the stadium and every race and nation bore its banners aloft. It happened that American Negro athletes were unusually prominent. Owens, little and lithe, won the 100 and 200 meter races and the broad jump, over world competition. The stadium thundered with applause. Woodruff, tall, thin and brilliant bronze, won the 800 meter run; and big, black Johnson soared to victory in the high jump. And then Hitler, who had paraded and poured praise on the white victors, failed to put in an appearance. It was a petty pout, but it spoiled Mansart's feeling of triumph, just as it shamed many Germans.

Mansart's guides, however, were careful that he should see just what the new Germany was doing.

"You must realize what Hitler has done for us. A year ago we had seven million unemployed. You must see the roads and homes which he has built. Remember what the Treaty of Versailles did to us and is still attempting to do. But, by God, we'll escape. Germany will rise again."

Then, there were also Germans whom he met who were more apologetic and knew that Mansart sensed that all was not well and that there was opposition to dominant trends. One professor at the University burst out in the midst of his defense of the Nazis and said,

"But there are limits. I will not be pushed too far."

He did not go into details and years after Mansart wondered how far he had been pushed.

Once Mansart was invited to supper at the apartment of a teacher in a gymnasium, as German high schools are called. There were six or eight persons present and Mansart could not help noticing that when after eating they relaxed for conversation, the curtains were lowered, and during the rest of the evening the voices remained low. The teacher said bluntly:

"I am ashamed of what we are doing to the Jews." Then immediately he began some justification. "Of course, the Jews themselves are in part to blame. They have bought up lands and property. They are pushing the small German shopkeepers into bankruptcy. They are flooding the professions. I know, I know, but that does not excuse the treatment some of them are getting. I am ashamed!"

Mansart listened during the evening to charge and counter-charge, and to overwhelming excuse and bitter regret. Mansart listened and wondered. He knew in a general way that Germany had a Jewish problem. He had intended to find out how far this problem resembled the Negro problem in America, but hitherto had seen no opportunity. Now he suddenly remembered the letter from Max Rosenfels which he had not yet delivered. Next day he excused himself from the planned itinerary and went off by himself. He rode up Friedrichstrasse across the Spree to Oranienburgerstrasse and there found, after some search, in a basement the number he was looking for. It was a dark and uninviting bookshop. There were no customers and apparently no attendant. He browsed a while and finally, raising his voice asked in German:

"Anybody here?"

A thin man finally emerged from the back, dressed in a long black gown and spectacled. He said softly, "Did you want something?"

Mansart handed him a list of several books which he had decided he ought to read, including Marx' *Capital*, a *History of Jews in Germany*, some books on Russia, and others. The man scarcely glancing at the list handed it back to him and said,

"Sorry, but we have none of these," and turned to leave.

But Mansart addressed him again. "Are you the proprietor of this shop?"

The man looked at him suspiciously. "No," he said.

"But," said Mansart, "I have a letter for the proprietor."

The man stopped, took the letter, read it and rushed into the back of the shop. After some pause he came back with an older man, and hurriedly, after looking out on the street, they took him into the back. While the younger man returned and lingered in the shop, the old man talked.

"Welcome," he said. "Welcome! Pardon our manners. We have to be very careful. I am glad to hear from my cousin Max. You must tell him when you go home that we are in bad way, that millions of Jews will die and be ruined before this world is much older."

And then they had a long talk. "You see," said the Rabbi, "German Jews for centuries have made common cause with the aristocracy and lost the sympathy, indeed invited the enmity, of the workers and shopkeepers. That was not entirely the Jews' fault. They were not allowed to work as artisans or farmers or to trade in earlier times. They became bankers and merchants, and in alliance with the privileged classes made their way and gained at least in part their freedom.

The French Jews made similar alliance with the leaders of the new Big Business and they're still prosperous. The British Jews joined in commerce and with the politicians. The Russian Jews had the foresight to join with the workers and forward the socialism of the world."

"Socialism?" asked Mansart. "Do you think Socialism will win?"

"Will win?" replied the rabbi, "It has won! We're all socialists now. Every country has some degree of socialism. Even your own Roosevelt is leading a socialist revolution. The difference you see is difference of leadership, of dictatorship. The ignorant mass cannot lead itself into economic emancipation, requiring scientific technique and capital, with the forces and classes now against it. Here in Germany, this Hitler has made alliance with the great corporations. They are going to give the mass of people as much socialism as will keep them quiet.

"In France, the state owns and governs education, transportation and almost all national enterprise. In England, the power is in the hands of the aristocracy, with help from the skilled artisans. Whether they will win through this partial dictatorship I do not know. You see, if such an experiment as the Russian should succeed, if the mass of the working people could really secure a dictatorship which would guide the state toward complete socialism, the more would be emancipated. But they can't. It will be impossible for people so ignorant and inexperienced as the Russians to choose or keep in power a dictatorship of the proletariat. They will fall out among themselves and then the foreigners will rush in."

"But I understand," said Mansart, "they are having some success."

"Some success, yes, I hope more; but I doubt it. I seriously doubt it. If they should succeed, then the dream of our Karl Marx might come true. The mass of people would be so well educated and trained, so experienced and so schooled in new folk ways, that they would not need a state. But that is a dream, a wild dream.

"But I am glad to see you, Mr. Mansart, because I want to call attention to one mistake that you American Negroes are making. You are trying to make alliance with the old planter class, and the new rich of the North. That's a great mistake. First of all, it makes the worker and the poor whites your enemies. They lead the mobs and do the lynching. You have got to change your alliances or you are going to lose."

Mansart was astonished. "I cannot believe it!" he said. "I cannot believe it! At any rate, I think after all I ought to see Russia!"

But Mansart had to remember that his chief errand in Germany was to learn of industrial education in the German state. To this he now turned as his time was growing short. He soon learned that Germany was not seeking to use industry as a means of education. It was using education as a means of carrying on and perfecting industry. So too, Mansart knew that in America the white philosophy back of the Tuskegee idea was not to use industry to teach Negroes, but Negroes to help industry.

In 1936, the electrical industry of Germany and a large part of Europe was divided between two great German corporations of which Siemens was the oldest and largest. It was capitalized at $100,000,000 and employed more than sixty thousand of the highest skilled workers in Europe.

By permission, Mansart entered this city within a city. Among the many factories was one large, seven-story building. The chief aim of this building was to produce a human product of the most careful and precise nature, to be used in the productive processes of this mighty industry. Industry here was dealing with men as it would deal with cotton: studying them, experimenting with them. Knowing exactly what it wanted men for, it proceeded with painstaking care, endless experiment and expert training to deliver a finished product which was unsurpassed in the world for efficient, delicate, precise and regular workmanship.

It takes from grammar school or high school graduates, 150 apprentices each year. They are children who have done their school work well, and the children of employees of the company were preferred. Only the very best material was selected. Those whom Mansart saw were from twelve to fifteen years of age, and were going to study four years after careful testing. The students were paid as they studied, not much but an increasing part of their living expenses were thus met as they proceeded through the course. They were entering a life work, would follow it all their working years and be pensioned after they were retired.

With a skilled working class, educated for a specific life work, it was evident to Germany that democratic control of the state could not be entrusted to them. Industry in Germany was to be controlled by a closely knit hierarchy for support of a wealthy class to whom the bulk of income and of power went. While these workers had some democratic power in their public life, in choice of local government officials and other smaller matters, on the other hand, in the great matters of government policy, general laws and the distribution of capital, of industrial aim and organization, of colonial administration, there was no democracy. The demands of the workers through their trade unions could not be wholly disregarded, but these demands were mainly in the matter of wages, and these wages and conditions of work must be improved and the cost of them taken from profits. This process, naturally, had to be watched carefully.

It was clear, not of course from what Mansart heard in the factory or from his interpreters, but from the newspapers and the broadcasts and from a colonial exposition which he visited, that the Germans thought they must have colonies and that the new colonies must not be simply those they lost in the First World War but larger colonial territory; that these colonies would supply this great industrial machine with raw materials raised on cheap land by cheap colonial labor.

The new colonial territory might be, of course, conceded by Britain or France in the face of the new German army and navy. But the chief idea of Germany in 1936, to Mansart's surprise, was that the new territory was to come from Soviet Russia, and it was Germany's growing thought and aim to take this territory. Consequently there was, while Mansart was in Germany, furious propaganda against the Soviets. Communism was denounced, its crimes were emphasized, and its inevitable failure foretold. Yet, and this is what intrigued Mansart, most methods which Russia had followed or announced were being imitated in Germany. Germany was a "socialist" state, in the sense that to an increasing degree the government owned and controlled industry. It controlled money and banking; it was moving toward ownership and control of land. Work and wages, roads and homes, were under government control. There remained only the question: Who will control the government?

When the dictators arose in Italy and in Germany, the industrial world of England, France and America applauded because they saw in the dictators an answer to Communism. Mansart was continually astonished at the way in which Russia was the center of German, if not of European thought. Before that, to Mansart's recollection, Russia had been significant mainly as a national problem which was going to be of tremendous importance to the world. But it was no threat; rather an experiment and a dream yet to be realized or to die with noble memories.

But in Germany in 1936 Russia was a fact; an accomplished experiment, so successful as to pose the immediate question of acceptance by modern culture or violent uprooting by every means. Britain was an enemy, but an enemy to be copied in success and method. France was an ideal which needed only German science. Italy was an ally. But Russia was something threatening which must be put under German control.

Here came Adolf Hitler, a psychopath and a dreamer, with delusions of grandeur, frustrated by poverty and war; ruthless in his idealism; bold, cunning, with a voice of brass and a knowledge of the human soul. This was the instrument which the captains of German industry picked out at the time of their defeat and despair to become master, not only of Germany but of Europe and possibly of the modern world.

Hitler was an artisan. He came from a part of Austria where the anti-Jewish feeling was strong, as was also his own economic rivalry with Jews as a worker. In 1932 Germany had been near anarchy. The next year, although still a minority, the Nazis attacked Jews, burned the Reichstag building and took power. Industry was frightened, the Junkers were frightened, the managers, engineers and small shopkeepers were frightened. They all submitted to a man who had been at first a joke, then a pest, and who now suddenly loomed as a dictator. Union labor, with its 8,000,000 members, proceeded to squabble as to whether to usher in the millenium immediately or gradually; through this squabble Adolf Hitler and Big Industry drove a carriage and four.

The greatest single invention of World War I was propaganda—the systematic distortion of the truth for the purpose of making large numbers of people believe anything authority wished them to believe. It grew into an art, if not a science. Nowhere was it used to such tremendous advantage as by Hitler in Germany. Newspapers, public speakers, the radio, expositions, celebrations, books and periodicals, every possible vehicle of information and training, including schools, were used on German people to teach them that they were the most remarkable people on earth; that the National Socialist government would be the best government for Germany, if not for the world; that other countries, especially Russia, were in the depths of misery and that Jews were responsible for all criticism heaped on Germany and for most of the other ills of modern countries.

All this Mansart learned while in Germany, while talking with his English-speaking companions, from several confidential interviews with German teachers and workers, from listening to the endless broadcasts as they were interpreted to him; and by walking, looking, listening. His stay in Germany could by no means be compared to his experiences in England and France. He made almost no friends. He came into no intimate contact with the people. But he did do much reading, and he began to understand Germany as never before. He got some glimpse of what it had been in the 19th century—a great country of science and education, of ideals, with music and art. A people which, rising from the utter depths of conquest under the first Napoleon became in its own eyes and even that of the world, one of the greatest if not the greatest country on earth, and now was in the midst of revolution.

CHAPTER IV

The Color of Asia

All this, of course, made Mansart eager to visit Russia, that weird land around which all revolutionary hope and fear were swirling, and thence to pass on for a glance at Asia. He had had Russia in mind when he first began this trip, but he had been advised by friends and people whom he had met in America, England and France that perhaps such a trip would not be wise; that Russia was in turmoil and that no one knew just how things were coming out. So he had given up the idea. But he was going to Asia, and the quickest way to Asia was across Russia by way of the Trans-Siberian railroad. It seemed foolish and too costly for him to go around by the Mediterranean. So he thought that perhaps he could spend a month in Russia and then go on.

This he found out was not possible. For some reason which he could not imagine, he was refused the right to stop in Russia. He did not know about the unfortunate experiences of the Russian Intourist effort; and of the new strains which the West was beginning to put upon this struggling country. So that the best he could do was to make the trip from Moscow into Manchuria without halt. This he finally decided upon. He wrote home as he started east:

> "It is October, 1936. I am in Russia. I am here where the world's greatest experiment in organized life is in the making, whether it fails or not. Nothing since the discovery of America and the French Revolution is of equal importance. And yet this experiment is being made in the midst of unexampled hostility; amid deep-seated bitterness and recrimination such as men reserve usually for crime, degeneracy and blasphemy."

He neared Mongolia and wrote:

> "We were nearing Mongolia, and already in the Province of the Buriats. The slim firs stood sturdily with straight heads and shoulders sagging with snow. The lonely silence of a Siberian night was about us. We climbed down a pass in the Black Mountains, following a river half hidden in ice. Suddenly the tempo of the scene changed. A large new factory blazed up in the night. Great piles of lumber lined the river bank. An electric road showed a beginning of modern road-making. Tracks of rails stretched wide on either side, until a modern railway yard was evident.

Then we swept into Vereudinsk, now newly named, and the world was soldiers. They filled the depot, covered the platform, crowded a standing train and marched about in overcoats to their heels, buttoned closely; some with guns, some with bundles. All was now clear. This was a frontier point of concentration against the threat of Japan.

"Ten thousand miles east of our East lies a land, lonely and dust-swept, pregnant with history in the dim past. Hence came the Mongol hordes that swept from Asia to Germany and Italy, and changed the history of the modern world. Brown men they were and yellow, with broad faces and flat noses and wild, straight black hair. They are here about me today, November 1936—perhaps 25,000,000 of them—in Inner and Outer Mongolia and in Manchuria.

"It was a new world. My color was nothing unusual. All the world was sallow, yellow or brown, except the blonde white Russian girls who waited on tables in the restaurants and on the dining car. The train swung out toward the East. I was in a Pullman car made in America. The porter was not of my own expert race, and I felt like giving him a few pointers. The roadbed was better than in Siberia. Always war hovered near us. They pulled down the curtains early. I wanted to look out but fortunately I first read the posted notices: 'Passengers between Hake and Agounor must not look out of the windows on penalty of severe punishment.' I did not look out.

"We swept along a great, wide plain, and the cold wind poured straight down from the North Pole. It was a desolate, barren land, and the seldom folk crept wearily along the lonely way. Then the whole scene changed as if by magic. We slipped out of the desolation of the northern desert. We flew easily on a perfect roadbed, ballasted with rock, and in Japanese cars better than Pullmans. The service was perfect. We were leaving the old border and haunts of the bandits, the modern successors of Genghis Khan. We came to Hsinksing, capital of the new Manchurian state, set up by Japan in 1932.

"I hurried on to China which was end and aim of all imperial planning, from America to Japan and from the 10th century to the 20th. In the morning I went down to the great harbor of Dairen. My friends handed me three colored streamers of farewell, and following the beautiful Japanese custom I and a dozen others held one end while the friends ashore unwound the other ends until a rainbow of colored strips of paper streamed from ship to shore and I bade Manchukuo goodbye.

"China is inconceivable. Here first a man out of the empty West realizes where the population of the world really centers. Never before has a land so affected me. China, to the wayfarer of a little week and I suspect a little year, is incomprehensible. I have, of course, a theory and explanation which brings some vague meaning to the mass of things I have seen and heard. I understand now as never before how I have believed the human history set before me and missed the whole meaning of a people. And this I know: any attempt to explain the world without giving China a place of extraordinary prominence, is futile. Perhaps the riddle of the universe will be settled in China, and if not, in no part of the world which ignores China.

"I write this standing on the Great Wall of China, with 23 centuries beneath my feet. The purple crags of Manchuria lie beyond the valley, while behind are the yellow and brown mountains of China. For seventy cents I have been carried up on the shoulders of four men and down again. And here I stand on what has been called the only work of man visible from Mars. It is no mud fence nor pile of cobbles. It surpasses that mighty bastion at Constantinople which for so many centuries saved Mediterranean civilization from German barbarism. This is a wall of carefully cut stone, fitted and laid with clean matching and eternal mortar, from twenty to fifty feet high, and 2,500 miles long; built by a million men, castellated with perfect brick, and standing mute and immutable for more than two thousand years. Such is China.

"I talked with a group of Chinese leaders and business men. We talked nearly three hours. I plunged in recklessly. I told them of my slave ancestors, of my education and travels; of the Negro problem in America. Then I turned on them and said: 'How far do you think Europe can continue to dominate the world; or how far do you envisage a world whose spiritual center is Asia and the colored races? You have escaped from the domination of Europe politically since the World War—at least in part; but how do you propose to escape from the domination of European capital? How are your working classes progressing? Why is it that you hate Japan more than Europe when you have suffered more from England, France and Germany than from Japan?'"

Mansart wanted to forestall the usual question and comment of foreigners on the Negro problem in America and instead elicit so far as possible information about China from Chinese lips. He continued:

"I saw today something on the streets of your city which reminded me of America. A well-dressed English child of perhaps six years was walking with his nurse along the Bund when he met some Chinese children, small, poorly dressed and dirty. With a gesture he ordered them off the sidewalk; they meekly obeyed and walked in the gutter. In general the whites here treat the Chinese just as we Negroes are treated in the Southern United States. I hear that only recently have Chinese been admitted to the Race Track which is the fashionable amusement center of your city. The white foreigners rule your city, force your children into separate schools and in general act as though they owned China and the Chinese. Why do you permit this?"

In later years, Mansart was deeply ashamed of calling this conference and asking these questions because he came to realize how abysmally ignorant he was of China and her history. He had never studied or read Chinese history or literature. In elementary school, China was a joke and its people "queer." In college he learned about the kings of England and France but nothing of the Han or Ming emperors. At this very moment, in 1936, Mansart had no dream of the frightful tragedy playing over China, or of the "Long March" of 8,000 miles, circling from Fukien to Yunnan, Szechwan and Shenshi. Just then, Chu Teh, of whom Mansart never heard, fleeing from capture in the freezing snows of Tibet, was starting out to join Mao Tse-tung in the future Red Capital of Yennan. The long-enslaved, raped and murdered peasants of China were at last reeling to their feet, covered with blood and lice, to rule a world. And yet, of their fateful history of three thousand years and its bloody culmination in the twentieth century, Mansart in his ignorance was questioning Chinese leaders in Shanghai as to why they let the West insult and rule them! They must have wondered whether he was fool or spy.

Of what the West had done to China since 1839, Mansart had heard little—of the Opium Wars to enrich England and reduce China to a colony; of the Chinese revolt called the Taiping "rebellion," in which the whoremonger and murderer, Chinese Gordon, began his saintly career which ended when the Negroes of the Sudan cut off his head; of the slave trade in Chinese coolies which sent cheap labor to America and the second frenzied revolt of the Chinese under the Boxers in 1899, when the Christian world united to steal China's treasures and partition her land. All this was either distorted or utterly unknown to this colored American. When he asked why they submitted to the West, there was a sensible pause quite as awkward for Mansart as for the five Chinese present at the dinner. Mansart remembered how often he had sat in similar quandary when well-meaning strangers had stripped his soul bare in public and blandly asked him why and how and what? Present with him today were five persons—the superintendent of the Chinese elementary schools; the president of a college, supported largely by missionary funds from the United States; a young banker; a well-to-do merchant; and a civil servant.

The school superintendent spoke first. "We are, sir, as you say, in a sense strangers and outcasts in our own land. That we realize each day. But we are not sitting supinely by and doing nothing. Oh, no! Europe is not always going to own and rule Asia. We have started a good system of schools, well supported, with Chinese teachers. There are not enough schools, to be sure, but they are growing. We share today in the government of this city as we did not a decade ago, and there is no longer exclusion of Chinese citizens from public places."

"But," said the merchant, "as you surmise, the chief difficulty is industrial. The Chinese are poor, miserably poor, and crowded into this city in a great hungry mass; foreign capital can easily get work done at the lowest wages and there is yet no effective effort to keep the income of the poor much above starvation. Such unions as we have are ineffective, and the Chinese employers cannot raise wages in face of foreign competition. But we are moving, as our banker can tell you."

"At last," said the banker, "we issue our own money and are not forced to use British currency. That is a start. But of course only a beginning, so long as industry is monopolized by outsiders. They own the factories and ships. But we have plans afoot. Down the river from Shanghai and nearer the sea, we are building a new industrial capital which will one day intercept the world trade which now centers in white-ruled Shanghai. You shall visit it this afternoon."

"Now," began the college president, "about Japan."

He probably sensed that Mansart had the Western prejudice in favor of the Japanese and knew nothing of recent occurrences. Indeed, when Mansart only that very morning had seen the monument erected in 1932 for the Chinese murdered in Chapei by the Japanese, he had not dreamed of what Japan had done to crush China as Sun Yat-sen struggled to free it. Before he left China, Chiang Kai-shek was captured in his night-shirt and made to promise to help China ward off Japan; Mansart knew almost nothing of this man whom our own General Stilwell called "a grasping, bigoted, ungrateful little rattlesnake" but who was given 3 billion dollars of our tax money—to become our "ally" in Formosa.

The president continued: "The Japanese are our kin. We gave them the civilization which they have developed. But today they despise us because we are victims of Western aggression which they barely escaped, and because of their power they propose to replace the West as our masters. It is explicable that we hate so fiercely our own Asiatic brothers who plan to treat us worse than the foreign devils from beyond the seas."

The talk proceeded and food and tea passed. Later the group visited the classes in the public schools where of course no white child entered. At last they came to that new ghost city beside the sea in the wide mouth of the Yangtze River. The marble city hall stood beautiful and empty; there were streets and stores, public buildings and parks, docks and storehouses. Almost everything except people. Mansart stared and wondered. When would the people come? When would the dream awake?

Yet, he also realized that the traveller must take with him much knowledge or he will never see what is before his eyes, or hear with his ears. He knew of British culture before he went to England; he knew much of France before he saw it. But of China what little he knew was mostly distortion. Through that false fog he saw little even when he stood with open eyes.

One of his final days he spent in Hangchow, that lovely city of islands and palatial homes, of tree and verdure, where the wealth of Chinese rests in peace. It was a singular echo of that other great monument at which he but glanced, that magnificent palace of the proud Empress Dowager where, with imperial gesture, this indomitable ruler of hundreds of millions of human beings tossed away the money which her nation gave her for a navy to defend them from the West, and instead built a fairyland of water, bridge and stone, of ebony and ivory, of flower and fountain and vine, of lovely couch and carved statue—to speak of Beauty and never of War.

Across the straits Mansart hurried to Japan, the one colored nation whose talent, industry and military might the white West feared. He looked on the island mountains with intense curiosity. He sensed a difference immediately. In China he had received every courtesy and yet he knew that China felt itself part of a white world and planned its future as part of that world. No sooner had he set foot in Japan than he felt himself in a colored nation who hated the white world just as he, despite all effort, did himself. He was received almost as a fellow-citizen. He again wrote home:

"I have never been welcomed to a land, least of all to my own, as I was welcomed to Japan. I was helped past the port officials, white Americans being politely but firmly elbowed aside, to their open-mouthed surprise. It was astonishing to be at last in a colored country, able and determined to run itself without white advice. And Japan considers itself colored and not white. I have already tested this in conversation and suggestion.

"What is Japan? I am, I admit, prejudiced in its favor. But I am trying to judge it fairly. First of all, it is colored. The blonde-haired world of my summer and fall is gone. The hair of the Japanese is coal black, with once in a thousand a faint brown. The skins vary from white to sallow, and then to yellow and brown. Casually, if I woke up suddenly in Japan, I should imagine myself among New Orleans or Charleston mulattoes.

"But the most extraordinary thing about the Japanese is not physical; it is spiritual. They are independent and self-reliant and self-sufficient colored folk in a world now dominated by whites. They have no fear of white folks nor secret envy. Whatever white folk do or have done, the Japanese are sure they can do better.

"It was the fear of England that was pushing Japan. England dominated China and India, Australia and New Zealand. But for the grace of God and the vigilance of the Japanese, she would own Japan. At one time during and after the Russo-Japanese war, recognizing the power and ability of the Japanese, England made alliance with her as an equal. Then, with no reason except the unstated one of color prejudice in America, South Africa and Australia, Britain broke the alliance in 1921, unwilling to link her fortunes with yellow people.

"Japan found herself between the devil and the deep blue sea; rapprochement with China, based on blood kinship and cultural likeness, was stopped by war and boycott, and reached unbelievable depths of hatred. Japan saw China kow-towing to the West, dragging whites about in human-powered rickshaws; she sensed nothing of the unbreakable strength of China, beneath a thousand years of humility. Europeans secretly and openly encouraged a split between these colored peoples which played directly into their hands. There seemed nothing for Japan to do but seek alliance with Germany and Italy, despite the fact that Germany despises yellow races and Italy's hands are red with the blood of black Africa.

"There is poverty in Japan; there is oppression; there is no democratic freedom. But nowhere in the modern world is there higher literacy, as newspaper circulations of one, three and even five millions prove. The Japanese laborer is not happy but he is not hopelessly discontended, for he belongs to the same class and family as the highest Japanese. They will guide and protect. He will obey.

"To me, the tragedy of this epoch was that Japan learned Western ways too soon and too well, and turned from Asia to Europe. She had a fine culture, an exquisite art, and an industrial technique miraculous in workmanship and adaptability. The Japanese clan was an effective social organ and her art expression was unsurpassed. She might have led Asia and the world into a new era. But her headstrong leaders chose to apply Western imperialism to her domination of the East, and Western profit-making replaced Eastern idealism. If she had succeeded, it might have happened that she would indeed have spread her culture and achieved a co-prosperity sphere with freedom of soul. Perhaps!"

In the dying days of 1936, while great Fujiyama still veiled its silver face, Mansart went down to Yokohama and set foot upon the sea. He sailed east into the sunset again to discover America, in his own thought and through the thinking and doing of other folk. Ten days he journeyed until he came, at Christmas, to an unbelievable land of raining sunshine and everlasting flowers, called Hawaii.

New Years, 1937, he stood in California of fact and fable, with the city of St. Francis of poverty and the birds before him, and lifted up his eyes to the hills beyond the Golden Gate. Lifted them and let them drop; two small years, two little years; suddenly he saw the whole world again aflame.

CHAPTER V

Color in the West Indies

Manuel Mansart was standing at the front gate of his campus in Macon, looking over the grounds. He was scowling a little and tapping his foot. It was a beautiful morning, one of those soft, glowing fall days of the South where there is no hint of cold weather and yet the heat of summer has gone. It was balmy, the trees were beautiful, and the breezes enticing.

The President had been back from his trip around the world for several months, and as he looked about he was beginning to ask himself, why are we here, and for what end? What is our duty and our ideal?

Just then he heard a sneeze and saw Jean approaching to begin her morning's work. They greeted each other cordially.

"You've got a cold," he said.

"Yes, I have. Perhaps I've been overworking a little. It wasn't really so hard while you were away, but of course there were some irritating matters. You know, our colored men I think even more than whites, are not yet used to seeing authority in the hands of a woman. They knew that I could do your work but they resented it—not so much in word but in various ways. They resented having me put over them, and also some of the trustees were a little doubtful of my beliefs. But there was no real difficulty because, after all, I knew the work and the details and they knew that I knew, and they let matters go on. But I did have to keep busy and watchful, and perhaps I'm a bit run down."

"I'm sorry you are," Mansart said. "I tell you what I think you ought to do. Take a month off after the holidays and run down to the West Indies and look about. I got a new slant on the West Indies while I was in France. A Negro named James gave me his book to read and it is revolutionary. We must include the West Indies in our survey. You'll not have time for doing much, but induce one or two delegates to attend our conference."

"I think I may," said Jean. And then she asked, "May I ask what you were thinking about? That scowl on your forehead was ominous."

"Yes," he said. "I came home from looking at the world with the idea that, after all, the object of our life is or should be Beauty, having lovely things about us. I think of those ancient wooden temples high in the forests of Japan. I think of that cathedral near where I lived in England. I think of the castles on the Loire in France. I think of so many lovely things. This world was meant to be beautiful. Beauty is, after all, the object of life."

Jean demurred. "Beauty? Yes, one object, of course. But not only beauty. In a way, not simply beauty. There must be people to know it and appreciate it, and they must have time to look and hear and enjoy. Looking about us here, how many people have time or training to enjoy a Titian painting or a great piece of statuary?"

Manuel was silent. Then he said slowly, "Nevertheless, for those who have time, for those who can, we must have beautiful things, even while we wait for more folks to enjoy them. And this campus is ugly. Oh, there are some good things; there are the classic lines of our Administration Hall. We have kept the old pillars of the South which the South in some curious way took from the Greeks. And yonder is a simple but rather fine façade."

"Yes," answered Jean. "Only one thing bothers me. The South in its better homes did keep simple, classic and beautiful lines. But have you ever thought that the Southern home never had space or a place for a kitchen, much as it needed kitchens? They had to be stuck on, apart from the main house."

Mansart smiled and said, "At any rate I'm going to have some grass on this campus, or something that looks like grass. I'm going to have some more trees planted, and then I'm going to have some pieces of sculpture. And in the halls some good paintings."

"Fine!" said Jean. "Only of course you must remember that the Trustees are going to ask about the cost of all this!" And laughing, she went into the building.

She realized that Mansart's wonderful trip around the world had broadened his outlook and broken down some of the barriers that had hemmed him in to a narrow racial world. Life had become beauty, logic, and comfort. But also Jean wondered if this very breadth was going to make Mansart forget or ignore the narrow demands of his exacting job from which he had glimpsed so fine a freedom.

Jean's cold persisted, and after Christmas she planned a trip to the West Indies. She remembered that from Virginia, through the Carolinas, Georgia, and Florida to Cuba, Haiti, Jamaica, and Panama, lay an unbroken country where Negroes and mulattoes were in recurrent majority groups. Whatever touched and influenced one part of this group, influenced the whole. Then she read James' *Black Jacobins* and Leger's *History of Haiti* and other books. She was astonished and thrilled. She wanted particularly to stand on that battlefield where Dessalines overthrew the power of France in 1803.

She went on one of those floating steamers making a round trip from Miami and touching briefly, all too briefly, at Cuba and Jamaica, Haiti, Puerto Rico, the Virgin Islands and the Bahamas. As usual, she travelled alone. She had no white friends with whom she could go, and of course colored friends could not secure accommodations.

She was first struck by the unbelievable beauty in these mountains stretching up from the depths of the seas into the heavens, with glorious foliage and flowers beyond description. And then, still amazed, she was depressed by the poverty, ignorance, and disease crawling upon them, dotted here and there with white vulgarity and tourist extravagance. Especially the tourists infuriated her—these droves of stupid, gaping fools intermingled with thieves, gamblers, whores, and idlers. All with money and few with anything else. Unaware of where they were and blind to what they said, laughing at the natives, sneering at poverty and ignorance; tossing alms like bones to dogs and revelling in menial service from cheap "niggers."

She glimpsed Cuba and Jamaica. She saw the same pattern: a colored and black aristocracy climbing desperately on the backs of black peasants in order to ape the wealth and extravagance of white Englishmen or Americans; while writhing below, great clotted masses of filth and sorrow, struggling toward the sun, but smothered with mist so that European race superiority and American robbery and rape looked like the uplift of man.

Jean debarked at Haiti, looked at Port-au-Prince and then went north to the Citadel of Christophe and his palace. Then she came to Cap Haitien and sat in the square. She met the man quite by accident in the neglected square of Cap Haitien. She had asked her way in passable French of a loitering boy, to the battlefield where Dessalines conquered Rochambeau. He did not understand, speaking only Creole; but the man sitting near answered.

Jean looked at him with interest and instead of immediately seeking the battlefield, started to talk. The man, Dr. Duval (he preferred writing it "du Val") was a well-known character on the Cape. Educated in France and long a teacher in Haiti, he was now retired on a tiny pension which hardly sufficed for his support. He spent his time in reading and study and sat almost daily in the city park with books beside him and pamphlets and papers in his pockets. His greatest joy was to run across some intelligent listener with whom he could discuss West Indian history. He gave information gladly and at length, but was sensitive at any patronage or attempt to pay him for what he regarded as simple courtesy among gentlefolk. A showy American tourist once handed him a five dollar bill after receiving his guidance for nearly an hour. The enraged Duval threw the money in the gutter and indignantly strode away.

"What the hell ails the nigger," sputtered the American. "Wasn't that tip enough?"

Today, the Doctor sensed in Jean an intelligent lady of breeding. He talked voluminously.

He first pointed across the square to the road leading to that last battlefield November 18, 1803, "when Dessalines and Capois overthrew the young Rochambeau, leader of the armies of Napoleon, who was seeking vainly a new empire in America."

"So Britain seized the West and the United States had Louisiana and the Pacific thrown into her lap for less than a song," said Jean. The man appeared gratified.

"Ah, you know something of history." Jean told him of her studies. "Hm!" he muttered. "But that is Anglo-Saxon history. The West Indies carried on the Renaissance; they formed a microcosm of modern history after 1500. But their story has been forgotten, distorted, twisted, and especially ridiculed—ridiculed and sneered into a mass of lies.

"Abbé Reynal said that labor in the West Indies 'may be considered as the principal cause of the rapid motion which now agitates the universe!'"

"But just how did this happen?" asked Jean.

"San Domingo was the finest colony in the world and its possibilities seemed limitless. After the independence of America in 1783, this French colony doubled its production in six years. In these years, Bordeaux alone invested 100 millions of dollars in San Domingo. The British bourgeois were the great rivals of the French. All through the eighteenth century, they fought each other in every part of the world."

"But the British stopped the African slave trade and eventually abolished slavery."

"The British colonies had enough slaves. San Domingo needed more. With tears for the poor suffering blacks, the new British bourgeois set up a great howl for the abolition of the slave trade, feeling their way to a greater exploitation of India. They began to abuse the West Indies as 'sterile rocks,' and asked if the interest of the nation should be sacrificed to 72,000 masters and 400,000 slaves?"

"But there was surely much real philanthropy in England?"

"Of course; and also faith that England was God's favorite. As one Englishman wrote: 'It seemed as if Providence, when it took from us America, would not leave its favorite people without an ample substitute.' Pitt saw a chance of capturing the continental market from France by East India sugar. The production of cotton in India doubled in a few years. Indian free labor cost a penny a day!"

As they conversed, Jean and her friend both stared across the great Northern plain toward the mountains where in dark and sombre beauty loomed the mighty citadel of Christophe. Dr. Duval was thin and yellow, shabbily but neatly dressed and a cultured gentleman in manner and language. There was about him no faint trace of servility, or thought that any woman of any color should not be honored by his attention. He pointed to the vast plain:

"Yonder the black slaves came, swept on like a hurricane; but what summoned them was the Wheel."

"The Wheel?"

"The Wheel, where they crucified the handsome Ogé, the mulatto educated in France where he fought boldly for the Free Negroes of Haiti. He said no word for the black slaves. Indeed, mulattoes, educated in Paris during the Seven Years' War, were often slave-owners."

"Why was Ogé attacked?"

"Ogé had sought status for Free Negroes alongside the whites of San Domingo as citizens of France. The whites would have no such alliance. They seized Ogé and Chavannes. They bound them to a great wheel; they broke their bones with bars of iron, and exposed them writhing and bloody to the burning midday sun until they died in agony."

"I remember," said Jean. "The whites and free mulattoes began to fight."

"But on the 14th of August, 1791, down from the crags and valleys of yonder sinister mountains and across that wide and fertile plain which for one hundred and twenty-five years had been making France rich and Europe envious—down poured four hundred thousand black men, most of them slaves, some freemen whose forebears had hidden in these mountains for more than a century. Over the long, green snake and the reeking entrails of a wild boar they had sworn allegiance to Boukman, crying in Creole to 'The God who created the Sun which gives us light; who arouses the waves and rules the Storm; who sees what the White Man does: watch over us and lead us!'

"In a few days one-half of the famous North Plain was a flaming ruin. From Le Cap the whole horizon was a wall of fire. From this wall continually rose thick black volumes of smoke, through which came tongues of flame leaping to the very sky. For nearly three weeks the people of Le Cap could barely distinguish night from day, while a rain of burning cane straw, driven before the wind like flakes of snow, flew over the city and the shipping in the harbor, threatening both with destruction . . .

"They, whose women had undergone countless violations, violated all the white women who fell into their hands, often on the bodies of their still bleeding husbands, fathers, and brothers. 'Vengeance! Vengeance!' was their war-cry, and they carried a white child on a pike as a standard!"

Jean looked at her companion and murmured:

"So the Reign of Terror came from France to Haiti."

"Oh, no, no! The reign of Terror started in Haiti; it did not reach France until three years later, when white French workers recognized their unity with black slaves and fought with and for them. Indeed, the French Revolution itself started in the West Indies, in the twenty-five uprisings of black workers which from 1523 to 1780 swept the West Indies and erupted in Paris in 1789."

Jean stared at her companion. What looked like disbelief in her eyes, was really resentment that in her study of history, in her attempt to know what the world had done, this central bit of history had been almost entirely concealed and distorted.

"You do not believe me!" he said.

"Oh, yes, yes!" she protested, "only the interpretation is so unusual—so new—"

He smiled and started to his feet:

"I will give you names of books; as you travel home, read them. But twilight falls. Before dark we have time to visit the battlefield which you wished to see."

Jean insisted on hiring a ramshackle cab and they rode west. As they rode Jean asked:

"After the uprising of the slaves, what happened?"

"Both Spain and Britain tried to seize San Domingo, while France strove to keep it. But its value was its slaves, and this threw contradiction into the lap of the Revolution. Toussaint appeared as leader of the slaves and Spain secured his services since he distrusted the French. The San Domingo planters invited in the English, and William Pitt seized most of Haiti and several other islands. Britain was on the edge of owning the rich West Indies. This would mean the re-establishment of slavery in the West Indies and a rich Britain could then overthrow the Revolution in France.

"But in France, Revolution reached its climax. The working masses of the French people took power in their own hands and the Reign of Terror ensued. The owners of wealth and employers of labor bowed to the workers. They declared hate for the 'aristocracy of the skin' and refused to drink coffee because it was stained with the blood of slaves. Then from the West Indies came a dramatic climax. In January, 1794, three deputies arrived from San Domingo—a white man, a mulatto, and a black man. When this black man, Bellay, finished his speech, the Convention declared the abolition of slavery in the French colonies!

"Immediately, Toussaint left the service of Spain and took charge of the French forces in San Domingo, proclaiming the freedom of the slaves. This black West Indian drove the British army out of San Domingo."

"But could Negro slaves oppose the British army?"

"They did. Fortesque, historian of the army, said the year 1795 was 'the most disgraceful year in the history of the British army.' The English in three years lost 80,000 soldiers in the West Indies, a loss greater than Wellington's in the Peninsular campaign. They spent $25,000,000 and General White advised withdrawal. General Maitland entered into negotiations with Toussaint.

"A convention was signed in which the English evacuated the island. General Maitland arranged a brilliant parade and royal banquet, after which he presented Toussaint, in the name of the King of England, a bronze cannon from the mansion of the Governor and superb vessels of silver and gold."

"What now was the real significance of Thermidor for black slaves?" asked Jean.

"The counter-revolution of Thermidor meant not only the triumph of the bourgeoisie over the workers, but the attempt to restore 'order' in San Domingo. French owners and investors wept. 'There is no longer any ship-building in our ports. The manufactories are deserted and even the shops are closed. Thus, thanks to your sublime decree, every day is a holiday for the workers. We can count more than three hundred thousand in our different towns who have no other occupation than, arms folded, to talk about the news of the day, of the Rights of Man, and of the Constitution.'

"Babeuf, a menial servant, preached communism, freedom for the blacks, and the unity of white and black workers. He organized the 'Society of Equals' but was executed in 1797. The owners and merchants raged. France tried to support the mulatto Rigaud against Toussaint, since Rigaud fought for slavery of the blacks. Toussaint triumphed again and the French bourgeoisie did not dare to try to re-establish slavery, but they began to fear that Toussaint might set up an independent island. The English encouraged this idea. But Toussaint believed in France and showed his faith in France by sending his sons there for education."

"And his reward?"

"His reward was eventual betrayal and cruel death in France at the hands of Napoleon."

They stepped out of the cab and looked about the bare field.

Jean went back in thought to the fall of the Directory in France and the establishment of the Consulate of Napoleon Bonaparte.

Duval continued: "It was clear that Napoleon hated and feared Negroes, and this despite the fact that his first step upward in Paris, came from his marriage to a West Indian octoroon. Josephine de Beauharnais had married into the French nobility. When her husband was guillotined, she found protection at the hands of friends of Napoleon and became the most glamorous figure in Paris society.

"Napoleon married her just before he started on his Italian campaign. He coveted for France its richest colonial possession, and was frightened at seeing it fall into the hands of the British. But before he could turn his attention to the West Indies, Toussaint had arisen and made himself practically independent of France. He had seized the whole island from Spain and in 1801 actually had the impudence to proclaim a constitution. He protested, and quite sincerely, his loyalty to France. But Napoleon, furious, determined to kill him. He planned a formidable fleet of 86 ships built in France, Spain, and Holland. It carried 22,000 soldiers trained under Napoleon himself and commanded by his brother-in-law, Leclerc.

"The fleet anchored at Cap Haitien in February, 1802. The city was under the command of Christophe. Leclerc ordered surrender in twenty-four hours. The reply was a volley of artillery fire and then Christophe burned the city, including his own home, to the ground. There followed two years of fearful war. The troops and the fever decimated the French.

"Leclerc soon was frightened. He wrote: 'My position becomes worse every day. Sickness carries off the men. Toussaint is not to be trusted, as I had indeed expected, but I have drawn from his submission the object I had expected.'

"Leclerc then resorted to disgraceful deceit. He lured Toussaint aboard his flagship on pretense of further negotiation. There the great black leader was seized and taken to France.

"Toussaint was murdered by cold and neglect in the snows of the Alps. This Napoleon thought would be the end, but it was not. First, Leclerc was in dread about slavery. He wrote Napoleon. Read here in this book: 'Do not think of establishing slavery here for some time. All the blacks are persuaded, by letters which have come from France, by the law which re-establishes the slave trade, by the decree of General Richepanse which re-established slavery in Guadeloupe, that the intention is to make them slaves again.'

"Then he screams: 'I have just discovered a great plot which aimed at raising the whole colony in revolt by the end of Thermidor. It was only partially executed for lack of a leader. It is not enough to have taken away Toussaint, there are 2,000 chiefs to be taken away. . . .

"'Although I have painted such a horrible situation I ought to say that I am not without courage. . . . For four months now I exist merely by adroitness, without having any real force; judge if I can fulfill the intentions of the Government.'

"On November 2, the sick and distracted Leclerc died. Of the 34,000 French soldiers he had brought, 24,000 had died, 8,000 were in the hospital, and only 2,000 exhausted men remained. Rochambeau succeeded Leclerc.

"Rochambeau was a ruthless beast. He received 20,000 new French troops after the death of Leclerc. He drowned so many people in the Bay of Cap Haitien that fish were no longer eaten. He hunted down the blacks with dogs. He burned Negroes alive, hanged and tortured them, and buried them to the neck in nests of insects.

"But Dessalines returned blow for blow. He hanged 500 white troops before Rochambeau's eyes. He burned the North Plain until it was a charred desert. On this spot here, Dessalines tore the white stripe from the red, white, and blue of the tricolor, and made the remaining red and blue, Blood and Sky, the flag of free Haiti. On November 16, 1803, the blacks and mulattoes gathered for a last attack upon Cap Haitien. A white slave-owner wrote a half-century later: 'But what black men these are! How they fight and how they die! I have seen a solid column, torn by grape-shot from four pieces of cannon, advance without making a retrograde step. The more fell, the greater seemed to be the courage of the rest....'

"'Those songs shouted into the sky in unison by 2,000 voices, to which the cannon formed the bass, produced a thrilling effect. The French too marched singing to their death, lighted by a magnificent sun. Even today after more than 40 years, this majestic and glorious spectacle still lives as vividly in my imagination as in the moments when I saw it.'

"On November 28, Rochambeau surrendered and took refuge with the British. He left the corpses of 60,000 French soldiers and sailors behind. On December 31, Dessalines read the Haitian Declaration of Independence."

It was dark as Jean turned to leave this bare old battlefield. As they rode back, her guide continued:

"Christophe, who followed Dessalines, could not hold the blacks and mulattoes in one government. It was no longer slavery that kept them apart, but a different conception of the state. The North under Christophe harked back to African communism, with dictatorship and discipline to ward off the white world of colonial imperialism. Hence the citadel of defense yonder at La Ferrière, one of the wonders of the world.

"But Pétion and his mulattoes in the south had their faces set toward the new democracy of the nineteenth century, as led by France and America. Pétion helped forward the independence of South America and sought in vain the good will of the United States. But white labor democracy in France and England, built on the exploitation of colored labor, repudiated all union with black Haiti, save as a quasi-colonial area."

The next day after thanking her guide and mentor cordially, Jean left the Cape for Port-au-Prince. She perused in the books loaned her the extraordinary story of Haiti. From the day when the English overcome the French in Asia and conquered India; when the French, rich from slavery in the West Indies, found their nation overthrown at home and threatened by a demand for the equality of workers, black and white; when the English tried to seize the West Indies; when Napoleon tried to enter Asia by way of Egypt and Toussaint L'Ouverture overthrew French, English, and Spanish; when the French workers tried to unite black and white in one struggle and the British subordinated the black worker under the white and bribed the white with higher wages, the color line stood until Russia abolished it and saved the world from a war of colors.

It seemed curiously clear now to Jean what had happened since. Great Britain had transferred her investments in the West Indies, and in the name of emancipation exchanged the West Indian plantations for new investment and expanded capitalism in African and Asian colonies. Thence came the industrial revolution and the new imperialism, born of the blood of Negro slaves.

CHAPTER VI

The Conference

Jean re-embarked at Port-au-Prince and sailed to Puerto Rico whence she planned to return home by way of the Bahamas. But at San Juan she left the ship again and went to the Virgin Islands. She wanted to be alone to read and think about the West Indies, and plan a message which she could bring back to Manuel Mansart.

On returning, Jean accomplished one goal she had long had in mind. She became dean of the college. She had long been this in fact and was acting dean when Mansart was abroad. On his return, the office of full dean should have been established, but in that case a man would naturally have been appointed. Since no man on the faculty seemed fitted for the job, the matter was dropped. Then Mansart got back in harness, and the need of a dean with authority became clear, especially as Mansart's mind and activities became increasingly engrossed in large matters outside the college. Quietly therefore Mansart and Coypel, head of the white University system and Mansart's superior, with the careless consent of Baldwin, voice of Big Business, succeeded in making Jean du Bignon titular dean of the college.

Outside her routine duties Jean now gave most of her time to the new organization for southwide study of race relations. She planned to have the first conference at the state college in 1938, including not only the teachers of sociology in the Land-Grant colleges and the private colored institutions of the South, but a few leading social thinkers of the nation. She wanted in that way first to settle questions of method and aim in sociology for the guidance of the colored colleges; and also to get various institutions more and more interested and involved in this movement.

First, she corresponded with the presidents of the colored Land-Grant colleges, urging them themselves to attend, and especially to send their professors of sociology or teachers of analogous subjects. Nearly all the colleges promised co-operation. Then Jean began writing to southern white institutions to invite their sociologists to meet with the conference as observers and advisers. A few responded. Finally, she sought to insure the attendance of certain leading Northern teachers and writers on social subjects. She induced Mansart to promise them expenses with board either in the college or at the white hotels in the city. Several consented.

Jean tried to keep central in her mind the object of this purely scientific program as the best way to ward off criticism and make sure of the co-operation of all the colored people and especially of the white trustees. On the other hand, no scientific work can function in a vacuum and Jean knew that inevitably the conferees would be considering in their own minds how and why the information gathered would eventually be used. In her own thinking she had assumed that the "socialism" of the Roosevelt era would be regarded as normal for the future by those who attended the conference. But in that case the more ticklish question of Negro political power must be in the minds of all, if not actually mentioned; for socialism could only be established by votes. Moreover, all the conferees must know that organized industry was increasingly going to center its efforts in the South because of its resources, its climate, its cheap labor and lack of labor organization. She conceived therefore that the trade union movement, particularly in the South, would be an object for her to investigate and, so far as possible, influence.

There was also the accompanying question of how far the American Negro, especially in the South, should try to develop as a self-supporting unit inside the white group. Already this path was recognized in music and art; it was venturing into drama, and it was manifest also in a distinct body of literature. But Jean saw that the economic aspect was as yet but partially conceived. There was, of course, the "Group Economy" discussed in the Atlanta University studies; and there was "Consumers' Co-operation" which the *Crisis*, organ of the NAACP, was pushing. But heavy industry and the trade unions, and the part and place of the Negro in this crucial development was not yet envisaged. Should separate trade unions be organized for Negroes, and a nation-wide Negro trade union movement be organized? Jean pondered long on these matters. What would be the relation of Negro business to the national business development? But all these considerations Jean put sternly aside from her main object in this organization, which was truth about race relations in the United States, gathered scientifically and presented to the world without bias.

But, Jean continued to reflect, here was Mansart's ideal of beauty, and here was the poverty that could not appreciate it. What was to be done about this? She kept thinking this over. Her idea, firmly fixed at first, was to achieve a scientific knowledge of the truth, even in sociology, a discovery of its rhythms, a realization of the possibility of prophecy. To this she still held.

Manual Mansart, while obsessed by his realization of the beauty and order of the world, was interested in the economic development of the Negro. He agreed with Jean's plans to study the Negro on a wide scientific scale. He wanted to plot the Negro's industrial future in this world which industry ruled. But he saw no clear path at present. Meantime, he wanted his college, his teachers and students, to realize what the world meant now as a place to live in.

First of all, he himself began to have a conception of the world as one unified dwelling place. He was escaping from his racial provincialism. He began to think of himself as part of humanity and not simply as an American Negro over against a white world. As he looked about, it seemed to him that one place to start was by beginning to make the State College at Macon a more beautiful and satisfying place than it had been, a better expression of the breadth and beauty of life. Interfering with this and disturbing his thought was the unrest in Europe, the premonition of possible war. Yet, he insisted on thinking of the broader aims of civilization, of the integration of mankind into the world; of the appeal to duty and order through peace. He did not believe, he could not believe, that there was going to be another world war.

He said to himself and repeated to Jean: "Surely it is quite impossible that civilization should try war again?"

Jean looked at him contemplatively and said: "I'm not so sure, President Mansart. I'm not at all sure. You see, the difficulty is that the problem which drove us into the First World War is unsettled, and that is the domination of the backward parts of the earth for the benefit of Europe and North America; and the use of the profit from colonialism to settle the problem of the worker in imperial nations. All that we settled or seemed to settle in the First World War was that Germany was not going to be admitted as an equal partner in colonial imperialism with France and England. And now, you see, that is rebounding. Germany and Italy are insisting not simply on world partnership, but it would seem that they want world dictatorship."

Manuel mused a considerable time. Then he said, "I think I have learned something new concerning nations, colonies and social classes on this trip. The classic division of classes within countries in the past left a great mass of labor at the bottom, working in ignorance and sickness chiefly for the benefit of a small hereditary aristocracy. This is still a pattern in much of the Middle East and in Central and South America.

"But in Western Europe and North America this pattern has changed. There, a considerable but a much smaller mass of ignorant and sick labor is at the bottom; and feeding on that, as well as subsidized by a powerful ruling oligarchy, is a large middle group of skilled and white-collar workers who think they have more to lose in any revolution than chains; they can lose homes and musical instruments, automobiles, electrical gadgets, servants, and the opportunity to live as superiors over lower classes. Their temptation to curb or overthrow the ruling oligarchy is modified first by the real chance that some of their own group may be able to join the rich, or negated by their share in the profit of exploiting not only the lowest classes in their own country but the majority of the working people of the world in Asia, Africa and South America."

Jean assented and added: "This turns most of the well-paid laborers of Britain, France and the United States into supporters of the ruling rich. In defense of their higher wage they join in oppression of the poor, and all the more cruelly because they so vividly know and fear poverty. Then, too, they consent to serve as well-paid soldiers to keep the poor peoples of the world in servitude to the rich. Thus, by higher wages and political power, they share in the loot of Asia, Africa, Central and South America, the Caribbean and South Sea areas.

"Especially in the United States, the middle-class well-paid worker has long been inured to oppression by living beside despised and exploited groups like Negroes, Indians and foreign immigrants. The law permitted this oppression and custom set few limits. Democracy was denied most such groups, and if war comes again, here lurks the cause."

Manuel went on with his thoughts and plans. First, he began to beautify the college grounds with trees, flowers and shrubs. He repaired and built fences and painted woodwork. Pictures seemed to have never been thought of in his college and indeed not often in the South. He found he could easily get large reproductions of the world's best pictures, and his students in their carpentry classes could frame them. So there began to appear in the halls and in the dormitories representations of European art: the older and greater painters, Michelangelo, Titian and Rubens, the dark visages of Goya, and some representation of the newer trends—Matisse and Gauguin and even Picasso. Especially, he wanted colored faces portrayed in a region where all skins were rendered white or caricatured. Works of colored artists like Tanner and Meta Warrick were sought.

To this, Manuel managed to add some large pieces of statuary. The trustees were not altogether in agreement here. They did not like naked white Greek figures. They thought it would have a bad effect on the morals of Negroes. But the Venus of Milo demanded entrance, and the Victory of Samothrace, and some Roman athletes. There were busts of Douglass and Booker Washington.

It then occurred to Manuel that he must do something more about the library. He really needed a new library building. And by arrangement with the New Deal Administration a rather fine building was erected in 1938, with both books and room to read and lounge. He secured a trained colored librarian with imagination, and began to buy books systematically. Back of the library a large room was set aside as a little theater, which thus brought a new and interesting member to the staff and resulted in entertainment for the students and some original writing.

In consultation with his daughter Sojourner, Mansart enlarged his whole music program. He forecast a school of music which not only would emphasize American Negro music but the music of Africa, the West Indies and South America, then go on to cover the great music of the modern world with Bach, Beethoven and Wagner. Some of the trustees thought this program overambitious; and the teachers had difficulty in gathering talent for orchestration, voices for singing and audiences to listen. But the work grew slowly. Colored singers like Hayes and pianists like Maud Cuney appeared in concert.

Jean's plan was to induce each Negro college to undertake continuous social study of the Negro population of its own state. This would be financed by the local institution itself and would be on as wide and intensive a scale as it could afford. It would take advantage of local and current studies of every kind, made by the state, organizations or private individuals; it would use the data of the United States Census, classifying matter which the census would not care or could not afford to use. Jean hoped that gradually these studies would become broader and more systematic and, following the criticisms of the sociologists gathered at the conferences, would also become more scientific and reliable. In time, Jean dreamed, there would emerge the largest and most complete, continuous study of the actions of a definite human group which the world anywhere was attempting, and out of this might come measurements for a science of sociology such as never yet had existed.

Naturally, the actual conference was disappointing. Only a few of the colored presidents attended. Most of the institutions, however, sent teachers of social science; but they were not a very promising group. The first step toward a realization of her project, Jean saw, would be to have better teachers hired and give them more time and money for this work. Four white Northern sociologists came and were very encouraging about the general program. They did not expect a Science of Sociology to emerge as Jean did, but they were sure that with care and some money, a most interesting body of knowledge might gradually be accumulated. The two white Southerners who came also expressed interest, along with some surprise. They wondered if Negroes could carry out such a plan. If they could, it would be an excellent effort.

There were only a few set speeches; most of the work was discussion, and that often was stimulating. There were few studies already in the making, and therefore few reports; but many plans were announced. Among the set speeches was one by a chance visitor.

Aba Aziz, who called himself in America, Alexander Abraham, was visiting the college. As was the custom, strangers of distinction, especially if colored, were welcomed at the college and entertained. This one seemed a man of education, and was asked by the President to stop over and to address the conference.

He was tall, thin, black of skin, with close-curled hair. His English was beautiful, as was indeed his French, German, Italian, Russian and Arabic; which last two languages he never used or admitted knowing when in the United States. His address was clear and short, but puzzling. He said:

"We admit that clear knowledge of Things is the best way to understanding. Yet an embarrassing question may here be asked: What do we really know of the Things we think about if indeed there are any real Things beyond our thought of them? Common sense comes to support Science and says, let us act as though this outer world really exists and proceed to know and measure it. On this hypothesis we build up a world of mass and energy which moves in Time and Space and shows astonishing regularities. Indeed, last century we had reached the place where we believed we were on the track of the Universal Laws of action among Things and closing in on analogous laws governing all life, vegetable, animal and human. Then in our day came a halting.

"This moving mass, at one end infinitely small and at the other a vast reach of stars, with earth between, when interrogated not only refused to exhibit the same regularities, but differed widely and disturbingly. They contradicted each other so that at least among the atoms we could speak only of Probability and even of sheer Chance which the pre-scientific students had rather infelicitously called Free Will. Time and Space seemed to be but aspects of one Thing and the universe could only be explained scientifically if we mathematically assumed that we had measured what was at present Unmeasurable unless and until we know what is now apparently Unknowable.

"All this the oldest, exact scientist resented, the Priest ridiculed, but the mathematician proved true by splitting and fusing atoms; while bending rays of light and blending motion and mass. All of which challenges the present day student. In this complex the present conference, as I understand, takes its place. It will, so far as it can, measure human conduct in a distinct and controlled area and there either discover Law or delimit the boundaries of Chance."

Mr. Abraham sat down amid a polite but faint applause. Few in the audience had any idea of what he was trying to say. Some of the white trustees consulted later.

"What the Hell was he talking about?"

"Sounded like nonsense to me."

"Who is he?"

"What does he really know about atoms? If so, how and why?"

"Let's get in touch with the FBI; he may bear investigation."

The FBI gathered in the next year an astonishing amount of knowledge about Aziz. The man was born in Yemen.

Where is Yemen? East of Egypt! But in what nation? Saudi Arabia.

Was he a Jew? Not of the orthodox types usually so known. But connected with the ancient rites—a Black Jew.

Educated? Oh, variously: in Cairo at El Azhar; in India at Calcutta; at Peking and the University of Tokyo; in Berlin, the Sorbonne and the University of London; also at Yale. He had taught short periods and on various subjects in Europe, Asia and Africa; in Spanish America.

In the Soviet Union? Oh yes, lived and studied for a year at Moscow. He had worked as an artisan in the United States—in electricity in Poughkeepsie and in a chemical plant in Chicago.

This information was easily secured and Aziz spoke frankly even about his change of name. But the conclusion was that he was either a spy or saboteur. He admitted that he was a Communist.

"I greatly admire the Russians and their system of education," he said casually, as he was taken to prison. Then he dropped from sight. A final report said that he had apparently been accidentally killed by falling from the walls of Alcatraz.

The trustees of the Georgia State College were on the whole gratified and pleasantly disappointed at the conference. The meeting was not radical or inflammatory. It enhanced the reputation of the State College. The chief result, beyond promise for the future, was the stimulation among the local teachers and the visitors of arguments and exchanges of views as to the future development of the American Negroes, especially along industrial lines. The place and future of the trade union movement came in for consideration, and then the general industrial policy within the race and over the nation. One of Mansart's most informing talks came after the conference, in a conversation with the Dark Dane, whom Jean had invited to the conference.

She explained to Mansart just what a Dark Dane was.

"The Danes, when they owned the Virgin Islands, used in certain cases to decree that individual Negroes of distinction were legally 'white,' with all the rights of Danes. Some descendants of such families still live on the islands and usually occupy high positions."

He was a black man, tall, with velvet skin and sharp features—a typical Scandinavian in all save color. A century since, the Danish government, ruling the Virgin Islands after Spain, France, the Knights of Malta and Britain, had decreed that his Negro ancestor was hereafter legally "white." His family henceforth was one with the rulers of the island of St. Croix. He had a good common school and high school education added to reading; he was familiar with the literature of Scandinavia and Britain, and knew something of the French. But he was insular. He had never travelled much, and his experience among men was narrow. He did not like white Americans and regarded their purchase of his island as a calamity. He met Manuel with grave courtesy which later ripened into friendship and considerable understanding.

"The West Indies," he said, "once were on the way to becoming highways of modern Europe to China and India. Beautiful beyond dream, with perfect climate, mountain, song and sea, they began to reflect European civilization in microcosm. Here culture, reborn in the Renaissance, lurched upward to new realization of a new world; new vegetation, free gold and such meeting of souls as once island Greece had known. Here Poverty, the scourge of Man, was to be conquered and Eternal Life achieved. Over these fortunate isles, out of Atlantis, the best of men started toward fabulous Asia, mother of human culture.

"But into this paradise the Serpent of Greed entered, and instead of an Eden for its own dark people and their European guests, arose Hell for the Indian, in blind effort to build a white heaven. But they made a mistake. They looked back; they turned back to Africa, the first of continents, so as to enslave its flesh and blood. They tried to forget Africa's past, malign its present and make its future a tale for beasts. To do this they had to blaspheme religion and lie to truth. The result was disaster: in slave revolt, human hate and degradation. All this brought revolution to Haiti, North America and France, and then came that revolution in industry which engulfed the modern world.

"This vast and fatal change in ways of making wealth and giving human service became more than successful in production but tragic in the way its results were divided among men. Not new culture in the dark West Indies, nor reborn civilization in China, brown India or black Africa became heirs of the new earth, but all these were forced to be sick, stupid, hungry victims of Great White Europe who tried to inherit the Earth. The world advance was twisted in Europe; Asia struggled and Africa shrieked until World War brought promise of utter disappearance of civilization."

Thus the Dark Dane spoke while Manuel listened in much astonishment, some doubt and a little agreement. He ventured at last to question:

"But what is happening in the West Indies, I cannot understand. I hear of undreamed of beauty in all these scattered islands; I hear of music and laughter and yet too, unease, sickness, unhappiness and the almost universal belief that real life and steady progress lie quite beyond these happy isles. Above all, the people: there is no people; or there are peoples of every sort, kind, and hue, and yet the bond between is so fragile and thin. They dislike each other so cordially!"

The Dark Dane counted on his fingers. "We are seven," he said. "The whites and the native whites; the mulattoes and the blacks; the Americans and Refugees; and the Tourists. Yes, God forgive us, the Tourists, who never belonged here and yet whom we invite and fawn on and let trample us to dust."

"But I thought—" said Manuel, astonished.

The Dark Dane interrupted. "You thought that the destiny of the West Indies was to be the playground of rich Americans where they could gamble, whore and get drunk at their sweet will, unhampered by law or gospel or even by the dictates of decent society; and above all where they could get rich on the ignorance, servility and poverty of the 'niggers.'"

"Well, no, not exactly that; but these hotels—"

"The chromium finish in Puerto Rico, in Cuba, San Domingo and Haiti. The cars and beaches, the dining, dancing and yachting, the shops and jewels—no, no! The West Indies should be center of a new and better world culture arising from and around and for their ten million colored folk and for such other human beings who wish to share their destiny as equal citizens and human companions. Impossible? Oh no! I've thought it all out. Listen.

"We would begin as a small compact group here in St. Croix; ten families, a hundred, a thousand, with a little money, able to read and write, trained to think. First on fair-sized plots of average land we would raise what we needed to eat, importing nothing but what we absolutely must; using brown sugar, unrefined by cheating Americans; eating our own abundant fruit and vegetables with no canned slop; balancing our diet according to science but avoiding fads. We would build our own outdoor homes; low, ventilated and sun-bathed. We would dare shake our fists in the face of Paris and New York fashion, and weave our own cloth from our own fibres. When we could we would learn to make and use the new synthetic fibres; but cotton, wool, flax and silk could cover us until nylon monopoly was broken. We would till the ground by inches, not by miles, and use hands and feet instead of tractors until better machines for simpler land culture were invented by our own brains or the brains of other human beings working for human happiness and not merely for profit.

"And all our object would be leisure, not work; time for thought, education, painting, poetry and sculpture; scientific exploration and invention. There would be no patents or copyrights but rewards, prizes and scholarships for individuals; drama and theater, visitors—not stupid 'tourists'—but artists and singers, poor in pocket, rich in talent and unwilling to barter their souls to the metropolitan tyrants; writers out of whom greedy publishers could not make money and therefore try to starve."

"But wait," interrupted Manuel. "You go fast and make fearful progress in words. But there are obstacles. First, land. The land of the West Indies either already is or is rapidly becoming monopolized. Where would your community live?"

"We would tax heavily all unused land and let each use tax free what land he needs for crops or homes. Property would be a social trust, revocable at will, with just compensation for any real sacrifice; ownership of property always known and publicly registered, and all income of everybody known to all with source and reason."

"But the power to do this?"

"We can vote."

"But my dear man, so can other millions; but they vote as the rich and powerful order or—"

"Are destroyed. But we would realize Democracy. We would vote as we wanted and we would learn and teach what we ought to want and how to get it."

"But do you realize how little of such democratic government there is in the world and how quickly and effectively that little can be nullified or done away with? And how in God's name can you get a voting body intelligent enough to know what is best for them and how to vote it in?"

"My dear President Mansart, do you actually doubt the possibility of human intelligence and the practicability of education?"

"Well, no, but universal popular education started a hundred years ago and where are we?"

"Did it start with the Reform Bill, or did we merely start talking about it? I tell you, it's possible."

"Moreover, your land program and rewards, and I suppose with Social Medicine and Old Age Security, public ownership of public utilities—all this sounds much like Communism."

"Like Communism?"

"You know, the Russian way—Iron Curtain and all that."

"Is that Communism? Why I thought Communists were murderers, conspirators and liars—at least so I have been told."

"And naturally believed it, as you will in future believe what you are told about other things. You see, dear friend, we are all at the mercy of what we are told, and ever will be."

"And education is impossible because Truth is unattainable?"

"Well—"

"It is not well; it is ill." The Dark Dane looked disgusted. Mansart served tea.

CHAPTER VII

The Southern Worker

Jean was thoughtful after the conference. She was at once disappointed and encouraged. Her main object seemed attained—that of securing co-operation from the teachers in the various colored colleges. But in conversing with the delegates and visitors she found surprisingly little sense of the use to which the facts of social investigation should be put. Some seemed to think that the object of the studies was the skills and training secured by the investigators. Of further use of this body of knowledge for social reform, their ideas were curiously vague.

Jean was aware that this was to be expected from her plan, and that this was her proclaimed object. But she realized that despite her own purely scientific goal, she was really most interested in the uses of information rather than just in obtaining it; that this was the only excuse for all this trouble in these critical times.

The more she thought the matter over, the more she herself wanted to become familiar with industry which dominated the world. It must dominate the world, for men must work for food and shelter before they could rightly think and feel. She was aware of how theoretical her knowledge of factories and real production was. The labor movement to her was mainly words and theory. What was true in her own case was even more true of her fellow teachers. They knew industry as brute toil, seldom as organized and planned execution. They knew of servants, laborers, teachers and professional men, but seldom of skilled factory hands, union members and labor leaders.

She determined, therefore, to take her summer vacation of three months away from the college to cross into the neighboring but far-off white world and learn what a textile factory really was. There was risk in thus crossing the color line. Hitherto, her chief difficulty had been to stay within her "race." Now she would use her opportunity and be for a time what she seemed to be—"white."

She knew that hiding would be easiest nearby, and so she just rode to Atlanta, and got acquainted with the members of the Textile Union. The union was not large. It had no valid contracts with the industry, and its membership was firm on the exclusion of Negroes. She learned that in North Carolina Negro tobacco workers and white union textile workers had found some common ground, but had been suppressed by the militia. The new CIO was working in the South, and large numbers of Negroes were coming into the general union movement, but not into textiles.

Jean rented a room in the white working section and began to talk to the women workers. She said that she wanted to become an apprentice in spinning and weaving. They laughed at her.

"Why on earth do you want to work in a mill? You've got an education," they contended.

"Yes," said Jean, "but I want to know how to do the work. I want to become a worker, and see if we can't organize for better wages and conditions."

"Well, we can't. If we go into the union and try to force the employers, first thing you know they'd have 'niggers' here working in our place."

"In that case," said Jean argumentatively, "I wonder if it wouldn't be a good plan to anticipate them and get some good reliable Negro workers into the mills."

The woman she was talking to sniffed. "I'd die first," she said.

Jean kept on. Over a period of three months she got the chance to work as an apprentice. Then she joined the union and finally spent a week working in one of the factories. She talked with labor leaders and found them discouraged.

"With whites and Negroes competing we can't get anywhere in the labor movement."

"Then," said Jean, "stop competing. Unite."

"I know it," he said. "That's what we ought to do, but that's exactly what we can't. It's the one thing that's quite impossible."

"I wonder if we couldn't try the impossible." Jean said. And she made arrangements the following summer to help in the state office as a volunteer.

After the winter had passed Jean returned to Atlanta. One morning Zoe Scroggs, who was now in charge of the state office, arrived to find a visitor waiting.

Zoe was the daughter of Coypel, the superintendent of Atlanta schools who had made Manuel Mansart head of the colored schools. It was Zoe who was in the street encounter which resulted in the beating of Mansart's son, Bruce. Eventually Zoe had married Scroggs, the labor leader, who once ran for governor and now headed the state labor movement. Zoe apologized for being late and quickly got to her desk.

"So sorry to be late. What can I do for you, Miss—?"

Jean Du Bignon looked at Zoe thoughtfully. She had come to talk with Joe Scroggs to learn more about the union movement, and also if possible to sound him out about the future of Negroes in the union movement. She had not known that Zoe was active in this work, and that put a new idea into her head. Why not try to enlist Zoe's sympathy? It would be a risk, and she might spoil her own plans. But Zoe looked intelligent and Jean knew something about her. She even sensed her contacts with Bruce Mansart, Manuel's ill-fated son. This might be providential; also, it might be fatal. She smiled and said:

"Officially, I am Jean Smith, studying about trade unions and seeking summer work. In fact—" she paused and looked Zoe in the eye; "in fact, I am colored and teach in the colored State College at Macon. My real interest is the future relation of Negroes to organized labor. My real name is Jean du Bignon."

There was a pause and Jean waited. She saw surprise, resentment, indecision and resolve chase themselves across Zoe's countenance. Then Zoe said slowly:

"I have heard of you from my father. I am glad to know you." Then she made the last gesture of surrender from a Southern white to a colored person: she held out her hand.

They talked for an hour on the union movement in general, in the nation and in Georgia. Then Jean began to talk about Negro workers. But Zoe stopped her. She hesitated and then blurted out:

"Did you know Bruce Mansart?"

"Oh yes; quite well. He was in one of my classes. I was at the college when the football game was played in Atlanta."

Zoe went white and was silent. Then she whispered, "He is dead?"

"Yes."

"How did—he die?"

Jean paused and lowered her eyes. "He was hanged."

Zoe gripped her hands together and shivered. But Jean continued: "It was for a murder committed in Missouri. The poor boy had gone mad. Indeed, I am sure that he was never wholly sane after that beating by the police in Atlanta."

"That is true; it must be true."

"And now what I want is to be sure in the future that boys like Bruce with a mechanical gift, and other Negro workers who can help in the world's work, get a chance to work beside their white fellows, so that together they can raise the working class to such respect and income that they can occupy their rightful leadership in the world."

Zoe, with tears in her eyes, said, "What a loss, what a horrible loss to the world, when a man like Bruce Mansart is driven from work to crime by senseless prejudice. We'll be pals. We'll work together. We won't tell Joe all of this yet. He wouldn't understand. He's honest and he's striving toward right. But he needs time and knowledge. I'll see you have a job here this summer. You guide my studies and I'll guide Joe. We'll reach the right if it takes a lifetime."

Then Zoe added, "You know that Angelo Herndon has been freed by the Supreme Court?"

"Yes," said Jean, "that was a queer case; I never understood it."

"It was white and black labor trying to get together; but you see, it was led by the Communists and my husband didn't dare take part. A colored and white group met one night to talk over a proposed strike and to unite blacks and whites in one union. Somebody told the police and they raided the house. Angelo Herndon was arrested and thrown into jail. That was in 1932. He was a nice-looking colored boy of 19 from Cincinnati. He was charged with having Communist literature and sentenced to 18 years imprisonment. He got out on $15,000 bail raised by public subscription. The Supreme Court turned down his first appeal in 1935, but young Ben Davis—do you know him?—fought the case until in April this year the Supreme Court, 5 to 4, declared the Georgia statute unconstitutional and Herndon is free."

"How splendid. And this Ben Davis, I must hunt him up. I know of his father."

"I believe he is in New York now and one of the officials of the Communist Party; but listen, have you heard of Herndon's brother?"

"No; gracious! how ignorant I am, on matters where I'm supposed to be expert!"

"This is about the Lincoln Battalion in Spain."

"Oh, Communists again?"

"Not exactly. Spain massacred striking miners in 1934, but the radical Left parties won the elections of 1936 and set up a republic. Civil war ensued, Franco leading, with Hitler and Mussolini helping, while Britain and the United States gave no assistance and allowed none. Then, in America arose that marvelous Lincoln Battalion—a miscellaneous mass of youth—from workers, writers and artists to bums and ne'er-do-wells—who threw themselves into a crusade for Spanish freedom. Among the first was Milton Herndon, brother of Angelo. Tall, handsome, quick to learn, he was commander of a section in the machine-gun company of the Mackenzie-Papineau Canadian Battalion when he left his cover to go to the aid of a wounded soldier. He was killed while dragging the helpless man to safety.

"Among the 3,000 volunteers who went to fight for freedom were other Negroes—Sergeant Joe Taylor, who sang Negro spirituals on the battlefield; Commissar Morris Wickman, of Philadelphia; Bunny Rucker, of Cleveland, a light-skinned Negro whose quiet efficiency won him the respect of the entire regiment; Roach, the Negro machine gunner from Provincetown; McDaniells, whom Spaniards called 'Fantastico.' I am told the Negroes loved Spain more than they had ever loved America, for in Spain there was no prejudice against their color. Of the battalion, 2,600 died crying, 'If Spain is lost there will be a Second World War!'"

"I heard parts of this story," Jean said, "but knew nothing of the Negroes save what I read in Shirley Graham's beautiful biography of Paul Robeson. He was in Spain when civil war was brewing, and sang especially to the workers. But why, why is so much of this unknown, hidden from the public?"

Zoe looked thoughtful. "Well, you see, so many Communists were involved. Even Russia sent aid to victims of Franco's bombs and barbarism. We in America are afraid of Communism, just as Hitler was in Germany."

"Then how on earth did you learn all this?"

"Well you see, I've been talking to young Ben Davis."

Jean returned to Macon just as Chamberlain returned to England from Munich where he had signed a treaty and proclaimed: "Peace in our Time." But in 1939 the world rushed to war. Franco triumphed in Spain, Germany and Italy united, Germany declared war on Poland, and Great Britain on Germany. But it was the sudden expansion of Japan which astonished Jean. Japan had already seized Korea and Manchuria.

Jean drew Mansart's attention to Japan. Manuel was, of course, interested but not alarmed. He admitted that Japan wanted to be one of the great nations of the world, and partners with Europe and America in exploiting Asia.

"And," said Jean, "I suspect that this exploitation will be just as bad and just as thorough as that which Great Britain and France have been carrying on."

"Oh, no," said Manuel. "No, this is going to be a different thing. This is going to be a colored folk taking charge of the development of colored folk; and because they themselves know what domination and exploitation is, they are going to do better. I am sure of that. Perhaps this is the beginning of the rise of the colored peoples of the world."

"Or," said Jean, "it is the ending of the old capitalistic exploitation with a few improvements. Moreover," added Jean, "you must not lose your interest in Germany. You know what Hitler was trying to do when you were there. Well, he is carrying it out and pretty soon the rest of the white world is going to make alliance with him. A Second World War is begun!"

"I doubt that very much," said Manuel. "I think he's going to find himself with strong opposition and that he will not dare face it."

"That," said Jean, "is not at all evident in his treatment of the Jews. The United States will soon be in this war and on which side I am not sure."

Mansart insisted that there was hope. In the case of American Negroes, there was progress. "There are things that Negroes can boast of. The NAACP still lives; there is one Negro in Congress and one state senator; there are 14 members of state legislatures and 12 members of city councils; there are artists like Hayes, Robeson, Bledsoe and Marian Anderson; there are little theaters among Negroes in four or five cities and one in Texas; there are 19,000 Negroes in colleges and 2,000 graduates a year. In the courts there have been some victories. Some Negroes' books have been published. The wife of the colored congressman dared drink tea at the White House; and there are triumphs here and there in athletics."

As Mansart voiced these considerations to his students and at teachers' meetings, inevitably a subject forced itself into discussion which ordinarily was not discussed, and that was politics. For forty years among the better class of Negroes in the South, it was not regarded good form to discuss politics. They were as a mass disfranchised, and while this situation could not and should not persist, yet as the dead Booker Washington had advised, discussion should not be insisted on at present.

But discussion could not be avoided. Jean said at Teachers' Prayer Meeting: "How shall Negroes vote next Fall—those who can vote? Remember that Negroes who do not vote are still the basis of each state's representation in Congress and somebody casts their ballot if they do not. It isn't a matter simply of doing away with the Negro vote, the right still exists; but it is exercised not by the Negro but by the white man, and not by the white worker but by the white landholder and investor, by capitalists and employers. With this increased voting power, the South can send to Congress the most reactionary defenders of wealth and monopoly, can hold the most powerful committee assignments, and this hard, immovable core of opposition cannot be met by reason or appeal."

"I don't quite see that," complained a professor.

Jean got a copy of the *Crisis* for 1928 and explained. "In the presidential election of 1920, a million voters on the Pacific coast elected 12 congressmen. In the Middle West, a million voters elected 13 congressmen. In New England, due to disfranchised foreigners, a million voters elected 16 congressmen. But in the

South, the poor and ignorant South, with Negroes and poor whites disfranchised, a million voters elected 45 congressmen. In five states of the Southern South, out of more than five million possible voters, four and a half million were disfranchised, leaving 600,000 actual voters.

"In 1932, because of the financial crash, Hoover was crushingly defeated and Roosevelt elected. He was re-elected in 1936. Now, in 1940, we American Negroes face the question of a Third Term."

"And," said Mansart, "in addition to that, the question of Socialism and World War."

Jean hastened to insist: "Our greatest problem is that of work and wage, and this not simply for ourselves and for our kin and color overseas, but for the laboring world."

There was a murmur against this, which a woman instructor voiced.

"But do we really have to plunge into the world labor problem and the inextricable tangles of Asia and Africa? Our problem is simpler. We want to be Americans. Other problems can wait."

"No. Becoming Americans does not mean automatic settlement of our problems. It means sharing the problems of Americans, and believe me, they've got plenty. These problems we must understand beforehand, lest we land as a dead weight and complicate the question we ought to be ready to help solve. We must not be content to loaf in a provincial racial enclave. We must emerge into the greater world even before we become Americans. Perhaps we can then lead them out of the woods."

"Nonsense. We can't lead ourselves, much less the whites."

"I'm not so sure. One of our Negroes once had a vision of a 'Talented Tenth,' that is, of trained, devoted men who would devote themselves to social uplift, not simply of themselves but of the world."

"A sort of set of dictators?"

"Yes, but not of a proletariat, because he did not know the labor group in industry. If he had, he might have gone another path. As it was, his Talented became too often selfish money grabbers."

"Was that in Burghardt's mind when he held the Pan-African congresses after the First World War?"

"No, not quite. I think he wanted Negroes to emerge into understanding of a greater black world and its problems. His plan even attracted Asia, India and Vietnam. China listened. But neither he nor they dared hope to get any chance to be co-workers in the white world. That world seemed then too self-centered."

"Isn't it still?" asked Mansart, smiling as he rose to leave.

Jean continued. "No, not quite. There is English labor, French art, and Russia and its dream. England must soon set India free and India will reach a hand toward us. This is a rapidly changing world."

In her own mind and with her Fall classes, Jean from time to time reviewed the history of the Negro in industry. Before the First World War, integrated ownership and control had largely displaced the skilled Negro worker in tobacco manufacturing, in iron and steel, in lumbering and mining, and in transportation, and confined them more and more to common labor and domestic service of the lowest paid and worst conditioned varieties. From the new textile, chemical and other manufactures, Negroes were nearly excluded. Just as slavery excluded the poor white from profitable agriculture, so freedom excluded the poor Negro from rising and expanding manufacture. On the other hand, the worldwide fall of agricultural income carried the mass of black farmers down to the level of landless tenants and peons.

The First World War and its wild aftermath seemed for a moment to open a new door. Two million black workers rushed North to work in iron and steel industries, to make automobiles, to pack meat, build houses and do the heavy toil in factories. They met the closed trade union which pressed them to the wall, into the low wage gutter, denied them homes, and mobbed them. And then the Depression met all.

In the Depression, Negro workers, like white workers, lost their jobs, had mortgages foreclosed on their farms and homes, and used up their small savings. But in the case of the Negro worker, everything was worse in degree. The loss was greater and more permanent; technological displacement began before the Depression was accelerated. The unemployment and fall in wage struck black men sooner, lasted longer, and went to lower levels. In the rural South their education almost ceased, while Southern city schools were crowded to suffocation.

Above all, in the Negro's case, local and federal relief helped him last. It was easily explicable human nature that the unemployed white man and the starving white child should be relieved first by local white authorities who regarded them as fellowmen and regarded the Negroes as sub-human. Then came Recovery through the New Deal. The CIO was formed. The Negro entered the ranks of union labor and, with the nation, braced himself for a new future. This future, however, involved the Negro's own inner development, which Jean must now study.

CHAPTER VIII

◆

The Free North

The owner of the *New York Age,* a Negro weekly, looked up from his bookkeeping with a frown.

"Jack," he said, "I'll have to put you on advertising, with a percentage instead of a salary."

"You know I can't make a living on advertisements."

"Why not? You know what advertisers pay."

"Yes, they pay for buyers, and Negro weeklies don't bring them customers. From Russworm's *Freedom's Journal,* away back in 1827, past Fred Douglass' *North Star,* in 1847, down to the 24 Negro papers from then to the Civil War and the hundreds since, they have all tried first to free and defend Negroes. This was and is a fine object, and the one I'm interested in. But it does not sell tobacco, liquor, food or clothes for white merchants. So they won't advertise with us and pay our expenses or more, as they do in white papers. You know that as well as I. Now, there is one thing we can try as the success of the *Crisis* has pointed out. And that is to increase circulation among Negro readers by printing more news about Negroes and pictures of them."

"That would cost money."

"Borrow and try—"

"No, I'm in debt already deep enough. Jack, it's either ads or you're through."

"I'm through," said Jack and went home.

Jack Carmichael had married a niece of Manuel Mansart's wife and together, on Mansart's advice, they had tried farming in south Georgia. Jack got into trouble with his landlord and had run away north, and was for a time lost. Betty had gone to New York, leaving her boy on the farm with his grandmother. She had studied nursing and sent for her boy and her mother. Then, almost by accident, Jack was reunited with his family and had gone to work on a local Negro weekly. Dismissed, he was now thoroughly despondent.

At home, Betty did not share in his despair.

"Jack, I've been thinking for some time that New York City is not the place for us to remain; it is too crowded and too Southern in sentiment. I've been looking toward New England, the birthplace of American independence and of Negro abolition. This morning, it happens, I see an opening. The city hospital in

Springfield, Massachusetts, wants more nurses and they have made me an offer."

"Springfield?"

"Yes, it's a city of about 150,000 persons in the west center of the state; a thriving manufacturing town, with excellent schools. It has a good government, two colleges and a United States armory. You've surely heard of the *Springfield Republican,* one of our most liberal papers."

"Sounds all right, but where do I come in?"

"Jack, let's go there and settle. If an honest, hard-working colored man can't make a way in Massachusetts, then we'd better quit."

Jack wanted to vote for quitting, but he could not disappoint Betty again.

Betty went first. The hospital authorities were a little taken aback when they found that Betty was colored, but they saw by examining the records that this fact had already been reported but forgotten or ignored during the ensuing negotiations. Of course, it should make no difference, but there were awkward questions about dormitory space. This seemed answered when the hospital authorities learned that Betty had a family and would live at home.

But that brought up the question as to where Betty could rent a place. She must be near the hospital and no colored people lived around there. The 3,000 or so colored folk lived almost entirely in a southern section of the city, by themselves. It was on the whole a nice neighborhood and well kept, and the Negroes lived there, as whites asserted and really believed, in order to enjoy each other's company. It was suggested that perhaps after all a home in this neighborhood might not be too far away, but Betty peremptorily refused to consider this solution.

"I have no objection in the world to living beside colored people or Jews or Italians; but a home two miles from the hospital is unthinkable."

Had it not been for an unexpected situation, this difficulty might have resulted in stopping Betty's enterprise right there.

"It is ridiculous for this nurse to insist on living in a white neighborhood," said the chairman of the Board. "Perhaps we'd better let her go back to New York."

That was impossible, for already Betty had taken over the care of Cyrus Taylor. And Cyrus was a character. He was one of the richest residents of the city, of an old and prominent family which had been active in Shays' rebellion back in 1786. Cyrus' son was high in finance and industry, which promised more wealth and prosperity for the city and state. Cyrus had long been a chronic and crotchety invalid and had recently dismissed the third nurse in succession, which the hospital, one of his philanthropies, had furnished him. Then Betty, the very day of her arrival, had been sent as a temporary substitute and seemed to be giving perfect satisfaction. Any thought of change just now could not be considered for a moment. So a small five-room cottage quite near the hospital and the Taylor home was secured for temporary rental.

The family arrived—the old grandmother, Jackie, a lively boy of eight, and Jack, the husband and father. There were soon some quiet protests chiefly on account of the effect which a Negro family might have on the value of surrounding property and less openly because this would put a colored child into one of the best public schools. Naturally, there were a few colored children in the public schools, but most of them went to one school which had a colored teacher among eight whites. It happened that no Negro child had ever attended the school nearest Jackie's present home.

It was delicately hinted that perhaps Jackie would be a bit lonesome among so many whites and that transportation—

The principal who ventured to make this suggestion to Betty reported, "She was almost insulting, and seemed to resent the plan. Mercy knows, I had only the best intentions, for I'm sure that this little darky is going to have a hard time keeping up in his work and enduring the treatment he'll get from the white children. But it's all right with me."

Jackie started in with three fights in his first term. In the first he was soundly licked but claimed that it took four boys to do it. He wanted no complaint made, so Betty said nothing. The second fight, a month later, was a draw and Jackie sported a black eye, as a sort of badge of courage. The teachers said nothing, for Jackie was a bright boy, above the average in all his classes and increasingly a favorite among the students—a favorite and a source of some apprehension because of his private enterprise in many directions and his efficiency in swearing and slang on occasion. The third fight, in late Fall, resulted in the so thorough beating of a very prominent young man that the principal thought he had to take a hand.

On his invitation Betty called and was prepared for argument:

"Yes, Mr. Principal, I know all about it and am glad you called me in. When three months ago a bunch of your hoodlums jumped on one little colored boy and beat him almost senseless, you had no complaint. I suppose you thought that would drive him out of your select school. It didn't. He wasn't brought up that way. The next time he had a better chance and came out very well. You didn't complain that time and neither did I. Now, however, one of your rich pets has had some teeth knocked out and you threaten expulsion. Go ahead and try. Here is the card of my lawyer whom Mr. Cyrus Taylor recommends. He thinks it might be a good idea to find out just who owns the Springfield public schools."

The principal quickly assured Mrs. Carmichael that expulsion was the last thing he had in mind, that he only mentioned it as possible so as to ward off any court action on the part of the incensed parents. All he was seeking was to restore peace and good feeling, etc., etc., to the edification of a score of teachers who just happened to be passing along the hall.

All this trouble over the house and Jackie was of little account to Jack Carmichael who faced the problem of earning a living. It was a curious situation. Springfield would have strenuously denied any real color prejudice. It had for a time harbored and helped John Brown. It would have admitted some animus against the Irish Catholics, and the 35,000 foreign-born mill workers were a problem in some respects, especially since the unions and strikes had challenged the old alignments of property and wealth. The small group of Negroes were mostly native born, with a common school training and good American culture. A few Southern Negroes had come in, but they were absorbed in the older group quite easily and with not too much complaint.

The work of this group seemed almost providentially laid out; they furnished house service and common labor. This work was well paid, but not extravagantly, and could not be raised since there was no other demand for services by Negroes. Many of them owned nice, well-kept homes. The others rented from white owners property which could not be rented to others and might be eventually sold to Negroes at a good price. Socially, Negroes had their own churches, and one of these, the Congregational, had organized a social center of which the town was justly proud. On the other hand, this Negro group of laborers had almost no connection with the foreign-born, neither social nor economic. The foreign-born—Italians, French-Canadians and a few Slavs—had come in as labor for the mills, which made electrical machinery, motorcycles, firearms and the new plastics. The Irish, their predecessors in the older woolen and paper mills, now considered themselves Americans; they held the best hand-skilled trades and went into business, the city services and white-collar work.

The difficulty came as these elements began to change their status because of education, income and property. This was most noticeable among the Irish and least among Negroes. When Mike Gibbons became partner in one of the old mills, when Tony Marcelli married into a prominent American family, the hundred thousand and more original Americans felt the economic and social pressure of lower groups and more or less resented it. But it never occurred to them that a colored man like Jack Carmichael would not want to be a servant. He was a nice fellow, well-bred and educated, but there was no job for him to do in the mills, no clerkships in the stores, and in fact a month's search opened for him not a single offer he could accept, except that of shipping clerk in a wholesale firm. And even this job had strings to it. Its former white holder resigned because a raise in wage and promotion was long denied. Jack was let do the work temporarily, because pressures of business had brought on an emergency. And the offer, as Jack found out later, was accompanied by the wage of a porter, not a clerk.

But it was a chance and Jack took it. He did a good job; so good indeed that had he been white he would have quickly been better paid and eventually promoted. As it was, his wages' were raised, but he was not recognized as a clerk and his application to join the clerks' union was turned down. Jack and Betty talked it over. It started with the matter of continuing the rental of their home. The owner said he wanted to sell and would no longer rent. The price he asked was high. The bank to which Jack applied refused a mortgage loan. Betty took up the matter with her patient, Cyrus Taylor. The owner lowered its price, the bank changed its mind, and Jack and Betty contracted to buy their home. This brought up again the question of occupation for Jack. They needed a better income if they were to live like their neighbors. If they did not live up to the standard of the neighborhood, the neighbors would rightly complain.

So Betty induced Cyrus Taylor to talk with Jack. Cyrus Taylor had been brought face to face with the infirmities of age and the changing economics of the twentieth century. He was upset in body and mind. To some of his older beliefs he stuck all the harder because of the revolution he could not stem in the main currents of his life. He had been an abolitionist almost from birth and never forgot the thrill of harboring fugitive slaves. He never admitted to any trace of color prejudice. When, therefore, Betty came and proved a good and understanding nurse, Taylor nearly broke up the household of his son where he lived, because his daughter-in-law wanted to treat Betty as a servant and serve her meals in the kitchen.

This insistence of Taylor extricated Betty from an awkward dilemma. The three servants were colored, a cook, a maid, and a chauffeur and gardener. They were nice people, clean, well-bred and efficient. But it was one of the basic principles of registered nurses that they were to be treated as professional persons and not as servants. The white nurses who preceded Betty had been so treated and had their meals served in a private dining room. It occurred to his daughter-in-law that the infliction of a colored nurse, whom this impossible old man perversely proceeded to spoil, might be in part balanced by her treatment as a servant. Then, to her surprise, the colored cook complained to Cyrus himself of the discrimination in treatment of the colored nurse and so before Betty herself had decided just what to do she found herself served alone in state and the cook making apologies. The daughter-in-law loved Betty even less than before.

Young Mrs. Taylor was a well-meaning woman. Indeed, in her own eyes, she was deserving and unfairly treated. As a girl she had never let a boy kiss her, had never listened to dirty stories and had attended Sunday School and learned to read, write and play the piano fairly well. She had helped in the housework at home but at her mother's wish had left the hard and dirty work to a servant. That kept her hands soft and her clothes clean. She had not exactly been presented to society, as her people had no such high social position; but after graduation from high school, she began to attend parties of the right sort. Her parents did not want her to take a job, preferring that she await suitable marriage and work in her own home. Her union with the rich young Taylor was a social triumph.

Personally she was frightened almost to death at the event, never having had the slightest instruction or information as to sex conduct or response. The result was disastrous. Neither husband nor wife had anything but embarrassment and frustration for months after marriage and finally retired to separate bedrooms. The husband kept a hotel suite in New York and used to run down on business once a month. He was astonished and pleased to find pretty women there who seemed actually to enjoy his caresses. His wife naturally had no such recourse. The few advances to her of men in her circle, she rebuffed with indignation and shame, wondering how her conduct had invited such frightful desires.

On the other hand, she did not know what to do with her time. She did not read much and did not enjoy what she read. The newspaper, except local gossip, was dull and hard to understand. Particularly, she was ignorant of history and references to the past of mankind brought no response. She had been brought up not to drink alcoholic beverages, nor to gamble. She gave parties, but they were insufferably dull, save as a few got into corners and talked about each other. She and her husband took a trip to Europe and she was surprised to find that the English used a language she could hardly understand, while the French actually understood no English at all. There was nothing to do but look at monuments, churches and pictures. The scenery was all right but she preferred New England.

Her greatest burden was her stepfather in whose home she and her husband lived. He was a foul-mouthed old tyrant, who swore and complained, and to whom nothing seemed sacred. She tired herself nearly to death waiting on him and then when they resorted to a trained nurse, she found that the nurse also had to be waited on. It was disgusting. Her servants had always been people from the colored settlement. They knew their places and she liked them. She could be intimate and confidential with them without having them take advantage of her. Sometimes she thought they were her only real friends. She welcomed then the chance to hire a colored registered nurse and prepared to turn her over to the other servants, when she proved more intractable than her predecessors.

Cyrus Taylor was breaking down physically, but his chief ailment was spiritual. He found himself living in an age which all his training rejected. He began to complain of this before Jack, his caller, was seated or could introduce his errand.

"Sit down, sit down! I know all about your plans. You want to go into business so as to be 'independent.' Well, my boy, you're born fifty years too late. There is no such thing as independent business any more. You know what I was once? An independent shoemaker. I repaired shoes and made them for special feet. It was a fine job and I loved it. I made enough to live on as well as I wanted to live. The old lady had a good home, a big kitchen, a back yard for the wash and a front yard with grass and flowers. We had three nice children. Then the oldest boy set up a shoe store in town. He sold a few of my shoes and more of the shoes made by the United Shoe Machinery Company. Then they drove shoe repairing and hand-made shoes out of business.

"Take my two sons. Neither of them ever did any real work, any straining of muscle or continuous hard thinking; or listening to wisdom or reading. Not them. The oldest never went to college. He got through high school after a fashion and went into business. That is, he began to scout around to see how quickest he could make the biggest income. He became clerk in a shoe store, where his pleasant manners sold shoes and got him acquainted with the Big Bosses. His shoe store became an outlet for my shoe repairs on the one hand and for United Shoe Machinery on the other. Then he sold out me and the shoe store. With my savings and his charm and adaptability he got a block of shares in the United Shoe Machinery Corporation cheap. The stock was split and watered and before I knew it, I was rich with nothing to do. It killed the old woman. She missed her kitchen and her washing. She just died. I'm still hanging about making trouble for everybody. Oh, the boy was no drone. He did not sit about loafing and feeding his appetites; but to call what he did 'work' of any kind, or 'sacrifice,' is a lie. Jan Matzeliger, the Negro from the West Indies, furnished the brains for the machinery which the company bought and patented, and now owns. Irish and French Canadians did the work, bright Irish and American salesmen distributed the shoes on percentages and salary, tasteful ladies set the styles, lawyers arranged ownership and tied it up so that we are rich. That's progress, I suppose, but I wonder if there wasn't something lost.

"Take that boy today. He's made money. He's making more; that's all he can do. He can't read and don't. He doesn't know one note of music from another. He can't tell a picture from a cartoon. He drinks whiskey and runs after women, not because he likes either, but to be a good fellow. He married and married pure and respectable, but it was just an incident in his life and still is. The other boy went to college, joined an exclusive fraternity, drinks, whores and gambles. He is receiving money which he never made and doing nothing else. To the real human service of letting men and women use their feet and letting shoe makers earn a living, neither of my boys are giving thought and never will." He paused and stared at Jack.

"Now, what is it you want?"

"I thought of starting a small neighborhood grocery store, to deal in good food and staples and so make a reasonable living, save a bit for the future and be my own boss."

"H'm, well, you might do something along that line down in the colored community."

"But Betty says no. She says it would not do to come into a free Northern city and open a 'Jim-Crow' store; even the colored people would object. I thought of taking a good corner near the mill district and serving colored people, of course, but aiming at the whole neighborhood."

"Fine, but crazy! If your store was poor you'd scarcely make a living. If it was good, the landlord would hike the rent and if you climbed over that, the big grocery chains would buy you out."

"Suppose I refused to sell?"

"You'd sell all right before they got through. But don't take my word. Try it. Go ahead! I'll see you get $5,000 credit with the wholesalers. But I tell you, Carmichael, you don't realize what a world you're facing.

"We used to go into business to serve our neighbors, by doing and making useful things. All that is out.

"Our whole idea of work, buying and selling, is changed.

"We used to work to do something for ourselves and for others. Now we work for wages. We used to make things for use; now we make them for sale.

"Success is not what a man does, but what he gets. The larger a man's income the greater his desert is regarded.

"If everyone works for his own advantage, we believe this will result in the best results for all; or in other words, universal selfishness brings universal happiness.

"It is bad business today to make goods that last; better make goods that wear out quickly and must be renewed. We say flatly:

"Don't save, spend; a penny saved is a penny wasted; a penny spent helps business and no matter whose business. Debt is wiser than saving; that's what saving is for.

"Don't pay as you go; pay as you come!

"Don't repair; throw away and buy new.

"Don't patch, don't mend, don't darn.

"Live in debt, gamble on the future.

"Drive out the tinker, the shoe repairer, the seamstress.

"Down with the miser.

"Modern life is buying and selling.

"Mass production of identical things drives us, kicks us, holds us in drab, tasteless sameness. We can't choose patterns of clothes, styles of cars, shape of shoes, texture of cloth, or color of skin.

"'Free enterprise' guided by mass production and monopoly reduces our life to dead uniformity without individuality. In our cities, homes and public buildings all gradually yield to offices, where goods are bought and sold; or rather where the ownership of these goods and the land occupied and the energies of laborers are bought, sold, or destroyed.

"Remember how that great and historic church on Fifth Avenue fell before a center for gambling in oil? Heard how a great music hall is to be sold for room to exchange foodstuffs between the West Indies and New England? A big railway station in New York is going to be turned from mere travel to a market place for buying and selling over the world.

"We used to cook in pints for individual taste; now we mix in tons and season with straw.

"We spend our savings not in improving products but in lying about them in great big picture magazines on a scale nobody dares resist.

"Our news is about selling; our art is about buying; our science is about getting wealth, and our religion about distributing it where it will do us good.

"Inventions and patents are not to make life easy, but to put wealth in a few hands.

"Politics is money and elections are bought and sold—

"But what's the use talking. You don't believe me; neither do my sons, or that daughter in Chicago. Or if they admit my facts, they say: so what? This is a new age, a new world. It is, but it's a damn sight newer than they dream. So go ahead. Who knows? You may start something!"

The grocery store which Jack opened was in many ways ideal. It was on a quiet corner, with middle-class white-collar workers near, mill hands two blocks west and colored folk three blocks south. The center of the city was four or five blocks north. Betty saw that the store was tasteful, with a touch of beauty. Jack made customers welcome and satisfied. He bought carefully and successfully at fair prices. He would not handle old or half-spoiled stuff. After careful inquiry, he extended some of his customers credit between paydays. Jackie, after school, helped deliver orders, and thus built up an astonishing circle of acquaintances. The very fact that Jack was colored and not Italian nor French Canadian, led to personal confidences and revelations which these foreigners would not have revealed to their own.

So, too, the colored group felt a sort of racial interest in a store which did not try to confine itself to colored folk, but still was run by a colored man. Then, too, here was a store which was run by a worker rather than by an employer or an investor. It became a center of gossip about employment and wages; about organizing the unorganized worker. Jack had much information about the West and South. Betty spent much of her free time in the store and as a registered nurse was eagerly sought for advice as to sickness among a group which could ill afford medical fees. On the other hand, the white-collar workers round about liked to trade at a good store where they could feel socially superior to the proprietor and to most of his customers. They became local aristocrats instead of unimportant people.

In Jack's new enterprise there were a hundred tricks of the trade to learn. He sought advice eagerly and for a time hired a former grocer to help out. From him he learned much about the storing of his stock and the selection of items. But the man wanted really to run the store and not just advise, so finally he had to go. There were difficult questions of buying. The wholesalers were used to unloading old and even partially spoiled goods on the small grocers in poor neighborhoods. They offered attractive bargains, which Jack avoided. The canned goods which Jack must watch often had labels newer than the contents. If, however, he bought first class goods guaranteed, the price was high and sale to poor people involved prices they could scarce afford. This meant a narrow margin of profit or sometimes no profit at all. It was a long, puzzling task, but Jack, with Betty and his son, did very well, and the store prospered.

Religion had to come into the picture of Carmichael's life in curious ways. There were in Springfield perhaps 50,000 church attending Protestants, who formed the upper stratum of owners, employers and officials. There were 25,000 nominal Catholics who were in more or less close touch with their church. The colored people were mostly Methodists and Baptists with a leading group of Congregationalists. And since the church was the center of colored social life it played a more active part than the white churches.

Jack and Betty at first refrained from close association with the colored churches. This was chiefly because they were both astonished to find that in this birthplace of abolition, the color line was clearer in religion than in any other social activity. On the street, in the parks, at the movies there was no visible color line; in the schools and colleges and politics and elections there were evidences of more or less color prejudice and in business and industry distinct color discrimination. But in church the separation was complete. Betty met it head on when she talked to the Reverend Mr. Reeves about joining the First Congregational Church. She especially wanted its advantages for Jackie. Young Mr. Reeves was delighted and offered to write a letter to Dr. DeBerry, the Negro pastor of the colored Congregational Church. Betty demurred. She knew Dr. DeBerry. He was a fine man. But she was proposing to join the First Congregational.

"But why?"

"It's nearest where I live, and besides, why do most of your communicants join this church?"

"Well, they are folk with common social interests—"

"Is your church a purely social organization?"

Mr. Reeves was affronted.

"Mrs. Carmichael, with whom would you associate in my church? What organizations would you work with?"

"Are you trying to say, Mr. Reeves, that your members will not serve God beside Negroes?"

Mr. Reeves arose. "Mrs. Carmichael, if you wish to join my church you may; but I warn you, you will not be happy. Most people prefer to associate with their own; if you are ashamed to do so, that is a matter between you and your God."

"I'll take up the matter with Him," Betty said. She joined the First Congregational and put Jackie in its Sunday School. She was careful to pay her church dues and now and then attended a sermon. On the few occasions when she was asked to serve on a committee or act with a group, she was so efficient that it was almost embarrassing. For instance, she worked with the public sanitation committee; she was soon elected chairman and launched such ambitious plans for city-wide action that the efforts had to be stopped or incur the enmity of the City Sanitation Board, whose chairman was a prominent member of the First Congregational Church.

Jack attended church seldom; but Jackie from the first became a regular and enthusiastic attendant of the Sunday School. He loved the beautiful room in which it met, sang the lively gospel hymns like a nightingale and joined in all activities; in most he was leader and planner, was elected to all sorts of offices and depended on by the teachers to put over their programs. Of course, these programs had to be such as Jackie personally approved. Otherwise, they simply did not work and the mass of other students backed Jackie in judgment to a man. Still, everybody liked Jackie, or at least all but a very few.

These incidents illustrated the status of religion in Springfield. Everybody "believed" in religion; most were by profession "Christians," that is, they "believed" in God, the sacrifice of his son Jesus for men's sin, and eventual reward of men in heaven or punishment in hell. They "believed" in prayer. But none of this professed belief had any real practical effect. Nobody or certainly very few believed that a request to God would have any effect on what would occur; few believed really in God as a powerful person who was conducting the world benevolently according to some great plan. Most people of Springfield regarded Jesus as a good man long dead, who left a moral program which nobody, least of all an American, could really live up to. And yet, this professed belief and practical rejection of its implications had a subtle but disastrous effect on honesty of character, telling the truth, and ability to reason clearly. People got so used to saying one thing and doing another, asserting honestly what they knew was untrue, and calling logic what was patently illogical, that religion as a real moral force was at a low ebb in the city. Moral standards existed to be sure, but they were based on hereditary culture patterns—the influence of persons recognized as respectable, and the actual results of current conduct on everyday life. Children were brought up in such an atmosphere of contradictions that they ignored, indeed had to ignore, advice and example. How could a man who was bad be called good? How could you love your enemies and refuse to speak to them on the street? How could you turn the other cheek and fight for your country, right or wrong? How could you lie and tell the truth for the sake of the same God? And who was this God, anyhow, and where was He and what should we do about Him, while ignoring His existence most of the time? It was such a situation that brought anger and frustration when a concrete question demanded answer, as in the matter of letting a family with dark faces join a group of professed followers of God, whose faces were whiter in color.

The church was a group of socially compatible friends who built fine church edifices, had pleasant meetings and listened to what they wanted to hear. The minister was a well-bred person, college-trained, who used good English, and was a welcome caller in homes. He preached sermons but seldom said anything one need remember, or which displeased anyone. Most of the sermons were "doctrinal"—that is, attempts to reconcile forgotten dogma with present fact, which was easy for those already convinced. Festivals like Christmas, gifts for missions to the heathen, and alms for the surrounding poor helped keep the parish busy. Add marriages, christenings and funerals, and the church had more than enough to do.

The Catholic Church differed somewhat from the Protestant. Its priesthood had nothing to do but promote religion among a large and loosely integrated group, kept in line by means of old folkways, emphasis on marriage and death, and insistence on the letter of the creed, while loosening calls for action. Thus dancing, drinking and gambling on a moderate scale were winked at, if not encouraged, and occasional attendance at services, money contributions and lip service to dogma were sharply insisted on. Ceremony, rich vestments and lovely music made brief church attendance popular. Thus, the Catholic clergy had a wide influence on, and a more intimate contact with, the mass of working people than Protestants—the purely social aspect of the church was less prominent. Problems of race and industry were settled often by the clergy and not referred to the laity. There were few Jews or other religious groups in Springfield so that their problems did not intrude.

What with their new economic status, their relation to the church, and Betty's successful nursing, the Carmichaels came to be regarded with mixed feelings; they were considered social climbers who wanted to "be white." They were "ashamed" of their own people. But a new and more weighty charge was that the talks about labor, wages and unions which began to center around the grocery were dangerous, since they involved so many diverse elements and races—the foreign-born, the colored folk, the clerks. Rights of labor, one big union, higher wages and shorter hours were discussed. All this focussed attention on the store and when the directors of the chief city grocery chain had their monthly meeting, the matter was touched on.

"Does he have a good set of customers?"

"Good and growing. His profit is not near as high as it might be, because he carries the best goods. Won't take left-overs or old stuff."

"His credit?"

"Good; he pays pretty promptly. Only he's playing pretty close to the line; if pressed he might have to give up. Trouble is he's thinking more of his community and their jobs than of his own business."

"Look him over, and sound him out!"

A week later Jack had a visitor who asked about the business and what he would sell it for. Jack was curt in his refusal to talk about selling. He'd never dreamed of such a thing, he said.

DeBerry visited him one night and with Betty they talked long. They liked DeBerry and agreed with him except on the matter of the white workers and mill hands. DeBerry was convinced from long experience that the white laborer, especially the foreigner, was the Negroes' worst enemy. His own friends and the supporters of his enterprises were the rich employers who, he was sure, would employ Negroes if it were not for trade union opposition. He continued:

"Mr. Carmichael, what I'm afraid of is your mill-hand customers. They'll leave you flat at the first excuse."

"I believe they'll stick by me as long as I sell cheap and good commodities."

"Even that won't do when the chains begin to put on the screws. How about your rent, haven't they raised it yet?"

"No, but I know the reason. Cyrus Taylor owns the building. He bought it when I moved in. I didn't know this until recently and then by accident. I've been asked to sell the business. I won't.

"You know of course that Cyrus Taylor is not well. He may not last much longer. But I'm sure he'll remember Betty in his will. He practically told me so."

And that was what Cyrus Taylor had both thought and said. But age made it increasingly difficult for him to come to decisions. He scribbled on bits of paper. Betty was a good woman and a fine nurse. One thousand dollars? Yes, at least. But what was that these days? Say $10,000. But what would she do with that much? It was not enough to let her retire and why should she retire? Well, he'd think about it. Whatever he gave Betty would of course go to help Jack. Now Jack was a good man but impractical. He would never make a business man. He thought too much of his customers as people, not as buyers. You couldn't do business today on that plan. Business was profit, not philanthropy. That was wrong, but it was a fact and in a world of private profit where would a merchant land who was thinking how his customers could live on their wage? What would a thousand dollars, ten thousand or a hundred thousand do in a competitive grocery business in Springfield or in the United States, if it was run to help the community and not to make the owner rich? So Cyrus Taylor did not make up his mind before the first stroke of apoplexy came. Betty saw the look of unrest come and go on his face, but he died peacefully before he acted. The will did not mention Betty. She was naturally disappointed. For the old man had more than hinted that he would "remember" her. The oldest son said:

"My father seemed by the various memoranda lying about to have in mind some gift for you, but there was nothing definite. However, I want to thank you for your devotion. Here is a little something." He gave her $250 in addition to her wages due. Also, when the two-year lease on the grocery building was up, he renewed it for the same rent but sold the property to one of the main city grocery chains. He could not be bothered with small investments like that. Betty went back to the hospital staff where she had plenty of work offered as visiting nurse and on various assignments.

But she worried about Jack. He was a good man, pleasant and with no bad habits. She knew that he loved her and adored Jackie. But he was restless. He was never satisfied. He always wanted to do something else. He wanted to dream and set his dreams on paper in word or line or color. It was this stretching out and away that always lured him from the job in hand. He realized this and fought against it. He worked hard and steadily and was so afraid that a second time he might fail his wife and son. He was desperately apprehensive of losing their respect. His wife sensed this and watched him almost furtively.

Jackie was unconscious of all this and went blithely on toward life. He had no problem, or if he had, they were problems of life, not of color nor status. His social contacts remained normal because at ten, sex had not begun to obtrude. He visited other children's homes and they his. His grandmother gave her life to him—to his delicious meals noted all over the neighborhood, to his mending and cleanliness, to his cozy room. His first knowledge of deep and unavoidable sorrow came when she died. Yet, he had his mother, and while she could not give him as much time as grandmother had, she knew a lot and told him much. His father, however, was his great possession and his pride. With him he spent all his spare time and came to feel himself a real companion and co-worker and not just a child to be ordered about. When, on his twelfth birthday, his father changed the sign to "Carmichael & Son," all in shining gilt, Jackie's heart burst with a pleasure so intense and deep that he could neither laugh nor cry, but only stand in mute ecstacy of perfect happiness. He made up his mind then and there to be a real partner and not just a helper.

That very week one of the chain store owners renewed overtures. A well-dressed and courteous man came and talked two hours. "I know just how you feel about selling. It is standard behavior in this era of business development. You have done a good job here and developed a good business. Extraordinarily good. It's just because of this that our chain must move in. The city as you know is covered by three chains. This area is sort of on the border, but we've had our eye on it for some time. You've developed it to the point where we must have it. There's nothing personal or racial about it. It's just a part of the business cycle. Mass manufacture, mass selling and mass buying are the inevitable steps. The individual simply cannot compete. We can buy cheaper and sell cheaper. We can't lose. You can't win."

"Sounds like socialism."

"Oh, no, quite the contrary, free enterprise; that is, free for those who hold the power."

"You say, there's nothing personal about this, neither race nor class?"

"Exactly. We are making you the same offer which we make white proprietors———"

"Except in one consideration. Doesn't the selling proprietor usually get an offer of management at least of his own store?"

The man paused and looked surprised. "Why—yes. Yes, of course. But you see in that case, in most cases—well, Mr. Carmichael, we might as well face it. Here we strike an aspect of American life which has nothing to do with grocery chains———"

"Except that in my case it has everything to do with my earning a living."

"Surely, but that you have in any case. We do usually offer a man whose store we're trying to buy, a job as manager of the merged business. But as you know, in this case you would be entering a job where the members form a closer social unit. Where if you made good we might want to transfer you. You might find yourself in charge of white workers———"

"And in such case?"

"It wouldn't do, Mr. Carmichael, you know it wouldn't. I'm sorry, but———"

"I'm more sorry than you are. And I won't sell. I'll fight until I lose all."

"You've made a bad decision. You'll lose all."

Within a couple of months a store for groceries, food and notions was opened on the corner opposite Carmichael. It was a capacious and well-equipped establishment. It was fully stocked and carried some widely advertised commodities which the manufacturers would no longer allow Carmichael to handle. Only one store to a neighborhood, the owners said. Also, manufacturers became unusually strict on cut prices for their goods. He could not say they were not just as strict on his competitor, neither could he be sure they were. Almost, he was sure they were not. For a time, the competition was steady, but Carmichael held his own. So long as prices were the same, he held his customers and the neighborhood applauded. Then, one afternoon Jackie ran in after school and cried,

"Father, the chain is advertising three pounds of potatoes for 15 cents. How can they when the cost is 20 cents?"

That was the beginning. The chain began deliberately selling below cost. Customers hesitated, but after all money is money. Jack tried selling some articles below cost; he tried buying from the chain and re-selling, but his co-conspirators were soon spotted and refused sales. It was a bitter, long-drawn-out struggle. The chain lost thousands of dollars, but they had the money to lose. Carmichael lost hundreds of dollars and could not afford it. At last, the wholesalers and the banks joined the fray and tipped the balance for the chain; until one winter night the sign "Carmichael & Son" came down and the store did not open next morning. That day prices went up precipitously across the street.

DeBerry was angry and disappointed. He talked with several of his rich white supporters.

"Mr. Bradley, you could help, if you would."

"Yes, I could for a while; but I can't hold back American business."

"But Carmichael is a good merchant. And we Negroes have so few chances to earn a living."

"I know, but why didn't he start business among Negroes, and not compete with white merchants?"

"Are we or are we not Americans? If we are, should we try to build a separate economy, with separate stores, separate transport?"

"But that's what you're doing in your church."

"No, no, that's not what I meant. There are some small areas of life—social intercourse, homes and neighborhood, where temporarily we try to live and act apart because of race prejudice. But you surely do not want us to develop as a separate Negro nation. That is preposterous!"

Carmichael and Betty took a long ride into the country up along the Connecticut River. He wanted to talk with an Italian truck gardener who had often sold him some of his best produce. He had a vague plan of a little farm where he could think and write while raising his own fresh, good food.

It was sunset when he arrived. The house was dirty and crowded. The family straggled in, dead tired, hungry and quarrelsome. The father, sweaty and soiled, looked at Jack and Betty with red, weary eyes.

"Welcome! Yes, yes, my friends, I know. You're both dreaming of the little farm with quiet, ease and rest. You're hunting in the wrong world, the wrong world. When my father brought me from Italy his one dream was a farm of his own in free America. How we worked and saved for this. We got it. It killed my father. It's killing me. It won't kill my children for they have revolted and left.

Only the two youngest remain with their wives and babies. Next year they move to the mills in Springfield. Why? Dear land, long transport, high prices for materials and low prices for product—and God!"

"God?"

"Yes. God with his rain and drought; his heat and cold; his wind and flood; his race hate. Eat with us and let me explain. Have some good red wine. Now spaghetti. Taste this chicken. Now sit out here. There, that is better. Listen. This land is good but it is not the best, and it was priced too high, far too high. The real estate men hoped to sell it to gentlemen who would farm as a pastime. They didn't want the damned Dagoes but if we must have it, we must pay the highest price. We tried. We are still trying. It proved too far out. It was too far for horses, and trucks cost in gas and oil. And then the market—the wholesalers, the stevedores, the squabbling for place, the price offered for the goods, the goods spoiled. We tried to sell directly to the customers; the city came with tax on taxes, rules of traffic and 'buy American'! And then God. Rain that never stops till it rots the work of a season; sun that burns until you see yourself burning in hell. Then the river turns loose and tears down from Canada with brown destruction and the wind whirls over from the Berkshires until the crop lies flat on the ground. And even when all is well, what can we do? How can we rest and play? What is there to see? Where is there time for music, dance and song; for comfort and dream? No, my friend, that is not the way. Believe me. I know. The consumers should pay more for goods? They pay plenty! But who gets it? I don't know, but I do know that we, the farmers, don't.

"Jack, if you have a big, husky family and work them like hell, you can make a farm pay with luck in weather. But you can't drive a family in America as we did in Italy and I guess that's right. Three of my children have deserted already. Those two scowling boys yonder will go this Fall. Now, if a man owns land and has enough money to buy machinery and hire outside labor, he can make money—on the machinery and labor, if he can find labor. Otherwise, there's only one answer: the mills. Mills are making money and paying good wages; with a strong union wages can be kept up and pushed higher as profits go up. This is the only democracy left to us in Free Enterprise; the close knit group organized to fight and fight hard."

"That's not democracy. Democracy means consultation and decision as to aims and methods."

"Sure, and trade unionism has little of this, only the faint beginning. It's not democracy. It's war or preparation for war."

"All right; that's it. Now, Jack, there's but one thing for you to do. Get a job in the mills."

"But I'd have to join a union, and most unions don't admit colored men."

"You'll have to push it. You see, Jack, through your grocery you made a lot of friends. You treated people right. The best union for you to crash is the machinists. That's dominated by the Irish Catholics."

"Fat chance I'd have there. The machinists have long led the fight to exclude Negroes from trade unions."

"All right, but the Catholic Church is wise. So long as that church represented the fight of poor Irish immigrants to get jobs in America and not be further pauperized by poorer Negroes, the Church paid no attention to black folk whom they regarded as incurable Protestants of the worst type. But things have happened among Catholics since then."

"I know it," said Betty. "I have been thrown with many Catholics and once made a study. Black St. Benedict of Sicily was canonized in 1807, and black Martin of Porres, in Peru, was beatified in 1836. The colored Oblate Sisters of Province began teaching in Baltimore in 1829, and another colored order in New Orleans in 1842. In 1884, the first colored priest was ordained in Chicago, and in 1889, came Bishop O'Connor's congregation for work among Indians and colored people.

"Then in 1890 came the real beginning. Katharine Drexel of the rich Philadelphia family furnished funds and the Catholic Church began deliberately to proselyte among Negroes. A mission board was established in New York City in 1907. After the war, in 1920, German priests challenged the church by opening a seminary for training Negro priests in Mississippi. In 1927, there were six Negro priests and 270,000 Negro communicants. And in 1937 came the Pope's letter ordering the American Catholic Church to proselyte by planned effort for Negro members."

"There you are. It's even better than I thought, although I had heard of some of this action within the Church. Now this is what you do. Get a group of the boys to back your application for an apprenticeship in the Machinists Union. Then go to the parish priest, not the Italian nor the French Canadian. Get the priest of the Irish group which calls itself 'American' to make an appointment with the Bishop. The Bishop is a big man. Talk with him. Will you do this? I tell you you can't lose."

Jack and Betty, with considerable advice from Jackie, talked long over this scheme. Betty said:

"The International Association of Machinists organized in 1888, excluded Negroes and the A.F. of L. on that account would not admit them; but in 1895 the A. F. of L. backed down and admitted the Machinists. The anti-Negro clause of their constitution was not referred to, but in 1899, one of the secretaries openly boasted: 'The Negro is not admitted.' Today when industry is increasing by leaps and bounds, when war demands increasing factory work, continued exclusion of Negroes is a vital matter."

Jack said: "I grew up thinking that a man's work was his life; his way of doing what he wanted to do, which was the same thing in my mind as to what the world wanted done. Of course, I soon learned better, but concluded that a man could easily find how his ability and desire could best help to do what the world needed. That didn't work out. So then it was a search for any useful work whether I liked it or not, provided it supported me and left enough time for me to do what I most wanted to do. Even that was denied. Now I'm face to face with doing what I am not interested in, or even hate working at, and having no time left for my own life. That, it seems to me, is the plight of the mill hand, and I don't like it."

"Perhaps, Jack, it will not prove as bad as that. Machinists get high wages; enough if work is steady to maintain a good life and with hours so limited as to leave something for hobbies and recreation. But, of course, first you have got to gain admittance to the union; then the union has got to fight for gradual betterment of its wage and conditions of work. This is not simply your problem, it is the problem of the mass of human beings today in civilized lands."

"How about the uncivilized?" asked Jackie.

"And ever after, until we are ready not only to help ourselves but all other workers of the world," added Betty.

"That'll be a long time."

"It's our job to see that it's not too long."

"And suppose," put in Jackie again, "the Bishop says come on in, but you'll have to become Catholics."

Jack and Betty looked at each other.

"Come, it's suppertime," said Jack, and Betty started toward the kitchen; but she said as she went: "Suppose we take that up when the invitation comes!"

The young Irish-American priest received Jack politely, but looked a little puzzled at his request.

"Are you Catholic?" he asked.

"No," answered Jack. "I come to you because I know that most of the machinists are Catholics and yet they exclude Negroes. I thought that perhaps you could persuade them to change."

The priest looked thoughtful. Then he said:

"Mr. Carmichael, this is a serious matter and before I try to do anything I would like to talk with the Bishop. I know that he is particularly interested just now in labor and race relations."

"I hoped you would do that. And perhaps you will get me a chance to talk with him?"

"I'll try and call you up soon."

The Bishop listened carefully and then called in the three chief officials of the Machinists Union. They were unanimously and definitely opposed to any Negro members.

The Bishop leaned back and touched his ten fingers together. "My sons," he said, "we're facing great changes in the world today. There was a time when the Catholic Church in America had the defense of Irish laborers as its chief and almost only task. That's true no longer. Italians, Spanish peoples and others have enlarged our flock. Where we had 127,000 Negroes in the Church in 1927, today we have nearly 300,000. And our growth among the dark peoples of Asia and Africa, added to our colored followers in Central and South America, and the West Indies, makes the mission of the Catholic Church more colored than white. Moreover, these colored people are forging forward; they are gradually ceasing to be the children of other days. This Carmichael is an example. Now, look here, I'm not asking you to be big-hearted and charitable. God forgive me, but I know better than that. You're human. I'm just saying, watch yourself and consider a small step in self-defense. If white labor doesn't begin to recognize and make common cause with colored labor, colored laborers will join employers and help crush you."

"But," answered the labor leaders, "there are no colored machinists in this town, and none coming. Even this Carmichael is no journeyman; he'd have to enter as apprentice."

"True, true. But there are colored machinists in the South and thousands of Negroes who can learn. One day machinery will come to a thousand million Asiatics and Africans—"

"But, Father, they'll never come here."

"No, but our industry may go there. Have you ever thought that while you are excluding Negro labor from the factories of Springfield, these mills may one day go to Mississippi where there are no unions, and where, if unions come, black scabs will stand ready to displace white workers? Think that over, my sons. Consider if it might not be wisdom to admit one black man now and here rather than face a national competition which will drive your sons into war or poverty."

It was a week before the Bishop asked Jack Carmichael to call and received him cordially. Jack was glum and prepared for disappointment, but the Bishop ignored that. He set out whiskey, ancient and good, and cigars of delicate flavor. Then he handed Jack a letter from the Machinists Union, accepting him as apprentice.

"Don't mistake this gesture," said the Bishop genially. "It is not a free gift. It's a small yielding to my request and to their own apprehension. But it may lead to something broader and finer. I'm glad to have been of some little service; but here again, I acted because I see the world on the edge of a struggle between races and colors which may tear civilization asunder. I want to do my bit to avoid that. No, no, no thanks! Good day and call again.

"And by the way, that boy of yours. I saw him at the city games. He's a fine lad. Tell him to visit our new gym. I think he'll like it."

Jack came home elated but Betty was silent. Several days later she came and sat on Jack's lap and thought aloud: "The problem of earning a living is probably now settled for us. As a master machinist and with steady employment you'll make more than a clerk or grocer and as much as most professional men. I'll have my nursing!"

"Good. Then why the gloom?"

"Because steady work for machinists will depend on making arms and materials for war. It's the threat of world war that is booming the arms factories and making the unions strong."

"I hadn't thought of it that way."

"I had, but what of it? In this crazy world it seems we must kill to live. We're helpless, especially we who struggle at the bottom of the heap. I'm all at sea, dear, but we've got to stagger ahead and peer toward the Light."

Jackie stamped in noisily and a bit late.

"Hello, all. How about food? Say Pop, that Catholic gym is a dandy. The fellows were swell. And do you know, the priests are not sissies. You ought to see them play tennis and box. Remember, the YMCA wouldn't let me use the tennis courts."

CHAPTER IX

The Itinerant Preacher

There was another visitor to Jean's conference of 1938, who dropped by almost accidentally—Roosevelt Wilson. Roosevelt's mother had "given him to God" in a revival after the Atlanta Riot and he had grown up with the Mansart children. He had later studied theology in New England and then worked in a large colored Baptist church in Atlanta. Then, in Macon he organized a Baptist church near Manual Mansart's college and married Sojourner, Mansart's only daughter. The expansion of the church along Roosevelt's line of thought had been hindered by race prejudice and the church membership itself. He had left the Baptist Church in Macon. He was now settled in Birmingham, Alabama, as an African Methodist minister. He had dropped over to Atlanta to talk with his bishop and sound him out on the matter of his running for bishop in 1940. He then passed through Macon to settle various small bits of business, and visited the conference. He was thinking deeply of his work and destiny.

Like an obbligato running above the development of a nation becoming socialistic, and at the same time being drawn into defense of colonial imperialism, went the apparently unheeded and untouched line of development among the groups into which the nation was divided. This was especially true among the Negroes.

There were the schools which Mansart represented, the expanding Negro business interests, the lawyers and physicians, the black white-collar workers. There was Negro labor beginning to penetrate the white unions, and there was the Negro church. Far more than among whites, the Negro church was more social than religious. It was a broad center of daily life in work and play. The Negro preachers were directors of this group to a much greater extent than among whites.

This Roosevelt Wilson had in mind when he left the Baptist church in Macon, Georgia, went into the African Methodist connection and accepted an appointment at Birmingham, Alabama. North Alabama was the center of a new integration of American monopoly. Here iron and coal were part of a new industrial empire reaching around the world; and here in mining, as once in cotton, the Negro worker was becoming an indispensable factor. Wilson hardly saw all of the broader economic picture, but he did see his church as stepping stone to high positions for himself as a social leader.

He took hold of a sprawling organization in 1936, in the midst of the "New Deal," and began to build it into the semblance of the sort of church that he had planned in Macon. This was a new church of working people, strategically placed. Into this church he and Sojourner enticed miners and artisans who had joined the new CIO unions and had some money to spend. In two years, they had erected a church edifice of which the Negroes were inordinately proud. Then came the social center, which was the only decent place in the city where Negroes were welcome to recreation separated from drunkenness and gambling.

He spread his organization and influence. He had a nursery school and a forum for discussion. He cooperated with labor unions. He became known in the white city as a progressive man with a certain independence. He did not beg for anything. He did not want charity. His church raised its own money and contributed to the poor and unfortunate.

And at the same time Wilson was building his fences for the Bishopric. At the next general conference, in 1940, he was determined that there would be no doubt but that he represented the most constructive and forward-looking forces in the connection.

Wilson found his hands tied more tightly than they had been in his Baptist church. Over him was a Presiding Elder with power, and over the Elder was a Bishop, all-powerful. He began to work on the Bishop, who was an old man but well-preserved. His knowledge of human nature was wide and deep. He was selfish and not too scrupulous, but keen, and he wanted his church to go forward. He watched Wilson, he listened to him. Often, with a certain ruthlessness, he swept aside the proposals of the Presiding Elder, and his objections, and followed the plans of Wilson.

Still, the demands of the Presiding Elder were influential. He was a big, loud man, jealous of Wilson and bent on increasing his own popularity with the Bishop by his contributions to "Dollar Money," and "Dollar Money" was the life blood of the church. Wilson became angry at the manifest efforts to reduce his social and charitable activities by larger contribution to the general church funds. A serious break was avoided only by the Bishop. He sided with Wilson on the distribution of funds, but secretly promised to support the Presiding Elder for the bishopric in the 1940 convention of the church.

This, naturally, Wilson did not know. His outstanding success made him believe that his own merits would elect him by acclaim. He attended the general conference in Chicago and was overwhelmingly defeated. His great handicap was that he was far too new a convert to this church. This ancient foundation demanded a long novitiate. He must serve as a worker in the ranks. He did not realize this. He did not understand that in this church his work as a Baptist counted as nothing. What he did realize was that the place which he wanted was literally put up at auction and sold to the highest bidder—the Presiding Elder.

Wilson came back to Birmingham and resumed his work but did not even try to conceal his dislike of the Bishop. The inevitable happened: at the end of the year, without hint or notification, he was transferred to Annisberg, Alabama—a poor, run-down charge. He protested. The Bishop was frank.

"You want to be a bishop? Then you must work for it and work long and hard."

"There were many men in Chicago who had worked longer and harder than your candidate."

"Sure there were, son. Most ministers can never be bishop."

"But," protested Wilson, "all my work in Birmingham is lost. Your favorite candidate for the bishopric gets it and I am thrown a run-down old church, to climb from the bottom again. Four years of effort are lost."

"Oh, no," said the Bishop, "not lost. The church will build on what you have done. It will be easy to get a man to carry this work on, but difficult to get a man like you to begin a new work. You'll have a chance to do this in Annisberg."

But Wilson was angry. "It is unjust," he said.

The Bishop looked at him coldly and said, "Take it or leave it!"

Literally, there was nothing else to do. He was caught in a machine. But Sojourner was not easily excited or upset and said quite calmly: "Let's go and see what it's like."

Annisberg was about seventy-five miles west of Birmingham, near the Georgia border and on the Tallahoosa River, a small and dirty stream. The city was a center of manufacture, especially in textiles, and also because of the beauty of some of its surroundings, a residence for many owners of the great industries in north Alabama. But it had, as was usual in southern cities of this sort, a Black Bottom, a low region near the river where the Negroes lived—servants and laborers huddled together in a region with no sewage save the river, where streets and sidewalks were neglected and where there was much poverty and crime.

Wilson came by train from Birmingham and looked the city over; the rather pleasant white city was on the hill where the chief stores were. Beyond were industries and factories. Then they went down to Black Bottom. In the midst of this crowded region was the Allen African Methodist Episcopal Church. It was an old and dirty wooden structure, sadly in need of repair. But it was a landmark. It had been there 50 years or more and everybody in town, black and white, knew of it. It had just suffered a calamity, the final crisis in a long series of calamities. For the old preacher who had been there twenty-five years was dead, and the city mourned him.

He was a loud-voiced man, once vigorous but for many years now declining in strength and ability. He was stern and overbearing with his flock, but obsequious and conciliatory with the whites, especially the rich who partly supported the church. The Deacon Board, headed by a black man named Carlson, had practically taken over as the pastor grew old, and had its way with the support of the Amen corner.

The characteristic thing about this church was its Amen corner and the weekly religious orgy. A knot of old worshippers, chiefly women, listened weekly to a sermon. It began invariably in low tones, almost conversational, and then gradually worked up to high, shrill appeals to God and man. And then the Amen corner took hold, re-enacting a form of group participation in worship that stemmed from years before the Greek chorus, spreading down through the African forest, overseas to the West Indies, and then here in Alabama. With shout and slow dance, with tears and song, with scream and contortion, the corner group was beset by hysteria and shivering, wailing, shouting, possession of something that seemed like an alien and outside force. It spread to most of the audience and was often viewed by visiting whites who snickered behind handkerchief and afterward discussed Negro religion. It sometimes ended in deathlike trances with many lying exhausted and panting on chair and floor. To most of those who composed the Amen corner it was a magnificent and beautiful experience, something for which they lived from week to week. It was often re-enacted in less wild form at the Wednesday night prayer meeting.

Wilson, on his first Sunday, witnessed this with something like disgust. He had preached a short sermon, trying to talk man-to-man to the audience, to tell them who he was, what he had done in Macon and Birmingham, and what he proposed to do here. He sympathized with them on the loss of their old pastor. But then, at mention of that name, the Amen corner broke loose. He had no chance to say another word. At the very end, when the audience was silent and breathless, a collection was taken and then slowly everyone filed out. The audience did not think much of the new pastor, and what the new pastor thought of the audience he did not dare at the time to say.

During the next weeks he looked over the situation. First of all there was the parsonage, an utterly impossible place for civilized people to live in, originally poorly conceived, apparently not repaired for years, with no plumbing or sewage, with rat-holes and rot. It was arranged that he would board in the home of one of the old members of the church, a woman named Catt who, as Wilson afterward found, was briefly referred to as The Cat because of her sharp tongue and fierce initiative.

Ann Catt was a lonely, devoted soul, never married, conducting a spotless home and devoted to her church, but a perpetual dissenter and born critic. She soared over the new pastor like an avenging angel lest he stray from the path and not know all the truth and gossip of which she was chief repository.

Then Wilson looked over the church and studied its condition. The salary of the pastor had for years been $500 annually and even this was in arrears. Wilson made up his mind that he must receive at least $2,500, but when he mentioned this to the Deacons they said nothing. The church itself must be repaired. It was infested with vermin. It was falling to pieces. It was dirty and neglected. It really ought to be rebuilt, and he determined to go up and talk to the city banks about this. Meanwhile, the city itself should be talked to. The streets in the colored section were dirty. There was typhoid and malaria. The children had nowhere to go and no place to play, not even sidewalks. The school was small, dark and ill-equipped. The teacher was a pliant fool. There were two liquor saloons not very far from the church, one white, that is, conducted for white people with a side entrance for Negroes; the other exclusively Negro. Undoubtedly, there was a good deal of gambling in both.

On the other side of the church was a quiet, well-kept house with shutters and recently painted. Wilson inquired about it. It was called Kent House. The deacon of the church, Carlson, was its janitor. One of the leading members of the Amen corner was cook; there were two or three colored maids employed there. Wilson was told that it was a sort of hotel for white people, which seemed to him rather queer. Why should a white hotel be set down in the center of Black Bottom? But nevertheless it looked respectable. He was glad to have it there.

The rest of Black Bottom was a rabbit warren of homes in every condition of neglect, disrepair and careful upkeep. Dives, carefully repaired huts, and nicely painted and ornamented cottages were jumbled together cheek by jowl with little distinction. The best could not escape from the worst and the worst nestled cosily beside the better. The yards, front and back, were narrow; some were trash dumps, some had flower gardens. Behind were privies, for there was no sewage system.

After looking about a bit, Wilson discovered beyond Black Bottom, across the river and far removed from the white city, a considerable tract of land, and it occurred to him that the church and the better Negro homes might gradually be moved to this plot. He talked about it to the Presiding Elder. The Presiding Elder looked him over rather carefully. He was not sure what kind of a man he had in hand. But there was one thing that he had to stress, and that was that the contribution to the general church expenses, the dollar money, had been seriously falling behind in this church, and that must be looked after immediately. In fact, he intimated clearly that that was the reason that Wilson had been sent here—to make a larger contribution of dollar money.

Wilson stressed the fact that clear as this was, they must have a better church, a more business-like conduct of the church organization, and an effort to get this religious center out of its rut of wild worship into a modern church organization. He emphasized to the Presiding Elder the plan of giving up the old church and moving across the river. The Presiding Elder was sure that that would be impossible. But he told Wilson to "go ahead and try." And Wilson tried.

It did seem impossible. The bank which held the mortgage on the old church declared that the interest was considerably in arrears, and the real estate people said flatly that the land across the river was being held for an eventual development for white working people who were coming in, and that none would be sold to colored folk. When it was proposed to rebuild the church, Wilson found that the terms for a new mortgage were very high. He was sure that he could do better if he went to Atlanta to get the deal financed.

But when this proposal was made to his Deacon Board, he met unanimous opposition. The church certainly would not be removed. The very proposition was sacrilege. It had been here fifty years. It was going to stay forever. It was hardly possible to get any argument on the subject. As for rebuilding, well, that might be looked into, but there was no hurry, no hurry at all.

Wilson again went downtown to a different banker, an intelligent young white man who seemed rather sympathetic, but he shook his head.

"Reverend," he said, "I think you don't quite understand the situation here. Don't you see the amount of money that has been invested by whites around that church? Tenements, stores, saloons, some gambling, I hope not too much. The colored people are getting employment at Kent House and other places, and they are near their places of employment. When a city has arranged things like this you cannot easily change them. Now, if I were you I would just plan to repair the old church so it would last for five or ten years. By that time, perhaps something better can be done."

Then Wilson asked, "What about this Kent House which you mention? I don't understand why a white hotel should be down here."

The young banker looked at him with a certain surprise, and then he said flatly: "I'm afraid I can't tell you anything in particular about Kent House. You'll have to find out about it on your own. Hope to see you again." And he dismissed the colored pastor.

It was next day that Sojourner came and sat beside him and took his hand. She said, "My dear, do you know what Kent House is?"

"No," said Wilson, "I don't. I was just asking about it. What is it?"

"It's a house of prostitution for white men with white girls as inmates. They hire a good deal of local labor, including two members of our Trustee Board. They buy some supplies from our colored grocers and they are patronized by some of the best white gentlemen in town."

Wilson stared at her. "My dear, you must be mistaken."

"Talk to Mrs. Catt," she said.

And after Wilson had talked to Mrs. Catt and to others, he was absolutely amazed. This, of course, was the sort of thing that used to take place in Southern cities—putting white houses of prostitution with colored girls in colored neighborhoods and carrying them on openly. But it had largely disappeared on account of protest by the whites and through growing resentment on the part of the Negroes as they became more educated and got better wages.

But this situation of Kent House was more subtle. The wages involved were larger and more regular. The inmates were white and from out of town, avoiding local friction. The backing from the white town was greater and there was little publicity. Good wages, patronage and subscription of various kinds stopped open protest from Negroes. And yet, Wilson knew that this place must go or he must go. And for him to leave this job now without accomplishing anything would mean practically the end of his career in the Methodist church, if not in all churches. He talked fiercely to Mrs. Catt.

"That place ought to be burned down!" he said.

She looked at him a bit wildly and said, "My dear pastor, that is exactly what I have done had in mind for years. Protest is nothing. We is in bondage to a house of shame. I'd hate to hurt those pretty girls. They ain't to blame. But if it should burn down there sure would be a big chance to make mighty loud protest before it was ever built again. I don't see what else we can do. It's gotta burn! God tells me!"

Wilson pulled himself together and looked at the wild-eyed woman. "My dear lady," he said, "I of course didn't mean that literally. You must—you must put it out of your mind. I—I was just talking in a general way."

Mrs. Catt looked at him calmly. "I knows just how you was talking and just what you really means. I thinks as I have thought for the last ten years. It's gotta burn!"

Wilson went to town and got a clear idea of indebtedness, of the lack of insurance of church and parsonage, and what it would cost to borrow more money. The cost was very high. He talked the matter over with his Board and tried to make plans for more regular and larger contributions. The response was not good. Mr. Carlson and the others seemed to think that they were already raising more money than they could afford, that they might possibly double the pastor's salary and make it $1,000.00 but not a cent more, and that on the whole they wondered if Mr. Wilson wouldn't be better satisfied with a church elsewhere. And Mr. Wilson told them flatly that he would not.

For several weeks he studied the situation. Nearly every Sunday he found himself turned back into the African past by the Amen corner, despite his cold, critical sermons. Moreover, he was receiving in the collection not even as much money as the church had been used to raising. Contributions from the whites fell markedly. He could see that he was being shoved out and back none too gently. He again had a talk with the Presiding Elder, who under the worsening circumstances listened more sympathetically.

Wilson took the train for Atlanta. There he sat down with the Bishop and went over the situation.

"My dear Bishop, there isn't a chance to do anything in Annisberg unless I can get rid of that Board of Trustees and the domination of Carlson. I want you and the Presiding Elder to help me do this."

The Bishop scowled, and just as he was about to say that this was more than he was willing even to attempt, there came a ring at his doorbell and a telegraph boy appeared with a message for Wilson. The telegram said that Allen church and parsonage, and some of the neighboring buildings in Annisberg, had burned down.

Wilson rushed back home. It was all too true. But there were other strange and disconcerting facts which he learned. The Cat, as his hostess was called, was dead. She had been seen setting fire to the church at sunset, spreading the flames with her torch from cellar to roof. Then she had climbed out on the roof of Kent House, wavered there and almost fallen, while, amid screams from the street, she set fire from attic to cellar, giving the inmates a chance to escape.

The girls had rushed out in every condition of dress and undress, and there had been a number of men who had run out at the same time. Unfortunately the mayor of the city, in his attempt to escape, had broken his leg. The morning paper praised him for his valiant attempts to put out the fire.

The chief of police came down and talked to Wilson rather truculently. "I want to know what you know about this fire."

"I know nothing at all. I have only been pastor of this church for a few months and have really made few plans and secured little power to direct it."

"Where were you last night?"

"I was in Atlanta talking to the Bishop of the Diocese."

"Planning this fire?"

"No."

"Have you ever heard anybody talk about burning down this church?"

"No," answered the pastor, lying bluntly.

"Listen, Wilson, this is serious business, and we have a suspicion that some of these darkies deliberately burned this church and Kent House under your advice!"

"Why, sir, should they burn Kent House?"

"I don't care why, but if they did somebody is going to jail for life."

"I should think," said Mr. Wilson, "this might be a matter of rejoicing on the part of the people of this city, that they have gotten rid of a house of prostitution right in the midst of their only colored dwelling district."

"If you dare say anything like that in public, Wilson—"

And Wilson bent forward and said, "I dare, and I'm going to."

The City Council took the whole situation under careful consideration. This was bringing into public discussion something that would hurt the city's reputation. Carlson, of the colored church, was starting an appeal to white friends for funds with which to rebuild, and Wilson learned that always in the past Kent House had contributed generously to carry on the church. He took a firm stand against appealing for funds to anyone who wanted this house of prostitution restored. And he went to the City Council to talk about it. But the Council would not listen to him. The banker was willing to furnish funds for the rebuilding of the church. The matter of the disputed Kent House was left in abeyance.

Then Sojourner went into action. She knew that there was planned a meeting of the Missionary Society of the city among the white women. It had to do with foreign missionary work in Africa. She went to the president of the Methodist Society and asked her if she would not like participation on the part of the colored people. She suggested, for instance, that she might bring a group to render some of the Negro spirituals.

Mrs. Dawes, who was a very pleasant and amiable person and not too bright, was delighted, and asked Sojourner to bring her group on a certain evening. When she brought the matter before the Missionary Societies she did not find quite the cooperation that she had expected. There was another matter that had to do with the question of inviting the Catholic Church and the Unitarian Church to take part. Finally, after rather warm discussion it was decided that they would not be included in the joint meeting. And after that, the weary meeting assented to having this colored woman bring her singers and give some Negro music.

Thus, it was that Sojourner went to one of the finer homes of the city, on the hill, and sitting in the back parlor where her girls would not be too conspicuous, waited for the signal for her little group to sing. It was a rather long wait and most of the ladies present were willing to have the singing put off to some other time. But they were tired and a little hungry, and so while colored servants passed around sandwiches and soft drinks, Sojourner arose and walking into the main parlor, said a word.

"I was thinking, perhaps, ladies," she said, "that you would not mind if I preface my music with just a word about one matter which is exercising us very much down in Black Bottom." She spoke in a low and cultivated voice and the ladies stared. And then she dropped her bombshell. She said calmly, "I refer to the proposal to rebuild in Black Bottom that house of prostitution known as Kent House."

There was an astounded silence, and then almost a scream of protest. But one large handsome woman arose in the back and literally yelled them into silence. "Listen. I'm going to hear about this! I know that talk has been stopped and I've tried in vain to get the truth. If this woman has anything to say, I'm for having it said right here."

And then Sojourner calmly told them that here was a house conducted by a Madam who had ample financial backing and police protection, and who kept in the house as virtual prisoners some fifteen or twenty young white women from out of town who were at the service of the friends and relatives of the ladies sitting right here. "And Christians of Black Bottom do not want that institution restored after God in his Mercy has burned it down."

Then, not waiting for the astounded ladies to recover poise or voice, she sat down at the piano and, gathering her girls about her, they began to sing:

"Let us all bow together on our knees. Let us all pray together on our knees. Let us all sing together, to meet the rising sun! Let us all sing together, if you please."

The meeting broke up in confusion, but the big, handsome woman tore into her home a half hour later, and when at the door she heard her husband's cheerful voice, "Hello, Rosebud, are you there?" she screamed back: "Can that Rosebud stuff! Jim Conwell, god-damn your soul to hell, if you let them rebuild that whorehouse in Black Bottom, so help me Jesus I'll leave you flat and I'll tell all Annisberg why!"

After this and during the next year in the city of Annisberg, the situation of the Negroes and their relations to the whites hung in dangerous balance. There could have been a riot at any time. Wilson was threatened with physical violence. The church tottered, with small contributions but with a break in the Sunday orgy. Then at last, by careful thought and work the re-organization wheeled into line. The old church was pulled down and a new one built, with a parsonage next to it. Some connection with the city sewer was made in Black Bottom, and the worst of the dirt and refuse cleaned up.

The black people in Wilson's congregation began to settle down and listen to what he had to say. New members came from without the immediate area and a demand for a Sunday School and for some social work. The contributions became more regular.

The colored people got more employment in the industries of the growing town. Although Wilson had been in black despair for months, it was Sojourner who had the vision and the courage to look forward to the development of this work and to realize what her position was as the wife of the pastor. She lifted him up bodily and completely and set him on his feet. His new church paid its debts, arranged for work for its congregation. The Bishop praised him, collected more money than was due, and again after three years shunted him to Mobile.

Then Wilson really rebelled. "By God," he said, "Enough is enough!" And Sojourner agreed. The motives of the Bishop were not altogether selfish. Wilson had rescued two lost churches and there were two or three other places which needed his energy and training and the cooperation of the kind of wife he had. Mobile won. It was a hard assignment, but three or four triumphs of this sort would make Wilson a very valuable man and perhaps rescue the church from the difficulties into which it had recently fallen. He therefore transferred Wilson without consultation, knowing that he might have trouble.

Roosevelt Wilson was in despair. There seemed to be no real future for him. If he went to an assignment and worked hard, he could build up a church. He knew that. He could build up a strong constituency which would regularly contribute to the support of himself and the church in general. He could, if necessary, build new edifices, with social rooms and modern conveniences, with no debt, with an income which would pay himself a reasonable salary, pay an assistant and a number of social workers. He could start institutions for old people and children.

But while he was doing this, the demands from the Bishop and the general church would continually increase. There was not only the dollar money as it was called, which was a tax of a dollar a head on membership, but there were all sorts of special causes—missions, domestic and foreign, especially missions to Africa. Some of these causes were good, some were frauds. At any rate, it was difficult to discriminate or refuse. It was dangerous to get in the bad graces of the Presiding Elders, and particularly of the Bishop.

The Bishop was well-nigh all-powerful. He not only received a good salary, but in addition to that he made forays and requests and demands of the district and of the church. When he came to visit, he expected not only free support but presents and money, clothes, shirts and shoes. In the course of the year these gifts to the presiding bishop or to other visiting bishops amounted to thousands of dollars. If they were not given, the minister need not expect a good appointment!

Of course, the Bishop must bow to local opinion, and on local opinion Wilson could count. His constituents always wanted him to return. Nevertheless, the Bishop and the Presiding Elder together could transfer him and at the end of three years by law they must transfer him. However, if he stood well with them he might possibly stay longer than that. He might stay almost indefinitely. But to stand well under such circumstances meant a tribute of money and subserviency.

Under these circumstances, it was natural for Roosevelt Wilson to redouble his efforts to attain the bishopric. He was by far one of the most successful pastors in the connection. He was well-trained, he had a talented wife and he was personally a decent man with high ideals. Moreover, he believed in the church and in its dogma. Not slavishly; he couldn't recite the Apostle's Creed, much less the Nicene Creed, and say that every word of it was true; but in general he accepted the Christian dogma. But he wanted to see it exemplified and typified in human lives, and he leaned strongly toward the socialistic state.

But beyond the personal ideas and decisions of the Bishop were the attitudes of the preachers who elected the bishop in the general conference. They were selected as delegates by their churches, and Wilson found that very widely they were seeking these places for the possibility of getting close to the bishop, and for the probability of actually getting paid for their attendance and vote.

In their minds, it was not exactly selling out—it was a means of support for people who represented poor folk. They were mostly getting miserably small salaries and working hard for that. If they were elected to the General Conference, the provision for their expenses was small, but there was always the possibility of going to the conference and being able to receive, not publicly of course, a definite sum of money if they would vote for a particular candidate. This bribery for the bishopric, Wilson found to his astonishment, was not only widespread but it was growing.

Wilson now tried another tack commonly attempted by dissatisfied ministers. He applied for transfer to another diocese. The bishop presiding over Texas welcomed him. He knew that Wilson was a good money-raiser and suspected that his hard experience would make him more amenable to advice. He needed such a man in Dallas where a prominent church was getting out of hand. He sent Wilson to the largest church of the connection, in Dallas.

It was a church of the colored prosperous and well-to-do. It had numbers of professional men, merchants, insurance men and contractors. There were some skilled artisans and some old and trusted servants of the rich whites. It had a beautiful edifice and a well-equipped parsonage and church house. Its surpliced choir sang well, but avoided for the most part the spirituals. The church contributed to the city Community Chest and did not solicit contributions from whites, although some donations could not be refused. It had a forum which discussed politics as well as general matters. It was a body, only slightly religious and not at all social minded. It had no debt.

It wanted a minister who would show off and emphasize its assured place in the community. It paid its pastors well. The Reverend Roosevelt Wilson at first sight seemed to fill the bill admirably. His first sermons were excellent—restrained, with learned allusions. The ones that followed, on social reform, workers and poverty, were less appreciated. The next talk, on trade unions, brought a conference with the Board of Trustees. The church was distinctly against unions. Its members had suffered from discrimination, not only in trying to join the unions but even after joining. Moreover, many of them themselves hired labor for personal service and for profit. They insisted that the subject be kept out of future sermons. Meantime, they suggested that Wilson ought to have an automobile for visiting his widely scattered congregation and for business matters. He could obtain one at nominal expense.

CHAPTER X

Bishop Wilson

Deterioration set in gradually. Wilson's ministry was comfortable. His salary was good and promptly paid. The raising of money was adequately attended to by the deacons. The church program was planned by the numerous groups, clubs and societies. Wilson's renewed suggestions about trade unions, boys' clubs, slum activities and other matters were listened to courteously and patiently. Then they disappeared "in committee" and if they emerged again they were transformed into something unrecognizable or merged with previous efforts of a singularly different type. The firm basis of conservative, respectable church life was not altered a bit.

At first Wilson protested. He objected, even rebelled, but this was gradually forgotten in a really charming social life. His calls on his parishioners were delightful, and there the policy of the church, long set, was explained to him and defended while he was attentively listened to.

The card clubs early took him in. There were dozens of them in and connected with the church, each with a score to fifty members, and varying from enjoyable social gatherings to respectable drinking bouts, with flirting and feasting. At all these social meetings, Wilson was flattered and praised.

As he aged, he looked more impressive; his skin grew sleeker, his bushy hair became a crown of iron-gray, his face dignified with lines of experience. His sermons slowly changed from crusade and invective and attacks on the white world, to description and reflection and suggestions of compromise, from the Bible and Shakespeare to current literature. He found increasing companionship in the church—doubters, cynics, pleasure-seekers, as well as earnest souls who dreamed of but recoiled from action and who, particularly in the face of the all-pervasive race problems, were not so sure of the ultimate answer as he was at first.

Especially, his almost forgotten attraction to beautiful women now began to evoke his own dormant interest. It was delicious to sip wine and munch intricate sandwiches in a modern living room with the rapt attention of a charming, well-dressed woman who had leisure and who was as entranced as he. Increasing portions of his spare time came to be consumed that way and he had less time for church and home.

All this Sojourner did not fail to notice. Naturally unassertive, tending to take refuge in thoughtful silence rather than in questions, and least of all in complaint, she felt the ache within her grow. She realized how deftly her music had been eliminated by the church. The Negro spirituals which she had revived in the services after long disuse were gradually relegated to new disuse by suggestions of classic melody, of modern music and form, all put forward quite kindly in the sincere attempt to increase the prestige of the church.

Sojourner for a long time acquiesced and voiced no protest. Her idea of the marriage communion was to help when help was sought, otherwise to wait and hope. But gradually, she began to realize that passive yielding was as useless in a church and family as in a race and nation. She began to think, plan and work.

Almost imperceptibly she began deliberately to split the church. Over against the gay, drinking, card-playing spenders and dressers she organized the singers and musicians, the readers, painters and actors. She gathered the youth and children from the parish and beyond, seeking talent even in the slums.

She organized her friends within and without the church. They took up Negro music as it was developing—Will Cook, Burleigh and Dett. She had them study the African drums that Shirley Graham had brought into her opera "Tom Tom," which a group of colored and white players staged as a city-wide venture in Cleveland. They followed Shirley's "Swing Mikado" which later entranced Chicago and New York until driven off the stage by the same capitalist theatre that killed WPA.

Then Sojourner organized a Negro Little Theater patterned after the Krigwa Players in New York and the white Little Theater of Dallas. Paul Green's play, "No 'Count Boy," was set for a Friday night, but it developed that the most ostentatious and extravagant of Wilson's card clubs had chosen the same night to hold a session at a new night club in the suburbs. It was an elaborate night club and represented a large investment. Several members of the card club were among the investors. They needed a flaming opening and the card club's party was just the thing; it was strictly private and cost $100 a member. The curious public would pay off on Saturday night following.

Wilson naturally had planned to attend the play at his wife's Little Theater, but neither date could be changed and the members of the card club, who wanted him to attend their party, brought up their heaviest artillery which included some beautiful and gorgeously gowned colored visitors from Chicago. A compromise was quickly reached. The Reverend Mr. Wilson's ticket was free, and he would come to dinner at six and leave early enough to reach the Little Theater by nine.

The dinner was quite late but delicious, the company was charming and more, and the party in exotic surroundings grew wild. It was an alluring place, the walls flamboyantly decorated with animals, scrolls and near naked dark and pretty women in seductive poses; yellow, crimson and gold suffused the room; soft music and lowered lights pervaded the scene, and waiters danced and sang on their missions. Liquor flowed freely from an open bar, with white-clad bartenders and half-naked flower girls. Wilson crawled into bed about four o'clock Saturday morning.

He awoke at ten with a splitting headache and a feeling of utter despair. For the first time in his life he had been drunk in public. He lay back in misery and stared at the ceiling. What had he done last night and who had witnessed his disgrace? Of course, Sojourner had risen long since and slipped downstairs quietly, despite the fact that she too must be very tired. Finally, she knocked softly and brought him a breakfast tray and the morning papers. She said nothing but kissed him gently and left.

She left and ran up to her secluded nest near the roof. She tore her violin almost roughly from its case. Hardly conscious of what she was doing, she played a poem, ripping from the instrument's entrails the pain and pity of her life. The first movement was rage and fury; she stripped the tones as gut cut gut and dissonance whined from the strained wood. Then came dark hate and dull despair as the violin grieved and quivered. Blending and low harmony followed with slow understanding of the deep roll of widened knowledge and high resolve. She rested, palpitating, and caressed the bow until finally melody crept into her soul and slipped softly over the strings—softly and sweetly—with forgiveness and love, the love that gives forever without return. Across the way, neighbors lifted their windows and listened. Carefully, at last she laid the violin in its bed. Silently she slipped downstairs to her work.

After a time, Wilson sat up. He could not eat but drank his coffee. Then idly he glanced at the *Express*. War had started in Europe—let it start! Roosevelt wanted us to enter; but why? Then he turned to the amusement page. There was a column of extravagant praise for Sojourner's play. Seldom before had Wilson known a white daily so to praise a Negro cultural effort. Wilson felt a mingling of exaltation and envy.

He threw the paper down and idly picked up the colored weekly. It had a front-page display of the new and fabulous night club and its opening, together with two murders and a hold-up. Inside was a half column on the Little Theater. On the back page was the gossip column. He started to throw the paper aside when he saw at the bottom a little squib:

"The Reverend Roosevelt Wilson did not attend the play last night. It is said he was rehearsing for the lead next week in his wife's 'No 'Count Boy.'"

Wilson got up slowly, bathed and dressed. He was in a white rage. This was a cooked-up thing—last night's dinner was purposely late and his drink must have been "spiked"! All right, so he was down! But by God he wasn't out! He sat down and wrote out resignations from every social club to which he belonged. He even sent a check in payment for his "free" ticket of the night before. Then he composed a sermon. He wrote every word of it by hand and then copied and corrected it. He would go down to dinner and before retiring for the night, he would commit every word to memory, even arrange the gestures. It would be the best sermon he ever delivered and his Church would be thrown back on its hind legs.

He was so full of his own scheme that he greeted Sojourner carelessly, picking absently at her very carefully prepared dinner and hardly glancing at her until with a cry of distress she tried to arise, then vomited into her plate. He was aghast. With help of the maid, he half carried her to bed as she, ashamed, protested and insisted that it was not any serious illness, but only something she must have eaten. The physician came quickly. He was a bright young man and had been at the party the night before. He emerged from the bedroom laughing and patted Wilson on the back:

"Congratulations, old man, your baby has got an excellent start!"

Wilson groped blindly into the bedroom and took Sojourner into his arms.

"We're going to have a baby in the family," he stammered, gazing into her eyes. But she whispered: "I don't want a baby, I want a bishop."

Wilson was not superstitious, nor did he ordinarily believe in signs. But the portents which within two days had poured down on his head gave him pause. He was going to make a sharp turn-about and re-orient his life. He was astonished to realize what store Sojourner still set on his election as bishop; now he saw but one straight unveering path ahead.

He had almost stopped reading and thinking. He had neglected Sojourner, partly for reasons of self-indulgence and escapism, partly because she had found a creative life apart from him and was making a success of it. What did he now propose to do? He would supplement Sojourner's work in music and drama by giving her a wider audience. Heretofore, she had been entertaining a church composed of professional men, white collar workers and servants of the white rich. To this, he intended to add artisans and common laborers. The church would fight this but such a fight now would be a fight against a considerable body of white public opinion which liked the new music-drama. There would ensue a hell of a row, but he was ready for it.

The rest of that Saturday and far into the night, Wilson sought out Negro trade union leaders and artisans. He visited saloons and pool rooms. On Sunday the church was crowded with strangers. There were mostly well-dressed artisans, but with them some shabby working people. Wilson preached on "Labor and Labor Organization."

"This is a new day. It is not sufficient to train our youth for business and professional life. It is not enough for us to serve the rich and powerful. Most of our people are workers. They dig and haul. They clean and carry. They do the fundamental work of mankind and in return are paid too little to live decently. This is true of the workers of the world and they are uniting to change this situation and see that the laborer gets a larger share of the wealth which he produces. From this day on, my work in this church will be directed to the uplift of Negro labor in Dallas by adult education, health promotion, and by organization for higher wage. If the church does not support this program, then I'll seek another church. To support this program, my wife will continue her work in music and drama."

There was open applause in the church that morning but there was also silent anger and determined opposition. A prominent colored contractor and trustee who paid his artisans "Negro" wages and knew they were threatening to organize a union, got up and walked out during the sermon. There was every element of conventional church strife—whispering about the pastor's morals; of his neglect of "old-time religion" and failure to stress redemption, sin and salvation; his sneering at miracles and conversion; his envy of the well-to-do and preference for the poor, criminal and lazy; his continual criticism of the rich whites and wooing of the despicable poor whites; his defense of strikes and unions; his wife's dragging in of slave music, resort to play acting, dancing and fiddles.

The trustees consulted the Presiding Elder and the Bishop. Instead of open battle, there was attempted compromise. The increased audiences continued, with larger collections and meetings of labor unions during the week in the basement. The Bishop talked to Wilson about a church in the working districts, nearer "the masses." Perhaps Wilson would like to transfer there? Wilson consented if he could have a large social center with a Little Theater. White people eagerly offered to contribute to such a project. But the trustees of his church objected. They were fearful of losing status. They decided it would be better to keep Wilson in his present place, then after his transfer next year, to keep the benefits of his expansion but gradually restore their church to normal.

Here, Wilson was back to his old quandary. He could do much here in lifting labor. But after that? Once again to the backwoods and everything to do over again. His mind veered again to the bishopric. What this great church needed was leadership from the highest levels to guide and support the local pastors who could learn his methods and ideals. It was the Bishop himself who started him on this line of thinking again, but whether deliberately or not, Wilson was never sure. The Bishop called Wilson in one day and said:

"My son, Wilberforce wants to give you an honorary degree."

Wilson stared. He had always opposed the cheap doctorates in "divinity" which many ministers sought so eagerly. But Wilberforce was the leading church college and its commencements were gathering places for leading church politicians; perhaps there a movement for social uplift led by the church might be initiated under his leadership. He consented and the Bishop added unexpectedly:

"While you are up that way, why don't you talk with your brother-in-law in Chicago—Douglass Mansart? He is a rich and powerful figure."

Wilson could not quite see how a man like Douglass could advise the church. But Sojourner added an idea:

"I think you ought to go. I was planning a trip. You see, we have about a thousand dollars profit on our theater, and I wanted to buy some scenery and properties in Chicago. I'm sure Douglass could get us discounts. Now, of course, expecting the baby I can't go. Perhaps you wouldn't mind talking with him."

Wilson seized on the idea. The theater and music were popular. Suppose the Church finally decided to get rid of him and give him neither the bishopric nor even a decent pastorate? He knew this was possible. He'd talk to Douglass about entering the entertainment field as a business. Think of what the Negro audience wanted in drama, moving pictures, music—entertainment without debauchery! Here was a career!

He ran up to Chicago before the Wilberforce commencement. Douglass welcomed him but discouraged his entertainment schemes.

"Brother, you don't know that business. They'd skin you alive. Now you've got no rent or taxes, no advertising, no trade unions, and an audience made to order. Once on your own, you'd be at the mercy of politicians and white theater owners. White movie magnates would tell you what pictures you had to run and when; stage hands would fleece you. No, Wilson, you'd have no chance.

"But see here, how about the church? Of course, you can do little in the pastorate, but you ought to be a bishop—could do a lot of good for the church. In fact," said Douglass reflectively, lighting a well-flavored Havana cigar and leaning back in his leather armchair, "in fact, I don't know how else you could reform the church. Talking won't do it. If you attack the bishops you will land without an appointment, and the bishops hold the power. Now, on the other hand—" Douglass paused and changed his approach. "Of course, it costs money to run for the bishopric."

"I don't see why it should cost much, outside of postage and some travel."

Douglass looked a bit impatient. "Everything worthwhile on this earth costs money. There's no use getting on your high horse and thinking of what you'd like to do. Fine thing it would be to have the bishopric offered you on a silver salver. Forget it. Naturally, you prefer to have this honor thrust upon you by acclaiming thousands. That won't happen in this hungry world, in a church of poverty-stricken workers. What you have got to choose between is whether you or somebody else will furnish this money.

"You'll need to provide some bread and butter for a whole lot of poor black ministers who come up, particularly from the South, and do not earn enough to live on. If they're not careful and are too delicate and sensitive, they will not get enough money to pay their board in Chicago and get home. You can call them 'venal' and 'dishonest.' But all that you really have a right to call them is 'poor.'

"Now, if you pay these ministers and pay them with discretion—not just throw your money around—you'll be bishop. Then, if you want to be big and broad you can see to it that the ministers, at least in your diocese, are better paid, that there are enough of them so that when they come to General Conferences they can tell most of the candidates to go to hell and can vote for the best man. Even that won't be easy to do. But that's the only way to approach the thing you have in mind. Now, I'll make you a proposition. I believe in you, I know you're a good pastor. I'll loan you enough to become bishop, and you can pay me back on your own terms."

Wilson listened with increasing distaste. At last, he said flatly, "No, Douglass, not that. I'm not in the market to buy office in state nor church."

"Have it your way," answered Douglass, "but let me know when you change your mind."

Evidently Douglass was prosperous and had money despite the recent Depression. He had an elaborate home and a summer camp; he had a beautiful wife and two children. Moreover, at first sight it wasn't at all clear whence his money had come until at last Wilson, who had a gift for inquiry and amassing information, suddenly realized that Douglass was one of the men back of the Johnson brothers' policy racket—the gambling on small payments against tremendous odds, carried on with the secret sanction of the city and state governments. In this ring, white and black politicians were making millions, and Douglass Mansart was in way of becoming, or indeed already was, a rich man. One of the results of the Depression had been to encourage gambling.

Wilson was no strict moralist. He was not too nice in his scruples. He recognized that this was a world where dishonesty was often successful. It was doubtful if the righteous man usually had the chance to "flourish like the green bay tree." On the whole, the man who was not too dishonest was the man who often got the chance at leadership and constructive work. But he made up his mind not to give up his hopes and ideals yet—not yet.

Wilson quickly made up his mind as to his procedure. He would continue his present work, and would let other pastors know about it. He would go to the General Conference and push the necessity of the Church taking a stand on labor and social problems. He might get wide support, might even develop such power that he would become a formidable candidate for the bishopric in 1944, or later. If not—if he was ignored or defeated—then he must think of another career, perhaps as a social worker, or even of a return to the autonomous Baptist Church in some industrial center.

He went to the meeting at Wilberforce University determined to observe how great a sentiment he could find against bribery in the General Conference, for a labor movement among Negroes, and a church movement that would fight for health and social security. This church, since 1850, had done much for education. Now that the city and state had taken over the schools—or were due to—could not the church turn to social reform?

He was at first disappointed at Wilberforce. The college had been almost entirely swallowed by the new neighboring state school. Its final demise seemed in sight. But on the other hand, Wilson met there a group of young ministers who thought as he did on social progress. They had several conferences. They criticized and suggested and when Wilson left, it was with a distinct understanding that in 1944, at Kansas City, he would lead a reform movement against bribery and for social uplift.

On reaching Dallas, he talked the matter over with Sojourner. She agreed of course, but to his surprise she had less faith in the Wilberforce movement than in Douglass. She said:

"A bishop of the African Church is a great and powerful man. In the past, good bishops built this greatest organization of black America. Lesser and smaller bishops have debased and nearly ruined this divine institution. It needs you. You are a good man. If you can get this place honestly, get it."

"Is bribery honest?"

"No, it is not. Neither is starvation. If, by helping poor and ignorant ministers, you can begin to overthrow this poverty and want, you ought to try it. This is not right, but it helps overthrow wrong."

"Jesuit!" murmured Wilson.

Then the birth of Sojourner's daughter dispersed all thought of everything. She was a dark and physically perfect baby, and Sojourner went through the ordeal far better than they had feared. When the baby faced her second birthday, in the Spring of 1944, Sojourner suggested a visit to Chicago. It seemed that the little girl needed to have her tonsils inspected with a view to possible removal. Sojourner did not trust the white hospitals in Dallas, where no Negro could rent a private room and where attention in the colored ward might not be the best. Wilson had come to be very fond of his little daughter and suggested a later trip when the treacherous Chicago weather would be milder. Indeed, they might go together in August, at the time of the General Conference in Kansas City. There was an excellent colored hospital there.

But Douglass, who had been consulted, wrote that at some pains he had secured the services of the best tonsil expert in the city and advised immediate consultation. So Sojourner and the baby went to Chicago. Douglass hardly recognized his sister. He had not seen her since her marriage and had hardly noticed her for many years before. He saw a comely, well-dressed woman, not handsome, not even good-looking, but who carried herself with quiet dignity. She could talk and had something to say. Her child showed care and training. Even Douglass' wife was impressed and re-arranged her guest room and re-assorted her guests. Since the baby's tonsils proved to be quite perfect and her general condition satisfactory, she was packed off to nursery school. Then Douglass and Sojourner sat down in his office for a talk. Sojourner immediately came to the point.

"Douglass, I want you to lend me the funds to finance my husband's campaign for the bishopric."

"Well, well! So he's come to his senses."

"No, he has not, but I have. The fight in our Dallas church is fierce and forbidding. I am sure that if my husband fails to be elected bishop this year, he never will be. Also, he will lose this church whose leaders hate him, and he'll have great difficulty in finding another or in finding any work which will satisfy him. On the other hand, he is beginning to believe he has a chance of election. There is really a ground swell behind him."

Douglass smiled. "A ground swell which, if added to by a careful campaign and enough cash will produce a Bishop Wilson. Otherwise, he'll be an 'also ran.' He'll get a good vote, but won't be elected. I know who's bidding against him and how much!"

"All right; but how much cash will be 'enough'?"

"About $10,000."

"$10,000! You're joking! It can't cost that unless you're proposing to go in for wholesale bribery."

"No, I'm not. But there's competition, fierce competition. The price at the last General Conference was about $5,000. But prices have gone up. And it's not all bribery, as you call it. There are quite legitimate costs of publicity if we go at this sensibly; there are some real personal expenses of travel and board which the friends of your husband cannot afford to meet. Then, there are a few out and out grafters whose mouths must be filled. Oh, I know it sounds pretty nasty. But, little sister, you're in a nasty world."

"But if I undertake this, which I now doubt, I couldn't possibly afford such a sum. I'd thought of a thousand, or possibly two. But ten thousand—Douglass, it's fantastic!" And Sojourner arose.

But Douglass pushed her gently back into her seat. "Wait, wait and let's consider this proposition. I'm a gambler and I believe in Wilson. He's a good man, which I'll say of few other preachers I know. And he's got a good, far-reaching program. I'll take a chance. Let me manage his campaign. If he loses, it'll cost you nothing. If he wins, I'll hand him the bill. And it'll be damn near ten thousand bucks or I'm much mistaken!"

"Done!" said Sojourner.

Of this scheme, Wilson knew nothing. He was pleased to hear good reports about his daughter's tonsils and assented to her and Sojourner spending the Spring in Chicago, with its musical and theatrical opportunities. He joined them in August, when, accompanied by Douglass and his wife, they all went to Kansas City. Wilson was encouraged. His mail was large. His proposals for a labor and social program were listened to with enthusiasm by the large audiences at the Conference, although the bishops and general officers said little.

Then, when the time for nominations came, Wilson heard himself nominated for the bishopric in a flowery but earnest speech, and not by a Texan but by a lay delegate from Birmingham, where he once was pastor. For a moment, his dream of a mass movement behind his program seemed to be sweeping the Conference, with him in the lead. A wave of exultation floated over him. He was to conquer Evil with Good. His lips trilled the old hymn:

"*Let us sound the loud timbrel over Egypt's dark sea;*
Jehovah has triumphed. His people are free."

He wanted to pray, but just then a tall Texas preacher bent over him and whispered:

"Er—Reverend—I'm afraid I have got to change my mind. I just told the Madame that a couple of hundred dollars would meet my expense. But I find it won't. I'll just have to have at least three hundred. I'm terribly sorry—"

Wilson arose and his face went pale. "Madame who?" he snapped.

"Why, Mrs. Wilson, of course. I thought you knew—"

"I didn't.' And Wilson walked off.

He was leaving the hall when he was elected bishop of the African Episcopal Church on the third ballot. But he walked on. He had gained the bishopric not by his character, not by his accomplishment and brilliant ideas, but by cash. How much, he did not know then, and it was not until a month later that Douglass' bill for $9,678.13 came to his desk. But now all he knew was that money had been paid for his position and he was in deathly shame.

He walked so rapidly that the Bishop of Texas had difficulty in following him. Wild ideas swept through his brain. He was tempted to turn back and re-enter that hall. He saw himself mounting the rostrum, facing the delegates, and hurling into their faces this soiled episcopal robe. He—but here, the Bishop of Texas overtook him, almost pulled him into his car, brought him home and made him eat and drink.

Then he talked to him. "My son, you bought the bishopric and you are ashamed of yourself. So am I. So is your faithful wife. Others have done the same and aren't a bit ashamed. Do not despair, son. Our church is not evil. This is not the first time bishoprics have been bought and sold in Christendom. Aye, and gotten even by knife and poison. Oh, no! Even today, in richer and wiser churches than ours—but never mind that.

"In our own church, all places have not always been put up at auction. But today we're in a jam. We've got things to do, many things and fast. And they cost money. With money comes evil. We're too poor to do what the world insists we must do. We resort to bribery. I'm sorry. I'm sorry you did. I'm more sorry that the church let you.

"One day, God willing and you and I helping, it will be so great a crime to sell a vote for the bishopric that none will dare do it and expect to remain in the church. But I'm glad it's you and not a lesser man that bought this high office. I do not judge your wife. Neither must you. Perhaps God told her what must be done, perhaps it was the Devil; but she did it. I could wish that, as a humble shepherd in some little Southern town, you could have served the Master. That was not to be. Instead, you are now the anointed of the Lord.

"Now you have to learn what this office really means. Hitherto, my son, you have had but little real belief in religion. You despise dogma and miracles. Church ceremony leaves you cold, save as emotional experience. I understand all that. All that I, too, have lived through. But do you understand or try to understand what religion has meant to most of your people? They found themselves in a world they did not know. Its vicissitudes, its evil, its irrational compulsions were absolutely incomprehensible. The world seemed ruled by Things. These must be appeased, obeyed, eluded. Before you were born, your fathers, or perhaps better, your mothers were led to believe that the explanation of this world was not simply a Devil of utter Evil, but also a loving Father who in his own good time would take his obedient children up in a chariot of Fiery Death to a world of Happiness. In the dirt, degradation, toil and license of plantations, under the fervor of black prophets, this solution of the puzzle of existence was revealed to them in brief moments of frenzy among a screaming mass of people singing:

'Shout O Children, Shout, you're free!'

"Then a miracle happened. They became free. But they were not happy. They were hungry and naked, and new preachers had to build a new church on top of the old. We tried to make this church a meeting-house where we could have what we lacked at home—heat, company, food, song. But not only this—there must be a Meaning. Gradually, that imagined heaven of slavery days must be brought down to earth, but not too swiftly. Conversion by miracle, shouting to God in person—the religious orgy must slowly disappear.

"You proposed to replace it with food and clothes and shelter. Fine, if you could; only you can't, at least not now. You can't even teach these children to read what other men have done and thought, at least not yet. But while we wait, and schools linger, and people starve—in that little interval of a century or two—what shall we do, you and I? Birmingham and Annisberg said, 'Work and Pray!' Dallas said, 'Eat, drink and be merry!' You tried both. Now, the salvation of the Lord has laid bare the way—the path of blood and evil. Arise, go and do!"

Sojourner was waiting. Long hours she had waited, clothed in her white nightgown and sitting in their bedroom with her back to the window and her eyes on the door. The room was dark. The clock chimed midnight as Roosevelt Wilson entered, and his wife loomed dark against the thin halo of the shining city behind her. Weary, and with eyes closed she was reciting and had long been reciting the Fifty-First Psalm:

"Have mercy upon me, O God, according to Thy loving-kindness; according to the multitude of Thy tender mercies, blot out my transgressions. Wash me thoroughly from mine iniquity and cleanse me from my sin. For I acknowledge my transgressions, and my sin is ever before me. Against Thee, Thee only, have I sinned and done this evil in Thy sight. . . . Hide thy face from my sins and blot out all mine iniquities. Create in me a clean heart, O God, and renew a right spirit within me. Cast me not away from Thy presence; and take not Thy Holy Spirit from me. Deliver me from bloodguiltiness, O God, thou God of my salvation, and my tongue shall sing aloud Thy righteousness."

Wilson started to approach her but she opened her eyes and held him back gently, while she sobbed and sang:

"O the Rocks and the Mountains shall all fade away, and you shall have a new hiding place that day; Sinner, Sinner, give up your heart to God and you shall have a new hiding place that day!"

Then the low recitative began again:

"O Lord, open Thou my lips and my mouth shall show forth Thy praise, For Thou desirest not sacrifice, else would I give it; Thou delightest not in burnt offering. The sacrifices of God are a broken spirit—"

She swayed in sheer weariness as he folded her close in his arms.

CHAPTER XI

Again World War

The Second World War astonished Manuel Mansart. It was something which could not happen—yet here it was happening. He had just travelled around the world. He had crossed the entire United States and if he had thought to have learned one lesson above all others on his journey, it was that all the world, and particularly America, wanted peace. Yet, here was war again and not, in truth, a new war but as was now suddenly clear to him, the same old struggle for domination of peoples, the same unjust, cruel and evil program of murder and destruction which for centuries had been the content of history. All the stirrings toward this, he had looked on, yet had not seen. Of what use was reason and effort and his dream?

Suddenly, he felt he wanted to get away. He wanted to go where he could get closer to the heart of the world, where he could talk with, question and listen to those who knew. He would take a trip to New York and there have a long talk with his son Revels, whose keen mind seemed to see clearly where his own groped.

First, there was the trip itself to consider. The black man in the South avoids the rail-trains when he can, for there he encounters color discrimination at its crudest. Usually, Mansart rode in his own motorcar, driving himself or with a student as chauffeur. But on a long trip such as this, he would have to take a fast train and have a Pullman berth. This was possible in the case of a prominent Negro like Mansart, especially one who was directing the spending of large sums of money, much of it going to the railroads for passengers and freight. But the task of procuring tickets and reservations meant going through a certain mumbo-jumbo in deference to racial etiquette. He would phone: "May I speak to the passenger manager? This is President Mansart of the Colored State College. . . . But this is urgent. . . . I must go on the noon train tomorrow." The clerk was abrupt. "He would see" and he hung up. Mansart then got the manager of freight traffic on the line and reminded him that the college had just paid a bill of over a thousand dollars. He must have that reservation tomorrow, and his voice was a shade more brusque than usual. He got the tickets that afternoon. He would have to take "lower one" berth at the end of the Pullman, and change at Atlanta for the fast through train. There, only a drawingroom was available at three and a half times the regular fare. Mansart took it. The colored porters were courteous; they all knew Mansart and he knew most of them. He transferred to his drawing room at Atlanta and settled down to rest. He did not attempt to go to the dining room—it would be full of white folk and it would be difficult to curtain off an alcove for "colored passengers," as the law required. That meant a long and humiliating wait. He would have his lunch served in his drawing room. He knew it would be late, for the white dining-car steward would wait until most of the whites had finished eating before he would send a waiter forward with a tray. So Mansart, settling himself comfortably on his pillows and staring out at the flying, changing landscape, began to collect and marshall his thoughts and attempt to think through this new and, to him, unexpected war aspect of the world in which he lived—England and her colored colonial empire, France with south Asia and north Africa, the United States and China, Japan, the West Indies and Central and South America. Then he came back to the United States, to his own people—where did they belong in this new phantasmagoria?

The waiter now brought his lunch and was solicitous in serving it. Mansart enjoyed it, then settled back again to rest and stare out on the darkening landscape. The world swept by—the dark loafers at the stations—the white girls in the factories—the burdened wagons staggering along dusty roads. Then, suddenly, with startling clearness, out there in the night he seemed to see a great green Spider nesting in Hell, weaving an impenetrable Web. It sat in a pool of blood, which had gushed down from China, flowed in from Spain and seeped through from Mississippi. The Spider seemed to be spinning out thin tendrils of American gold, linking strand to strand. To the drying, stinking mess, the Spider added clods of British dirt and moistened all with the slime of France, until the spreading Web grew wide as the Earth and high as Heaven. It was too horrible. It seemed to divide the Darkness from the Light and the White World fought the Dark World and both faced Death.

Here, the porter shook Mansart gently and suggested he make up his berth so that he could sleep more easily. Mansart slept soundly the rest of the night and next day breakfasted with his son Judge Revels Mansart and his wife, sitting on Washington Heights opposite the Jersey Palisades.

"Frankly, Father, I am especially glad you are here, and in the normal course of your work and not by special invitation. I wanted to invite you but hesitated lest I get you into a situation that would be unwise for you even to seem to be a part of, since war has again gripped the world. As it is, you have come without premeditation or invitation."

"Well, I'm glad I'm here. I like to come to New York, although I can't say just why. I feel nearer the center of things, and that is necessary today."

"That is in a sense true, at any rate after London and Paris. Perhaps in another decade—but as I was saying. There is going to be a meeting in New York of a peculiar character. I really know little about it. It was arranged by my Royal Arch chapter of the Colored Masons. It is not a Masonic function, but the Masons were probably asked to help because of their international affiliations, especially among the colored peoples. Hence the appeal to colored Masons, who are just now receiving unexpected recognition from the American whites."

"Frankly, I know little of the colored fraternities. The Odd Fellows in Atlanta have attracted me but only because of their insurance and real estate efforts."

"Well, away back in 1775, the British Army in Boston initiated 15 Negro Masons. The Grand Lodge of England set them up as a lodge and later they themselves organized a Grand Lodge. Now there are 35 Negro Grand Lodges with 150,000 members and 14,000 in the Royal Arch. This Negro American Masonry today is recognized the world over. One of the high echelons of this organization was recently approached to assist in providing a meeting place for a group of colored leaders. As I say, I know little of this meeting. But at the request of friends, I have undertaken local arrangements. I have confidence in the character and objects of those who are convening this conference. You know I don't go in much for meetings and not at all for Negro organizations. But I believe this is important and timely, especially since the world for a second time in a generation has gone to war."

Quite unexpectedly to Mansart, the conference took place high up on the northern end of Manhattan Island at the Cloisters—that magnificent collection of works of French medieval art assembled by George Barnard and given by the Rockefellers to the Metropolitan Museum of Art. As a member of the Museum Board of Directors, and through other influence which the Judge had brought to bear, there was to be held in one of the chambers of the Cloisters, closed and especially set aside for that purpose, a meeting of about one hundred delegates representing the Colored Peoples of the world, "to take council as to their situation in this war and in its aftermath." This was all that Judge Revels had to say and his father inquired no further.

The delegates gathered quietly at noon. Lists of names were distributed to each member, which were to be returned upon adjournment. About twenty-three groups were represented. Some, like Africa, India and China, each had four delegates; South America and Japan each had three; American Negroes had two delegates; some seven other groups had one each. Each delegate was identified by a number which he wore on a medal conspicuously displayed on his breast. One alone among all wore no number. He presided, sitting rather back in the shadows. He was small and thin and white turbaned. His eyes were caverns of gloom. His voice was low, clear and beautiful. Opening the session without ceremony, he said:

"There has come upon the world a Day of Doom, the most momentous since Mohammed's flight to Medina 1,320 years ago; or comparable to like dates in the history of other faiths. A World War has been unleashed which will cost the lives of twenty-five million human beings, mostly youth whence our world gets its strength and dreams. It will maim and wound and drive insane or weaken with disease fifty million more men, women and children. And it will cost one billion dollars. Its weapons will be horrible. We will rip from the bowels of Hell weapons deadly enough to wipe life from earth and I am told these scourges will first be tried out upon us—the Dark World. What shall we do? What can we do?

"In the world's childhood, we used to blame God for such catastrophes, and then excuse Him by attributing them to some inexplicable purpose of His, which

He did not reveal. During the youth of science, despite our inability to prove this, we tried to account for human action as the result of mechanical law. Now, as we approach, albeit all too slowly, scientific maturity we admit wide ignorance of the real nexus between cause and effect, but we work slowly and waveringly forward by use of scientific hypothesis, probing, changing and rejecting, by incessant testing of facts until bit by bit truth emerges. Our greatest and most useful hypothesis is that the conscious action of human beings can change human history. Still clinging to this hope and conviction, we approach this new crisis of mankind to inquire what action caused it, what action can cure it.

"First we will listen to a condensation of the most important of the voluminous and complete documentary reports deposited with us. We may foretell that Britain will free India within a decade; the United States will seek to reduce China to colonial status; black men will save Africa from Hitler, but Britain and France will try to keep her chained. Japan will free us from Europe but try to keep us in slavery to herself; South America will long lie divided and prostrate under Europe and the United States.

"The documents relating to these matters and to a score of others will be given you as you depart. We will separate in small groups and during the next weeks meet elsewhere in smaller gatherings. Meantime, in farewell, watch and wait: Remember that Hitler's most dangerous gift will be not war, but the Big Lie—making truth inaccessible by the monopoly of communication. Against this we must set the promise of the Soviet Union never to hold colonies, nor to join with colonial imperialism, and to outlaw every vestige of color and race discrimination within its borders. Finally, it should be our bounden duty to seek Peace through Non-resistance. This, as I firmly believe, is our only path. Go, with God!"

Mansart found himself leaving with his son and a young Japanese. He began to ask questions and the Japanese said, "I am a Nisei, an American citizen of Japanese descent. You wonder why I am here. Few know just what we Japanese, born in the United States, have suffered and what suffering is planned. We have well-developed industry, land for raising and selling fresh vegetables. Our competitors will make this war an excuse for seizing our property and even imprisoning us in concentration camps. Our material losses will reach millions. Our souls may be wounded beyond repair."

On the ride home, Mansart talked with Revels.

"My son, this meeting may have been a Communist plot!"

"That is possible."

"We know the real names of none and certainly not of that remarkable man who presided, and whose prophecies seem preposterous. I think I recognized him, although I may be wrong. He is either Mahatma Gandhi, or much like him physically and spiritually."

"Gandhi? It couldn't be. He has never visited the United States."

"No; once he planned to when he was in England a few years ago, but his American friends, like John Haynes Holmes, advised against it. They said that a little ugly brown man, dressed in a loin-cloth, who had fraternized with African blacks, would be insulted and despised in the United States. For that reason, he gave up the idea. But it may be possible that today he has come incognito, for the simple reason that colored folk are not 'news' in New York and colored visitors attract little publicity."

"Extraordinary, if true. But surely, the catastrophes he foretells cannot come to pass. I do not believe we will enter this world war."

"I do not know. Germany is moving on Western Europe in force. France and Belgium have succumbed and Britain has scurried home from Dunkirk. Roosevelt thinks that the defense of Britain is an even greater duty than the development of the welfare state in America."

"But may not this whole thing be subversive and dangerous?"

"It may be. But on the other hand, it may not be and may prove of the utmost urgency. If so, it had to be secret and this very fact warns us. The Colored World, Father, may be face to face with new dangers of oppression and of utter subordination. If so, we must know it and act. There was in this meeting a note of sincerity and authority. I know personally many of its promoters and sympathizers. My belief is not easily won. I am by nature cynical and suspicious. If I had not believed in this movement, I would have had no part in it. This is the reason I helped it take place. I shall do nothing further without more knowledge than I now have. But—I shall watch and wait."

And then Judge Mansart added to himself: "It is quite possible that this meeting, held so secretly, is already well known and reported to those in America who are in the seats of power."

This was true. Certain Negro Americans had brought circumstantial reports to Wall Street where, in the Morgan bank, a committee had for some time been in continuous session. The members represented most of the chief international cartels which controlled the production and distribution of goods the world over. There were British industrialists and bankers, French business men of the type which originated the cartel idea, German army officers and representatives of Krupp and Thyssen; the Japanese ambassador was there and, of course, the chief heads of American corporations in steel, oil, food, fibers and power production.

They were all not only well-bred gentlemen but consultants of a peculiar sort. They not only must confer frankly and without losing their tempers on matters over which they were in serious disagreement, but they must reach some degree of agreement; else, as one put it, "Socialism will sweep the world and private capitalistic enterprise will disappear."

They were discussing the new war beginning in Europe. The reports on the secret meeting of the colored folk were reassuring. There was as yet no conspiracy and the mirage of peace and nonviolence still guided them.

"In the long run, the darkies are right," said an Englishman. "But we must be sure that the present run is not long but short and quick."

As the hosts, the Americans set down their demands first. "America must enter no world war until our profits are high and certain and there is nothing left for government financing of industry. We cannot be asked to restore the former British monopoly of world trade and finance. America must share. We oppose socialism in Britain, western Europe and particularly its extreme form in Russia and the Balkans. We will cooperate with Japan in reducing China to complete exploitation provided, of course, we receive our rightful area of participation."

The British made notes and consulted and then laid down their demands. They were holding in leash a mild British socialism but would oppose any further push toward socialism in Europe or America, and particularly in Russia and southeast Europe. They demanded preservation of the hard-won British trade opportunity and financial guidance in Asia, Africa and South America with reasonable exchange of advantages with Germany, France and America. As to Japan, they would recognize her productive power but could not admit her to British markets without due and reciprocal action on her part.

The Germans were definite and firm. "We have become since recovery from war and depression, one of the most efficient producing nations of the world. We need raw materials and markets. This is largely denied us in a world dominated by British, French and American capital. We demand entrance on reasonable terms. As to socialism, we dominate it at home and will completely put it at the service of private capital in Russia and the Balkans within a few weeks. We are ready to support Japan in its demands for trade in Asia similar to ours in Europe."

A small core committee reported after lunch. "There is one area of complete agreement, several areas of partial agreement which can be adjusted, and one matter still requiring debate and serious decision. We all agree that Russia must be eliminated from modern civilization, and Socialism everywhere strictly curbed. There is a different question that remains to be studied and resolved, touching the division of production, trade and finance in the world between Britain, France, Germany and the United States. We feel, however, that this can be worked out.

"A more serious problem is connected with Japan. Europe cannot consent to be supplanted by Japan in Asia, nor to let Japan flood Europe with cheap goods. This question must be explored and perhaps an equitable basis of division of capital, land, and labor control can be arrived at. But because of the fundamental question of the equality of the yellow and white races, the time for agreement may be unduly prolonged.

"Meantime, certain delegates have put forward a startling proposal, which we lay before you. In the United States there is a hard core of opposition to war as such. It is due to an Asiatic philosophy of submission brought in by Jews and to the same doctrine of peace and non-violence which the current colored conference adheres to. Supporting this thesis are the socialists, the liberals, and the New Dealers. All this may make it difficult if not impossible to get America to go to war.

"On the other hand, those whom we represent must have war. War alone will insure our present profits and bring greater profits and power in the future. If, of course, there could be progress without war, we could consider peace. History has proven that impossible. By war alone can socialism finally be conquered. Now by curious contradiction, Roosevelt, champion of the welfare state as outlined by the socialist, Harry Hopkins, wants war, because only by war can he retard or stop the fall of the British Empire. All we need then, is by a strike of capital to hold off war until Roosevelt is defeated. He must of course be put out of office by the vote of the people next November. Once Roosevelt is defeated, we will move in and enter the World War on our own terms and for our own objects. This will mean the end of the New Deal and alliance with Germany to wipe Communism from the face of the earth. It will mean cooperation with Britain for the halting of socialism in Europe and the restoration of colonialism in Asia and Africa. This is clear. But we must face facts—Roosevelt might win a third term. His hold on the American public is strong. In case then, and against all probabilities, he does win, what then? Over this point, we argued long until a brilliant proposal came to us from Japan." The speaker paused and wiped his forehead. Then he continued: "Japan proposes, if Roosevelt wins, to attack the United States suddenly and without warning."

There was a gasp and silence. The Japanese ambassador rose unsteadily to his feet, but the little unobtrusive colleague beside him growled an order and the ambassador sat down. A Frenchman asked: "What would be the effect of such an extraordinary move?"

The chairman of the executive committee continued: "The proposal when first made startled us. But listen to its logic. On one matter alone today can American opinion be stampeded and that is race and color. On that matter there is a national unanimity unequalled on any other. There is wide difference of opinion on the allowable extent of the government in business, on private profit and the welfare state. Socialism is gaining but it is far from being in majority. American attitude toward England varies, but there is no enthusiasm for using our strength to restore the British Empire. Americans believe that Russian Communism is bound to fail, but there is no unanimity on being willing to make this happen by force. Even in matters of race, there is less dogmatism today than 75 years ago. Still, an attack on white America by yellow Japan would unite the nation like a giant catalyst. War would be declared the next day. Moreover, it would be war for one object alone, to conquer Asia which is our object. It could not be a Roosevelt war to restore to world power a socialist Britain, but it would be a war to restore the British Empire of Victoria, with the United States in close partnership, and to smash Russia completely."

"But what would become of Japan. Would she not face annihilation by America?"

"Only if we permitted it. Japan is ready to take our word that in the end she will gain equality with Europe, and co-rulership in Asia!"

The small unobtrusive Japanese sitting beside the Japanese ambassador now arose and introduced himself as the direct emissary of the Imperial Rule Assistance Association, which was now in supreme power in Japan. In excellent English, he reaffirmed the promise of war on America.

"But," stammered a British merchant, "what might not such an act start in world reaction?"

A German general spoke up crisply: "It could start nothing which German military might united to Japanese versatility could not turn to the advantage of this body. Before the Japanese-American War was well started, Hitler will have conquered Russia and be facing the West with invincible force. We guarantee here and now the integrity and survival of Japan as a recognized great world power. And we have already made offensive and defensive alliance with her."

The discussion lasted long toward twilight. But in the end there was substantial agreement. This was (in case Roosevelt won a third term):

1. To ask Japan to attack the U.S.A. without warning.
2. It was guaranteed that when Russia was conquered, Germany, Britain and France would protect Japan from injury and grant her necessary access to world trade.
3. When the U.S.A. declared war, British industry and finance, with the cooperation of American business interests, would see to it that the U.S.A. did not attack Germany or help Russia.
4. After the war, France and Italy as well as Germany were to be recognized as co-partners with Britain and the U.S.A. as leading directors of world trade, industry and finance.

The November election came and Franklin Roosevelt was chosen president of the United States for a third term. Judge Mansart exulted and a week later arranged for a small group to meet at his home. Jack and Betty Carmichael came down from Springfield and brought Jackie. He met young Revels for the first time and together they went to see Jackie Robinson play ball. Sally Haynes, the young white social worker, was there. She had been in Europe on vacation and managed to get out the August before, as war was declared. Betty and Sally had many notes to compare and Jack and the Judge's wife talked over his experiences in Springfield. The Judge marked time by silent attention for he expected another guest. It was late when Hopkins finally came. He talked frankly and was enthusiastic about the recent election of 1940. He said:

"The people of the United States have given Franklin Roosevelt, by a vote of 27 million to 22 million, an election to an unprecedented third term in office, thus confirming a mandate for him to proceed toward the establishment of a welfare state leading to as complete a realization of socialism as satisfies the nation. It was decided that an intelligent nation used to free democratic methods of government could thus achieve socialism without revolution or dictatorship. Some countries, like Russia, oppressed for centuries by serfdom, ignorance, disease and priestcraft, could bring uplift only by force and violence, especially if opposed by a world in arms. But intelligent America has a better way."

"But," asked Judge Mansart, "isn't this change to war which Roosevelt wants, a sudden and a serious turning from social reform in the United States to pulling out of the fire the chestnuts of Britain and France?"

"I know what you mean and at first I was inclined to shrink from the war in Europe and insist on sticking to our muttons right here. But there were two mighty objections: first, the deep-seated belief of FDR, my friend, that England is the prime example of modern freedom and democracy; and that if ever we achieve socialism by democracy, Britain must lead; and second, the increasingly clear fact that in a world dominated by Hitler and Mussolini, joined openly by Japan, there can be no freedom, democracy or socialism for America or any other land."

The Judge smiled and remarked: "Some of us, Mr. Hopkins, expected that you might be a candidate in the last election."

Hopkins was frank. "For a time I thought so, too; and FDR promised me his support. But just as soon as it was clear that he could be persuaded to run, I withdrew. Of course, he was the only logical candidate. Now, my only fear is for his health. These next four years may kill him."

Sally Haynes said: "My fear is that this awful war will not only divert Roosevelt from developing socialism in the United States, but also to the support of colonialism in the rest of the world."

"And just here," said Judge Mansart, "I was depending on Japan. I thought she was leading the way to drive Europe out of Asia."

"That's just what she is attempting," answered Hopkins, "and in so doing, she started the Second World War back in 1931. After the crash of our stock market and the collapse of European capitalism, Japan started to invade China. But not for socialism; not for the plans of the dead Sun Yat-Sen in China. No, but for a Japanese capitalism exploiting the millions of Asiatic workers."

"Perhaps that was the key to the Chinese situation which father missed in 1936," said Revels, "and yet, yet—"

"Remember that Hitler became chancellor in 1933, just after Japan had attacked Shanghai. The very next year, Italy seized Ethiopia with the tacit assent of Britain and France. Then Hitler and Mussolini joined Franco to kill socialism in Spain and keep it out of Africa. The European Axis thus was aimed not simply at the West but at the Balkans and the Middle East. In the far East, Japan further penetrated Asia and joined the European Axis."

"But," said Hopkins, "there are curious complications. American Big Finance does not want us to enter this war on the side of the British Empire. It wants to supersede Britain as master of the Eastern world and, because of this, favors Germany. Our present business connections with Germany are colossal—artificial rubber, chemicals, dyes and steel are all tied in with the Reich. All that FDR could achieve until 1939 was neutrality. Roosevelt believed in England even more than I do. He feared the fall of the British Empire, and to him Britain was civilization. I and others doubted.

"A successful welfare state for our masses would be better than a realm on which the sun never sets in peace. But my personal loyalty to a friend prevailed over loyalty to an idea. Moreover, I see a vision. There is a chance that the American welfare state may combine with a socialized Britain and a Communist Russia to beat back the dictators who claimed the earth for European colonialism and for the profit of American Big Business. The difficulty here is that Big Business in the United States and Britain are both bitterly opposed to a welfare state, and are openly and secretly bound to colonial imperialism even to the extent of flirting with Japan. They had vowed war to the death against any success for the Russian Revolution. This is the paradox of 1940."

Harry Hopkins leaned back and reaching his glass for more beer said:

"Here's something else. Einstein, the great physicist who has just come to Princeton, has written Roosevelt. He warns him that Hitler is working on a secret weapon and urges us to start work on atomic power. This may be why the Germans have not yet closed in on England with full force."

"There's another matter," said Sally. "I was in Europe last Fall. I heard that Britain, France and the United States as well as Germany were sounding out the Russian leaders. They wanted investment concessions in Russia or at least no opposition to capital in the Balkans. In return, they offer alliances of various sorts and kinds."

"Further than that," asserted Hopkins, "Japan is sending a plenipotentiary to us offering deals to Big Business, and Business is approachable. On the side, he's talking peace and cooperation to Secretary Hull. I have a feeling that if Business is not able to deliver, Japan may attempt open force. Well, I must go."

None can say how far Franklin Roosevelt would have gone in reorganizing the economy of the nation if the work of the first eight years of his reign had continued and expanded. We might now live in a different world. But war intervened and once again, as so often in the past, ruined the future of mankind.

On the strength of his third triumphant victory, in 1940, Roosevelt forced the nation towards war by gift and agreement, by lend-lease, annexation and warships. He took Republicans into his cabinet, got millions appropriated for defense, and with Churchill he drafted the Atlantic Charter on old and nearly forgotten terms of no new territorial annexations, self-government, free trade, free travel, better labor conditions and world government.

Big Business conspired to wring every ounce of profit from the economy. It continued its alliance with the German cartels in rubber, aluminum and steel. Even when material was furnished, the prices and conditions were impossible. Owners of copper mines like those managed by Barney Baruch made extravagant profits; a billion dollars were spent on airplanes before a single one was delivered. Steel plate costing $318 a ton was sold to the government for $400 to $600 a ton. The government spent over $100,000,000,000 for nitrates but got none before the Armistice. Four hundred million dollars were spent on contracts for shells which never reached the firing line. Shipping lines sold ships to the government for $2,000,000 each and later bought them back for $300,000.

President Mansart often wished, in the ensuing five years, that he could have spent more time in New York, to learn more of just what was going on in the world. It was literally years before he realized that Hitler had murdered six million Jews in Germany—that it had really begun back in 1933 and continued even while he was listening to Wagner in Bayreuth and talking to the old Rabbi in Berlin. He had been told this but could not realize it—how could such a horrible thing happen in the civilized world amid such indifference and such silence!

In Atlanta, the news was scarce and contradictory. France fell and Belgium gave up. There was the tragedy at Dunkirk—but why? Neither the United States nor Britain seemed to want alliance with Russia, and suddenly Germany did. It was a long time before Mansart understood that Hitler had outbid the West by offering the Soviets the eastern part of Poland in return for the certainty of not being attacked in the rear when he started on his Western foray. The West offered the Soviets assistance only if the Soviets gave up Socialism, at least in part. Even in such case, their offer was guarded. So Hitler won the gamble and marched West. Mansart heard indistinct reports of the terrible bombing of Britain from July to December.

In 1941, in June, Mansart learned to his dismay that Germany had invaded Russia. This sudden change of policy seemed to him inexplicable. He could not believe that this reversal on the part of Germany was simply because British airmen were fighting back more fiercely. When a strong man meets resistance he does not usually turn his back. There was something unexplained.

Western Europe, however, began to breathe more freely. It hoped that Hitler would leave it in peace while he attacked Russia. For this they were willing to give up the League of Nations, yield Manchuria to Japan, let Germany re-arm and take Austria, Czechoslovakia and the Rhineland, give Ethiopia to Italy and Spain to France. Our own ambassador said, "It would be the wish of the democratic countries that armed conflict would break out in the East between the German Reich and Russia. . . . Germany would be obliged to wage a long and weakening war." The *Diary* of our representative in Berlin said that "Britain, the Nazis and Bullitt favored dividing the world, with Germany dominating all of Europe. Japan was to control Asia." Then like a clap of thunder, came Pearl Harbor!

The United States had stubbornly stayed out of actual war until, with unbelievable effrontery, Japan attacked the United States. Japan was colored. The United States had browbeaten her, cajoled her, insulted her, admired her, but refused her recognition as an equal, and induced Great Britain to withdraw her first step toward such recognition. But these little brown men had persisted, had built a mighty empire and demanded partnership with the white world. Japan's military might and her marvellous expanding industry was making her a feared rival of white imperialism in Yellow Asia. Finally, Japan made alliance with Germany and Italy. Withdrawing from a plan of war she signed a non-aggression pact with the Soviet Union, and, during peace negotiations with the U.S., she destroyed our sea power in Hawaii. This made war not only possible but imperative, backed by American color prejudice.

Japan was aware of the chink in American armor. Mansart before the war had met Yasuichi Hikida. This well trained young Japanese had visited Negro schools, translated books on the Negro problem into Japanese, and made friends with colored people all over the nation. He did nothing subversive in act, and he tried to convince Negroes that the Japanese people sympathized with their struggle against race prejudice, indeed that the Japanese were fellow sufferers.

Later, Judge Mansart made the acquaintance of an American white man who had married a colored woman in New York and, with funds which probably came from abroad, purchased two of the oldest American magazines, the *Living Age* and the *North American Review*. Whether this effort was Japanese or German, Judge Mansart never knew. Personally, he had no part in it. But he never forgot Japanese hospitality to his father at the time when he had no dream of war.

Meantime, Japan talked earnestly for peace and friendship between these two nations, for future profits and future exchange of culture, and talked all the more persuasively because their envoy, Kurusu, believed what he said and had no ulterior motives. But the Japanese military junta achieved complete control of Japan in 1941. By secret division of the world cartels, it became the role of colored Japan to divert American power from helping Britain, while the Nordic supremacist Hitler, holding his hand from giving Britain the *coup de grâce* with the help of the coming Secret Weapon, was to turn suddenly and annex the Soviet Union to Greater Germany.

What really happened at Pearl Harbor December 7, 1941, none will ever know completely. There was and is grave suspicion of treachery or treason. Roosevelt himself was accused by Congress but absolved after his death. Here was a great military establishment equipped at vast cost to make the nation secure. Here lay 86 American warships with marines and officers alert in a world already at war. Yet, when 100 Japanese airplanes flew out of that December morning with attendant submarines, there was neither warning nor planned resistance. Everybody seemed elaborately doing nothing—dressing, parading and saluting. The timid report by a private who thought he heard planes was brushed aside. To this day, the gold-braided admirals dispute as to what each did or ought to have done. One black man, Dorie Miller, a messboy on the Arizona, who could join the American navy only as a menial, put up a real fight. Seizing a machine gun in the use of which he had received no training, he shot down four Japanese planes. But the Japanese on that fatal day shot down 177 American planes, destroyed ten warships, damaged eight others, and left nearly five thousand American boys dead, wounded and missing.

Japan was on the warpath—she struck at Indo-China, the Philippines, Singapore, Hong Kong, the Islands of the Pacific. She stretched her empire thousands of miles in three months.

Siam fell, then Guam, then Wake Island. The Philippines gave up in May, with MacArthur running away. By this time the Japanese had spread over Malaya and had sunk two British battleships. They captured the Dutch East Indies with its oil and rubber, then took Rangoon, the capital of Burma, and Mandalay. By February, 1942, the Japanese flag had swept over 6,000 miles from the Aleutians to Australia. It was the greatest uprising of Asia since Genghis Khan.

In Macon, President Mansart and Jean Du Bignon discussed these utterly unexpected developments. They went back and tried to piece together events which had happened two and three years before and which only now revealed their real significance. Jean emphasized the role of Italy.

"Look at northeast Africa. Here, Italy was promised her colonial empire in the Treaty of London, which tempted Italy into the First World War. This Clemenceau and Lloyd George repudiated and Italy never forgave them. In 1934, when Hitler had the West backed against the wall, Italy seized her chance and her pound of flesh was Ethiopia. The League of Nations threw Ethiopia to the dogs, despite the moving appeal of her exiled emperor. Then in 1940 Italy made alliance with Hitler and began the movement eastward toward Egypt, the

Suez Canal, Greece, the Balkans and the Middle East. Beyond lay the British empire in Asia. By October, Italy was on the march."

Meantime, down in the French province of Chad, 2,500 miles due south of Alexandria, which Graziani was about to seize, there was a black French governor, Eboué. He decided to support the Free French, and not Vichy. From his four open harbors on the Atlantic, he could import American war materiel and on 150 planes a day send it to North Africa. On nearly 2,000 miles of stone-surfaced roads, rubber, tin, lead and zinc, with cotton, coffee, cocoa, palm oil and wood could roll North to the British soldiers gathering to hold and redeem the highway to Asia. Behind these supplies marched thousands of black troops.

By January, 1941, the tide began to turn. British Somaliland and Eritrea were recaptured and Haile Selassie returned to Ethiopia. Rommel with his German Afrika Corps rushed to the rescue. The British were pushed back, but black Ethiopia and black Eboué reinforced British Montgomery and at Alemein, in October, 1942, the Axis armies fled west and met the British-American invasion.

"That movement of ours to North Africa, instead of against the bare back of Hitler, has always puzzled me," said Mansart.

"Elementary, my dear Watson," said Jean, with an apology for her impudence, "don't you see, Churchill, the Machiavelli of London, wanted first to save the empire which he did not propose to liquidate. He wanted to make sure of that empire after Hitler and Stalin had destroyed each other. He proposed then to waste no time helping to stop what he regarded as the inevitable collapse of Russian Communism and the equally certain fall of Nazi imperialist colonialism. Back of him, American Big Business was ready to leave all to Churchill's fine Italian hand to convince his friend Roosevelt that both were framing an Atlantic Charter based on Four Freedoms. This, Roosevelt sincerely believed. What Churchill really believed, he wasn't saying!"

In Europe, Hitler's plans seemed perfect. From June to October, his armies captured six great cities and surrounded Leningrad. He announced that Russia was crushed. But the cold came down from the Arctic, the worst in one hundred fifty years, and 200,000 Germans died trying to reach Moscow—which they never entered. They whirled south to the Caspian Sea and surrounded Stalingrad in August, 1942. Here, gradually, the steel hand of the Russians slowly closed until in January, 1943, Hitler had lost his great gamble—the Soviet Union remained unconquered.

It was a fearful victory. The Germans destroyed 72,000 towns and villages, leaving 25,000,000 people homeless. They demolished 32,000 industries: they tore up 40,000 miles of railroads with stations, telegraph and telephone offices; they destroyed 40,000 hospitals, 84,000 schools and 44,000 libraries; they ransacked 100,000 farms and drove off 70 million head of horses, cattle sheep and goats. Their damage to state industrial enterprises has been estimated at $128 billion. Sixty-one of the greatest power stations were blown up. Coal mines and oil wells were destroyed. Public buildings, museums and churches were ruined. The Soviet Union lost seven million of its people in war, and perhaps as many more in civilian life. The British Empire lost a million persons and the U.S.A. about the same. The Germans lost at least ten million. The war cost the Soviet

Union $200,000,000,000. The U.S.A. gave her in net Lend-lease about five percent of this sum. Never before in the history of man had a single nation sacrificed so much for the salvation of the world.

Jean noted with some apprehension that President Mansart was giving more time and thought to the war than to the college. But of course, she herself was tremendously interested in the great drama unfolding abroad. Both she and the President were thrilled by the incredible march of Japan—a colored people was challenging the most powerful nations on earth. Mansart watched in fascination. He knew how Japan hated white folk—for the same reasons which made Mansart himself still shrink from them when he forgot his broader principles.

He watched Japan in that fateful year of 1942 in amazement and apprehension—the Great East Asia Co-Prosperity Sphere. He tried to show nothing in his countenance. But he and Jean alone in the office, could not restrain a certain exaltation as they witnessed the amazing uprising of Asia against Europe to oust the European masters.

It was some time before President Mansart seemed suddenly to become aware that once again American Negroes were going to war.

"And what are they going to fight for?" he asked in despair.

Of course, they were going to meet discrimination. Possibly they were going to be more integrated into the army and navy than they were in the First World War. This proved true. After some preliminary hesitation, discrimination was abolished from the officers' training camps. Even in Georgia, Negro officers were trained. At first a few, but at last at the rate of several hundred a month. Still, why were Negroes fighting?

The teachers of State College discussed this matter and although careful, the bitterness spilled over.

"Well, here we go again—fighting nobody for nothing."

"For the British Empire!"

"And what has that empire done for us?"

"It stopped the slave trade which it started—when the trade ceased to pay. It emancipated slaves when Toussaint made slavery too dangerous. It changed chattel to wage slavery."

"It stands for democracy!"

"For whites only—never for the blacks and browns and yellows who form most of its realm."

"It may free India after this war."

"It will if it must—not otherwise."

"War will stop our welfare state and increase the power of wealth."

"Unless we can depend on Russia to beat Hitler."

"A broken reed!"

"So Napoleon thought."

Then, rather suddenly, there was an unexpected opportunity for Negroes to voice their boiling inward revolt. The role of government in industry had widened during the Depression. There was a chance that it would permanently become much wider. Yet, Negroes were discriminated against openly, even in government contracts. There were, in 1941, over a million Negroes unemployed. They began to ask for the opportunity to work, especially in war industry.

Philip Randolph, a colored Socialist who had been hounded and imprisoned and finally lured to trade unionism, had organized the Pullman porters into a union and was fighting for its recognition in the American Federation of Labor. He now dared to demand of President Roosevelt that in the new war industry Negroes be accepted on equal terms with whites. Randolph declared that unless the President yielded, he was going to organize a black army of 50,000 black agitators to "march on Washington." The Negro race all over the country was aroused and began to prepare for the march. Some Negroes and many white friends protested. They saw this was no way to get concessions.

But down in Macon, Jean was pleased. She said, "You know, President Mansart, Randolph has chosen a strategic time. Here, the United States is on the brink of entering the Second World War on a large scale. They must have a united country behind them. Many Americans oppose the war. The loyalty of Negroes means more today than it did even in the First World War, and in the First World War it was indispensable. I have an idea that we are going to see some yielding on this matter."

Mansart was skeptical. "We are, after all, only a small part of the nation and smaller than our numbers when it comes to education and wealth. We are in no position to demand."

But Jean tossed her head. "We are in no position not to demand," she said.

Roosevelt was thus faced, in 1941, by realization of the fact that 12 million American citizens, an increasing number of whom could vote, might be led into opposition to his program and party. Moreover, as Hopkins pointed out, the demand for equal treatment in government-controlled industry was absolutely fair. Since, however, Roosevelt did not dare ask Congress for a law compelling the admission of Negroes to war industry, he induced his friends to discourage immediate pressure.

Mrs. Roosevelt, Mayor LaGuardia in New York, and others tried to allay unrest and persuade Negroes to wait. But preparations for the march went on. Headquarters were opened in New York and in other cities. Monies were raised. The date for the march was set for July 1. On June 28, the President called Randolph and a number of other Negro leaders to Washington. He met them, along with several Cabinet heads and members of the Office of Production Management. They discussed the situation earnestly. Finally the President, knowing that he could not get action from Congress and realizing that the Negroes would not yield, offered to issue Executive Order 8802 to insure "full participation in the national defense program by all citizens of the United States regardless of race, creed, color or national origin."

A commission to enforce this order was appointed, including two Negroes and, as chairman, the white principal of the Negro Hampton Institute. Randolph and his friends called off the March on Washington. Thus American Negroes won one of their greatest victories since Emancipation. And Franklin Roosevelt in this way secured the almost complete backing of American Negroes for him and the Democratic Party. This was even more important than equal distribution of relief funds. It was the culmination of the Roosevelt attitude toward Negroes.

So to the astonishment of Mansart, the celebrated Fair Employment Commission came into being. Many whites protested. There were strong words in Atlanta at the great camp which the city had built. There were strong words elsewhere, but on the whole the order was obeyed. It was a singular victory. And yet when Negroes sat down and took careful account, what had they won and lost?

Yes, lynching almost disappeared. But something worse than lynching had taken its place, and that was systematic and nationwide injustice in the criminal courts. Negroes, forming twelve percent of the population of the United States, composed from 30 to 80 percent of the prisoners held in jail. They invariably form the great majority of the prisoners for life, and of 3,219 persons in the country executed between 1930 and 1952, 1,732 were Negroes. All this meant that Negroes were being arrested more often than whites, were being railroaded to prison and given longer terms, and publicly killed twice as often as whites. Compared to lynching, this record was far worse and more degrading and fatal for black folk.

And what about the basic matter of earning a living? Negro slaves earned nothing beyond subsistence, from 1619 to 1863—a span of 244 years. From 1863 to 1900, the wage of Negro workers, if not stolen from them, was paid at the rate of $200 to $400 a year for each family. After the war, the average might be half the average wage of white workers.

They were beginning to vote and hold office, and yet the majority of Negroes in America were still disfranchised by law or custom or by fear of violence or denial of work.

CHAPTER XII

Black America Fights Again

The American army in the Second World War, had 500,000 colored soldiers, with 5,000 commissioned colored officers, including 500 in the Medical and Dental Corps, 150 chaplains and 200 nurses. The navy had 100,000 colored seamen, including 16,000 in the Marine Corps.

When the Allies at last landed in Normandy these black boys manned barrage balloons and big guns, loaded and unloaded ships, and drove thousands of trucks carrying supplies and troops on the French highways to the front lines. They had already helped largely to build the 1800-mile Alcan Highway in Canada and the Ledo Road in Burma. Colored pilots bombed Sicily, Italy, Germany and Rumania, and thirty of them earned the Distinguished Flying Cross. A colored artillery unit helped hold Bastogne in Belgium when McAuliff's 10,000 men were entirely surrounded by Nazis. The colored 92nd Infantry Division in Italy bent but did not break before a Nazi counter-offensive. Negroes built airstrips in New Guinea, fought against Japanese at Bougainville, against Germans in North Africa, and served in India, Persia, Alaska, France, Holland and the Philippines.

These Negroes thought deeply as they served, and some wrote home:

> "We thought about conditions as they exist in the States. We were elated to go into battle and perhaps die for rights that we, as Negroes, had never known. But the heart-breaking part about it was that the people we were to fight against could get better opportunities in our own country than we could. All they had to do was to get there."

A little sister wrote poetry to her black brother in the ranks:

"Or it the world just upside down
The right all on one side.
One group of kids can buy war bonds
But cannot buy a ride.
Or will this all be straightened out
through blood and prayers and tears,
Or will it just go on and on
As long as there are years?"

A soldier aboard a transport wrote:

> "We were responsible for getting out the evening meal. This was a good six hours' job, and the heat was so intense that we worked stripped to the waist. We were bitter because, with at least four thousand men aboard, only our black battalion was required to perform this drudgery every day. Some of our non-coms protested but they were only reduced to privates and sent back to the job."

Still another said:

> "The battle of the Bulge was the last and almost successful effort of Germany to rule the world. In that battle were black soldiers and because of the need there was greater integration of black and white troops than ever before."

Naturally there were some touches of human joy, as when one black correspondent wrote of his troops entering into Paris:

> "I have never been kissed so much in all my life. Almost every woman I meet on the street stops and kisses me on both cheeks. It is a beautiful custom."

The West was surprised and bewildered by the resistance which the Soviet Union exhibited to the fierce onslaught of the Germans. The British suggested American lend-lease to the Soviets; it would not save them, of course. It was never meant to save them but it would give Britain a longer breathing spell and forward that mutual annihilation of two enemies which might save the world for them. Americans went further and said, "Suppose the British Empire and the vast dominion of France fell, who would be their heirs but America?" It was the American Century by logic, and there was no need for fighting for it—let fascism in Germany and Communism in the Soviet Union kill each other off, while we inherited the earth!

Almost deliberately, therefore, Britain and America, subtly led by Big Business, sacrificed France to Germany. Britain, despite all her respect for French culture, had hated the French for 900 years, and her own ruler had long styled himself "King of France." America held France in contempt, thought her sex crazy even for "darkies," though at the same time exquisite in food, manners and dress. This compelled at once almost slavish compliment and bitter jealousy. Let the Bosch discipline the Frogs. Here, too, America would "take over."

But if America was sluggish in the European area of the war, she rushed fiercely into battle in the Far East. Here, her pride and prestige were hurt and her color prejudice lent strength to her arm. The navy in which American Negroes at the time could enter only as menials saw the disgrace of the Britannia which had so long ruled the waves.

There were black boys a-plenty who crept through all the mud of the tropical islands from Hawaii to Japan, who died in Iwo-Jima and on Okinawa. They suffered from fever, brutality and race hate. But their voices did not carry far and few came back to talk. In the Philippines they remembered their black brothers of the Spanish war and they saw the great bandmaster, Walter Loving, drop dead and unavenged before the guns of Japanese guards.

At the battles of the Coral Sea and Midway, early in 1942, the United States began the annihilation of the Japanese fleet which had been overextended in annexing the vast new Japanese empire. The American army had begun a long, slow, roundabout and costly approach to Japan which would take years but was sure to be fatal if left free to develop. After all, Japan with 83 million people and limited resources was fighting alone the richest nation on earth with 150 million inhabitants. Japan must have help.

It was late in 1942 that a Japanese gentleman called on Judge Mansart in his New York offices. He professed to know a certain Indian whose interests Mansart had defended successfully many years ago. He was a well-bred person of rank and education and said he was about to leave the country by special passport. He talked generally and then confidentially.

"Judge Mansart, in strictest confidence, do you think American Negroes would be disposed to help Japan if they had opportunity?"

"In what way? By sympathy, political support or by—espionage?"

"Not only in these ways, but by—revolt?"

"No," said the judge, "I do not think so."

The Japanese continued imperturbably. "I have heard," he said, "that a slave psychology still hampers your people and that no insult, no discrimination can bring among them aught but whimpered tears and prayers."

"That is in part true; but more than that, these tears and prayers, along with hard work, patience, repeated appeal to reason, and successful organization have brought us such progress that we hope in time to reach full equality in this nation."

"At the present rate, when will you reach that goal? A hundred years or a thousand? Pardon me. I do not mean to be discourteous. We Japanese know only too well how long it takes to make the white world admit the equality of colored peoples. We are fighting today desperately to hasten the rate of progress. I take it that you do not think your people can help?"

"You are right. I see now no practical way."

"Others do not agree with you. Your jails are full of bitter victims unjustly incarcerated. Your streets are full of poor and neglected persons of your race whom the New Deal helped last or quite forgot. There are 300,000 American Indians left from the million of 1500; segregated mostly, and forgotten on reservations. They do not love this nation. There are a quarter of a million Nisei, American-born Japanese, largely robbed of their property and herded into concentration camps. They are ready for anything. There are millions of white Americans—a third of your nations—so degraded and disappointed that they can feel what we feel. Judge Mansart, is this no sound basis for revolt?"

"It might be, if conditions get worse. But if they get better—"

"They will not get better," said the Japanese. "I beg your pardon. My wishes have rushed my words beyond my discretion. There are factors to spark this huge body of revolt. There is a Negro Congress and a Communist Party. There are Pullman porters led by a socialist whom the A. F. of L. repeatedly has slapped in the face, who once threatened to march on Washington. These folk daily thread this land. But I say too much. Do not, I pray, think that I am a conspirator. I have made no plot nor do I know others who have. But I see the material ripe for a fire. We Japanese today need such a fire. Please forgive me. Please forget all I have said, until the day when remembrance will be a pleasure."

He looked earnestly at the Judge, who bowed and shook his hand. He sat long after his guest had gone. He was not sure whether he had been probed or informed. He was beginning to question much of his past belief. Especially, he saw a world ruled by industry and banking in a colonial imperialism of monopoly, reaping wealth from war. It was becoming clear to him that the concept of business as service to mankind was yielding to the idea of business as power over men. We were working not so much to fulfill the wants of men as to rule men and enable the comfortable few to use the miserable many.

His Japanese visitor hastened to the pier where he met some searching questioning. It appeared that he was a Japanese citizen in transit to his home and on a trip begun before the opening of war between the United States and Japan. His credentials were in order although his travel seemed to have been suspiciously slow. But the war itself perhaps explained that and he was finally allowed to sail. He landed in France and was immediately received by the Vichy government. He was soon in possession of a diplomatic passport and accredited directly to the Fuehrer, Adolf Hitler.

He passed through a distracted land, inwardly torn, yet alive and almost hysterical with laughter that choked back tears. He entered a war-beset Germany, muscles taut, eyes glaring, loud-voiced and harsh, dropping with the blood of Jews. Then more slowly he fared across the plains of Russia, burnt, torn and ravaged, bleak with snow, with dead unburied, and with people hollow-eyed and hungry. It proved difficult to locate Hitler. The Germany army, on its long march of 1,500 miles, had reached the shores of the Black Sea, but its troubles were not over. When the Japanese special envoy at last reached Hitler's camp, the fatal siege of Stalingrad was in progress and Hitler was in a fury.

Beyond the ruins of ancient Kiev with its bulbous towers, and the treeless fields outside the city, the Germans had built a camp, wide and ordered, with uniforms and trumpets. The Japanese was led to an elaborate canvas mansion, where sentinels clicked their heels and challenged pre-emptorily:

"The Feuhrer? Your credentials! Pass, Heil Hitler!"

"Who?" Hitler roared as the Japanese was ushered in.

The Japanese bowed low. "Sir, I have the honor to bring you a special message and appeal from my august master, Hirohito, Emperor of Japan!" He proffered his red-sealed message but Hitler brushed it aside.

"What is it?" he yelled. "I'm busy. Speak!"

The Japanese saluted and said: "Sir, Japan is hard pressed. Our navy is outnumbered and in danger. A large American army is approaching slowly but steadily, and it is well-equipped. My august Master prays for help from the German nation. If you will turn back now and subdue England and the American forces resting there, the pressure on Japan will be lessened. Simultaneously, black revolt may break out in the United States.

"While this diverts both Britain and America, we will consolidate our new possessions and attack Russia in the rear. After your fatal blows, Russia will soon surrender to our might, backed, as it will be by that time, by the hundred millions of China. The great Fuehrer of Germany and the Sun-God of Japan will then rule the world."

Hitler whirled about. He frothed at the mouth and screamed: "Get out. Get out, you yellow dog! Do you think that I will even tolerate you Japanese monkeys in my back yard? Emperor of Japan—Sun-God—indeed! I am German Emperor, President of France, and when I will, King of England and President of the United States. Do you think I am going to share my rule with darkies? Get out—go home! Tell your God-damned emperor to stew in his own vomit!"

Guards hustled the envoy out of the tent.

He was pale and trembling, but dignified. He asked to be escorted to the front lines and soon left in the direction of Stalingrad. It was a week of travel in snow and ice before he was in the presence of Joseph Stalin. Stalin was ten miles from the besieged city in a peasant hut; but he did not seem busy or worried. He received the envoy pleasantly, who now presented another set of credentials addressed to Marshal Stalin. Stalin had them carefully translated and listened quietly.

"The Emperor of Japan asked that the treaty of neutrality now in existence between Japan and the Soviet Union be changed forthwith into an offensive alliance. Japan would send her armies and airplanes to help drive back the Germans, and together they would rule the Eastern world and beat back the West."

Stalin paused over his tea to read a dispatch. Then he said calmly, "Thank you, sir, and thank the Emperor very much; but you are too late. The Germans have surrendered at Stalingrad!" It was January 31, 1943.

The Japanese envoy politely took leave, refusing the proffered hospitality for the night. He walked out into the black and bitter cold toward the great city flaming yellow and crimson beyond, alive with the roar and scream of cannon and bomb, streaks of colored lights illuminating the sky. The reek of death and the stink of putrid flesh filled the field. The envoy threw away his astrakan cap and let the snow sift into his hair. He unbuttoned his jacket and vestcoat until his bare flesh under thin silk was bared to the chill night. Then he drew out his sword, raised his hand in salute to the East, where 5,000 miles away the shrines of Kyoto gleamed warmly in the sun. He said aloud, "My Emperor, I have failed!" and plunged the sword deep into his bowels, twisting it as his body writhed in death.

In the United States, unrest was stirring among the black folk. It was, as Judge Mansart had said, not revolt; but, as President Mansart down in Macon knew, it was deep and bitter unrest and it might grow to something more dangerous to all America, black and white.

In Detroit came a terrible outburst. Among the half million immigrants who came to find jobs in that mass production capital since 1943, were 50,000 Negroes. They had had to fight for their jobs; and in June, beating, killing and destruction of the poorest and blackest began until Roosevelt, over-riding the hesitant governor, sent 6,000 Federal troops to quell the riot.

Two months later, in Harlem, came an inexplicable riot, with stores looted and torn apart. Even the people themselves did not seem to know what was happening, and why. Yet, it was in reality clearly part of the pattern which had spurred the president's effort to open industry to black workers. It was one aspect of the world-wide colonial exploitation of colored folk. Harlem was being persistently exploited, and its black folk wanted bread and jobs and less clubbing by the police.

Except in the case of the well-to-do, the mass of colored workers were segregated in the worst sections and houses at the highest rents. Food which could not be sold downtown was disposed of in Harlem at high prices. Harlem schools were crowded and poorly disciplined under inexperienced teachers. At the stores into which Negro consumers crowded no Negro could work save as a janitor or servant. Gambling and dope and prostitution were almost uncurbed, and the gains went mostly to whites. Merchants were rude to black folk and policemen ready to club them mercilessly. In this seething mass of discontent and revulsion, the most trivial incident could suddenly be sparked into a roaring flame. The retail district of 125th Street was half destroyed at the cost of a million dollars—an expression of the despair of the people living there.

Judge Revels Mansart was particularly upset by this New York riot—not only because of its general implications and questions connected with his position, but also on account of his son, Revels Jr. Young Revels was of draft age and was soon going to be taken out of college and put into the army. His father and mother were both upset and wanted him to take the officers' course, but he objected. They began to chide themselves for not having sought a home and environment better suited to his development, so that he would have had a group of friends and a pattern of activities to guide him. But where? How? What community wanted a Negro family, no matter what their status and character? Their advent meant lowering of property values through white fear and hysteria, and invited ostracism if not violence.

Or, suppose this phase passed—where would friendship, neighborly intercourse or social recognition enter? Who would invite them to tea, dinner or dance? They must be outcast and alone. The elders might stand this, but what of an eager youth of eighteen? If this was true around New York, was it better in New England, the Middle West, or California? Los Angeles was a "Jim-Crow" town and so was Portland, Oregon. Many unions in San Francisco excluded Negro labor, and the whole South was caste-ridden and insane with color hate.

They had even thought of migration, but where? Canada would exclude them and Mexico welcome them only if they were rich and did not need to work. In Europe, the world was too upset and competition among youth too fierce for strangers and especially those of a different race to intrude. South America held open some hope, but the political conditions there and the poverty repelled the Mansarts. In the West Indies, struggles of class and color were already too fierce for strangers to be able to live there happily at peace. The Mansarts were glad that they had but this one son when the last blow fell—he volunteered for the air force.

Young Revels had read of the flying squadron of Colonel Davis, a young Negro officer. He came home one day from meeting and seeing some of the cadets in Harlem, and calmly announced that he had enlisted as a private in the flying corps and was going to Tuskegee for training! His mother was aghast and used every argument to deter him from so dangerous a mission. But his father looked at it philosophically.

Here, at last, there seemed to be something which was of real interest to the boy. Up to this time, Revels Jr. seemed to express no interest in anything in particular. He went through high school making a passing grade, attracted by athletics in a general sort of way but taking no part, having no particular hobbies and showing no interest even in girls. For him, the girl problem had curious phases. The colored girls in school were mostly from poor homes, were ill-dressed and homely. The white girls were richer and better dressed. They expected to be noticed but he ostentatiously refrained from giving them any attention whatsoever. He was determined that no one of them was going to get the chance of snubbing him. There were rich and pretty colored girls to be found, but why spend time on such a quest?

He had entered college with the half-expressed desire that he might take up the law and follow in his father's footsteps. But even his father was not enthusiastic about this, because Junior did not show the drive or the interest which seemed to him to be necessary for this profession. He thought of medicine and mentioned it, but young Revels wanted nothing to do with ailing human bodies.

Flying was different. He tried it experimentally. It was the most marvellous experience that he had ever felt, this soaring above the earth and all its little nasty things. So Revels Mansart II went into the Second World War as a flier. He travelled by way of the college at Macon, sampled "Jim-Crow" for the first time, and spent a week there on his way to Tuskegee. He especially liked Jean Du Bignon because she did not try to dissuade him from his chosen job. She just took it for granted that his mind was made up and that he was capable of deciding for himself, and then she talked about life from there on. He grew very fond of her during his short stay. If he ever came back, he wrote to his parents, he would like to sit in her classes. She understood fellows like him.

Jean drove him to Tuskegee and was there when, experimenting with one of the old rattle-trap planes which the Government had palmed off on this Negro school, Revels felt the machine dissolve beneath him. He promptly baled out, soared safely to earth and into the arms of an almost fainting Jean.

"Nothing to it," he said jauntily, and in an hour was aloft again.

Jean drove swiftly home. This generation! He was a boy who might have been her own son. Thank God she had no sons!

Revels pictured himself sailing over Germany to burn the backs of Hitler's stormtroopers, who were spewing their hatred of Jews and "Niggers" and storming Russia. To be sure, he knew little of Communism, but quite enough to contrast it with Britain's role in Africa and Asia. He liked French treatment of colored troops. He had read *The World and Africa* and *Black Folk Then and Now*. He was eager for his mission when, to his bewilderment, his squadron was ordered to Africa, and not to West but to North Africa. He growled:

"What the hell are we doing here? Why don't our army jump on Hitler while his back is turned?"

"Shut your mouth," whispered his pals. "You're in the army now."

He stood one morning in January, 1943, with a young French Resistance officer looking out on the ceremony when Churchill, De Gaulle and Roosevelt met in Casablanca, North Africa. The Frenchman glowered.

"Where's the fourth chair?" he growled.
"For whom?"
"Eboué!"
"And who is Eboué?"
"The black man who made this possible!"

Revels looked blank. The young officer lighted a cigarette and talked. "Recall 1940? Hitler had Europe. The French surrendered in June, and Britain was bombed for six months from July on, after the treason of the Belgian king and the disgrace of Dunkirk. Italy already had armies in Ethiopia and Libya. Britain was in Egypt, intent on saving the carcass of its precious empire—whether Germany or Russia won. All North Africa, with Algeria, Morocco and French West Africa followed Vichy in surrender. The fatal port of Dakar, nearest to America, was unprotected from German seizure. There was but one link missing in the encircling chain—Equatorial Africa, in the very center of the continent, south of Libya and nearest to the forces of Britain in the Anglo-Egyptian Sudan. Through Chad could flow materials from its four Atlantic harbors; here black troops could be assembled and sent north to Egypt. Who held Chad, held Africa; who held Africa at that moment, held the world.

"The governor of Chad was a black man, born in South America, in French Guiana, educated in France, once governor of Guadeloupe. The white governor general of Equatorial Africa was bribed by Vichy and named Commissioner of all Black Africa, with headquarters at Dakar. The white governor of Gabon followed.

"But Eboué, black governor of Chad, called his officers together. He said: 'We were sitting around the radio in the club at Fort-Lamy, the night of June 17, 1940, to listen to Pétain's broadcast. With me were young French army officers, graduates of Saint-Cyr, several department heads and other officials of Chad, and some of the local merchants and functionaries. When Pétain had finished, a silence, born of great pain, fell upon us all. But the pain was stilled for me because I sensed that all Chad stood together in its determination not to yield. I proposed to those gathered about the radio that we serve notice that, whatever the cost, we would continue to fight. I gave them a choice—to follow Vichy or De Gaulle. All but a few chose De Gaulle.'

"A French general later declared: 'If Eboué had followed the example of Pétain, Laval and Weygand, disaster would have followed. . . . Because he did not do so, British and American planes were landed and assembled at Nigeria, flown eastward through Fort-Lamy to Khartoum in the Anglo-Egyptian Sudan, thence northward to the Middle East. Had there been a day's delay, nothing could have stopped Hitler!'

"Eboué offered De Gaulle soldiers, minerals and money. His poor black peasants collected 24 million dollars for the Resistance at a time when they were nearly penniless. Already, Eboué had built one of the largest and best airports in the East and nearly four thousand miles of roads. One hundred and fifty airplanes a day flew from Eboué's airport to the Middle East with troops and supplies. The soldiers he trained marched 1,700 miles north to fight in Tunis and Tripoli. Later, they were among the first to enter Paris."

Revels gasped and looked at the assembled guests. "So that is why he's not here today?"

The young Frenchman growled. "He's not dead yet. He'll present his bill for services rendered."

"Will it be paid?"

"Hell, no! Not if Britain and America can help it!"

Revels hung his head.

The flyer stood flanking the road as President Roosevelt and General Eisenhower explained the expedition and assured the troops that despite the seizure of half of Russia by Hitler, the defeat of Rommel at Alamein meant that Britain and the United States were now in the fight and were going to close in upon the Germans, even if four years late.

On the whole, Revels liked the Air Corps. There was less race segregation among the fliers than in other branches of the service. Negroes were and almost had to be treated like other men. He made acquaintances, not deliberately but unconcernedly. He took men as they came, white and black. Some were interesting and some were not.

Then came the turning. After Stalingrad, the United States army turned north to Italy. Leaving Britain to push to the East and her colonial empire, America went north to take Italy and be in position to help the Eastern front should Russia march to London. Revels flew on wings inspired by all the dreams of his youth.

It was a day in June, 1944. Summer was trying with golden sun and silver water, and with the emerald green of her foliage, to burst through the blood and degradation of war. Revels had landed in Sicily, July, 1943, and flown on to Italy. Waves of sorrow and sympathy sometimes swept across him but he did not let them remain long. After all, Italy was an enemy. This was the country that smashed Ethiopia and began the world war, that hated "Niggers." So Revels flew with careless and magnificent efficiency; he had a feeling that he was going to get an even greater chance at revenge.

General Clark ordered Revels' squadron to accompany him to the attack on Rome. Revels had just heard of that conference which Eboué had called in Brazzaville, not far from the Atlantic coast in Equatorial Africa. It had met in January. De Gaulle had flown from Algiers to open it and all the French governors, administrators and technicians had taken part. The conference represented three and a half million of the four and a half million square miles of French colonial territory, and 25 million of the 70 million French colonials. Eboué had presented his demands for black Africa.

"We must declare war on illness; we must abolish poverty and ignorance. We must end the robbing of the natives by big planters and companies who are determined to continue colonial exploitation. French Equatorial Africa needs doctors, technicians, teachers, scientists to help develop its people and its resources. And we are going to get them."

Eboué died in May; this was June. Revels felt the recklessness and despair of youth plunged into the disaster of war. He saw the blood-splashed murder at Anzio under that curtain of crimson flame which the Nazis poured down daily from the overhanging caves above. He flew above them to Cassino. High in the heavens, he knew that children on the earth below were toddling along the roads gnawing on anything they could find that looked like food, swarming after the trucks, begging the soldiers to throw them something to eat.

"Nothing to eat, nothing to eat," they screamed.

He thought of yesterday when he had bargained with a man. For a can of army corned beef and some hard biscuits, the man was to furnish him with a woman. He had asked casually, "Is she decent—is she young, good-looking?"

And the man answered with low voice and blank eyes, "She is beautiful. There's nothing common about her. She's my sister."

Suddenly, he was sick of it all. Even enemies were human. This, then, was war! He was not punishing enemies. He was not striking against armed and evil men. He was starving little children, raping young girls and crucifying their old fathers and mothers. He laughed as he received his final orders to fly to Rome. Eternal Rome! He rode out and soared into the sky.

He flew up straight and swift, above and beyond his fellows. He dropped burning Hell on monastery, priest and people. In his mind's eye, he saw the blood of women and children spurt and fly. He laughed wildly at planes in pursuit until, outdistancing all, he was alone in the heavens and all his gas was gone. He had watched it as it ran out, and then swiftly curving the nose of his plane earthward, he fell ten thousand feet, closing his eyes as the plane drove its nose a hundred feet into the ground of Italy.

Judge Mansart received his son's letter long after the boy's death.

"Dear Mom and Pop:
"When you receive this I shall be dead. I simply cannot stand this. I know now what war is. I am no longer deceived by fairy tales of glory and victory. War is dirt and mud, hunger and death, rape and lying. I have killed enough of my fellow-men. I have scattered the guts of women and children over the earth. I have seen blood spurt, red and thick, to feed the soil. I will not live in a world like this. Tomorrow I am going to carry out orders and fly as near heaven as my engine will take me and then I am going to turn and drop straight into the earth. I shall soon be dead. I never expect to see you again but I greet you. I know what you have tried to do for me. I am deeply grateful. My love to you both and to Aunt Jean.

Goodbye."

There was no funeral. On the Sunday morning after the news, a few visitors met in Revels' living room. A citation lay on a crimson throw across the piano. His picture hung on one wall. A baritone sang:

"I stood on the river of Jordan
To see them ships come passing over.
I stood on the river of Jordan
To see them ships go by.
O mother don't you mourn
To see them ships go passing over.
Shout, Glory, Hallelu!
To see them ships pass by—
I stood on the river of Jordan!"

CHAPTER XIII

Roosevelt Dies

The death of their adopted son had shaken the Mansarts to the depth of their lives. Both grasped blindly after some sort of escapism to hide the terrible void. Mrs. Mansart found it eventually in re-union with her estranged relatives in Charleston, South Carolina. Her only sister, older than she, had torn the family pride by openly consorting with a white man who eventually became governor of the state. Her family were light mulattoes, old and well-to-do and related by blood to the best white families of the state, but it had been more than a century since any white person had consorted with this proud clan. Their price was marriage, open and legal. Despite this, one of their most beautiful daughters had become the known concubine of a well-born young white lawyer. They lived together in a fine mansion where she was officially "housekeeper," but with three children—a boy and two girls. When the man became governor, an aunt presided over the official mansion, but he continued to live mostly at his old home. When, however, the young governor proposed to go to the United States Senate, the couple had to face facts. The young governor had been chosen to lead the revolt against the Democratic Party in the South, against the Roosevelt New Deal. It was not only resentment against Roosevelt's recognition of the Negro, but also the rise of the fight against socialism in a region where big business was about to play its boldest role in oil, sulphur and textiles. A revolt looking toward a third party in the South was due and the young governor was the man to lead it. But for this, he must rid himself of his colored family—either that, or the South would ruin him politically, socially and financially.

"This thing could be carried on a half century ago. But today with the women voting, it can't be faced. What do you say?" asked his supporters. And now he stood in his home with the tensed body of his common-law wife in his arms and said to her: "You know I love you. I have never loved anyone else. You have been brave and true. I do not see how I can live without you. But I must. You see it, don't you? I must." She made no answer. There was none to make.

He pensioned off his colored family and married a young white woman of the current aristocracy. The colored woman and her children came to New York and bought a house on Riverside Drive. The son, quite white in appearance, was eventually taken into a white manufacturing firm and disappeared into the white world. The elder daughter, with darker olive skin, married a rising young colored lawyer, a protegé of Judge Mansart. Mrs. Mansart had for a long time taken no notice of this family of her sister. But the youngest daughter, after the suicide of Mrs. Mansart's adopted son, called. She was fifteen and of dazzling beauty—cream of skin, black-haired with liquid eyes, lovely features and faultless form. She came with the young lawyer brother-in-law at the suggestion of Judge Mansart. Mrs. Mansart, forgetting all her anger at her sister, the girl's mother, was drawn to her immediately and clung to her as to a new-found refuge. The girl was intelligent, well-bred and ambitious, but she was lost in New York. Her brother and sister were older and the companions of her childhood were far away in Charleston. Her mother brooded darkly in dark seclusion. The girl felt deep compassion for Mrs. Mansart and in turn Mrs. Mansart came to realize what a wife this girl would have made her dead son; and despite his death, she found herself continually treating the girl, Marian, like a prospective daughter.

The Judge, on the other hand, found increasing escape from his pain by gradually entering a new world. He refused to run again for the judgeship, even when the possibility of promotion was held before him. He reduced his private practice to a minimum, taking only cases which particularly attracted him. He increased his library and began systematic reading of books and current periodicals. Marian, his wife's niece, got in the habit of using his library, and finally became his secretary, helped by a stenographer. The Judge found a new world in a Hungarian restaurant not far from his office on the East Side. Here, he fell into the habit of regularly taking a long lunch and meeting foreigners of education, experience and knowledge who received him gladly as a companion, without exhibiting that patronizing effrontery which white Americans think it proper to use when they meet a black American whose position they cannot entirely ignore. Thus, Mansart was gradually transported into a new and hitherto unknown world.

He learned how Russia was striving to achieve democracy. In this desperate, heart-breaking struggle with weak human nature, with crime and selfishness, the Soviet leaders could count on no aid or sympathy from the decency and religion of Europe or America.

Judge Mansart listened to this explanation with a good deal of surprise. He never had the situation put to him in this way. His whole idea of the Soviet Union, as he thought it over, was quite the opposite. The aim of the Soviets, he had thought, was largely murder and purges. Stalin was said to be a ruthless scoundrel. Yet, here was a contradictory explanation. The Judge said to himself, "Where did I get my information about Russia?"

He began to realize that he had gotten it largely from the American press and Leon Trotsky; that when Trotsky came to Mexico the American press was thrown open to him and American liberals swarmed about him. So that for years it was Trotsky who made up the minds of Americans on Russia. All this, of course, could not have been spontaneous. It must have been promoted and paid for. All American periodicals, all news services were open to Trotsky. The liberal movement became his agents.

Moreover, now, whether or not it was necessary to change one's attitude toward Russia and one's interpretation of the current results of the Russian revolution, whatever was necessary, was difficult because of the changing place of the newspaper in the life of ordinary Americans. There was a time when the judge read the *New York Times* and *Tribune*, looked over a few standard magazines and now and then read a book. He then felt prepared with knowledge, basic knowledge of what was going on in the world.

But he began to realize that this was no longer true; that the newspapers withheld news, interpreted the facts in curious ways and even, on occasion, deliberately lied. This must be because of the influence of the business interests and powerful banks on newspapers and magazines, which went to the extent of actually owning them or distributing the materials which they must have—the newspaper print, the use of the great news-gathering agencies. Judge Mansart saw, therefore, that he could not depend upon newspapers as formerly. He must, so far as it was possible, get his own sources of information.

Judge Mansart began to learn what most men learn slowly and some never—namely, that when we live through a great series of human events, we do not necessarily see them, even less do we really understand them, nor can we arrange them to fit logically into the world we already know. Perhaps (and this complicates understanding even more) current events clearly show us that our interpretation of the past has been wrong, that only through the present can we see the past. Time, in other words, shifts—future is partly the past and the past is future. Judge Mansart began to look back and to try to classify and rearrange his memories and experiences.

The main school of his re-education in the meaning of current events was the little Hungarian restaurant where he began to meet men with a first-hand knowledge of the world, and who talked frankly about it. He must get further information, by conference if necessary and even by correspondence. It was difficult and annoying, but manifestly this was what he had to do. So that he and Mrs. Mansart and Marian, who was often at their home, made special efforts to acquire and constantly expand their own collection of facts and impressions concerning the world developing about them. Marian was soon to finish her course at Wadleigh High School and planned to enter Hunter College.

Because of his acquaintance with Harry Hopkins and the fact that he had met him once or twice, Judge Mansart paid special attention to what the press reported Hopkins as saying; to his mind, Hopkins was an honest, straight-forward man who tried to tell the truth as he saw it. Everything therefore, that Hopkins said, Judge Mansart followed with keen interest.

Mansart recalled that he had had another chance to talk to him, just before Harry Hopkins went to England. He realized then that the United States was at last willing to become a partner with Russia against Hitler and Mussolini.

Lend-lease had been debated for months and was finally adopted as necessary to save Britain, Greece and China. There was a hard fight, but the President stood firm and finally obtained the power to extend Lend-lease to the Soviets if Hitler or Japan attacked her. Hopkins' friends rejoiced. They hoped that this thin, anemic man would have the courage to stand up for this program while in England. And, grinning appreciatively, Hopkins told them he would.

A few weeks later, this son of a harness-maker appeared in the Kremlin and sat down with Joseph Stalin; they talked as man-to-man. He did not bring, as Stalin expected and as his predecessors had, terms calling for the entrance of private capital into the Baltic areas and the Balkans. He offered only to help beat Hitler, and the next thing the world knew, the United States was granting a billion dollars of Lend-lease to Russia.

Looking back over the history of these events which, at the time they occurred, he had not understood, Judge Mansart realized that his son had died because not until July, 1943, had the British and Americans attacked Italy; they were still inching their way to Rome, in June 1944, when young Revels plunged to his death.

Secretly, Churchill feared victorious Russia. Knowing what he himself would have done under such circumstances, he was convinced Russia's victorious hosts would never stop at Berlin but would march on to London and Paris. Later, Mansart learned that Churchill had even ordered Montgomery to stack the captured German arms for eventual use by a new army to be composed of German prisoners.

When the Peace effort began after Stalingrad, Judge Mansart concluded that Churchill still feared Russia. Hopkins wrote:

"If the West had responded by an equally strong push on Hitler's bare back the war might have been settled in 1943. But the World and its military experts, and especially the Americans, refused to believe their eyes and were sure that Russia must eventually be completely vanquished."

Later Hopkins said to America:

"The thing the American people must look out for is that there is a minority in America who, for a variety of reasons, would just as soon have seen Russia defeated in the war and who said publicly before we got into the war that it did not make any difference which one—Russia or Germany—won. That small, vociferous minority can take advantage of every rift between ourselves and Russia to make trouble between our two countries. There are plenty of people in America who would have been perfectly willing to see our armies go right through Germany and fight with Russia after Germany was defeated. They represent nobody but themselves and no government worth its salt in control of our country would ever permit that group to influence our official actions."

Roosevelt who, as Judge Mansart came to see, was a greater man than Churchill, rose to statesmanship. He set out to build friendship with the Union of Soviets and dragged Churchill with him. The only man in the world at the time capable of getting the trust and friendship of Stalin was Franklin Roosevelt; and this he accomplished by frankness and honest dealing. He knew that Stalin was neither fool nor barbarian. He knew that Russia had just demands and was capable of enforcing them. He knew that Stalin kept his word but was not to be misled by flattery or double talk. Personal conferences were arranged between Roosevelt, Churchill and Stalin at Teheran and Yalta, but at a cost in sheer physical strain which later killed Roosevelt.

A young man joined Mansart and others at the "Stammtisch" in the spring of 1945. He seemed well known to many of those present and talked freely.

"There were strong and curious currents at Yalta," he said. "I was there and heard and saw. Subtle, tragic and world-shaking things were in mind. Not least was the role of the Soviet Union, led by the cool, unwavering Stalin. Stalin knew Churchill, and knew him as a ruthless liar who had used every weapon he could lay hands on to overthrow the Russian Revolution. It was he who had held back the Allies as long as possible, so that Hitler had every opportunity to crush Russia; and he had finally yielded only when he had to.

"Stalin liked Roosevelt because of Harry Hopkins; but Stalin knew that Roosevelt was largely in the power of those same Big Business interests which Hoover formerly represented. He knew that this clique stood behind the landlords of Poland and the Baltic states who had organized among them a nest of lying and intrigue against the Soviets. With Poland, they formed the '*Cordon Sanitaire*' of Clemenceau for conquering Russia whenever the opportunity offered. Poland had for centuries been the most dangerous center of greedy landlords in Europe, sucking the life out of millions of helpless peasants. Poland's hordes of soldiers, led by buccaneers like Pilsudski, had for decades swept into Russia and often overwhelmed her. Czechoslovakia and Hungary and all the Balkan states had for a century been centers of European exploiters of the peasants."

Judge Mansart learned that we had given fifty billions of dollars to help Europe stop Hitler; thirty-one billions of this went to Britain and we promised more and eventually gave it; ten billions went to France who laid down her arms and needed more help than she gave. But only eleven billions went to the Soviet Union which bore the main brunt of the fighting. This gift deserved at least to be doubled as Russia lay bleeding alongside her 15 million dead. But having nearly died to save us, she was doomed to crucifixion.

In March, 1945, Roosevelt reported to Congress:

> "The structure of world peace cannot be the work of one man, or of one party, or one nation. It cannot be just an American peace or a British peace, or a Russian, or a French or a Chinese peace. It cannot be a peace of a large nation or of small nations. It must be a peace which rests on the cooperative efforts of the whole world."

Mansart listened attentively to the young man's further comment:

> "Tremendous additional agreements were necessary and the implementation and refining of those was agreed on in principle. Had Roosevelt lived, this had every chance of being accomplished, not without friction but with faith, understanding and good will."

Harry Hopkins wrote later:

> "We really believed in our heart that this was the dawn of the new day we had all been praying for and talking about for so many years. We were absolutely certain that we had won the world's first great victory of the peace—and, by 'we,' I mean ALL of us, the whole civilized human race. The Russians had proved that

they could be reasonable and far-seeing, and there wasn't any doubt in the minds of the President or any of us that we could live with them and get along with them peacefully for as far into the future as any of us could imagine."

Judge Mansart had listened to the discussion with deep interest especially to the account of the young eye-witness of current events.

"Who was that young man?" he asked as the luncheon broke up.

Someone answered, "I think his name is Hiss—Alger Hiss."

It was the very same afternoon of this conversation that Mansart noticed a newcomer in the restaurant. He was a young man in his twenties and drew Judge Mansart's attention not only because he had never noted him before, but because every young man of this age, especially one with a touch of color in his skin, reminded him of his lost son. This young man was visibly colored and unusually handsome; broad, well-built and stocky, with beautiful olive skin and clustered curly hair. As he arose and glanced toward Mansart, suddenly something vaguely familiar seemed to leap out from his face. It was a proud, young face, and its appealing beauty and self-reliance caught Mansart like a sudden grip. Where had he seen and known that smile? And Judge Mansart's heart almost stopped. He staggered forward and, hurrying, caught the young man almost roughly as he opened the door.

"I beg your pardon. But someway, somehow I thought perhaps I knew you—had met you somewhere." The young man's face grew almost stern, but he answered courteously.

"No, Judge Mansart, I have never seen you before. But I came here today because I have a letter which I am commissioned to give you. I lost my nerve when I saw you looking at me. I'm sorry." He felt carefully in his inner pocket and produced a long envelope. "This, sir, is for you, and should have been delivered some time ago. And here is my card. May I call on you—perhaps tomorrow?"

"But certainly. At my office or home."

"I would prefer your office. Say at four in the afternoon? Thank you, sir." He left abruptly and Mansart was disappointed. There was something about him that drew old memories from the past. What was it? He looked at the card.

Mr. Philip M. Wright
General Electric, Poughkeepsie, N. Y.

Mansart scowled at the card; it was no one he knew—then he rushed to his office and opened the envelope.

> "My darling Revels:
> I shall long be dead when you read this. But it will, I fondly hope, be given you by the hands of our son, Philip Wright Mansart, or, as he calls himself, Philip Wright. I will not try to bring back the awful tragedy of our parting. I know that all these years you have thought that I left you voluntarily. How could, O how could you after all we once were to each other. I never dreamed you would believe this until your demand for divorce came. Then I knew. What message they left

you, I do not know. I was kidnapped by my brother and his friends; put into an ambulance, gagged and transported to a sanitarium where I was committed legally as an incompetent.

Their plans were frustrated when it was discovered that I was three months with child, as I had long suspected but hesitated to tell you. I made a bargain with them. I was to keep the baby but never to see you again. Otherwise I declared I would kill myself. It was a long battle, but I with my parents' help won, if that could be called winning. I went to cousins in Maine and bore my beautiful child. Later I returned to my home and parents and brought up our boy in my home town. Then came your appeal for divorce. I granted it, of course, but soon afterward they discovered cancer. From this I shall soon die, but with one wish: that you know that never, never have I ceased to love you. And that you must know and bless our son. Mary."

"Mary" was that Mary Wright whom Revels Mansart had married in 1921 after he returned from war and whom he thought had deserted him a year later. Now he knew that she had been forced to leave and that the demand for divorce was not hers but had been made to seem to come from him. With dumb distress he now awaited the call of young Wright, his son.

Marian, Mrs. Mansart's niece, was now a senior at Hunter, with an outstanding record. She had for some time become accustomed to spend afternoons at her uncle's office, using his library and assisting in systematizing his work. She was there the afternoon when Philip Wright called—half-way up a ladder where she was seeking a book.

Wright had made up his mind not to visit Mansart's home and become socially involved with him and his wife. But he had promised his mother to talk with his father and now he must do so, although he had small liking for the task. He entered the well-furnished and impressive offices just at sunset, before the lights had been put on and the soft colors of evening were brightening the mahogany and brass. The stenographer had gone for the day, but Marian was there, poised on the ladder. Her arm was uplifted, her neck turned, and the soft light poured across the cheeks of a face that seemed to Philip the most beautiful he had ever dreamed of. He paused a moment and then, moving quickly forward, took her hand to help her down and half whispered: "I think you are the most lovely thing I have ever seen!"

Marian was used to being stared at and called beautiful in all sorts of tones and every kind of word; but now she was speechless and moved as never before. She had never seen a man who so filled her every ideal of what a human being might be. His face was soft cream; his hair curled and dripped over his wide forehead; but above all he had manners and intelligence and he so evidently meant what he said in such deadly earnest. Both were standing voiceless, when Mansart came out from the inner office. He was still so full of emotion over the letter which he had read, that noticing nothing, he grasped the young man's hand and pulled him into his office. He began to talk almost hysterically.

"Believe me when I swear that I never doubted but that your mother had left me voluntarily. I did not for a moment question her right and duty to do this after what she had suffered. But I never asked for a divorce; I was told she had applied and I knew that it was her right to do so. For ten years I lived unmarried and then at last married a good woman, not for love but because we both needed companionship. That we have had. But, O my boy, had I known—had I dreamed you existed——"

The young man's face was gray. "The girl out there," he said, "is she—your daughter?"

Mansart stared and answered hurriedly:

"O no, she's my wife's niece and assists me——"

But the young man was gone.

Mansart sat down heavily. It was what he deserved, but God how it hurt! He could see now every lineament of the face he once loved so dearly, in the countenance of this young man of whose very existence he had never known.

He dropped his head and sobbed:

"O my son, O Philip my son, O Mary my dead and tortured wife——"

Marian talked excitedly of the young man who had called, then left so hurriedly. Mansart told both her and his wife who Philip Mansart Wright was; he begged Marian to make him return. She had no difficulty. He was back the very next day and had a brief conversation with Mrs. Mansart, but he seemed to have little time for anyone but Marian and she hardly a thought for anyone but Philip. This went on for a week. Then one afternoon they came into Judge Mansart's private office, hand in hand. The girl's face was flushed and the boy's face shone.

"We are going to get married, sir," they said.

Mansart staggered to his feet and clasped them both in his arms.

Mrs. Mansart was not one who as a rule believed in love at first sight or trusted the sudden impulses of youth. But this mutual attraction of her niece and her husband's newly discovered son made her infinitely happy. It seemed to bring back the eternally lost. She assented to the marriage, and made the elaborate wedding a family reconciliation, at which the silent and brooding elder sister, Marian's mother, appeared, as well as the young lawyer and his wife.

Philip, who in lieu of military duty, had an assignment at General Electric, secured a leave of absence for their honeymoon. On the very afternoon of graduation, Philip and Marian Mansart-Wright drove South in the Judge's big car to the bride's relatives and old companions in Charleston; from there they went on to Macon, Georgia, to meet President Manuel Mansart.

In Macon, President Mansart was also becoming aware of the new post-war world. He realized how deep was the resentment against Roosevelt in certain circles because of his attitude against wealth, his friendship for workers even if black, and his "appeasement" of the Soviet Union. It cropped up again in Warm Springs, where the tired man tried to recuperate and help others afflicted like himself to do the same. President Mansart had seen him ride by on his way to Warm Springs.

"There is death on his face," he told Jean, and she reminded him of rumors in the air.

It was the year of Stalingrad when a white man accosted a Negro employed on the grounds at Warm Springs.

"Why, hello, Jim; you working here?"

"Yes, sir, I'm helping the President's valet."

"Pretty good job?"

"Oh yes, sir, mighty good. I like it fine."

"What do you do?"

"Well, when the President comes often he wants to be wheeled about after lunch or in the night when he don't sleep. I often pushes him in his chair; we wanders about the grounds—down by the pool and up by the highway."

"Alone?"

"Oh, no—they's always his guards about!"

"Then you take him back and put him to bed?"

"Oh, no. I just takes him back. Only his valet touches him. He wouldn't have nobody else. I tell you that man carries a burden inside and out—pounds of iron and steel. I don't see how he does it. But he don't never complain, though sometimes he does look beat."

"Any colored folks treated in these Springs?"

"Oh, no sir! Only whites."

"I thought the President was such a friend of your people."

"He is; but this is the South and he can't interfere——"

"Can't, or won't?"

"Can't, leastways not all at once. He's got a lot on his mind besides such matters. Well, I must be moving."

"Do they pay you well?"

"Pretty well—at least a heap better than I was getting."

"You could use more?"

"Oh yes, sure, sure—good night."

The white man walked slowly back to his car. When he reached the hotel he talked to his companions.

"I know the 'nigger' who helps groom Roosevelt."

"So what? Can he tell us anything we don't know?"

"No——" the man paused and looked his two companions squarely in the face. "But he is alone with him now and then, at night."

"With the Secret Service in good sight," replied one.

"Lurking about of course, but inside those grounds——"

The other froze. "But—you don't—you can't!——"

The man was silent behind his hard scowl. "There's nothing I wouldn't try with that bastard!" he growled.

American corporate finance, centered in an ever-growing network of powerful banks, was developing wider control of industry and trade. Into its power fell the owners of property, the technicians, the newspapers, editors and publishers; the broadcasters and actors; even the laborers. The great and growing monopoly of money and credit was moving toward the absolute rule of the nation and even the world. This super-power hated Franklin Roosevelt with perfect hatred. They cursed this crippled traitor to his class, who after refusing Hitler's blackmail, joined Communists to prevent American business from corralling the earth. These insane seekers for power swore by earth, heaven and hell to kill the God-damned meddler and wipe his memory from history.

This was the interpretation of current history to which Jean Du Bignon gradually came. President Mansart could not wholly believe it but he listened; he listened also to the strange story which was whispered secretly on his campus:

"It happened a week later at nightfall, near the pool at Warm Springs. What happened, few knew. Of those who did, none ever talked. But next morning a colored man named Jim was found shot dead near the pool. He had struggled furiously and shrieked in protest. The President was not harmed and never mentioned the incident. A white man was also reported found dead on the grounds.

"The President was indisposed for several days after and he rode out no more after dark. But there were men who growled: 'He'll die at Warm Springs yet.'"

One black man talked, but none believed him. He said, "There were men who met down there in total darkness so that none could see the others' faces. They whispered, 'He is sick—he must be made sicker. He must die. Before the United Nations is born, he must be buried. Five persons are close enough to touch his body—they must be reached. One of us must be assigned to get to know each of these enough to tamper with them. There is influence, pressure, fear. There is money—there is no limit to the money. By hook or crook; by knife or gun; by poison or drug; by God, Franklin Roosevelt must die before April 25, 1945.'"

Men said this is a fairy tale and cannot be true. Others replied, "Not literally perhaps, but in substance it cannot be false." For Roosevelt died April 12, 1945, in the 63rd year of his life and in the twelfth year of his reign as President of the United States.

Jean Du Bignon shut herself in and thought. The end of the world seemed to have come and she was deeply discouraged. She had never seen Franklin Roosevelt, much less met him. But she had heard him—all the world had heard him. She wrote rapidly:

"This was a man, a great man but not too great to be human, with healthy human frailties. His was an education of contact with well-bred persons, but with husky, salty folk as well. He might have had broader, deeper study, reading, learning, but he never stopped developing—he was always growing so long as he lived. Always, he was torn between his boyhood loyalties, inherited from his wealthy, well-bred family, and his broadening knowledge of mankind and its dwelling places in all ends of earth. Had not life pressed so fast and furiously upon him, he might have achieved rare wisdom. But much wisdom he did achieve and he accomplished truly great deeds. I am glad I lived to know him a little from afar and to share his tremendous era.

"He saved the British Empire and the French Republic by firmly grasping the hand of the Soviet Union and letting her pull them and his own America out of defeat. He was father of a family which, from mother to grandchild, posed for him every problem of life which can try a man's heart. He neither whined nor whimpered, but backed Heaven to Hell to protect the Right. In all and with all, he kept his soul serene, met mornings with a smile and talked to the hearts of his countrymen as never Presidents had talked before. He died in harness—that harness of pounds of steel, under which he grimly bent every waking hour. His reach was not wide but his grasp was mighty. He 'never dreamed though Right were worsted, Wrong could triumph.'"

CHAPTER XIV

The Nations Unite

President Mansart and his assistant enjoyed the visit of Philip and Marian. It was a breath from a new young world full of faith and force, and they were blissfully unaware of the testing of heart and soul which they must face in the next decade. Jean especially realized that these young folk were ready for change and movement and she knew that this was what the world was about to see. When they left, she began to sense the meaning of the great march from the Revolution of Roosevelt to the Counter-Revolution of Truman. It was unbelievable. Here was a man suddenly made master of the world, grasping in bewildered surprise at the program of his leader which he never understood, nor ever would. It was a fantastic and awful commentary on naive American belief that any man—at least any white man—could do anything; a belief which might one day ruin the world.

It was at this time that Mansart's son Douglass, from Chicago, visited his father. Mansart and Jean were both glad, for none was more conversant than Douglass with current politics in the Middle West. Douglass had come to bring his son, Adelbert. The young man, it seemed, had decided to come to the State College for further study, a rather slim young man of medium height, brown, with a discontented face. Indeed, he bore a startling resemblance to Mansart's lost son, Bruce—there was the same black, loosely cured hair, the same unsettled and hesitant manner. Mansart could not quite understand why Douglass' son had chosen to leave the North and his well-to-do family to come to Georgia.

Dougass' explanation was vague, but Mansart was so glad to have a grandson here at school that he did not press the matter and welcomed the boy, letting Jean take charge of him. Meantime, he took up most of Douglass' short stay with questions about Truman, who had suddenly become President.

He found that Douglass had become rather corpulent, but was very well-dressed and evidently prosperous. He was expecting to go to the State Senate next year and was the political boss of the chief colored Chicago Ward. Of course, Douglass knew Truman—he knew all the politicians in the Middle West.

"I saw him in France during the First World War. He was a good-natured, fun-loving guy who played the piano and had a good time. His rank as captain, which he got at the close of the war, rather went to his head, but he was better than most such officers. Back in Kansas City, he became one of Tom Prendergast's gang and that was a worse outfit than our Big Bill Thompson's. Truman gave up his men's outfitting business which had failed anyway, and 'went into politics.'

"As Prendergast's boy, he became county judge, then went to the United States Senate. He was the club that beat Wallace to the Vice-Presidency in the campaign of 1944 and was early chosen to change Roosevelt's policies in case Roosevelt died, which he did. So reaction is on top now. We have got as president a man with elementary school education, no cultural background and rather big ideas of himself due to his success in a provincial western city. Much will depend on the advice he gets and on his own headstrong impulses toward self-assertion.

"But Truman's real handicap, and one he will never escape, is his lack of a fundamental and broad education. He is essentially a good-natured man who wishes most folks well. He has ability and a clear mind. But he does not know the world. History, to him, is a closed book. He has no conception of science; he does not read; he does not listen to the world's real teachers. He never learned how to study. He was always, essentially, a 'show-off.'"

Jean listened with interest to Douglass' account of the new president, Harry Truman, but she was even more interested at the moment in his son. She wondered how Douglass' married life had gone, for she had not seen him for many years and this son, who was not happy, intrigued her. It took a little time to gain young Adelbert's confidence and learn why it was that he had left Chicago and the opportunities of the North, his home and the schools open to him, to come down here. But gradually it came out. He did not like his home. He particularly disliked (in fact he said "hated") his mother. He did not like his sister. His father was good enough but had hardly any time for him.

It turned out that the real trouble centered in the fact that Douglass' first child was a girl, light-skinned and pretty, whom the mother adored and exhibited. Her hair was brown but very krinkly, and her mother from the first had had it straightened and oiled and pressed weekly. And then the second child, good-looking and a boy, was disliked and almost disinherited in his mother's affection because his skin was dark. He was quite as dark as his father, with loosely curled hair which was, of course, a natural quirk of colored heritage.

In consequence, however, while mother and daughter often went to town, sight-seeing or to theaters and restaurants and enjoyed themselves in many ways, the dark little boy was never taken with them. He exhibited too clearly his Negro blood. From early childhood, then, he grew up hating his family and the world. His father sensed this but there was little he could do. He was busy with his business and his developing political career. True, he gave the boy money, sometimes took him along on automobile trips, but the boy grew up largely by himself.

His father had had both children enrolled in white school districts. This suited his sister who ignored him, but it made little difference to Adelbert. He kept away from his white fellow students. Then, when he came of high school age, he insisted on attending Wendell Phillips High which was in effect a colored school in a Northern city where schools were not supposed to be segregated by race. The school was crowded but well-equipped and had good teachers. He was interested in most of his studies and did well. He liked his colored fellow-students.

Approaching his graduation from high school, when the question of college came up, he determined to go to his grandfather in Georgia. He wanted to live in a colored world which was satisfied with being colored. The idea persisted that perhaps his grandfather would turn out to be a different kind of a man than his father. Douglass was astonished at the boy's decision but on the whole was rather pleased with it. His mother was both relieved and affronted. And so, the boy, who had always been a problem to his Chicago family, suddenly appeared in Macon.

Gradually, he began to fit into the life of the school. He was particularly interested in drama and drawing and he wrote English well. One or two of his little plays were staged and Mansart began to look forward to the time when his grandson would become a teacher in the school.

When an invitation came to attend his sister's wedding, Adelbert was firm in his decision not to go. He said he knew Dr. Steinway, the physician she was marrying, a man nearly twice as old as his sister but very successful, very, indeed. He had been trained in Chicago and practiced there for some time; then he had gone to Los Angeles. He had insisted that this was a growing part of the country for Negroes, being nearest to the Spanish world of South America.

He became what was sometimes called a "commercial" physician. He had no deep human sensibilities or sympathies. He was strong, and callous. He calculated on making his profession "pay" in every way. He "strung along" those of his patients who could pay well for numerous visits over long periods of time. He was careful to select patients who could pay well, and to these he was always attentive. Poor patients he got rid of in various ways—by curing them quickly or sending them to the city clinics; sometimes by simply saying that he could do nothing for them.

He split fees with consultants and specialists, even with druggists. He made out prescriptions at high prices when the same medicines were available in patented form at a much lower price. He was a good diagnostician but did not waste time on diagnosis when he thought a hastily prescribed pill would do. A variety of machines, gadgets and medical apparatus was installed in his office, all calculated to impress his patients. He often turned patients over to the nurses who put them through treatments which required the use of these various machines. This did them no harm, but it cost them more money. He had no scruples about recommending operations by surgeons with whom he had worked out business arrangements and often sent his patients to hospitals when it was not absolutely necessary.

Young Adelbert probably gave a rather too unfavorable picture of the physician. But there was much truth in his description. Dr. Michael Steinway was especially opposed to "social medicine" or to free medical service of any kind whatsoever. He firmly believed in what he called "the democracy of persons choosing their own physicians and paying them." He was a large, good-looking man, yellow in color, with straight hair, always well-tailored and groomed, and with a perfect bedside manner. He was a good "mixer," collected and told excellent stories, and had a wide acquaintance with persons of wealth, influence and power, white and black. His political connections too were wide.

He had put off marriage until he could have the kind of establishment which he wanted. That he found in Los Angeles where he bought, on Harvard Boulevard, one of the elaborate mansions which its former white owners could no longer afford to keep up. There he established his office and nurses, and installed an excellent household which included a gardener, cook and maids. Then he looked about for a pretty girl and a young one, with money in the family. He found her on a visit to Chicago in the daughter of Douglass Mansart.

The mother was delighted. It meant that she would make annual visits to Los Angeles and would not have to spend the cold winters in Chicago. It also meant that her social career there would be pleasant and notable. Douglass did not like the idea at first, but after all, what difference?—perhaps an older man would take better care of his daughter than some young whippersnapper who wanted to get hold of Douglass' money.

So the marriage took place without Adelbert. It was elaborate and costly, and some phases of it very beautiful. It was held in a prominent Catholic church because Mrs. Mansart had joined the Catholics early in her career for various reasons, some of which were obvious and some not mentioned. The bride was pretty and gorgeously gowned; the gifts were costly and many of them quite appropriate. The going away on the Santa Fe "Super-Chief" train was an event which even the white papers noticed with deference.

Manuel, who attended, did not exactly enjoy the occasion. The mansion on South Boulevard was very beautiful, costly and well-run. But there was in it very little that could really be called "home life."

While he was in Chicago, Bishop Wilson wrote him asking his father-in-law to return by way of Dallas and suggested they both attend the organization of the United Nations in San Francisco. The Bishop was a "consultant" of the UNO and Douglass easily arranged for his father to get a similar appointment. The position carried no power and little influence; but it gave them the right to attend the sessions and hear delegates discuss and answer inquiries in small groups. Mansart was eager to go, for he had high hopes in the UNO.

Bishop Wilson, immediately after his election in 1944, prepared to go to Africa where it was the custom to send newly-elected bishops. It was a sort of penalty which young black bishops paid. But it wasn't as bad as one might suppose. Most of them went to Africa, stayed a few months, returned home and rested the balance of the year, or even of the quadrennium. Others went there determined to do something—which was extremely difficult in a country unfamiliar to them and which had its own culture and religions. If the assignment was South Africa, there was the worst interracial situation in the world to face. This was often a challenge, and some bishops actually did accomplish something. Even in those cases, however, after six or seven months of effort, most of them returned home and spent the rest of their term in America.

But Wilson, partly of his own accord, but more because he was impelled by Sojourner, planned to go to Africa and stay four years with the distinct idea of doing something towards its redemption. He could not do much, he realized, but he would do something. What he could bring to Africa he did not know.

Could he attack its problem of poverty? He did not see how. He felt he could help in education and perhaps fight against disease.

Sojourner was even more determined to try. She would take music to Africa and bring music out. She would appreciate the beauty of the land. She would dream its future. She would make her years in Africa seem like a holy pilgrimage, and when they both came back and spoke to audiences in America, whites as well as blacks would be thrilled and uplifted, and a vision of a free Pan-Africa would be conjured up before them.

However, before beginning his trip the Bishop had to await the end of the war. He spent much time in reading, correspondence and study; and he planned to attend the UNO. Thus it was that in the summer of 1945 President Mansart and Bishop Wilson rode through Texas. Texas was waste, waste, grey wet waste; mud and sand, scrub and stumps; tired pines, sluggish waters, brown coarse grass; nothing human, nothing beautiful save the flood of bluebonnets here and there. Then came a sudden frenzy of huddled, crowded activity of tense, hard-faced white men, smooth, silken white women; smoke, steel, oil, sulphur, machinery, grinding, screeching; white and black workers squatting in squalor; hurried, breathless, huddling. Texas!

Mansart, in the Bishop's new home in Dallas, had talked with him of Africa.

"Something new," the Bishop said, "is coming out of Africa in the last half of this century. There will be revolution in West Africa, and blood in the East. Ethiopia will regain its seacoast and curb white investors. The ancient Sudan will be an independent state, and a new Egypt will be free of Britain. South Africa will start a war of races when less than three million whites seek to chain ten million colored and blacks. The United States will furnish capital for the whites. If any nation furnishes arms to the blacks the end will come soon."

"What nation will?"

"India or the Soviet Union—or West Africa."

"I am amazed—I cannot believe that in either case———"

"In a life and death struggle will Negroes ask or care who sends them arms? I tell you, something new is coming out of Africa."

"But what of Central Africa?"

"If and when white South Africa falls, then Central Africa—the Rhodesias and the Congo will go the way of West Africa."

"And French Africa?"

"Will go the way of Indo-China."

"But will France ever surrender Indo-China?"

"She will. I know all this sounds fantastic, but believe me, President Mansart, this prophecy is near the truth. It's simply a matter of time. But what bothers me is, what are black leaders going to do for the people of those countries? As I see it now, what they want to do is to replace the white exploiters, the people who have been using Africa for the comfort and luxury of Europe and America.

"The ascendancy of black men, trained in England, to some degree in France, and a few but an increasing number in the United States, is going to transfer some of that comfort and luxury to Africa. I wonder, however, if the mass of Africans are going to be better off? Probably, and yet not well off. Black West

Africans, for instance, want to be the black rulers of an African world, doing exactly the same thing that white rulers have done for three hundred years. I do not like it, President Mansart, I do not like it."

Then the Bishop added, "I have one commission from Africa and that is to induce American Negroes to renew their interest in Africa. They want to hold a fifth Pan-African Congress in Paris or London this Fall. The NAACP, you remember, initiated these congresses in 1919. I wonder if it will help renew them now?"

"I doubt it," said President Mansart. "The NAACP is in a difficult position just now. It is trying to carry on a progressive program and avoid being attacked as Communist."

"But I don't see how it could," said the Bishop.

"Nobody else does. But while we are in San Francisco we'll have a chance to inquire."

Manuel Mansart and Bishop Wilson sat in the Opera House at San Francisco and witnessed the effort to organize the United Nations. Mansart felt uplifted. He seemed to be seeing history in the making. Seated directly behind the President and the Bishop were three persons—a young colored man, a white middle-aged man and a white girl. The colored man was a former student at Mansart's college and introduced them to each other. He explained that he was temporarily representing the Urban League whose secretary would arrive next day. The white man was on the board of directors of the NAACP and the young woman was Sally Haynes, the young friend of Harry Hopkins, whom he had met before.

As they walked away together, Mansart mentioned Alger Hiss who had presided.

"I met him before. I like him. A good, clean-cut American with no airs; honest, if I know an honest man. Stettinius I never liked. He seems to me like a rich man's spoiled brat, with no depth or breadth."

"Did you notice," asked Grey, the white man, "how popular Molotov is? He may be wrong but he has the poise of knowledge and the dignity of confidence."

The Bishop recalled the variety of the world's peoples who daily sat in the great auditorium. He was never weary of watching their coming and going—British Eden and French Bidault; the turbanned Arabs and dark Ethiopians; even the contradictory Smuts, slave-driver and humanitarian. Sally, however, was critical and uneasy.

"I see something which I fear none of you noticed. Observe how stubbornly they fight over colonial trusteeships?"

"But the Charter," interrupted Mansart. "That splendid Charter. Listen to this: 'promoting and encouraging respect for human rights and for fundamental freedoms for all without distinction as to race, sex, language or religion.'"

"Yes, but read on," said Sally, "and sense the flat contradiction in the paragraph on trusteeships for the little people of the earth; in the Trusteeship Council the imperialists can never be outvoted. I smell a rat—a big, filthy, evil rat. You see, my friends, I know Big Business. I grew up with it—I'm one of its products. Of this new ruling class, my father was a prince of the blood—a ruthless banker who gambled in human beings until he lost a huge fortune and blew out his own brains.

"I tell you, there is evil in the air. We are in today for a scientifically conceived and directed propaganda which will put Goebbels to shame. Listen, I was at Dumbarton Oaks last September as an ornamental guest whom most of those present regarded as a spy. I was not housed in the decorous old manor house with the officials—no, I was at that other mansion back in the forest. There the rulers of the earth gathered and listened and plotted. There were wires and wireless which connected us with every center of power in the world. Messengers and messages were endless and uninterrupted. We held our breath, whispered, shouted and celebrated. What a web those spiders began to weave.

"I know you all think me a dope, talking through my hat. I am telling the exact truth, save for names. I am trying to say that because I was my father's daughter, left penniless by his death, and because I worked with Harry Hopkins, I was confidently counted upon as eager to betray Hopkins and Roosevelt. I sat for a time in the inner sanctum of the men now plotting to overthrow and rule this nation and the world. I was with them that midnight last month when Roosevelt died. They drank champagne and shouted for joy."

Sally's listeners were uneasy but said nothing. Later, down in the harbor, the five had dinner together near a window looking toward the craft-laden sea. The food was good and varied. They lingered to smoke and talk.

Bishop Wilson said slowly:

"One thing in which I rejoiced now brings me pause. That is the veto. By the veto which six nations have in the Security Council, the white people hold the world in leash."

"You forget yellow China."

"That is just the point; the whites own and control China. The day they lose that control or fear its imminent loss, comes the Third World War, by whatever name it may be called."

There was a long silence and then Mansart, turning to Grey, brought up again the matter of the renewed Pan-African movement and the possibility of the NAACP supporting it.

"I'm a newcomer to the NAACP and cannot speak with authority. But we are in a singular jam. On our initiative Truman is going to appoint a Civil Rights Committee headed by Big Business, with both the NAACP and the Urban League represented. I have good reason to believe that such a committee will make a very strong report. If it does, this will indicate that Big Business is willing to compromise with Negro leaders and grant them civil rights if they in turn will keep out of the labor movement and give up the socialism of the New Deal. If the NAACP refuses to play ball it may be branded as communist and persecuted, just as they plan to destroy the Council on African Affairs and the Civil Rights Congress."

Both Mansart and Wilson were not only amazed but skeptical.

"It isn't possible!"

"I can't believe it."

Sally said, "You are due to see in America before long much that is now unbelievable."

It would have been interesting to this group if they could at this very moment have listened in at a conversation taking place at the Hopkins Hotel on the heights above. In an exclusive suite on the top floor, with a gorgeous view of the harbor, sat four white men in close conversation.

"Wilson, that's strong stuff!"

They were discussing a report for President Truman on Civil Rights for Negroes.

"It is strong."

"It means some day intermarriage and social equality between races."

"It does——"

"Then, by God——"

"Wait; either this, at our own time and in our own way, or we develop in our midst a group of bitter enemies, daily growing smarter and more united and richer by internal cooperation; open to any proposal from anywhere for secret revolt or armed rebellion—fifteen million here plus ten million in the West Indies plus at least 25 million more in the South and Central Americas!"

"Hell, they'll never revolt——"

"And never have revolted, I suppose—at least if you let us tell it; but remember Haiti, Cuba, and a dozen other islands; remember D'Ayllon, Old Providence; in New York and New Jersey and a dozen times in Virginia, South Carolina and Louisiana. Remember Vesey and Nat Turner; remember a hundred thousand fugitive slaves and a half million black soldiers, laborers and spies who settled the fate of the Civil War; remember the Chicago, Washington and Detroit riots? The majority of living human beings today the world over hate our guts. Shall we help them out by building a black atomic bomb in our own insides?"

"So you are going to let your daughter marry a 'nigger'?"

"What I want won't make a damn bit of difference to her, especially if Russia, China, India and all the Dark World get strong enough to step on our faces. And too, my dear friend, what the hell are you bellyaching about? You've got colored cousins now in every Southern state; a few more in 25 years, or a brother-in-law in fifty, won't kill you. Meantime, with just this report—not even carried out—Negroes will be frantic with joy. They'll do our will; they'll hate labor unions and fight Russia. They'll desert Africa and China. They'll worship the white rich and despise the black poor."

"Well, I still don't like it!"

"Neither do I, but what else can we do about it? It's equality or war. I say get their leaders, annex their brains; honor and promote them; separate them from their ignorant masses—separate them from boiling Africa and Caribbean upsurge. I tell you there's nothing else to do! Besides, we promise today; we start to fulfill in ten years; we step forward in 25 years. Boys, this is a program for a century."

"You mean the donkey and the carrot act?"

"More than that, boys; this is no donkey and we've got to put up more than carrots."

"I wonder," said the fourth man, hitherto silent, "I wonder! Perhaps we must offer more than carrots, but surely not as much as social equality. At least not for a long time. Admission to hotels and the social gatherings open to the public will satisfy the dark social climbers for a long time yet. You see, the Negroes have small alternatives. Their internal social structure, while extensive, can be shattered by only a slight giving in on our part. Who will attend the Alpha Phi Alpha Christmas gatherings or balls or parties, if they can go to a Waldorf-Astoria public New Year's dinner along with the ordinary white social climbers? And yet, this will be far from inclusion in the Social Register. Let's be sensible. We must yield, but such yielding can be stretched over a hundred years!"

Such was the conference at the Hopkins Hotel. Our group did not hear it.

The Bishop and President parted after the UNO conference at San Francisco. The Bishop started east, stopping in New York, where he had already accepted a place on the Board of Directors of the NAACP. He first noticed that the organization had in effect been divided into two parts. The Legal Department, with separate offices and funds, was attacking the question of color discrimination, especially in education and voting. It was having notable success, destined in the next decade to become phenomenal. The main organization, on the other hand, faced difficulties. The Civil Rights Report was still only on paper; the FEPC had received no impetus from President Truman, despite his promises; and the old question of relations with trade unions and the labor movement still faced the old hesitation.

If, now, the organization were to begin pushing agitation for civil rights beyond the program of the Legal Department; especially, if it now were to join the labor movement and help the progressives toward the new aims of this world-wide movement, it would without doubt be charged with Communism and, like most current movements for social uplift, be publicly proscribed as "subversive." In these vital fields, therefore, the organization was cautiously marking time and waiting and, at the same time, with difficulty keeping its more reactionary elements from joining the national witch-hunt.

The Bishop was puzzled, but being a newcomer on the Board, ventured but one suggestion, and that was that the NAACP take part in the projected Fifth Pan-American Congress to be held in England in the fall of 1945. With some reluctance the Board of Directors authorized Bishop Wilson to attend the Pan-African Congress as their representative. The Bishop eventually thus came into the international labor movement.

Early in 1945, the World Federation of Trade Unions was formed in Paris, and there were representatives of various African provinces and countries present. There arose some difficulty over the right of these African trade union representatives to speak for themselves and not be spoken for by the trade union organizations in the mother countries—the English trade unions, for instance, wanted to be the mouthpiece for the British Africans. Otherwise what might not colonial labor demand? After a considerable struggle, the Africans won their right to speak for themselves.

Then various of these African representatives proposed that immediately following the labor congress there be called another Pan-African congress. They thus took up the idea which the NAACP had started back in 1919, under which four Pan-African congresses had already been held. It was first proposed then, that a Fifth Pan-African Congress be held in Paris in the fall of 1945, but certain difficulties developed, partly connected with the war, which made it necessary to transfer the meeting to London. The Fifth Pan-African Congress, to which Bishop Wilson was sent, was thus scheduled to meet in London.

Here, new difficulties arose, undoubtedly instigated by the government, which made it impossible to find adequate halls in which to meet or to secure suitable boarding accommodations. Finally, a local organization in the city of Manchester undertook to grapple with the matter, the Congress was called to convene in Manchester, and in October, 1945 the Fifth Pan-African Congress was held.

The Bishop planned to visit the Pan-African Congress with Sojourner, intending then to go to West Africa to devote himself to his church work. It had been arranged that during their absence, their little daughter would stay with the wife of Judge Mansart. But at the last moment this plan was changed and the little three-year-old girl, named "Africa," flew with her parents to England and went with them later to Africa.

More than 100 delegates met in Chorlton Town Hall, Manchester. For the most part they were delegates sent directly from African colonies. Represented were Gambia with 200,000 Negroes, Sierra Leone with a million, the Gold Coast with four million; the Union of South Africa with seven and a half million natives and other colored people; Nigeria with 30 millions and representatives from still other colonies in North Africa and the West Indies.

The delegates were young men, some of them immature and enthusiastic, others with considerable experience in colonial life and social development. The proceedings were of great interest, the speakers exhibiting not only the natural and sometimes emotional eloquence of Negroes, but also an illuminating substratum of knowledge of hard fact and careful judgment.

One could trace in the speeches two clear tendencies; self-criticism, warnings against inner class conflict; urgings to sacrifice as the beginning of reform. The other, and the stronger, a demand—sometimes arising to bitterness—for self-government and even independence. The basis of these demands, as developed in many of the speeches, were an exposition of colonial conditions that astonished even many who knew something of what colonies mean. It was emphasized, for instance, that in West Africa, under the controls of the War Administration, ginger, which used to sell at 25 pounds a ton and rose in wartime to 100 pounds, was bought from the black farmers, under compulsion, at 11 pounds and 30 pounds. Representatives of 300,000 farmers of the Gold Coast complained bitterly of the cocoa situation and the refusal of the new Colonial Secretary of the Labor Government even to listen to proposals that involved any change in the Economic Controls then in effect. Each speaker emphasized the poverty—the grinding poverty—of West Africa, of families receiving an average of 5 pounds a year for their work, and skilled labor toiling to earn barely 2 shillings a day.

Among the persons whom Bishop Wilson met at this congress were several whom years afterward he had cause to remember. There was Jomo Kenyatta, a tall, bearded man from Kenya, leader of the native movement. There was Kwame Nkrumah who, a few years later became the first prime minister of the Gold Coast. There was Wallace Johnson, the trade union leader in Sierra Leone, and several other black men from South Africa and Liberia who were destined to play important roles in the African liberation movement.

The final resolutions said in part:

> "The delegates of the Fifth Pan-African Congress believe in peace. How could it be otherwise when, for centuries the African peoples have been victims of violence and slavery. Yet if the Western world is still determined to rule mankind by force, then Africans, as a last resort, may have to appeal to force in the effort to achieve Freedom, even if force destroys them and the world.
>
> "We are determined to be free. We want education, the right to earn a decent living; the right to express our thoughts and emotions, and to adopt and create forms of beauty. Without all this, we die to live.
>
> "We demand for Black Africa autonomy and independence, so far and no further than it is possible in the 'ONE WORLD' for groups and peoples to rule themselves subject to inevitable world unity and federation.
>
> "We are not ashamed to have been an age-long patient people. We are willing even now to sacrifice and strive to correct our all too human faults. But we are unwilling to starve any longer while doing the world's drudgery, in order to support, by our poverty and ignorance, a false aristocracy and a discredited Imperialism.
>
> "We condemn monopoly of capital and rule of private wealth and industry for private profit alone. We welcome economic Democracy as the only real democracy; wherefore we are going to complain, appeal and arraign. We are going to make the world listen to the facts of our conditions. For their betterment we are going to fight in all and every way we can.
>
> "The Fifth Pan-African Congress, therefore, calls on the workers and farmers of the Colonies to organize effectively. Colonial workers must be in the front lines of the battle against Imperialism. Your weapons—the Strike and the Boycott—are invincible.
>
> "This Fifth Pan-African Congress calls upon the intellectuals and professional classes of the colonies to awaken to their responsibilities. The long, long night is over. By fighting for trade union rights, the right to form co-operatives, freedom of the press, assembly, demonstration and strike; freedom to print and read the literature which is necessary for the education of the masses, you will be using the only means by which your liberties will be won and maintained. Today there is only one road to effective action—the organization of the masses.
>
> "Colonial and Subject Peoples of the World—Unite!"

These proceedings the Bishop duly reported to the NAACP in America: but such a program was too forthright for this organization to dare espouse at that juncture. It therefore quietly dropped this entire program.

During the next three years Bishop Wilson, moving on to West Africa, watched the world in considerable perplexity. First he saw the American and western trade unions try to smash the new Federation formed at Paris; ostensibly to oppose Communist trade unions, but also, as Wilson knew, to still the voice of colonial unions and forestall demands for wages more nearly equal to wages in the home countries. In both West Africa and the West Indies, the Negroes hesitated lest they be charged with Communism. But Wilson saw revolution in West Africa and unrest all over the continent. Meeting Padmore, the black English leader, the Bishop ventured to visit Liberia in a plane which used the great airport which the United States built for the Republic of Liberia.

Wilson looked down upon the vast rubber plantations which Firestone leased, and on forest, river and land which Stettinius and his associates controlled forever.

He said, "I am not sure I am right, but I feel as though I was returning home as a missionary from Africa to America."

He and Sojourner came back to talk about what was happening in Africa and what might happen to the colored people in the United States. It was a great event for Judge Mansart and his wife in New York. And in Macon President Mansart and Jean celebrated the return by a concert featuring African music which Sojourner conducted.

The Potsdam conference, the second peace effort of the reorganized world came just as President Mansart returned from San Francisco. Jean noted with distress that Truman, utterly ignorant of foreign affairs, was himself going to replace Roosevelt at the conference table, taking with him as Secretary of State, Byrnes of South Carolina.

"Byrnes? Isn't he a rabid enemy of our people?"

"Certainly. Remember how he defended lynching in Congress? But worse than that he is the last man to deal with the Russians. He was trained to despise workers, black and white."

"But Roosevelt liked him!"

"Yes, but as administrator in the war effort at home—never as negotiator with Stalin."

So it happened and Mansart saw the peace conference turn into the beginnings of new war. Atlee displaced the astonished and disgruntled Churchill, but Churchill made friends with Truman and flattered him. The war of worlds was reborn because Truman held the greatest secret of the modern world. It gave him a power which drove him wild. He was sure the United States was master of the universe. At Potsdam he only whispered it but the arrogance with which he conducted himself was unbounded.

The United States had the secret of splitting the atom and releasing its giant energy. Where Roosevelt would have shuddered before this power and stood humble before his terrible responsibility, Truman got arrogant and Byrnes "got tough"! It has been agreed by the victorious powers to disarm Germany and make her pay indemnity for ruling half the world. But the United States did not mean to keep its word. It had started on another path. A week later, without warning, American planes dropped on the unarmed women and children of Hiroshima and Nagasaki in Japan, a frightful catastrophe, killing 150,000 persons and maiming others to the second and third generation. It was the most awful deliberate mass murder that modern civilization had ever seen. It smashed Japan and made Soviet aid to America unnecessary.

Truman and Churchill immediately determined to crush Communism and regain control of the Baltic states, and eventually of Russia. This program Churchill soon published in the United States at the invitation of his new friend, Truman. Truman found himself in the powerful hands of a new regime; the big bankers, spokesmen for the New York Stock Exchange, the life insurance, steel, oil, railroad, and automobile interests entered his cabinet. Lend-Lease to Russia was stopped, payment for it was demanded and loans refused for restoration of the ally who had won the war for the West at terrible sacrifice. Already, Truman knew he had China, led by Chiang Kai-shek and the Soongs, in his pocket.

One other thing Jean made President Mansart think of, partly because due to convention he had ignored it, but also because it seemed to her really important.

She said, "Joe Louis has been in the front lines entertaining the soldiers."

Mansart listened. Of course he knew about Joe Louis. Louis had been a new person in the Negro world, of whom President Mansart heard while in Germany—and tried to forget. But on his return, he found that ignoring Joe Louis was impossible. Joe Louis loomed in the nation, in the world, and was without doubt regarded by public opinion as the greatest man in the Negro race. He was both hero and legend—this poor, unlettered Negro boy from the plantation slums of Alabama, who had not spent a single day in school and had worked like a dog for Henry Ford.

Then the sportsmen and gamblers saw his magnificent bronze body; under their guidance he had through sheer skill and dogged endurance risen to be first Boxer of the world. His vast strength, carefully trained and artfully guided, had knocked out Carnera the Giant, Braddock the American, and Schmelling the German, in good, clean fighting. Mansart knew this was not the greatest career for a man, but who could stand and protest in a world of war not only not clean but unfair, deceptive, dirty? If they didn't like Joe's profession, why didn't they train him for another? In his sphere he achieved greatness.

Then too, Joe Louis with his silent, expressionless face, traveled 30,000 miles to entertain the distraught soldiers of world catastrophe.

Jean said, "He should have a Congressional Medal."

Mansart was silent. He had never countenanced boxing in his school. He had never mentioned Joe Louis in his talks to the students. He felt guilty. In this rotten world Joe stood high among men!

Bishop Wilson and President Mansart talked earnestly about what was happening in the United States. Greater civil rights for Negroes seemed certain although the President was still doing little to implement his promises. There was aid for Turkey and Greece, or was it for control of oil in the Middle East—oil for war in face of the world cry for peace? In China our State Department was boosting and aiding Chiang Kai-shek. Was that truly aiding China?

Above all, the Bishop wondered about the Union of Soviet Socialist Republics.

"I cannot believe that Communism is simply a conspiracy."

"Nor," said Mansart, "do I. But are you quite fair to American Big Business? I realize what a marvellous technique we have, what tremendous factories and industries. We must give credit and much power to the creators of this industrial miracle."

"Yes, indeed we must, but we must not let American business choke us, destroy our souls, prevent democracy and ruin taste and art. Mass production is too often mass slavery and stoppage of progress. Americans used to be able to choose different types of autos. Now they are all alike. Shoes have not altered since 1700; they are still wide at the heel and narrow at the toe, while the human foot is just the opposite. In clothes, homes, buildings, individual taste is captive to profits for mass manufacture. There can be no mending, patching or repairing; we throw away shirts, trousers, pots and pans, waste wool, tin, copper, and steel to rape more from the earth for more private profits. We build roads for speed not for scenery; we erect buildings for floor space not for comfort. We hold inventions off the market if they threaten profits. We use patents for monopoly, not to encourage ability and genius. We are slaves of our industry instead of its masters. Is this necessary? Can we not improve it? And must we fight the Soviets to help ourselves and the world?"

CHAPTER XV

The Attack on Mansart

The luncheon at the Womens Club in Atlanta, in the fall of 1950, was most successful. There were six persons present—all white of course, three of them Southerners. Clair, the representative of the new Maloney Fund said, as the coffee came, that his fund would gladly give $50,000 now for a new study of American Negroes and more if needed. He was a Northern man of sixty who had just retired from automobiles and entered philanthropy. The white Southern college president, a vivid man of 45, explained that his institution would undertake the research.

"Fine," said the politician, now 37 and sure to be the next governor of the state. "For a time the Negroes controlled the study of their race in America, and they put out some vicious propaganda; which, even if true, was bad for publicity for the South and for the white race. We can now know the truth and publish as much of it as is good, and color it our way."

Clair looked a bit uneasy, and the President hastened to explain that naturally the work of investigation would be strictly scientific—

Mrs. Emery, a clubwoman, interrupted. "Naturally, naturally; who could doubt that! Yet, it is better to have reports made with some reference to our good name and recognition of our intentions. The world must not continue to think that the chief industry of the South is lynching."

The Northern sociologist remarked: "And it is the Negroes' own fault that their studies were given up. Atlanta University started them in 1897, dropped them in 1915, tried to revive them in 1938 and then let them lapse entirely. Of course, white students can do them much better."

"Now," said the chairman, "this is the situation. Negroes have been complaining of not getting their share of educational expenditures, state and federal. It was true. But a determined effort is being made to remedy this. Unless it succeeds, this race separation in schools will lapse because of lack of funds for a double system, or even by court decision."

Mrs. Emery declared, "That must never be!"

The politician added, "If it comes, the South will rebel!"

"Oh no!" said Clair hastily, "but we must get enough funds to meet the cost of equal educational systems."

"It will take a lot," volunteered the sociologist.

"At any rate, we must try," said the politician. "Our state of South Carolina is leading and will persist."

"Already," added the chairman, "we have enough figures to send out a report which will show that the two systems are so rapidly approaching equality that complaint will soon be absolutely unjustifiable."

"Splendid," said several. And Clair added, "Make it a book. We'll give it wide circulation."

"Suppose, however," said the sociologist, "that the Supreme Court should forbid public school segregation?"

The politician was firm. "They'll never do it. Or if by unthinkable chance they do, it'll be a four-five decision and immediately reversed. Moreover, the 'niggers' themselves don't want integrated schools. The black teachers would lose their jobs and the black children suffer hell!"

The college president demurred. "It is true that no decisive Supreme Court edict is probable, but in the unlikely case it came, then remember that Negro opinion would force all Negroes to demand the right. They have been yelling for equality too long to refuse it when offered."

The sociologist again ventured advice. "Remember, however, that if equality keeps on being refused, the Communists will continue to make capital out of this and the Negroes will more and more listen to them. Moreover, we'll continue to build up a dangerous group solidarity right within our borders based on that very race pride which we have preached and they have lately accepted. I tell you, they've got us over a log."

Mrs. Emery sniffed. "You are giving Negroes too much credit for brains. Think of what will happen if the Supreme Court should be so crazy as to order integration of the schools—the Negroes could then blackmail us into complete social equality on pain of going Communist."

Both Mr. Clair and the college president intervened.

"There's not the slightest chance that the Supreme Court will interfere with the present long-established pattern of race separation in the United States. We now have only to see that school appropriations become more equitable and that this is widely known."

The president, however, added thoughtfully, "Of course, we are facing the upsurge of the colored peoples and we cannot minimize that fact. Britain has freed India. Who would have dreamed that ever possible! China has the bit in her teeth. This country must see that she drops it soon. It was a mistake for America and Britain to assume that the fall of Japan left China helpless in their hands if power stayed in the grasp of Chiang Kai-shek, their puppet. Silently, irresistibly, China arose. No power or plot of America sufficed to hold her and the arms furnished Chiang dropped into the hands of the Communists. I am not so certain as some that Formosa can be depended on. Of course, the Chinese Republic will eventually fail."

"It won't fail!" The gruff interruption came from the oil millionaire, Vanderburg. He had been expected to be present and to flaunt his power; but as usual he was late—he was used to having people wait for him. "China won't fail in our day and Chiang is finished. The Supreme Court is bound to stop segregation—if not this year, then soon. We've just got to give up this foolish notion that we have the earth by the tail or that we own all the brains. We don't. 'Niggers' and 'Chinks' are as smart as we if they have the chance. What we've got to do is to see they don't get that chance.

"Continued segregation here in the United States means inevitably building a closely integrated group with leaders, organizations, plans. This mustn't happen. We've got to integrate 'Niggers' into our group and work them into positions under us, but below policy making and giving orders. We've got to cut down, for instance, the power of these Land-Grant college presidents and keep power in our own hands to be carried out by our own puppets, in place of the present gang who've got too much brains. I've just got myself elected to the Board of the State College at Macon. I'm going to get rid of Mansart. Don't fool yourselves—unless we're smart the darkies of the world are going to give us hell. We didn't lose China; China kicked us out." And Vanderburg, with an abrupt nod here and there, marched out.

The group was astonished, but their convictions were not altered at all by this outburst.

Clair smiled deprecatingly. "I'm afraid our friend exaggerates."

"He certainly does," echoed the college president, while the sociologist disdainfully sniffed. The meeting closed after a few more pleasant exchanges and encouraging remarks. As they drifted out, Mrs. Emery shook out her gown and eased her girdle. Pursing her rather full lips, she let fall a few words out of the side of her mouth into the receptive ear of the politician.

"I understand that Vanderburg's high opinion of Negroes extends even to their women's beds."

Meantime, down in Macon signs multiplied of coming trouble for President Mansart's administration. Though he had not forgotten it, he did not let his mind dwell on an occurrence at the first Board meeting following his return from San Francisco. A well-signed petition was brought before the Board demanding a stadium in which competitive athletic games could be played. Manuel had never encouraged athletics and was particularly opposed to intercollegiate sports. This attitude was not unrelated to his memory of his son, Bruce.

Sports brought a species of inter-racial mingling which he feared. The white people of Macon, especially the merchants and white collar workers, were starved for entertainment and flocked to the colored games. There, separate seats had to be furnished and some of the local citizenry thus had their feelings of race superiority prodded. Incidents of race clashes occurred frequently; they were seldom serious, but Manuel disliked the situation.

Also, it seemed to him unusual that this petition, signed in the main by his own college alumni, instead of being brought to his attention first, came up in the Board from the hands of a white oil man from Texas—Vanderburg.

Betty Lou Baldwin had died in 1947. Just before her death, she had summoned a cousin of her daughter-in-law, from Texas. Her son John was failing in health and her grandson, Lee, needed more guidance than his mother could give.

Betty Lou thought that Vanderburg, as the nearest male relative, representing the tremendous industrial upsurge of the Southwest in chemicals, sulphur and especially in oil—with its tax-free bonanza—might be a good influence to introduce into the Baldwin family and its many interests.

Vanderburg acquiesced. He opened an office in Atlanta, became a director of Baldwin's bank, and was soon elected to the Board of Trustees of the Colored State College. Then Betty Lou died, not exactly in peace but at least not without hope.

John Baldwin had by no means retired, but he was glad to give up smaller duties to others, and his family relations were far from pleasant. Vanderburg quickly took over supervision of the state school, although Baldwin continued to visit it now and then.

Vanderburg had ideas about Negro colleges. One of them concerned Negro athletics and he accompanied his proposal and petition for a stadium by a gift of oil bonds with a face value of $100,000. Such a gift had to be received with thanks. Mansart put the bonds in the college safe and took no immediate action.

Mansart's calls away from the college were, as he knew, getting to be too many and he meant to curtail them. But another annual meeting of the presidents of the colored Land-Grant colleges, to be held in Atlanta, was coming up, and he felt obliged to attend. He felt he wanted to consult his collegues on many urgent problems of which inter-collegiate athletics was one. He hurried off to Atlanta.

The day after he departed, a woman entered the Dean's office with a letter of introduction from the benevolent oil man. She was a light mulatto, striking in appearance, well-dressed, and carried herself with assurance. Her English was perfect and she evidently had a keen, well-trained mind. She said, after greetings:

"I was sent by Mr. Vanderburg. Some time ago I applied for a position as teacher here."

Jean remembered that Vanderburg in 1949 had pressed the appointment of Mrs. Grey to the faculty to teach social science. The matter had been postponed for further inquiry. Mrs. Grey had a master's degree from Chicago and seemed well qualified. But social science was Jean's own field and she had no wish to share it. She was easily able to do all the work of the department, even after her appointment as dean. But this was because the world war had stopped the development of her cherished Plan of Social Study by the Land-Grant colleges. When and if this plan was revived, as she was determined it should be, Jean would have little time for undergraduate teaching and another teacher would be needed.

All this flashed through Jean's mind as she looked Mrs. Grey over. She did not like her. Why, it would have been hard to say. But hitherto the faculty had been carefully chosen and was on the whole harmonious. Friction, of course, had arisen here and there from temperment, envy, and ambition. But Mansart's character, backed by his great influence and Jean's advice and knowledge, had kept relations pretty good—with one exception. At the time the President had gone to Chicago and thence to the UNO in San Francisco, an appointment had been made in "Business" which Jean still regretted.

John Jacobs was quiet and presentable, but he was not interested in the school as an institution of learning. He might be playing a part for forces outside—of this Jean was not sure. She could not confirm her suspicions and planned to talk to Mansart about it. Meantime, under pressure from the white members of the Board, Jacobs became bursar of the college. He was a thin, dark man, unobtrusive and accurate, and taught bookkeeping. His wife was a silent, black, mouse-like little woman.

Yet Jacobs did not exactly fit in. He seemed to feel that his office was not accorded the recognition it merited. As bursar, he felt he should be consulted more often on major policy decisions. Jean saw that there was some basis for this complaint. The President and she had long been accustomed to run things without much outside consultation; because they understood each other so thoroughly and agreed so completely on policy, further consultation seemed unnecessary. If Jacobs had been more companionable and had evidenced a deeper understanding of college problems, he might easily have grown to occupy a more important place. But because of his attitude toward the institution as a machine rather than a group of human beings and his slow, reserved, almost sensitive ways, it became customary on the part of Jean and President Mansart to ignore or even forget him.

The proposed appointment of Mrs. Grey had been pressed lately but decision had been avoided only because of Jean's insistence that the President had not yet had time to reach a conclusion. No appointment had ever been made by the Board without his recommendation. Vanderburg was nettled and showed it, but the Board had too high an opinion of Mansart to rush the matter through.

Meantime, Jean tried to obtain some information concerning Mrs. Grey, and, quite accidentally, found it in the story of a student. This student had been employed during the summer in the office of Mr. Vanderburg in Atlanta. He assured Jean that Mrs. Grey was a frequent visitor there and that there was much talk about her. No, he could not obtain testimony or sworn statements, but her general reputation was not what one would call good.

This information Jean relayed to President Mansart. He had made up his mind what he was going to do. There was no use resorting to detectives and secret photography or similar methods. On the contrary, he made up his mind that a visit to Mrs. Vanderburg in Atlanta would not be amiss. He telephoned for an appointment, identifying himself as president of the State College.

She was surprised to find him colored. So far as she remembered, no colored man of this type had ever asked to call upon her. But she was not narrowly prejudiced and, after all he was from the college in Macon. She was interested. She received him at the front door but seated him in the hall; she continued with the burnishing of her nails during the conversation.

"President Mansart," she said after he had explained his visit, "you have asked me something that ordinarily I would not talk about. And yet, I do think that you need protection in this case. Mrs. Grey, to be quite frank, is a bitch. She and my husband for some years have been, shall we say, seeing a good deal of each other. She is a brilliant woman, and besides entertaining him she does dirty work of various kinds for him. Ordinarily, she would be about the last person to have at your school.

"On the other hand, let me give you a frank piece of advice. If you don't have her, you'll have someone else. This is the great age of spying and lying. They're going to plant somebody there to find out about you or to make up plausible fairy tales. It might be the wise thing for you to accept a person whom they nominate and whom you know."

"Thank you for calling." And Mrs. Vanderburg arose.

As they walked toward the door, she said, "You will, of course, wonder why I endure Mrs. Grey. The reason is simple. By not interfering with my husband's affairs in business or love I keep my own freedom. I associate with such persons as I wish, I spend as much money as I want to, and I go where and when I will. Of course, I could imagine something much finer than this without money and without freedom, but the choice has not been given me. I trust you understand, President Mansart?"

President Mansart said he did, and thanked her humbly. And the appointment of Mrs. Grey to the Department of Sociology in the Georgia State Colored College went through. From then on, President Mansart and Jean made it their business to give much more careful and concentrated attention to the college and to the currents within it of opposition and disintegration. First of all, the stadium must be built. All his fellow-presidents had advised this for many and differing reasons; not least among which was the unusual gift of bonds. Unobtrusively, Mansart had plans drawn and surveys made.

Meantime, Mrs. Grey moved swiftly. She organized her program of teaching and taught well; she learned all she could about the college, its personnel, their relations. It occurred to her, or was suggested, that John Jacobs, the bursar of the State College, might be useful for some of the plans she had in mind. Vanderburg was impatient. He had an over-simplified idea of public institutions and of state officials. He was in a hurry to locate the graft in this college—who got it, how it was worked, by whom. He had no doubt that Mansart was getting more than his small salary—otherwise he was a fool.

Vanderburg wanted to increase his control over the college. Its funds, its attendance and its reputation were growing. Up to this time, nothing wrong financially had been discovered. The college was well-run, although its accounting methods were not exactly up-to-date. Still, there was no patent dishonesty. On the other hand, if there really was no dishonesty, then it must be manufactured—and Mansart removed.

Mrs. Grey soon observed that Jacobs, the bursar, was not happy. He was quiet, unnoticed, usually alone. Mansart ran the financial affairs of the college himself, with Jacob's role limited to that of top clerk. Nevertheless Jacobs did retain certain responsibilities. He kept accounts, had access to important papers and to the safe. Mrs. Grey, therefore, made a distinct set for Jacobs, which was something so unusual in his life that it almost frightened him.

He lived in a home in the surburbs of Macon, back of the college—a nice site but undeveloped. The house was old-fashioned, comfortable, but in no way striking. It was a simple, two-story residence built on stilts in the Southern style and without a cellar. His wife, a meek, dull-faced brown woman, obeyed her husband without question. She kept house well, was a good cook and punctual, but neither did nor said anything out of the ordinary.

Mrs. Grey began to put her plans into effect. First, after an apparently fruitless search for lodgings, she proposed to make her home at Jacobs' house. He was pleased, but for that purpose Mrs. Grey asked that the second story be substantially rebuilt and refurnished. Under her guidance, this was tastefully and comfortably done, but it called for more money than Jacobs could spare. Mrs. Grey gladly loaned him the money on his note. She then proposed that he ought to build a basement and furnish a playroom where he could entertain his friends and neighbors at cards. She had in mind the need for a place where meetings might take place far from the attention of the public, colored or white.

Again Jacobs hesitated, and again Mrs. Grey was accommodating. She managed, without commitment of any definite word or gesture, to make him begin to think of the possibility of something romantic entering into his bleak life, even daring to believe that this very elegant and striking woman was actually *personally* interested in him, and that somehow, a future life might be shared between them. He hastened to agree to her playroom, but had to borrow so much more money to build it that without realizing it his promissory notes were soon transformed into a sizeable mortgage. His wife signed the mortgage without reading it and without asking questions.

A cellar was dug beneath the home, and a cement foundation and tile floor and walls put in. It was nearly finished save on one side where the tile had reached only half-way up to the ceiling. There was left between it and the yard a wide, excavated hole. This was to be finished in the next few days.

It was at this stage that Mrs. Grey found an opportunity to sit down in the cellar and speak confidentially with Jacobs, beginning to unfold her further plans. She did not realize that her voice could easily be heard through the thin partitions of the floor of the kitchen where Jacobs' dull-faced wife sat sewing. Mrs. Grey was encouraging Jacobs to talk about his position and duties. Yes, he kept books—that was about all. He did not sign checks. He was seldom called in to discuss plans such as, for instance, the projected stadium.

"Where, by the way," asked Mrs. Grey, "are those bonds kept that were given to build the stadium?"

"In the safe, or at least they were."

"You have the key or combination?"

"Yes, and so do the President and Dean."

Mrs. Grey hummed. Then she said, "John—— Oh, pardon me for using your name. . . ."

Jacobs assured her it was a pleasure to hear her call him by his first name. She proceeded.

"John, have you by chance noticed the daily quotations on these particular oil bonds?"

Jacobs had never noticed the prices of bonds of any sort, and said so.

"Well, these bonds are steadily rising in price. Moreover, you know that I have inner sources of information. These bonds will continue to rise markedly for another week; then they will suddenly drop to a very low point."

"But——"

"Wait; when they are at or near their highest, if the bonds were in my hands for say, 24 hours, I could clean up from fifteen to twenty thousand dollars and restore the bonds intact. But their value would be by that time far below par and the college would lose money. It might later leak out that somebody had meantime made money on them. The President or even that prissy Dean might be suspected."

Jacobs looked scared. Mrs. Grey continued.

"They couldn't suspect you for the deal would be carried out in Atlanta while you would be here. Moreover, in any case you would be protected by powerful friends whom I know. Suppose now you secure those bonds and put them in my hands for 24 hours?"

"They'd never think of President Mansart's taking them if he denied it; he's absolutely honest. He'd vouch for the Dean."

"Of course. But he might be accused of criminal carelessness in the handling of bonds destined for a project which he never favored."

"I suppose so."

"Certainly so. It would hasten Mansart's retirement. And,"—Mrs. Grey leaned nearer and lowered her voice—"John, as he goes out we move in, understand?" Her bosom touched his chest; her lips, subtly perfumed, brushed his cheek. There surged in him a rush of passion such as he had never known before.

"Listen, John," she said, "I want you to take those bonds and give them to me."

"And go to jail for theft?"

"Certainly not. Mansart is responsible for the bonds, even though you and that Dean have access to the safe. But it is Mansart who alone is responsible. If the bonds disappear, he will be the last to accuse or suspect either of you. You will not have left Macon. He will suspect thieves, and the Board will, at the least, accuse him of carelessness, especially since he opposed the gift."

"But suppose the bonds are traced to you?"

"They won't be. I shall leave Macon Friday and not be seen until Monday afternoon at my one o'clock class. I'll slip back Saturday night and get the bonds from you. No one will see me but you. I shall take the bonds to Atlanta and hand them to Mr. Vanderburg who gave them to the college. I assure you, dear John, no one will suffer for the disappearance of these bonds but Mansart."

Jacobs, the sweat streaming down his face, promised to "think it over." Mrs. Grey gave him a week; then they talked again. Jacobs had not been consulted by the President and the Dean as to the future stadium or their plans. He felt more affronted than usual. Mrs. Grey took his hand and said:

"Listen John. I am going to Atlanta this weekend on some business. After I have gone, not before, just open the safe and take out those bonds. I will slip back secretly and take the bonds back to Atlanta."

"Why go away at all?"

"So that I cannot be connected with the disappearance of the bonds if discovered, and you cannot be connected with me!"

Jacobs was afraid, but the idea kept turning over in his mind until Mrs. Grey went north on a Friday afternoon. The next night she was to return secretly.

Meantime Jean, almost by accident, had noted the rise in oil bond quotations in the morning papers, in the course of checking some of their bond holdings. She waited until the lunch hour when the executive offices were empty and then, securing the bonds, compared notes. The bonds they held were quoted currently at 117. If they were going to fluctuate like that, she thought, they should be sold. She hurried over to the president's home and interrupted his nap.

"We should sell those bonds today. If they drop, we will be held responsible for any loss."

"But we cannot sell here. Atlanta is the only market with New York connections."

"Tomorrow is Friday. Suppose I drive up to Atlanta tonight and go to Baldwin's bank tomorrow morning. When the Board meets Tuesday we'll not only have plans ready for the stadium but $117,000 cash with which to build it."

Mansart agreed and Jean went to Atlanta late that afternoon.

On the following Saturday night the little dull-faced wife of John Jacobs was sitting in her living room motionless. Sometime after dark she heard the gate open and saw Mrs. Grey slip softly through it. She used her key to enter the front door, then went down to the playroom to see how matters stood. She looked at her watch, wandered about, then got up on the scaffolding where the tile foundation was being finished, to look over into the open hole. Suddenly from behind came first a gentle and then a strong push. She fell headlong into the hole and on her fell a wheelbarrow of cement intended for use in finishing the wall.

The little brown woman went swiftly upstairs and outdoors. She began shoveling dirt into the hole. She worked furiously for four hours until she had covered the wheelbarrow and cement and reached almost to the height of the wall. Within the hole there was no sound or motion. Then she went back into the house and took Mrs. Grey's handbag, searched for her keys, went to her room and found the mortgage. She burned it in her stove.

Jacobs came home quite late. He did not bring the bonds. He had opened the safe soon after the President and Dean had left Friday afternoon. He often stayed to clean up odds and ends of the day's work. Slipping his hands quietly into the safe he reached for the bonds. They were not in their accustomed place. He looked about. He could not find them. Perhaps they had been taken out for the committee meeting Tuesday, he thought, and left carelessly on the President's desk. He could not find them there and did not dare force the lock. Besides, this was unlikely and the President had said nothing.

Reluctantly, Jacobs left and locked the safe. He was almost afraid to face Mrs. Grey, but the fault was not his. He realized more and more that what he had tried to do might, if he had been successful, have put him in jail, and certainly would have ruined President Mansart. His feeling for Mrs. Grey was strong, even tumultuous. But he was not a fool. He resolved to go no further with this extraordinary plan. He lingered in town, went to a movie and finally returned home late. Mrs. Grey was not there. Finally, he woke his sleeping wife.

"Mrs. Grey come yet?"

"No," she said.

"Heard nothing from her?"

"Not a word."

He waited for Mrs. Grey until nearly dawn. Still she did not come.

"That's queer," he said, and reluctantly went to bed. It remained queer. Nothing more was ever heard of Mrs. Grey.

Vanderburg, awaiting her in Atlanta, was beside himself. When he arrived for the Board meeting Tuesday he summoned Jacobs, after failing to find Mrs. Grey.

"Where's Althea—Mrs. Grey?"

Jacobs said he did not know, and then seeing the rage on Vanderburg's face he blurted out the whole plot which he was sure Vanderburg already knew.

Vanderburg yelled: "But the bonds were sold Friday in Atlanta at the top of the market. Today they're down to 87 as I planned they would be. Where the hell is Althea? Has she been murdered and the bonds stolen?"

"That Dean got them bonds and sold them," said Jacobs. "She must have murdered Mrs. Grey and stole the premium."

"All right, when she reports to the Board today we'll know."

Jacobs went as Vanderburg stormed out. But the Board meeting revealed nothing except completed plans for the delayed stadium. The Dean reported that she had sold the bonds at a premium at Mr. Baldwin's bank in Atlanta Friday morning and that the college had $117,000 on hand for the stadium building fund. Vanderburg sat dumb. He could not ask how the Dean got the bonds from Mrs. Grey; he was naturally not supposed to know Mrs. Grey ever had the bonds, if indeed she ever had. Whether she had or had not, she had been fouly done away with.

He sought out Jacobs who was equally distraught. He had never given Mrs. Grey the bonds for they were gone Friday night when he tried to get them. But Mrs. Grey—poor Mrs. Grey had met foul play. But how, where and from whom?

The college and President, especially the Dean, made every effort to trace Mrs. Grey, without success. Her car was safe in her garage. Had she gone to Atlanta by train? The train hands had not seen her and she was a noticeable figure in the "Jim-Crow" car. Where had she gone and when?

Vanderburg was suspicious of everybody. He quickly sent for private investigators from New York. They searched Mrs. Grey's office. They searched Jacob's house from cellar to attic; they tore her bedroom apart. They ransacked her car. Mrs. Grey was never found. Also, to Jacobs' unanswerable distress, no record was ever found of the mortgage which she held on his house. It had never been registered nor was payment ever demanded.

But always John Jacobs waited for her. He glimpsed her in crowds or dissolving in the darkness of night. The play room was finished and Mrs. Jacobs kept it immaculate. But no company was invited in. Often Jacobs sat there alone in the dim light. At such times he often thought he heard the footsteps of Althea Grey and caught a whiff of perfume.

Disturbing as this occurrence was, neither the President nor the Dean were as much upset by it as by what they perceived and guessed concerning the world about them. From the day that Harry Truman announced as his doctrine the crushing of "Communist aggression," both watched events tensely. The campaign of 1948 looked like the one way out of inevitable war. More than that, it would be a return to the New Deal and Wallace seemed like the man chosen for the job.

President Mansart thought it unwise to take a political stand or to go to Philadelphia to the founding convention of the Progressive Party. But Jean slipped away; she saw the enthusiastic throng. She heard Shirley Graham bring them shouting to their feet with the cry: "Jim Crow must go!" The campaign swept on, and Wallace fought for Negro freedom as well as Peace. The South was torn in two, almost in three. It was the fight of the New Deal against its betrayal since Roosevelt's death, and Tom Dewey typified that betrayal.

What happened was not simply the defeat of Dewey—which the voters desired—but the election of Truman who never himself dreamed of election. The rotten borough voting system did it—democracy simply could not work. Those who wanted to vote for Wallace could only vote for Truman where Wallace was not on the ticket.

But this was not clear to the public, least of all, to Truman. He leaped to power with a flourish. "I am FDR and all his plans," he pompously announced. And with his cry came the shadow of death. His cabinet and his policies were changed before his face by the vast forces which he himself had nurtured in the past seven years. Finance capital, monopoly industry, colonial trade, the Pentagon of War seized the reins and were just settling themselves in the saddle when they were slapped in the face by China.

China, of all thinkable powers, could be counted upon as already belonging to the U.S. as a first installment of that colored world of slaves which our nation would own and drive and bleed. It took the State Department a year before it could realize that the yellow millions were actually following the Soviet Union and not the U.S. Why? It must be treachery—betrayal! Washington swung around just in time to hear that Russia already had the atom bomb. That was it. That explained all, and the only answer was war and war now!

Truman's Secretary of Defense, heading an irresistible war machine capable of immeasurable destruction—this man who stood for ships, planes, guns and atom bombs and who represented one of the world's greatest owners and purveyors of capital, the Dillon-Read bank, ran half naked along the streets of Washington shrieking, "The Russians are coming!" and when taken into custody leaped from a sixteenth-story window. Paul Robeson, forty years before, had broken Forrestal's nose in a football game.

It looked as though with Forrestal, the President and the whole nation winced. The State Department formed NATO to build within the United Nations an inner bastion against the Soviet Union; Churchill was invited to egg our students on to war. The Marshall Plan was set up to rescue European capital from loss by war and the demands of labor unions. Then, the government turned back to its home front with fury: eleven Communist leaders were sent to jail for no crime but thought of what might lead to crime; ten Hollywood writers were sent to jail on charge of "contempt of Congress;" the persecution of Alger Hiss was unleashed.

The nation—the thinking nation revolted. The best of our thought and will lent their names to a national call against war, and tried to gather in New York the best intellects of all the world to plead and argue for peace. This seemed to President Mansart so obvious a move that he gladly accepted an invitation to attend. In a great meeting like this—held at the Waldorf-Astoria—here, he was sure, was the solution. It conformed entirely to what he had learned on his trip in 1936 and to what he had been trying to preach and do since. First, Peace, and then increasing world understanding and realization of Life, Truth and Beauty.

It seemed to him that the conference at the Waldorf-Astoria was a tremendous success. But in the face of the bitter, hateful and sudden flare of opposition which followed the universal attack, he was left speechless. Why was it that New York and the nation utterly repudiated this meeting of some of the greatest men of the world? How could one of our greatest universities refuse to let Shostakovich give a concert on its campus? If it was spontaneous reaction, it was ominous. If it was planned propaganda, perhaps that was even more threatening. He returned South in silent distress.

Somehow it seemed to him that his students as individuals, and the seething dark millions back of them were melting away from his touch, were getting further and further from his influence. Once they were all his people. He had had his arms about them and was protecting and guiding them. This was no longer true. Other things, the world itself, had intruded, had come between him and the Negro people. He had been sucked up into greater and wider causes—Peace, Socialism, the meaning of all life. He wanted now to rid himself of diversion and get back to the Negro problem, to concentrate all his energy and hope there. And yet, if he and his folk were part of this wider world, how could he or they ever be really separate?

CHAPTER XVI

The Dismissal of Jean Du Bignon

In the spring of 1949 Jean Du Bignon broached to President Mansart the idea of her taking a trip to Europe. It was shortly after the meeting at the Waldorf-Astoria in New York, which had taken place in March. Jean was far more upset by the extraordinary repercussions of the meeting than was Mansart. She believed she saw deliberate organized opposition to any effective peace movement. If this were true, what was the reaction in the rest of the world? She wanted to know and she was sure that America was not prepared to tell her. She had received an invitation to a World Council of the Partisans of Peace in Paris and suddenly here seemed a chance at one time to probe the progressive forces of the world and to fulfill her long wish to see the Europe of which she had read so much and through which she had guided President Mansart. He assented without question. Peace which failed in New York might triumph in Europe. And so Jean Du Bignon sat among the 2,000 people in the Salle Pleyel in April, 1949. She had seen some of these types of peoples and races many times; but these Africans, Algerians, South Americans, Moroccans—they were not simply types for the inspection of Europeans—they were men and women, talking, arguing, demanding Peace.

Jean stood and cheered wildly with other thousands when Paul Robeson came striding across the hall from his concerts all over Europe. It seemed to her so appropriate for him to declare: "My people will never fight the Russians who have outlawed race prejudice!" The applause was tumultuous.

It was years before Jean realized the tremendous implication of this statement if ever it was implemented. It meant the splitting of eastern Europe from the white world and adding it to the power of the colored world to assert autonomy and independence of European imperialism. It led later to a fierce persecution of Robeson in America—almost to his crucifixion and the refusal to let him travel abroad or to sing at home save under restrictions. This Jean did not sense at the time, but she did later.

She began to realize almost shamefacedly how thoroughly White and American she was in thought and reaction. That afternoon she lunched with the Russian writer, Ilya Ehrenburg. She had met him while he was traveling in the southern United States and they had many notes to compare. As they were leaving the restaurant, he asked:

"Have you seen Picasso's 'Guernica'?"

She looked puzzled—"Guernica?"

He looked surprised and explained: "You know, the Spanish town which was bombed."

She did not know; indeed, she realized she had not known much. But now as she saw the mighty mural, she heard Ehrenburg tell what civilization did to the struggling workers of Spain. Britain, France and the United States let these ragged, starving women and children drown in their own blood, under the bombs of Hitler and Mussolini. It was a horrible tragedy. It was obscene!

For the first time in her life, her loyalty to the land of her birth faltered. She said nothing and would not see the tears in Ehrenburg's eyes. They returned in silence to the Salle Pleyel and she sought her seat. She sat a space in silence and found herself listening in astonishment when a woman from Viet-Nam was called to the rostrum. She looked like a rare and precious Chinese doll. She seemed hardly more than fifteen, yet she was a matron and talked the language of all civilization.

"Like other peoples," she cried, "the people of Viet-Nam want no more war. They know too much of murder, ruin, devastation not to long for Peace."

Viet-Nam? What and where was Viet-Nam, Jean asked Gabriel D'Arboussier as she listened. He was a dark West African. He answered: "The people of Viet-Nam, like the peoples of Madagascar, Africa, Asia and Oceania, see in the new masque of the French Union the old face of the French Empire. The Marshall Plan, the Atlantic Pact and the proposed Pacific pact are all designed to distribute to France and other colonial governments, money which enables them to hold, conquer and exploit their colonies."

Jean sat perplexed. Like most Americans she had always regarded the Marshall Plan as an attempt to help the needy. She had never attempted to understand the Atlantic Pact. She had thought of most of the world's peoples as backward, uncivilized, perverse—problems of civilization and also victims. She could not help but be thrilled when, knowing that Chinese and Korean delegates had not been permitted to attend the Paris Congress, she learned they were holding a simultaneous congress in Prague. She rose with the delegates when the Prague Congress announced the fall of Nanking.

It was the climax of the congress when over the wires came the voices of that Congress sitting in Prague where 213 delegates from 13 nations, excluded by the fears of the French government, had met in unison simultaneously to fulfill the world cry for Peace. The voice of the leader of the Chinese delegation, Kuo-Mo-Jo, thundered down the aisles and through the balconies of the Salle Pleyel:

"We march! We will continue to march! We will march around the world!"

Like many others, Jean's attention was centered on the Russians. In looks they were impressive: the white-crowned Metropolitan; the madonna-like mother of two war heroes; the suave writer, Fadeyev and the fiery Ehrenburg. She knew in a general way why the United States disliked and feared Russia; but what she was curious to know was why so many other countries, new nations and little folk, Africans and Asiatics, seemed to place their hopes for salvation on Communism.

The magnificent and awe-inspiring spectacle at the Buffalo Stadium answered some of her queries. Here were massed at once 200,000 human beings, and at least 500,000 during the afternoon passed through. It was not an organized spectacle. She was sure that the Napoleons and the German Wilhelms had often offered more grandiose and glittering performances. But she doubted if ever before the mass of unorganized peoples had poured out their hearts as strikingly and desperately in a plea for human uplift. That cry for Peace rang in her ears for days and months.

She did some sight-seeing in south France, but had to hurry for she had not much time. And then she had the good fortune again to meet Ilya Ehrenburg. Ehrenburg beamed upon her in his sort of enveloping and fatherly way and said,

"Why not look at the Soviet Union before you return?"

She hesitated a moment and then said, "Yes, of course. I'd love to!"

And so it was that on a morning in midsummer she saw the buildings of one of the greatest cities of the modern world, with magnificent boulevards, great public buildings and afar the site for a university. Here and there, behind and aside, were relics and remains of the old city in ruins and by-ways, but the new and good were growing. There were parks and the most beautiful subway in the world; there were stores and emporiums, factories and working people's homes and a curious shift of daily human interest from the rich and luxurious to the worker and intellectual. Then finally at the Bolshoi Theater she saw dramatic art at its highest—Tchaikovsky's "Swan Lake" and its magnificent ballet. And she came back with new hope and vision to Macon, Georgia.

Jean was expected in September, after three weeks abroad; but before she arrived there came the extraordinary story of the concert of Paul Robeson at Peekskill. It was announced for the last of August, and Judge Mansart of New York wrote his father of the mob which stopped the concert which he and his wife had ridden up to attend.

> "The press is here to see the great lynching, every New York newspaper, their crack writers and photographers, but not one policeman and not one state trooper—not one."

This seemed inexplicable to President Mansart until he realized that it was a protest against what Robeson had just said in Paris as well as resentment long brewing against Negroes and Jews intruding in this Westchester vacation area. The postponed concert, it was said, would be given under police protection in early September.

The news of the September effort was even more disturbing to President Mansart. Warned by the police, Judge Mansart had turned back on his way to the concert which was given, guarded by Robeson's friends, wielding ball bats and ranged arm-in-arm to protect the large audience. A friend of Mansart reported that there was an organized attempt to lynch Robeson and maim as many of the audience as the white mob of war veterans and anti-Semitic hoodlums could reach with the aid of the police. The friend wrote:

> Hell was at work; cops, in a craze of hate, were beating cars with their long clubs, smashing fenders, lashing out against windshields, doing a dance of frenzy as the autos rolled out of the place. Even through our closed windows we could hear the flood of insanely vile language from the police, the unprintable oaths: "Jew, Kike, darky, Nigger!" The slime and filth of America's underworld of race hatred compressed into these "guardians" of the law. There were about thirty police grouped there at the entrance, and they flogged the cars as if the automobiles were living objects of their resentment.

Policemen routed other cars through the woods where the mob beat and wounded the hundreds who tried to drive home.

It was of this story that Mansart was reading when John Baldwin of his Trustee Board was announced. Baldwin had not visited the school or a Board meeting for a year. He was in bad health and worse temper and asked the President peremptorily about the rumor that the Dean, Jean Du Bignon, had gone to a "Communist Peace meeting in Paris, and that the President himself had been at that Communist gathering at the Waldorf in New York."

Mansart said that these visits had been made; but that neither meeting was, to his knowledge, "Communist" and both were most worthy of attending.

"You must realize, Mansart," stormed Baldwin, "that things in this country are coming to a showdown. We are going to stop this Communism. We are going to turn this country back to its normal path."

Mansart interrupted: "Don't you think that what we have called 'normal' is really abnormal? Wasn't the New Deal leading us right?"

"No, it wasn't. It was interfering with private business."

"Which," said Mansart, "had already been ruined by private greed. Mr. Baldwin," he continued, "I'm an American just so far as I am allowed to be by law and custom. I want the best for America. I want America to be the best. But I don't like some things in America and I don't like what some Americans do. And I won't say I do. For instance, there's Ben Davis. I knew him. I knew his father before him. When I was a student at Atlanta University little Ben used to come daily to school. He was a good boy. He grew up to be a good man, men black and white tell me. He was one of the best councilmen New York ever had.

"What Ben believed and what he planned, I do not know and I do not care. He was not even accused of doing any wrong. He had a right to believe in Communism. But to punish a man not for what he did, not even for what he believed, but for what his beliefs might lead to, was not justice. It was a crime."

"Mansart, you are going too far."

"The Supreme Court went too far."

Baldwin scowled. "Mansart, we have been counting on the southern Negroes as a conservative force in this country. We are going to see that they are or we are going to smash them. I have particularly depended upon you and you've done a good job. Don't spoil it now. It was a mistake for you to attend that meeting of fanatics in New York."

"But Mr. Baldwin, they were not fanatics. They were some of our best Americans, and the foreigners—why we had a great musician from Russia, with two authors, and men of science."

Baldwin brushed all that aside. "They represented Communism, and Communism has no place in the United States."

"I'm not saying that it has. I'm saying that we ought to have a democratic exchange of ideas. This was stopped by a mob, and normal exchange of ideas was absolutely prohibited. Imagine, Shostakovich being refused the opportunity of giving a concert on the Yale campus!"

"President Mansart, I am not going to discuss that with you now. All I am going to say is this: it was a mistake for you to go to New York. It was a greater mistake for that Du Bignon woman to go to Paris, and as I understand, even to Russia. She is a firebrand I am afraid, and we have got to get rid of her. Now Mansart, if you want to play along with us we want you to remain here as president of this institution. Otherwise, we are going to get someone else. I want to make this plain to you. The Board has made up its mind." And Baldwin left.

Mansart was dismayed by this interview, yet the eruption in 1950 of the Korean war, possible prelude to a Third World War, so utterly astonished him that he gave more thought to the world situation than to the future of himself and his college. He wrote letters, he attended meetings. He spoke, openly and freely, and as he made his stand clear, the stand of his Trustee Board and of the powerful interests in the country back of it hardened. In several conferences Baldwin and other merchants and bankers emphasized their point of view among themselves.

"The old plans," said Baldwin, "which young William Baldwin, president of the Long Island Railroad, expressed and emphasized in the South in 1900 were to develop Negroes as a separate working force, with jobs different from that which the skilled whites were going to do. Unorganized, uncontaminated with foreign ideologies, they would balance each other so that we could continue to have a cheap, efficient working force.

"Well, all that's gone out the window. It is impossible not to realize now that Negroes are getting education; more than we had planned and more than we can stop. Moreover, the whole method of industry has so changed that the distinction between ordinary labor and skilled labor is disappearing. It's labor, mass production. Now what we have to look forward to is an integrated labor force, white and black. There'll be opposition, and we can use race prejudice to keep unionization and race integration at a minimum. But race distinctions which interfere with industry eventually must go.

"What we've got to do is to see that in neither group of white or colored labor do foreign radical ideas penetrate. We have got to keep labor organization in hand and the labor unions down; curtail their political power in such a way that this mis-called Democracy disappears under the dictatorship of Big Business.

"I do not think that Mansart is going to play along. And I know this all-too-influential white woman who is helping him and who calls herself colored has got to go. Mansart's a good man. We must keep him as long as possible. But we've got to cut his nails and we've got to do that now."

Meantime Mansart, instead of listening to the gossip of what the Trustee Board was thinking, and guiding his actions as he was used to doing, was utterly upset by the drafting of his grandson Adelbert, Douglass' boy, who had graduated from the college and who had become one of the assistants in the Little Theater. Despite Mansart's influence, Adelbert was drafted and sent to a camp in Biloxi, Mississippi, where the full force of Mississippi race prejudice slapped him in the face. And then, soon after, he was on his way to the mud and blood of Korea.

Manuel Mansart never, to the day of his death, could logically and satisfactorily explain to himself the year of 1950. Sometimes he thought it must have been the result of headstrong vagaries of one man with power and responsibilities far beyond his brains or education; then he shifted the blame to Truman's fastidious and stiff-necked Secretary of State; at other times, he was sure everything was the crime of that vast, crawling and spiderlike octopus of industry and trade, held vise-like in a half dozen magnificent ganglia of money and credit which almost owned and certainly ruled a great part of the earth. Yes, this was the master criminal—or was there no master—simply embodied, encysted Evil?

In December, 1949, the pale wraith of China became disembodied from the enveloping mists of two years' strife. By January, 1950, most of the world had recognized a new republic in China. America would not believe it. Too long had it held Chinese in utter contempt. Could the great corporate business in Korea, which the Japanese sold to Wall Street, have sent John Foster Dulles to that front trench to watch over the tungsten deposits which, in his fevered imagination, the North Koreans threatened?

So North Korea took up arms to stop the American agent, Syngman Rhee, from marching north. Then Harry Truman started what narrowly missed being World War III. It was, as he said, his most important decision, when without authority of any sort, on June 27, 1950, he ordered American troops to "take police action" in a foreign land. He did not consult Congress. He had no mandate from the United Nations. But the United Nations, with the Soviet Union absent, consented eleven hours after MacArthur was on the march, and Congress never dared object.

So Harry Truman within a year sent 50,000 American boys to their death, maimed a hundred thousand more, and plunged Korea into a bloody hell that took at least 5 billion dollars in the first year, from education, health and housing which the nation sorely needed.

Jean returned from her trip abroad at the beginning of the new school term in the Fall of 1950, and Manuel and the teachers were deeply stirred by her reports. MacArthur had crossed the 38th parallel and rushed to the Manchurian boundary where he was not only bombing China but Russia. Jean pointed out how seriously this changed the war and waited to hear how China would answer. Evidently Washington was worried and suddenly, in October, Truman rushed halfway round the world to talk with his autocratic pro-consul.

According to the papers the interview was eminently satisfactory and our troops kept rolling north, killing and spurting flaming oil until, as it later was revealed, on November 24, MacArthur again threw his might across on the border.

Then it came, and to the astonishment of the world and the rage of MacArthur, China struck back. In late November, six thousand American and Korean troops lay dead and 32,000 wounded. On November 28, as MacArthur cried, it was indeed a "New War." The United Nations army reeled back and ran. The UN had opposed the United States drive across the Yalu, and Attlee had rushed to Washington when Truman almost nonchantly, had threatened use of the atom bomb. The UN now asked for a "cease fire" and Truman declared a "National Emergency." The question of evacuating Korea entirely was discussed in Washington.

Jean gave her idea of the situation. "MacArthur was frightened into panic and his army made the longest and most headlong retreat that any American army ever made. Then MacArthur, with his troops 70 miles below the 38th parallel, realized that the Chinese had stopped following. They were not rushing to Pusan and seeking to drive him 'into the sea.' No, they had stopped at the 38th parallel and were ready for peace."

The demand for peace was growing all over the world. Four great Peace Congresses had been held in New York, Paris, Moscow and Mexico in 1949 and 1950. The Stockholm Peace Appeal had gone forth in March, and in April a Peace Information Bureau had been established in New York. Its "Peace-grams" were flooding the country and as the Korean war opened, 2,500,000 Americans had already signed the petition against the use of the atom bomb.

Five days after Truman opened the war, Acheson emitted a blast against the Stockholm Appeal which the Peace Information Bureau stoutly answered. It revealed that 200,000,000 people in all parts of the world had signed this appeal, led by some of the greatest personages of the day.

This was serious for MacArthur's plans. He was trying to arouse the fighting spirit of America by luring the Chinese south and then administering a smashing blow; or, if this led to further defeat of his forces, he would secure for himself unlimited men and war materials and carte blanche for further operations. For this he wanted Chiang Kai-shek to come from Formosa and join him on the mainland. The American phase of the war would then be over. Most of his ground troops could go home. But with American airplanes and artillery, and with atom bombs; with Chiang's troops and the Chinese bound to flock to his banners once he reappeared, and with the American navy raking the coast and wide rivers, he and his troops, backed by American Business, would march into Manchuria, and then to Peking, Nanking and Shanghai, and down to Canton.

Chiang, under expert guidance, would know how to wipe out the peasants west of Hankow to Chungking and bomb them out in Shensi and Szhechwan and even Sinkiang and Mongolia. At last, Asia would succumb to America. But for this Chiang was absolutely necessary; he would be the symbol for China, putting down Communist rebellion, helped by American traitors. He and his followers would know customs and language. MacArthur insisted on Chiang and wrote not only to Truman and the Pentagon but to the powerful China Lobby, with its fat supply of Soong funds; finally, he made the mistake of writing even to the Republicans after their gains in the recent Congressional elections.

Meantime, as Jean pointed out, since the Chinese did not fall eagerly into the trap MacArthur had so liberally baited by evacuating Seoul and retiring toward Pusan, he adopted other tactics. Having already express permission again to cross the 38th parallel when he so decided, he clapped a deep censorship on his movements. There ensued a pause of a month, when thoughts of peace spread.

MacArthur tried to get the right to bombard Manchuria. He did not succeed, but he got the right to cross the 38th parallel again. Secretly in February he sent his troops across, and finding no Chinese army he ordered the navy to bombard Wonson for 41 days, longer than any city had ever before in history been so attacked. American flyers poured lead and flaming oil on unarmed men, women and children until, as the triumphant admiral told the press, "You cannot walk in the streets. You cannot sleep anywhere—unless it is the sleep of death." The population became "suicide groups" and Songjin and Chongjin, cities nearby, were given the same treatment.

But in the narrow neck of Korea, MacArthur was held as by a stone wall. Writhe as he would he could not advance north. The Chinese Army, which he had enticed to Pusan, was at the 38th parallel and there it stayed. Then, Jean unfolded the morning paper and pointed to the astounding news that on April 11, Truman had recalled MacArthur.

Mansart read the news in the utmost astonishment. "But why, why?" he asked.

Jean explained. "Truman was in a jam. The little 'police action,' which had looked like a fine piece of publicity ten months ago, had now begun to be more than a hot potato. In the first year, it had cost five billion dollars and involved seventeen nations and 700,000 men. This was not merely a 'police action'—this was heading to world war, as our allies were not slow to emphasize.

"The peace demand was growing right here in the United States, as the elections showed. The atrocities of the war irked Truman, but as the boasted soldier he thought he was, he would not admit that. The cost of the war was making taxpayers writhe, but he dared not yield to such considerations.

"MacArthur had impudently disobeyed his orders. This Truman angrily denied. But when MacArthur appealed to Martin, leader of the Republicans in the House of Representatives—where the Democrats had only a majority of two—this, to Truman, was political treason and he seized on it as an excuse."

Jean talked to Mansart as often as possible, not so much about Paris and the peace movement as about the things she had seen in Prague and Warsaw and particularly in Moscow. He listened with interest but mounting distress. It was true, as Baldwin had insisted. Jean was going radical. This would be a danger to her and to the school. He must in some way talk this out with her, and yet she was doing most of the talking, filled with the enthusiasm of what she had seen and learned. She talked freely to him and to her students.

One morning in the fall of 1952, soon after Jean's return, and as she was overflowing with her experiences abroad, a new student, a tall, bright-eyed yellow boy in the back row of her class asked, "Miss Du Bignon, what do you think of the Rosenberg case?"

Jean had been reading since her return of the young couple accused of treason. She was aghast as well as indignant. She resented what seemed to her an attack on womanhood, an affront to motherhood and especially a denial of the clear processes of justice. She spoke frankly and heatedly.

"I am amazed at this case. I am sure the accused will soon be released. It involves first the right to think. Perhaps the Rosenbergs were Communists. I do not know. I do not care. I have just returned from visiting a nation of Communists. I saw millions of fine people. I believe in freedom of thought no matter what it believes. Actions alone are punishable, not beliefs.

"The Rosenbergs were decent people so far as all testimony proves. They had studied together in school. They had fallen in love and married, built a home, worked for a living and brought up two fine boys. They are accused of conspiracy to commit wartime treason in time of peace. The testimony against them is from a confessed criminal, whose testimony was bought by what I call bribery; that is, by a reduced sentence for confessed wrong-doing.

"Just what the Rosenbergs are accused of actually doing is not revealed. What was it? Was it anything they could have done? What proof of their doing it exists, outside the word of a criminal? What is 'conspiracy' to commit when commission is not even alleged? This brutal sentence cannot stand, I am sure."

There was silence a moment. Then the same boy asked, "Do you think it was right to send Ben Davis to jail?"

Jean hesitated a moment. Perhaps it was not wise to discuss such matters in class. But why not? Was this not the place to teach truth? If not, where? Jean said: "Ben Davis is a fine man. He was born right here in Georgia, up in Dawson county; he took his high school work at Atlanta University and then went to college at Amherst, in Massachusetts. He studied law at Harvard. He secured the freedom of Angelo Herndon in Atlanta. He served two terms in the city council of New York and did excellent work.

"I have no doubt but that Ben Davis fears, just as you and I often fear, that nothing but force will ever set our people free in this land. At the same time, I'm sure that neither he nor you ever laid plans or took action to start violent revolution. He was never charged with that. He was charged with being a member and official of the Communist Party, and that he freely admitted.

"I have heard him thank the Communist Party for the way it had treated him and for what he had learned from Communism. But belief in Communism does not mean that all Communists always believe in immediate revolution. They believe that there are times when revolution is unavoidable, but not necessarily here and now. A man's thoughts, his beliefs, are his own and he is free to hold them. If at any time his thoughts lead him to illegal actions, he must stand ready to take punishment, not for what he thinks but for what he does. For these reasons I think Davis' sentence and that of his fellows was unjust and unconstitutional."

When Miss Du Bignon finished her answer the new student in the back stood up and quietly departed. He had only recently enrolled and belonged to a well-known colored family in Washington, D. C. His father had long been a clerk in the office of the Attorney General. He ran through the corridors into the street, caught a street car, left the car at the Union Station and took a cab for the airport. A few hours later he was closeted with officials in Washington.

Several months went by. And then one day Miss Du Bignon was surprised to receive a visit from a Federal official who handed her a summons. It seemed that she had been ordered by the Attorney General in Washington to register as a foreign agent. She was surprised and indignant. She immediately told the president and he summoned the college lawyer. He was a respectable Macon white man, conservative and careful, but broadly sympathetic with Manuel Mansart. He read the subpoena and hesitated. "I am afraid, Miss Du Bignon," he said at last, slowly, "that you may be in considerable trouble."

"But how and why?" she asked. "I have never been an agent of a foreign power or done anything that by any stretch of the imagination could be called subversive or illegal."

"Didn't you some weeks ago discuss Communism in your class?"

"Yes, I did. Is there a teacher in the nation who has not? I also talked about peace; about Ben Davis and the Rosenbergs."

"Well, I imagine that story got to Washington. Now there are some other things which I must ask you, because without categorical answers I'm afraid I can't handle this case. Miss Du Bignon, have you ever been to Russia?"

"Yes—in 1949 for a month."

"One other question—are you a Communist?"

"No," she said, "frankly, I'm not. I have studied Communism, and I certainly sympathize with its ideals. If what I believe is true in Russia, Poland, Czechoslovakia and other 'Iron Curtain' countries, then if I were a citizen of those countries I should certainly be a Communist. In this country I have never thought of joining that party. I never lived where it had an organization and have never been invited to join. I have assumed that in Russia past conditions were so bad that Communism by revolution was the only answer; that on the other hand in the United States with more intelligence and less poverty, we could work out fundamental reforms such as we need by peaceful evolution."

"You admit that dictatorship and violence must be the program of any Communist Party anywhere?"

"I admit nothing of the sort. I believe a man may be a Communist and neither desire nor plan violence. Violence may be necessary to start any reform, as for example reform in taxation in 1776, but violence or revolution is certainly not the object of Communism. Moreover, a man may be a Republican and plot revolution."

"Thank you, Miss Du Bignon. I am going to take your word that you have never been under orders to act for any foreign power."

"You have my word."

"Then I advise you to refuse to register. I will associate myself in your case, but not as chief counsel. President Mansart knows well that my acting as counsel for his college has been no easy job. It has cost me some clients and certain social losses. These things I do not mind too much although my family sometimes complains. For me not to act in this case would hurt you. But new currents are moving in this nation and for that reason you must hire as chief counsel someone better prepared to defend you. How about Mansart's son in New York?"

Mansart wrote to Revels and asked his help. Revels stayed in his office reading the letter and looking at the picture of his son in flying uniform. Then he wired to Mansart and offered to take the case. The Atlanta attorney was willing to associate himself with Revels.

After a short interval, Jean was indicted by a federal grand jury in Washington for refusing to register. It became clear that the Justice Department was trying to prove that Jean had gone to Paris to consult with the "Communist conspiracy"; that she had then gone to Moscow for "orders" and that she had come back to the United States to spread in her teaching and administration the overthrow of the government of the United States. It was a fantastic charge, but she had to go on trial.

Meantime Mansart had spent some time in Washington and brought into the case as his personal assistant a young colored woman recently admitted to the well-known firm of colored lawyers, Cobb, Hayes and Howard. The young woman, tall, brown and well-tailored, was frank. She said, "The Government has no case and they know it, unless they bring in a hired informer to swear that Miss Du Bignon is a Communist. There may be strong influence back of this prosecution that demands conviction. If that is true, then Miss Du Bignon will go to jail."

"But can lying testimony be had and be believed?"

"It can in America today at $50 a day, and Government protection. But we'll wait and see."

Jean appeared in Washington a month later and to her astonishment as well as curiosity she was in the prisoner's seat, accused of something that looked like treason. She talked very frankly. Yes, she had "Communist" books in her library: how could she teach the facts about Communism if she did not read such books? And how could she teach social science today without touching upon Communism? Yes, she deeply sympathized with the objects of Communism. No, she was not a member of the Communist Party. Yes, she had met Americans who were members of the Communist Party. No, she had not been under direction of Communists either in this country or any other country.

Of the discussion in her class, she thought it was proper to put before students the conclusions which any honest person made from the facts which he had gathered. Certainly, if in the future she discovered other facts that proved or disproved what she had said, she would say so. She certainly did believe that certain Americans had been guilty of violence; as a Negro—(and when she said that there was a stir in the court)—she had seen dishonesty, cruelty and betrayal, as well as violence and murder.

The charge that Jean was herself a Communist was delayed because none of the paid informers which the prosecution had at their disposal had ever seen or heard of her in the centers of the Communist Party of America. At the last moment, after all the accusations were in and Jean herself had testified, there was hurried into the witness stand, a well-dressed and intelligent white man. He calmly deposed that he was an undercover agent of the federal government; that he had been stationed in Paris to cover the Peace Congress of 1949. He had met Miss Du Bignon; in fact they had lunched together several times, alone and with well-known foreign Communists. She had attended secret meetings at which he had been present and that without doubt "she was a party member and a spy and agent for the Soviet Union."

Jean sat stunned and incredulous. This plain lie surely could not stand up in court! She looked appealingly at her lawyers. They looked away. The examination continued.

"Is this person in the courtroom?"

"I am told she is."

"Could you identify her?"

He thought he could. He arose and looked at the table where Jean and her lawyers sat. Directly beside Jean sat the young brown lawyer who was Judge Mansart's assistant. Now in fact, this paid stool-pigeon, secured at the last moment, had never before seen Miss Du Bignon, but knew of course that she was colored. When she had been pointed out to him sitting at the lawyer's table, he naturally assumed that the colored girl was the accused and not the apparently white girl by her side.

"There she is," he said confidently, pointing at the girl. The prosecuting attorney leaped to his feet but Mansart was ahead of him.

"Will you touch her on the shoulder?"

The witness complied and Mansart said:

"Your Honor, we rest our case, and ask dismissal."

The Judge with a look of disgust assented and Jean Du Bignon was free.

Outside the court, there were certain men who talked together. On the whole, they concluded that this woman was not a Communist conspirator. At the same time, the very frankness of her beliefs and her outspokenness were a source of danger. And, too, on the other hand, she might be a Communist spy unusually intelligent and resourceful.

It seemed, therefore, on the whole, to be wisest to drop the case and then over a space of time, a year, perhaps ten years, to keep her under careful surveillance; to see that she did not get work or leave the country; to read her mail; to watch her contacts. This would be the best way of finding out the truth about her.

Jean was delighted and her attorney greatly elated. The Atlanta lawyer said that this was a complete vindication for her, but he warned that hereafter she had better not touch upon the subject of Communism, and see that no further accusations could be brought against her. She looked at him in astonishment.

"Do you mean that in an institution called a university, the subject which is the greatest matter upon which mankind today is thinking must be slurred over and omitted? Are you advising me not to study Communism any further?"

He was uncomfortable and did not think that Miss Du Bignon's statements showed a sensible attitude. He simply added, "I am telling you that today it is not wise even to study Communism!"

Revels Mansart said little. He received her thanks gravely and refused compensation. He only remarked cryptically, "This, my dear friend, is only the beginning, not the end."

Jean returned to Macon with her sense of triumph dampened by these words. Her apprehension was confirmed by a communication from the Board of Trustees which was already on her desk. Due to the fact that she had been even suspected of treason, the Board thought that her usefulness at the State College was at an end and she was summarily dismissed. There was no mention of a pension after her thirty years of service.

This was the first time that Manuel Mansart lost a cause before his Board of Trustees. He saw from the very opening of the meeting that he had no chance. The Board evidently had already been in consultation, and both the colored and white members had made up their minds. They listened to him respectfully, even when his plea found him so filled with emotion that he could not speak with ordinary calmness and incisiveness. When he was through they attempted no rebuttal. They simply passed the edict of dismissal.

The thing that hurt Jean most was that her plan of a continuous sociological study of the American Negro was thus stopped. The colleges which had united in this project for various reasons found it expedient to withdraw. Most of them, after all, had no clear conception of what this study might have meant to the American Negro and to the science of sociology.

After the Board meeting, Mansart called Jean to his office and said, "Jean, I need not tell you how grave an injustice I know you have suffered. But there is one thing that I hope you will let me say. From the first time you came into this office until now, through all these thirty long years of struggle, you have been in the center of my life and work.

"If I had been a younger man and if there had not been between us this startling contrast in the color of our skins, I should have long ago asked you to marry me after my wife died. But I felt first that to mention any such thing would be a sort of betrayal of my position as employer and spiritual father, and that you would have a right to resent it. Any resentment or recoil on your part would have seemed to me like death.

"But now the situation has altered. In the midst of your fine career you suddenly are placed where you cannot earn a living. And I wonder if under these circumstances you would not let me at least have the name of being your husband, so that I could continue to have the benefit of your counsel and be able to protect you."

Jean arose and put both hands upon his shoulders and kissed his forehead and said, "I am deeply honored, Manuel, by what you say. I am going to refuse not because of the silly matter of age, which has nothing to do with my love and affection for you; nor because of the disgraceful fact that a difference in color in America must for a moment move us, but for the plain truth that your marriage to me just now would mean loss of your own position. You're going to have a hard time to hold it even as it is, and at the same time to keep your own soul. But marriage with me now would be interpreted as deliberate defiance of the Board of Trustees. No, it cannot happen. Moreover, what you have named as the chief reason for this marriage does not exist.

"You know, I told you some time ago of my working in Atlanta with the Textile Union. I never used my real name there. I have been offered the position of secretary of the state union organization. This will give me employment, and outside of the possibility of my race coming up and losing my job on account of that, I can earn a living. What I am going to do is to return to Atlanta, lose myself in the white race, and try to lead them gradually to admitting Negroes to the Textile Union and so begin that integration of the laboring force in the South which, in the long run, will settle the economic problems of the nation.

"In the meantime I shall keep in touch with you. I shall continue to love you as I have for these long years, and perhaps finally when you retire we can find a place and time to live together as man and wife."

Manuel looked at her in astonishment. "But if they find out you are colored?"

"I have told the secretary and some members of the Board."

There was nothing more to be said. Jean went to Atlanta. Thus, she embarked upon her new—and to what all the world would have called her impossible—job.

And yet, was it so impossible? From the formation of the CIO in 1935 to the FEPC in 1941, the Negro had made long strides toward integration in the American labor movement. Unions like the Textile lagged; but could they keep this up? The pull of lower wage scales in the South on the hard-won higher wage of New England was directly traceable to excluding the Negro worker from the Southern unions. The end must be admission of Negroes. The answer lay in the length of time white labor could afford to pay for the cost of color prejudice.

President Manuel Mansart on his part turned to the task of conciliating and rebuilding his Board, which seemed quite possible but which proved in the end to be a fruitless endeavor. He had talks with various members of his Board. He realized very soon that it was not so much a desire to get rid of him personally that was moving them as that they had in mind a man who could better carry out the kind of work which they wanted done at the State College. He was the young president of the Land-Grant college for Negroes in Northern Louisiana. It had been subsisting on small appropriations from the state and from the federal government.

President Limes had not offended the authorities by continual importunity and by protesting what was given him. On the contrary, with what he was granted, he had expressed thanks and gone to work to do what he could. And what he could do was to appease the local community, to furnish them with house servants and with a number of helpers in agriculture paid by the United States government; he had given himself the job of inducing the colored people to stay on the farms, to work for the wages given, and to improve the quality of farming in various well-recognized ways.

Now, this was the kind of man John Baldwin and the white members of the Board were very much pleased with. With larger funds and greater power this man could be an influence among the Negroes. He could restrain feelings of discontent. He could stop organized agitation. He could be armed with concessions to the Negroes for the right to vote. They could even, in some instances, be allowed to enter the "white primary," and so long as they voted for the dominant Democratic Party, this would strengthen conservatism and reaction there. Thus, the new Negro vote, gradually integrated, could be a distinct advantage to the employers and to big business in general.

There would be more funds for Negro education and it might even happen that separation by race in schools might eventually be given up. That would save money, gain votes for industry and clip the claws of the white unions. All this was not voiced loudly; but it was a matter of secret and earnest consultation.

Thus Mr. Limes, suave and pleasant, influential among colored people, knowing how to woo them and persuade them, and being young and energetic, could do a much better job than could be expected of Mansart. Mansart was getting old and used to having his way; he was undoubtedly listening to, if not entertaining, new and dangerous ideas.

The method, then, decided on for getting rid of Mansart was not to level false charges or have a row, or arbitrarily force him out. It was the perfectly logical decision that in the colleges of the South, particularly those helped by Federal funds, there should be a recognized age limit for the Presidency. Mansart would be seventy-five soon. It could therefore be decided that at 75, all presidents of Land-grant colleges should retire. This would get rid of Manuel Mansart, and there could even be appropriate recognition made of his work, and a pension suitable for a colored man given him. The transition would be made without difficulty and without criticism.

Jean, despite her brave words, walked out into the world with a shiver. She had a strange distaste after the long years again to enter the white world as one belonging to it. She had lived too long with her own black folk. She felt completely bone of their bone and flesh of their flesh. She did not wish to leave them for a moment. Even the contemplation of it was revolting to her. Not that they were always lovable, always right in decision and broad in outlook. Oh, no. They were often narrow, selfish, wrong-headed human beings. But they were hers. She belonged to them and they to her. It was hard to leave them even for a short time.

She went to Atlanta, found a room in the factory district and reported for work at the labor office. Then, having an afternoon to herself, she took a walk. She walked out to Peachtree, as almost everyone does. It was changed, but always interesting. About four in the afternoon she found herself at the fork in the road fronting the Episcopal cathedral. People were gathering, and she paused at the crossing. An elderly lady paused beside her and said, "Could I take your arm? I'm attending the funeral, too, and my sight is none too good."

"But of course," said Jean.

"He was a great loss," continued her companion, "but perhaps he had outlived his usefulness."

Jean hesitated and then glanced at the black-broidered program slipped into her hand. John Baldwin was dead at 73, and this was his funeral. She said nothing but went into the church, and they sat together. The old lady commented in whispers now and then:

"His wife is still beautiful, but so cold, always so unfeeling. I'm glad Betty Lou went on before. Oh, there is the boy; Lee will never amount to much. Perhaps his marriage may help, but I doubt it. Who is she? Oh, some Russian princess, so they say. There seems to be such an astonishing number of Eastern European nobility now. They say she was flirting outrageously for a time with John the father. His wife apparently never noticed. Now the engagement with the son seems almost announced. There she is! Just a shade too spectacular for my taste!"

She sank to her knees as the organ pealed. Jean sat through the services and helped her friend down the steps.

"Thank you so much. My car will pick me up at the corner. Pardon me, somehow your face seems familiar."

"I'm a Du Bignon, of New Orleans."

"Yes, of course. Why once I met old Mère Du Bignon. What a great lady she was! Won't you come home with me to tea?"

"I'm so sorry," said Jean as she left, "I fear I haven't time!"

CHAPTER XVII

Adelbert Mansart and Jackie Carmichael

In the winter of 1951 Adelbert Mansart, Douglass' son and Manuel's grandson, was in Korea. A few days before he had been dashing north in a swaying, creaking jeep. Now he was stumbling blindly through the snow and ice. He had left behind destruction in ashes and flames. Around loomed dark mountain crags half-hidden in wind and dust. Stretching ahead, they said, was the Yalu River and Manchuria. The soldiers, clinging to each other, were yelling and singing and weeping. The Third World War, so far as they were concerned, had begun. Adelbert gritted his teeth, hung on perilously and tried not to see the half-burned ghosts of men covered with napalm, nor to hear the shrieks and wails. It was thus that Adelbert Mansart, a boy of 19, saw war—a war of whites on colored folk; the attempt of the United States to conquer China—far from home, in cold and snow. He had never before seen violence on any scale. He had known deep inner hurt, but not violence nor death. At every stop he saw the drunken whites smash the heads of men, kill children and chase screaming girls.

"Damn the Chinks and Gooks and all other Niggers," they yelled and cursed as they gulped strong liquor to fortify themselves against the freezing blasts.

Adelbert heard these jibes and they knew he heard. He saw with open, agonized eyes, white men rape colored girls on the open road, and curse and kill them. Hospital patients were bombed as they fled; civilians were machine-gunned, and children flying from burning houses were slaughtered by low-flying planes. Towns, bridges, water systems and railroads were blown up, and ripened crops destroyed in the fields. Prisoners were buried alive; flaming petroleum was poured on helpless refugees; forests were destroyed; naked women beaten and chased through the streets; cartridges exploded in men's mouths and heads split open with axes because these were "Communists." He saw a colored captain refuse to lead his troops to certain death; and later learned he was court martialed. He could do nothing; he could not even protest. He was a soldier and must obey.

Then suddenly all changed. There came a pulse of weird silence, but not for long. Seemingly without forewarning, the troops wheeled in their tracks and came smashing, dashing back, driving the panicky soldiers aside to the gutters.

The whole army was turning. The war had stopped, the fighting ended, the retreat begun. Yellow China was pouring into brown Korea.

The commanding officer, General Walker, roared by swaying in his jeep. Suddenly the jeep reeled, rose and overturned. The army leader lay crushed and dead. Who did it, how did it happen, why? There was no time to ask. Adelbert's own jeep stalled in a ditch. The men jumped out and floundered through the mud and snow, yelling and cursing. The wind shrieked and the dying shrieked back. Adelbert stumbled, he staggered on and fell. Someone stepped on his head and thrust it far down into the slush. He tried to turn and rise when a great iron wheel rolled over his right arm. He heard the bones crack. Exquisite needles of pain rose and gripped him and he knew nothing more for endless time.

When he awoke he was aboard ship and screaming—why, he did not know. A blurred figure jabbed narcotic into his arm to stop him. This happened several times. At last he lay silent and through a small porthole watched the curling sea. An officer bent over him. He tried to salute but he had no right arm. He rose in terror. He had no arm! Again a scream struggled in his throat and again he fell into a stupor of sleep.

Days went by; at last he lay calmly. He was in Japan. He had lost his lower arm and was going home. His head, too, was not right. It ached continuously, a low, sullen ache. He was aware that the nurses thought him crazy, but he was not. He knew that. But what would he do at "home"? The thought made him suddenly laugh aloud. Arrived in Seattle in early May, he was rushed to a hospital and when he awoke the rest of his right arm was gone.

After many weeks, he became calm and normal. He boarded a train for Chicago and went straight home. The beautiful, three-storied mansion sat back from the boulevard, with a wide lawn in front and at one side. There were chairs and tables and gay umbrellas. Hundreds of people were milling about—beautiful women of every color, richly coiffured and gowned; colored men in well-tailored suits, light and tinted in shade, some soldiers in uniform. White waiters threaded through with laden trays. Many in the through glanced at Adelbert as he pushed his way in.

Adelbert wondered why he had come. What was it he was so set on doing? Something, something, something very important; but he could not define just what. But he must see his father. He glimpsed him in the throng and called out loudly. His father was fat and gray, perfectly clothed in a tan tailored morning suit with crimson tie and spotless linen. He had a baby in his arms—his daughter's new child but a few months old. The lovely daughter in a Paris gown, with her distinguished-looking husband, stood near.

Douglass Mansart heard the hail and looked up. He saw a dark young man with long, uncombed hair; clad in dirty, disarranged khaki, and noticed immediately that the youth had but one arm. His first impulse was to summon the police patrol who were vigilant in the background, when his daughter suddenly started and rose from her chair with a cry. His wife blanched, then hurried forward. The soldier stiffened a moment as he saw her, then crumpled and sank to the earth.

Adelbert spent six months in a sanitarium in up-state New York. Manuel Mansart and Jean came up to see him several times while they stayed with his uncle, Judge Revels, in New York City. They talked of life and war and of Adelbert's future. He was firm on one point. He would not stay in America—he hated the United States.

Manuel argued: "I know how you feel, son. There have been times when I have felt the same. But you are wrong. This nation has been cruel to us—cruel and unfeeling. Yet at bottom, its heart is right. It will yet do justly, love mercy and walk humbly with its God."

Adelbert's face was stone and Jean intervened. "My solution," she said, "is France. A year, perhaps several years in France. Heal your own soul while France is healing hers. It should be a fine experience."

At Manuel's request, Douglass furnished the money, and Adelbert went to Paris in 1953.

It was spring. Adelbert left the great hall of the Sorbonne quietly, and sauntered into the courtyard. Within, the learned professor was still droning over new aspects of International Law. It would seem the United Nations had changed the basis of this law, or would change it; but then again it hadn't, at least, not yet. The first step toward effective change would follow the new Atlantic Pact; that is, if it was followed, as it must be, by a Mediterranean and Pacific Pact.

"In fact, if European dominance or the rule of——" he had paused there and had not added, "the White Race," as logically he would have had he not become conscious of the colored faces before him. Curious, the thought struck him, how colonials and Asiatics and Africans were crowding into the universities since the war. Well, it was a tribute to civilization and to the white peoples. . . . It was here that Adelbert left. What the professor had been saying seemed to him pure poppycock. In fact, education as it was called in the world and as it unfolded itself around him, was becoming increasingly distasteful.

He was short and slight, with a face of dark chestnut brown and hair long and curled. His features were straight and sharp and his eyes black and glowing. He was well but carelessly dressed and had an air of being used to good living which brought waiters scurrying as he lounged over to a corner of the café. He had but one arm.

"What rot!" said a companion who joined him, a young Englishman. "What's the old buffer driving at? The same old slop—Europe is civilization!"

"Britannia rules the waves," added Adelbert. "The idea dies hard."

"It does; but it dies. It must die willingly or be killed."

Adelbert looked up lazily. "Haven't we had enough killing?"

"Not of ideas. There a massacre is still due."

"I wonder. Ideas don't need violent killing. All they need is slow starvation—forgetfulness, oblivion."

"And how soon this side of never-never-land will that take place, so long as our schools are dominated by anachronisms like this fossil?"

"That's what gets me. I'm wondering how much more of what is called 'education' I need or can use," said Adelbert. "You see, my father was hipped on 'higher education.' To avoid argument, I went to my grandfather's college in Georgia. I did it to escape a northern college—for reasons you wouldn't understand."

"Perhaps I do," said the Englishman calmly. Then he paused. He wanted to hear the story of this somewhat arrogant but reticent young colored man who seldom spoke of himself. Now, the Englishman was eager to hear more.

Adelbert paused, lighted a cigarette, and watched two passing girls, who glanced responsively his way before going on. Then he continued.

"Well, yes, of course you know our famous 'color line.' It hit me pretty hard. As a child, my intriguing father got me placed in suburban schools with well-to-do whites. They, or most of them, had little or no background of race discrimination and I had almost no color consciousness. We played and studied together, visited each other's homes. We were conscious only of good companionship. Of course, now and then the outer world intruded. Once we came to blows over a football match with another school when I was refused entrance to the shower. We practically tore the plumbing out. There were also one or two girl episodes which were embarrassing; but in those years I cared nothing for girls.

"Well, I insisted on changing to a high school which despite the law was confined to Negroes. I liked it that way and determined that if I must go to college I would go where I would find the complete race segregation of the South. My grandfather was head of such a college and there I went. I liked the people and the work. But I came to realize that in my native land I was destined forever to be a pariah, an outsider, a 'nigger.' I was wild to escape the Color Line. I did. How? I was drafted in the filthy Korean War. I lost my arm and my soul. And I saw the world. My God! What is it? Have you found out?"

The Englishman slowly re-lit his pipe and got it going. "No, I have not, but I'm groping. Sometimes I think I descry a faint glimmer in the darkness. The center of the world is undoubtedly moving East. We must move with it—in thought certainly, if not body. The trouble is—" He paused.

"The trouble is," added Adelbert, "that the human beast even in the East is not attractive."

The Englishman shifted uneasily. He said, "Of course in time—"

"And time," added Adelbert, suddenly feeling the weight of his twenty-two years, "is not something we have in unlimited quantities."

"Which reduces itself to the pressing necessity of finding what to do with what little we have."

"Or with chucking the job entirely and having another Pernod."

"No, no, not that," began the Englishman. But Adelbert had already risen and beckoned to the waiter. He started off, waving a careless good-bye.

Crossing the Boul'Mich' he entered the Luxembourg gardens and sauntered down one of its ornate flower-lined paths. He found a chair and for a long time stared at the dark gray façade of the Palace. Its columns held an answer attempted two hundred years ago—beauty and gracious life built on toil and misery. He saw a lady emerging between the portals, coiffured and curled, groomed and painted and dressed with an elegance distilled from the rags and disease of a thousand beggars, a chain of pearls about her neck, pearls which were the nodules of syphilis.

So what, he thought. Had we bettered this? Not a whit. We had moved our poverty and misery out of sight of fastidious eyes and simply stored it far away in Africa and Asia and the islands of the sea "where every prospect pleases, and only Man is vile!" The number of rich and well-to-do living on human misery, thought Adelbert, is far greater than it was in 1789.

Here now walks a Paris girl of the better class—a hundred Chinese coolies starved to give her stockings. How many Australian black men sweated to make her skirt? That leather belt around her slender waist—it must have brought tuberculosis and hunger to how many shacks among the gauchos of the Argentine? And her scanty, delicate underwear, wasn't it wrought in the mills of Carolina by children working through the night? Who put that jewelled wedding ring on her finger but a million black African families torn asunder and scattered in thousands of dank, dark mines. What she will eat at noon, peoples, races and nations plant, tend and send abroad while their own children starve. This is the French empire! This is merrie England! This is God's country—America—land of the free!

He arose angrily from his seat and swung out on the Rue Vaugirard where, pausing for traffic, his eyes caught an old poster: "Congres Mondial de la Paix." He stopped to admire Picasso's dove, then walked on pondering; finally he hailed a taxi and went to seek his friend, D'Arboussier.

Gabriel D'Arboussier was a copper-colored African, French to the core in education and culture, but fanatical in his devotion to his native land. He had talked much about the Peace Congress, and Adelbert, his interest suddenly whetted, felt he wanted to learn more about what had taken place there. He ran into D'Arboussier dashing out, just as he himself was stepping out of his cab. They both re-entered the cab.

"Good! I was hoping I would run into you. Come with me. This is something you must see for yourself." D'Arboussier pointed up to the purple streamers festooning the avenue. "Today they are burying Eboué in the Pantheon among the great dead of France."

"Did you know him?"

"He was my friend, my leader. I still follow him!"

"Did France reward him?"

"No, it neglected his warning words. It delayed his great plans. But afterthought has come. This re-burial of his body marks the re-birth of his plans for Africa."

The solemn music of the band playing a dirge drew near as they left the cab; then the funeral cortege, led by heads of state, appeared and entered the portals of the Pantheon. Eboué was borne aloft in his great bronze casket.

They turned back, D'Arboussier talking animatedly of France and the ferment in Africa. Hardly had they turned when they encountered a woman, obviously Asiatic, graceful and slight. She stood very still with head bowed and face veiled, until the casket had disappeared within the great portals. Then turning swiftly, she glided away. It seemed to Adelbert that D'Arboussier had recognized her and was about to speak, but she disappeared too swiftly and neither mentioned her. D'Arboussier invited him to a meeting, but Adelbert declined. He knew D'Arboussier was a Communist and always ready to discuss peace. But wasn't this contradictory?

"To get peace, weren't the Chinese waging war?" Adelbert insisted. "Wasn't war the only answer to peace?" It seemed to him idiotic and quite futile. Then he asked D'Arboussier what he thought of Russia. How did his black world propose to emancipate itself? Could it do it alone? To whom could it turn for help? They remained talking and arguing until sunset, then parted with promises to meet again soon.

Adelbert had hitherto hesitated about associating himself too much with the African blacks because he regarded herding simply on the basis of skin color as silly. He had no "race pride," only "human" pride as he expressed it, and indeed it was not quite that—rather pride of individuality and of interests based on like individual tastes and outlook. And yet, in this worldwide movement there had arisen a new thing—here was a common human cause, peace. Here were human beings of every variety, united to secure life when life was threatened by annihilation and the frightful deformations of war. This common cause made him feel a kinship for such folk greater than any bond he could feel for Negroes as such. Perhaps in the time of his grandfather, Negroes as slaves or as new freedmen had some mystic bond of "race" that made them one. But now? Except for a certain similarity of color, what had his father in common with a Mississippi field-hand? Barring that color, his father was a white American making money, buying votes, using "influence" as other Chicagoans did. Now, in Africa . . ."

He suddenly became conscious of the woman. It was, he was sure, the same Asiatic woman whom he and D'Arboussier had seen two hours ago. He dimly remembered seeing her as he turned from the Rue Vaugirard toward his lodging on a narrow street which led off to the right. She had followed him, or at least seemed to, until he started to turn. Then, under the street light he met her face to face and was startled. At first he thought she was the lady from Viet-Nam pictured in the press as hurling fiery words at the Peace Congress. Then he saw she was not; but she had the same doll-like fragility, the same small exquisite feet and hands. She was younger but not young. Her face was comely, not beautiful, but strong and set and there were deep lines carved upon it.

Coming swiftly around the corner she was upon him before she could stop. She paused, drew back with an almost snake-like quiver, stiffened and looked him unblinking in the eye. Although she was rare in look and race, he thought he knew her kind, and raised his hat easily. She walked straight toward him and passed him without a word or gesture, disappearing silently around the corner. He was puzzled; was it that he did not look rich enough to be her quarry or had she mistaken him for another? If the latter was the case, he was glad he was not in that other's shoes—there was something like murder in her face. He forgot her and climbed wearily up to his room.

Next morning he came to two conclusions, on one of which he wrote his grandfather:

> "*Dear Granddad:*
>
> *"It's no use. I can't stick it. I don't like study; I don't like universities. I don't like life. I have an experiment in mind. If it turns out to be feasible I'm off on my own. If it fails or does not continue to attract me (which is the same thing), I may come crawling back home. I may not. So long."*

President Mansart was worried about Adelbert's letter and immediately sent it on to his son Revels. Judge Revels received it in the same mail with a communication from Betty Carmichael, in Springfield. He had not heard from the Carmichaels in some time, but understood they were getting on quite well. He knew that young Jackie had graduated from high school and then attended college at Yale. The Judge's wife somehow had gathered that Jackie was going to marry a white classmate in Springfield, but they had no definite word of this. Jack, the father, was now a man of thirty-four and the Judge was curious to learn how he had turned out and what he was doing.

Betty came down from Springfield to talk to her relatives.

"We are doing well in everything, I suppose, that really matters, and yet there are clouds. Jack has his job in the factory and with the war work, he earns over five thousand a year. However, the factory is threatening to move south, where it can have cheap land, unorganized labor, low taxes and even some free capital furnished by the city and state. This is making the unions anxious but nothing has happened yet, except what unions in war work must fear, and that is, peace. My nursing has gone well; I am in a new research laboratory with interesting work and good pay. We have a lovely home, a car and a servant."

Nevertheless, she was worried. Jackie had graduated from Yale in 1950 with a good record. Since high school he had been engaged to a pretty white classmate of Irish descent, a Catholic in religion. There were difficulties at first. But Jackie had many Catholic friends and Betty had nursed the girl's mother through a dangerous illness, and all were at least resigned to this inter-racial marriage.

"While Jackie was in college, I noticed that matters were not going smoothly between the pair, and before his graduation the engagement was quietly broken although Jackie insisted that they still remained good friends. I am not, as you know, wild about our men marrying white girls, but if the couple are compatible, I see no reason in mere color of skin for it not to take place.

"But this was broken off without consultation with me. Then Jackie went west to a technical school for post-graduate work. We saw nothing of him and he seldom wrote. Jackie's college record, at least temporarily, secured him exemption from military service. After graduation he worked in electronics and physics. He was studying and working hard, summer as well as term time, and was earning enough to pay his own expenses. He was also interested in biochemistry and nuclear physics.

"I planned several times to go out and see him but he or I were always too busy. Yesterday, like a bolt from the blue, came a wire saying that Jackie is married and leaving for work in—of all places—Mississippi! Moreover, because time presses he wants to have a wedding reception here in your apartment—next Tuesday. He says he won't have time to come to Springfield. I don't know what to make of all this. Is it pique at being jilted by a white girl? Is his wife white or colored? And who in God's name ever heard of an educated young Negro settling in Mississippi? I hardly know what to ask in regard to this self-invited reception."

The Judge smiled, and lighted another cigar.

"The white South has always argued that equal rights to Negroes would be the straight road to intermarriage. We protested but the South was right."

"But," said Betty, "I always thought that our pride of race, our memories of the past, would so bind us into a self-respecting group that cases of intermarriage would be few until the day when nobody cared."

"And yet, in the face of this we want to meet—indeed we must meet and know—our white neighbors. We live beside them if we can afford to or are not kept away by law or force. We push our children into schools with white children, and we must if we want them well educated. Take Jackie. In the rural South, he had almost no children to play with. In Harlem, he had too many but of every degree of poverty, disease, debauchery and misfortune. You yanked him away. In Springfield, you fought to put him into the best school, with the best whites. He's a handsome, intelligent boy. What did you expect?"

"But what will become of colored people if their successful individuals are continuously lost to the mass of whites, while the dark residue is allowed to wallow alone in the dirt? Besides, Jackie did not associate closely with the upper-class New Englanders, but with the mill hands' children, and his fiancee was a Catholic."

The Judge laughed aloud. "Which is religious prejudice added to race," he said. Then he grew solemn.

"It is not merely a matter of religion," he said. "It is rather that in our day the political activity of the Catholic Church has raised important questions—the way Catholics have supported colonialism in Africa and Asia; their crushing of Spain's effort to be free; the narrow escape we had of seeing a world crusade against the Soviet Union; and here, among us, the enormous growth of parochial schools and the way in which the public schools have become controlled, with so many of the best Jewish and Protestant teachers driven out. And finally, the subtle way in which the admission of Negroes to higher political office has come to be restricted to Catholic Negroes. Here is that 'foreign' rule right here in America about which, in the case of Russia, we have railed and jailed so furiously. What's sauce for Spellman seems poison for Vishinsky."

"But, my God," said Betty, "surely we are not in for another anti-Catholic crusade?"

"A great and ancient human institution is by nature good, bad or indifferent. But to attack it as a whole is always wrong. Not to attack its evil is also wrong. To claim for it infallibility is to claim what no human institution ever attained. To assert its complete evil is mere ignorance.

"We must more intelligently recognize and help the efforts which Catholics themselves are making inside the Church to suppress evil. Many Catholics raised their voices to halt the world crusade against the Soviets. Catholics are helping to bring education to the natives of Kenya, Nyasaland, the Congo. South America is showing signs of refusing further to follow the rule of reactionary North American investors working in the name of the Church. Catholic labor in the United States stopped in its tracks the attempt of the Catholic hierarchy of New York to fight union labor in the cemeteries of Brooklyn. Yes, and one day Catholics will repudiate Budenz and his kind; they will refuse to let liars teach morals in a Catholic university."

The bell rang and Jack Carmichael entered. He had just arrived from Springfield. Not yet middle-aged, he was already slightly grey and solemn in mien. He did not join in the talk but listened seriously. After dinner they relaxed in the library and waited.

It was nearly nine at night when the bell rang and Mrs. Mansart opened the apartment door. Jackie and his wife stood there. Jackie, a big, husky, cream-colored man, vibrant with life and faith, strode in like a fresh breeze—but one foreshadowing a whirlwind.

"I expect you do not remember me, Sir? I am the grandson of your mother's youngest sister. You remember how your father helped my father settle in South Georgia? Oh, hello, Mom, Hello, Dad!"

Mansart remembered only too well. How vainly his father had dreamed of Negro farms in the South leading the dark millions to freedom! And now they were heading by the hundreds of thousands to the greater freedom of Harlem and Chicago's South Side.

Beside Jackie stood a woman nearly as tall as he, well-proportioned, with a brilliant dark brown skin and long black hair. She was simply but tastefully dressed and one saw at a glance that she was reserved and intelligent. Her manner and bearing remained calm even in a situation which could not but be trying to her and her ease and perfect poise dominated the scene. Betty stared open-mouthed—it required a desperate effort to find a few words of greeting. Mrs. Mansart came forward with some conventional phrases which she knew sounded stilted and empty. The Judge simply reached out both hands. The bride smiled graciously, then leaning forward, kissed Betty lightly on the forehead.

"Jackie has talked so much of his mother," she murmured. Mrs. Mansart kissed her and Jack took her unconventionally in his arms. She smiled gratefully at him and then turning slowly to the Judge began to speak. She spoke a clear musical, distinctly enunciated English, which had a slight accent and yet was in no way foreign.

"You must forgive us, Judge Mansart, for this unwarranted intrusion. It was entirely my fault. You see, I am the granddaughter of Hiram Revels, once Senator from Mississippi, after whom you are named. From childhood I have been eager to meet you. Nearly all my family are dead and you seemed more than a relative. American? Of course I am. I was trained at Alcorn and then at sixteen went to Denmark, whence I returned only three years ago. I am thirty-two," she added. By this time the group had thawed and soon Jackie was talking.

"Ann," he explained, "Mother is still bursting with that broken engagement in Springfield. You see, Mom, Kate was a nice girl. I think she was the prettiest thing I ever saw on that commencement night. Of course we ran into all sorts of difficulties, but we were madly in love. But then, while I was in college I began to think. Trouble was about what we were going to do when we lived together. Kate was American—much more American than most Americans. She had not the slightest interest in Ireland. She wanted a beautiful home, a big car, servants and good ones, clothes in plenty and a good time. She had a heavenly love of pleasure; her laugh was divine. All this I liked. I think too I could have earned enough money to carry it out. But after that, WHAT?

"This matter of inter-racial marriage bothers me. We may look at it as a way of settling the race problem by letting the Negro race gradually be absorbed into the white and thus disappear in America. I think Mom sees it this way. That means that all which the Negro as such had to contribute to this country would be lost. I don't believe in race pride, as we call it, but our contribution rests on our experience and memories, our suffering, our music and laughter. This is important. It is a massive bundle of human history from which the world can learn and be guided. Then too this disappearance by absorption would mean the death of Negro women; the Negro men for the most part would marry whites; the Negro women would languish as spinsters and lonesome, bitter outsiders. This would be a terrible loss. No people can lose their womanhood and survive.

"Then, too, contrary to the current American philosophy, marriage is not mainly and cannot be entirely sex. Marriage is friendship and cooperation in work. This nation is striving madly to make sex appear as the only real life and the result is divorce, broken homes, deserted children and nasty orgies with alcoholic and drug stimulants. I know this because I've watched and thought of women now for ten years. I saw college life continually ruined by absorption in sex. I saw human intercourse diverted into sex. And in contradiction, children, instead of becoming cherished and planned for, became more and more neglected, mis-educated or lost in abortion. So I gave up the idea of Kate. We loved each other but it was an attraction of sex, not of ideal and work. It was the lure of the unusual. More and more Kate craved excitement. She loved gambling—you should have seen her at a horse race—and could she drink whiskey! When I met Ann, there was something different. I was drawn to her not because she was brown—although that made it easier—but because we wanted the same things, remembered the same things, and were trained to do the same work, and that work we thought of supreme importance.

"Then comes the thought of the Indians—the forgotten, disinherited, murdered, and debauched American Indians. You see Ann is part Indian. Her father married into that Indian tribe that still lives out on Long Island. I knew nothing of Indians until Ann taught me. Here in the United States, slowly, inevitably the Indians are disappearing into mere Americans, without enriching America or saving their own souls and culture, which deserve saving. But Indians survive. In Central and South America are a hundred million or more people who are predominantly of ancient Indian blood. That blood and culture has swallowed Spaniard and Portuguese, Italian and Jew, and with Negro blood it will give South America a new civilization which the world will hail. The United States, helped by white Europe, now dominates and exploits these millions and keeps them in slavery with the connivance of Indian traitors, rich and ambitious. But change is coming, precipitate and complete change. Ann and I await that change with enthusiasm. We seek other Negroes to work and wait beside us. I suppose all this is a sort of egocentric, spiritual nationalism which the world today fears. Yet, for us it is self-defense, a determination that we and our thoughts and dreams shall not die but live for the world's good."

Ann took up the theme: "Grandfather had a plantation on the bluffs above the Mississippi River. He bought it in Reconstruction times and we've held on to most of it. The soil is worn out and the buildings falling down. But the location is excellent, with river and road to the world. There are old families around, Negroes long associated with our family as friends, tenants and laborers; even some poor whites are long-time friends. Many of the younger folk have gone North and been educated; some we've got hold of and others we are in touch with. What we plan is a small rural group led by young educated men and women. We want to farm and raise stock; but beyond this we want to start local industry in the homes to begin trade with our neighbors and the nation. We want a village with a hospital, a good school and work for everybody. Just so far as possible we'll discriminate against nobody; whites and blacks can attend school if they want to and will be welcome to the hospital.

"We are not fools; we know the opposition will be strong—ignorant government in which Negroes have little voice, habitual mob violence, and Big Business, gigantic and growing, determined to make Mississippi and Louisiana the greatest modern center of industrial exploitation in the nation with no effective trade unions. We are prepared for violence—we are going to be armed even to submachine guns. But we know full well that if our survival and progress depends on arms, or just so far as it so depends, we are doomed. If by care, industry and thought, by science and education, adult and youth, we can found and run a small co-operative enterprise, we are started toward a future. It's a gamble. Perhaps as wise men have said, no such peaceful, democratic path to social progress is possible without revolution. I don't believe that yet. And Jackie and I are ready to give our lives to prove it's not true."

"Ann has spoken for me," said Jackie. "I know what we're up against and the chances are not good. But we may win. These are some of our immediate problems: can we get a good Negro physician to come to Mississippi and work for health, not money? Can we change the local Negro church into an adult education institution with a minimum of dogma? Above all, can we in peace apply chemistry and physics, horticulture and psychology in a region long depressed by ignorance, poverty and disease?"

Judge Mansart stared at these devotees and a lump came to his throat. He thought of all their predecessors—Brook Farm, New Harmony, Hopedale, Zoar and Aurora. Well, what of it? We fall to rise and without effort, even hopeless effort, nothing is ever won. "Go to it,' he said, "and we will always be ready to advise and help." Mrs. Mansart added: "It is simply magnificent. I wish that I could have seen such a vision in my youth!"

They became conscious of a noise in the hallway, then the bell rang furiously. Jackie winked. "The gang," he said, and rushed to open the door. A dozen young white folk poured in. They were gay, almost tipsy, and swarmed enthusiastically around Jackie and Ann. A tall, strikingly beautiful and gorgeously gowned girl rushed forward. She threw her arms about Jackie and kissed him.

"Jackie, darling! So terribly glad to see you; and Ann! So you're the girl who finally landed him. Say, you're pretty swell—that color and that gown, my, it's tops. Who designed it? We've been having a grand time—that new musical, I forget its name but it's swell. Then supper at the Stork Club—the champagne was divine. Now, we've come to take you to the airport since you won't stay over. Then we'll finish up somewhere until dawn. And Jackie, don't forget—Hal's father is lousy with money and we don't know how to spend it. If you need money for your crazy Mississippi bubble, write me. Don't forget, just write or wire!"

They poured out as swiftly as they poured in. Ann was the last to leave; she turned and kissed Betty and held her close. "I'll take care of him," she whispered.

Betty sank speechless into a chair and stared toward the door. "These children," she gasped. The Judge suddenly exclaimed, "I clean forgot to show Jackie Adelbert's letter. I must send it to him."

"Please enclose this with it," Mrs. Mansart said. "It is a letter which President Truman has just received from a woman whom I know."

The Judge read:

"Dear Mr. President:

"There has come into my hands—and I have just read—the Report of the Women's International Commission for the Investigation of Atrocities Committed by U.S.A. and Syngman Rhee troops in Korea.

"Mr. President, I have never, in my forty years of life, been so shocked and horrified as I was today upon reading this documentary Report of the utter depravity of the sex-crazed troops under our command in Korea.

"'... 26 hospital patients burned to death from incendiary bomb fires ... 30 mothers and children killed ... systematic machine-gunning of civilians trying to extinguish fires ... children machine-gunned from low-flying planes while running from burning homes ... hospitals, tramcars, bridges, water systems blown up ... women and girls "caught" on the streets and taken to army brothels ... a native beaten by the Americans because he hid his wife from them ... the Americans led her naked through the streets ... North Korean prisoners of war put into a field, petrol poured on them, set afire and burned alive ... mountain forests destroyed by American incendiary bombs ... imprisoned women beaten by Americans, 20 raped ... victims killed by American cartridges exploded in their mouths ... in King Won alone 2,903 women raped by American and Rhee troops ... chased into rice field, violated, shot. ...'

"How long, how long, Oh mighty President, must this bleeding, killing, murdering, torturing, destroying, maiming, this infanticide, homicide, genocide—this travesty on justice—continue?

"America's 'leaders'—by their own definition in World War II—are making themselves war criminals, perpetrators of dastardly crimes against humanity for which they may yet be made to pay with their lives by an enraged world opinion.

"At the head of that parade of the despised clique of fanatical 'anti-Communists' and would-be atomic annihilators of life on earth and destroyers of the civilization which took millions of man-years to create, will march—in chains, perhaps—the ONE man who could have stopped it all but didn't—Harry S Truman, unless ... unless you do something tangible and effective immediately before it is too late.

"If that day comes, Mr. President, you can contemplate in retrospect a certain longish 8-page letter dated Wednesday, September 19th, 1951, in which the 'Terrible End' was 'prophesied' by a little-known, now-dead-and-gone-and-forgotten, little nobody who signed herself,

"Pleadingly yours,

Vena."

CHAPTER XVIII

◆

Back to Africa

Adelbert, after writing his grandfather, telephoned his friend D'Arboussier and accepted the invitation which he had just declined—to attend a meeting of the Rassemblement African Democratique. He decided that he wanted to see what these men were planning, what made them so enthusiastic, so sure. The idea of Russian Communism in Africa was too fantastic—but just what did they plan? Was it anything that could arouse his interest? Probably not. He had no deeply conscious roots in Africa. Generally speaking, he did not particularly like black folks and felt as alien to a black Georgia tenant as to a white British navy. Both seemed to him to belong to an alien race.

The meeting took place in a restaurant on the Left Bank. There was evidently a higher level of culture here than at similar meetings of colored folk in America. The members were nearly all university-bred and belonged to many races. There were Sudanese and West Africans, some with their tribal marks on their faces; there were mulattoes from Africa and the West Indies; there were Asiatics; and Adelbert was startled to recognize the same fragile Asiatic girl whom he had recently encountered. If she recognized him she gave no sign, and he was careful not to notice her too obviously.

"Tell me," he said to a man seated at his table who had been introduced to him as a citizen of Timbuctoo, "Do you Africans expect to escape from European control without war?"

"Perhaps not, but it is possible."

"And do you aim, in case of war, to conquer and control whites as whites have conquered and controlled you?"

"Oh, no. You see, war as an instrument of progress is unthinkable. As a measure of last ditch defense, we may have to resort to it from time to time. We are certain that by planning and knowledge, and by democratic control, we can organize our people for their own welfare, progress and enjoyment, and not let them be regimented for the enjoyment and progress of Europe."

"Benevolent fascism might do that, but——"

"Fascism can never remain benevolent. Eventually it must succumb to its own greed and idiocy. Only democratic control insures eternal benevolence—a people must seek its own welfare."

"But is not democracy mob-rule? And will the mob ever be wise enough, in the broadest sense, to rule benevolently?"

He heard a voice from the table behind him. It was a soft yet firm voice, a woman's voice speaking in a tremulo vibrant with strength and faith. He turned and was astonished to see that it was the young Viet-Namese woman speaking:

"Democracy is and always must be mob-rule, even though the mob must be led, must be taught by word and command. There is no other way. Your West has bribed the mob with small concessions and big illusions. The East must plead with it, persuade it, imbue it with the self-sacrifice and discipline necessary for its own salvation."

Adelbert stared at her. Her eyes did not waver. D'Arboussier broke in: "Let me illustrate. Europe, by enclosing the common land and bribing the feudal lords, separated the peasant from the soil; and by monopolizing tools, made the people slaves to employers. We Africans have not yet surrendered our tribal ownership of the soil. Starting from there, can we not raise our own food, process our materials for our own needs, educate our masses by an education aimed at life and not simply at power? Once the majority of the world's peoples start on this path, can they be stopped?"

Another broke in: "Moreover, the white race is already so envious of itself that it is committing suicide. When it discovers that the prize it covets, namely the slave labor and valuable materials of Asia and Africa, can no longer be obtained, wars will cease for sheer lack of cause."

Adelbert smiled incredulously. "First, all this self-education and self-control is easier imagined than realized. After all, Blacks, Browns and Yellows are no angels! We must expect to be betrayed by our own people. . . ."

He sensed the weight of the silence which greeted his words. The atmosphere changed and though the conversation turned to a lighter note and the wine continued to be passed, Adelbert knew he had unwittingly touched a deep wound. He arose and strolled about until he found himself near the Viet-Namese. His vanity at first tempted him not to speak. But they both turned at the same time. She showed no trace of coquetry as she said,

"The other night I mistook you for another. You are very like in build, and he used to live near."

He smiled. "I am glad I wasn't he," he said.

"So am I," she answered coldly, with no trace of a smile. She did not enlarge further and as they sat down she returned to her thesis. She was sure that the Western laborer had sold his political power for comfort and mechanical luxury, then had turned soldier to conquer and enslave the colored masses for more power. Adelbert insisted that the colored folk, too, would under similar circumstances yield to the same temptation.

She was silent and her slender arms, tensed under her mental earnestness, fell to her lap, the wide sleeves falling back. Then, for the first time, he noticed. He had heard of it, had even seen the scars on coarse, hairy arms. But here, on a wrist that might have belonged to a child, were the tatooed numbers of the concentration camp—71,942. He stared down and then took her hand gently in his.

The beginnings of tears started in his eyes—he felt so utterly anguished that he had no words. She let his hand lay on hers for a space, then said:

"You see, I was educated in France. When the war came, of course, I helped the partisans and was—betrayed. They took me to Germany."

He wanted to know everything, to ask about all that happened to her but could not; nor did she offer to tell. She arose at last and looked into his eyes with something nearer to a smile than he had ever seen.

"Goodbye," she said with a certain finality. "Trust the people!" And she was gone. He suddenly realized that he did not even know her name.

Adelbert never forgot the ordeal of decision he experienced in the next week. His grandfather had written pleadingly: "Don't be crazy. Please come home!" He would have every chance—his father had money—more perhaps than Adelbert thought. He had influence. "Don't be a fool!" There was more in the letter; but to Adelbert all was too clear—nobody in America wanted or needed him.

The handful of leading Negroes were getting rich—the mass of poor Negroes were getting poorer. All that the leaders aspired to was to be like white Americans—wealthy, loud, swaggering. Yes, he could be one of them. But then what? He did not have to swagger and boast—he was perfectly sure of himself and of his worth. He was not concerned about what other Americans or other Negroes thought. But he did want something worthwhile, something meaningful to do—some vast chance on which to risk a life. He began to feel he had found it. Of course, he was not sure—could anybody be sure of anything in this damned world? But why not take a chance? Throw all to the winds and *try Africa?*

He leaped up and grabbing his suitcases, began to pack. He had just piled his fresh clothes on the sofa and was kneeling over his largest valise when the door opened softly and quickly closed. He turned—the Viet-Namese woman stood there. Her robe was torn, a bloody knife was in her hand and her face was pale as death.

She stared at him. "You!" she gasped, and staggered a moment. He started toward her but she stiffened and touched her lips with a finger. He heard a commotion in the hall. There was a peremptory knock on the door. Without a word he turned and, pushing her on the sofa, threw a pile of clothes over her; she was so fragile that the addition scarcely showed. He quickly turned the blood-smeared doormat and said gruffly: "Entrez!" busying himself with the bags and scarcely looking up.

"Monsieur," said the polite Paris gendarme, "I believe a woman just entered your room."

Adebert turned casually and the police officer noted his fine linen shirt and tailored trousers.

"Sir," he said as he brushed off his hands and lighted a cigarette, "a lady left at six this morning. She has neither returned nor been replaced. I was expecting that damned concierge to help with these bags, and thought it was he when you knocked. Did you happen to see him?"

"I did not, Sir. But pardon me, a dangerous murderess has escaped and is in this house. Would you permit me, Sir, to look through your apartment?"

"With pleasure, Sir, only don't disturb my things. I've been up half the night arranging them."

The policemen searched the bedroom, the little bathroom, the oaken armoire; he looked under the bed and behind doors. Puzzled, he profusely begged pardon and hastened away, bowing politely as he backed out of the door.

The bundle of clothes did not move, did not even tremble. When Adelbert lifted them the woman, stained with blood, lay still as death. He was seized with panic. Quickly filling the bath with warm water, he lifted the little body, stripped off the torn clothes and lowered her into the water, rubbing her body gently and massaging her temples, cheeks and neck. She lay like a golden idol, infinitely beautiful, of perfect form. He was sure she was dead and for a moment was horrified at the predicament he would be in. Then he thought he detected a faint pulse beat. He opened a bottle of cognac and poured a few drops between her lips. She stirred slightly as he lifted her in his arms and placed her on his bed, covering her warmly and stroking her forehead and temples with gentle hands. Then he poured a few more drops of liquor into her mouth until at long last she was sleeping gently, her heart beating regularly.

He turned to gather up and destroy her clothes. Suddenly, as he gazed down on the torn and blood-smeared garment, the full horror of the situation dawned on him. Neither squeamish nor given to nerves, Adelbert was no stranger to death and murder. Death—if sudden and violent—was news even in Chicago; in Korea, it seemed to him, he had seen nothing but death. War was murder and murder was war. It made the world dirty. And here it had touched with tainted hand this lovely wisp of a woman who had affected him somehow as no woman ever had before. She was beautiful, yes, but not innocent—she had deliberately transgressed the commandment: "Thou shalt not kill."

He stood up slowly. He made a bundle, as small as possible, of all the blood-stained things. Carefully he climbed the attic stairs—paused and looked around. There was a policeman on the roof. He returned, left the bundle hidden among his packed clothes, then sat down to think. He must see D'Arboussier. He started for the door and paused. He tiptoed to the bed. It was after midnight. She was still asleep, breathing regularly but faintly. He started to make himself a bed on the floor. Then alarm seized him again. Suppose she should die in the night? He partially undressed, lay down beside her on the bed and enfolded her gently in his arms. Thus they slept.

He awoke with a tremor. He felt her slight body nestled against him. But though her eyes were closed, he knew she was no longer sleeping. He looked at her face. Her skin was smooth, pale gold, her features perfect. She was not as young as at first glance she had seemed to him. She was perhaps twenty-five. The lines on her face were faint but strong and fixed. She had known sorrow and despair—she had suffered. What was it about her that drew him so inexorably? He had always disliked or faintly despised women, even when they catered to his appetite. He lay his head back in reverie, easing her gently in his one arm. She yielded but made no move.

He supposed his dislike of women arose from his old feeling of resentment toward his mother. From his birth, his mother had resented the fact that he was so dark. She was olive-skinned and pretty and quite vain, and if he had just been cream-colored, with his curled hair and beautiful features, she would have had him on constant exhibition. As it was, she was ashamed of him—he was "too black." He was always relegated to obscurity. Even his father had noticed it, but she knew how to bring father around with her kittenish ways.

If his mother had been lovable or even really beautiful in his eyes, Adelbert might have suffered more. As it was, he rose indifferently above the situation. He found he could easily get his way in most things, and his mother was least among the things he admired or envied. He grew up unscathed by what his friends called love. He kissed girls and sometimes petted them; as he grew older he indulged cautiously his sex instincts, but he himself always remained untouched in his deeper self, and always half indifferent.

And now—he raised his head and looked at this woman. Her eyes were looking frankly and clearly into his. A moment he lay still. Then he kissed her long and gently and she yielded to his caresses. Quickly he arose and stepping to the bathroom, bathed and dressed. Then he came back, bringing her some of his underclothes and a suit, together with his sewing kit. She thanked him softly and he stepped into his living room, shutting the door behind him. Then he sat down to think. Yes, he must see D'Arboussier. He must also manage to keep the concierge out of the room until he returned. There was, too, the danger that the police might return. He must risk that. Above all, he must first see D'Arboussier, although he was not sure in his own mind why he considered it so imperative.

The door opened quietly. There entered a young man with ill-fitting but not altogether poorly arranged clothes, his head topped by a rather large beret. Adelbert was startled to recognize the Viet-Namese. He arose and smiled. She smiled faintly back and said, "I had better go now, don't you think?"

"No," he answered, "there may be policemen still watching. I'm going to summon D'Arboussier."

"That would be well. Phone from some corner store and say little. If anyone comes, I shall know what to do."

Going to the armoir, he fumbled a moment, then brought out a snub-nosed automatic. She refused it. "I shall not need that," she said quietly. What did she mean? That she would peaceably surrender or that she had other weapons? He nodded and went out. At the window of the concierge he paused and said casually.

"Leave my room alone until I return. I'm packing."

He hurried as far as the Rue des Rennes where he telephoned D'Arboussier, giving no name but stressing the urgency of his request. He stuffed croissons into his pocket and started back. As he approached his lodgings, his heart jumped—a policeman was talking to the concierge. He buried his face in his morning paper until he was abreast, then nodding indifferently, walked up the three flights with bounding pulse. Entering, he saw no one, but in a moment the Vietnamese stepped out of the armoire.

"I hid here," she said, "when the concierge entered; but I am small and you have so many clothes. The fur overcoat completely enfolded me."

He sat down and wiped his forehead. Then he arose and began to make coffee. She silently relieved him, but for herself poured only a small cup, which she drank without sugar. Up to this time neither had mentioned the tragedy which, to him, seemed to poison the air. He waited for her to speak, but she simply kept still, as though there was nothing she could or even ought to say. It was to him inexplicable. He arose impatiently and stepped to the window, his back to the room. Then she began to talk. Her voice was low, yet distinct and firm.

"I am Dao Thu. It will be hard for you to understand. This generation has learned to hate the killing of a single person and yet to accept the slaughter of masses of people. It is perhaps the greatest anomaly of the twentieth century—an infinite contradiction. It is more than wrong. Masses of men are never guilty. The victims of Hiroshima were not guilty of wrong. Those who dropped that bomb were murderers. We build monuments and cast medals for men who kill indiscriminately in wars we call 'glorious,' yet condemn to shame the man who strangles his daughter's seducer.

"We, in Viet-Nam, arose and took back the country which foreigners had stolen. France fought by murder, torture and starvation, helped by England and America. We fought on.

"While studying in Paris in 1938, before the war, I met our great leader, Ho Minh. I acted as his secretary while he was negotiating with the government for our freedom. It was then we met Eboué, just summoned home from his governorship of Guadeloupe. We knew what he had done for the workers, their homes and wages. We sought his help and sympathy. He promised aid. He believed in France, but France did not believe in him. He refused to be a tool of Mandel and as punishment was sent to Africa. But he was glad. He had already served there five years. He assured us of his help and of the good faith of France. He knows better now.

"During the war, I tried to help that part of France which resisted Germany, and could surely sympathize with Viet-Nam. I was right. But the crime and criminal appeared in our ranks. Spies and traitors appeared to sell us to our murderers and traducers. Was there the slightest doubt of their guilt? Were they not worthy to die? Must they not be killed if Viet-Nam was ever to live?

"One there was—I knew him well; tall for our land, handsome, educated, gifted. We were in school together in my land and met again studying in Paris. We were in love and planned to marry. But he went with Pétain, I with the Resistance. For a time, Phan Hu pretended he was still on our side, but spying on Vichy. In this way, he betrayed me to the Nazis."

Adelbert tried to take her tattooed hand in his, but she withdrew it gently. "No," she said. "I did not kill him for that. I would not murder just for myself. But when I learned that he was planning to restore control of France over my country by means of a degenerate puppet prince who was gambling at Monte Carlo; and that his were the brains engineering this plot, I knew Phan Hu must die; not because personally I hated and despised him but because he was leading the traitors of my land.

"I gave up my education. I gave up my state scholarship. I gave up my profession of medicine. I became the hand of God and of my country to remove a man worse than a murderer. I stalked him a year; that is how I first met you, mistaking you for him. Last night I found him. I killed him. My work is finished.

What happens to me now is of no account. Least of all, my friend, would I have you stain your hands with a crime in which you had no willing or conscious share. I want to go now and surrender to the French police. I would have done so last night but it might have involved you."

She started to rise when there came a knock at the door. They paused and stared at each other. Then quickly, before he could prevent it, she opened the door. D'Arboussier stood there. They were silent.

"May I enter?" he asked, smiling. They came to life and grasped his hands. He bowed, kissed the hands of the lady and murmured, "God bless you, Dao Thu; you have served well!"

He listened to what had happened, then said, "Now for your escape!"

She shook her head in despair but before she could say a word, again came a knock at the door. Adelbert almost lifted her bodily and carried her into the bedroom. D'Arboussier calmly opened the door. A telegraph boy stood there with a blue message for Adelbert. D'Arboussier paid for it, then burst into laughter.

"Boy," he said, "where'd you buy that uniform?"

The boy, somewhat taken aback, answered suspiciously. But D'Arboussier continued smoothly.

"We want to play a joke on a friend—send him a telegram by the hand of his own sweetheart disguised as a messenger. How about lending us your suit for an hour. It's worth—oh, what's the difference—here's a thousand francs."

The boy hesitated. Another thousand franc note appeared and the boy quickly shed his suit. In a minute or so Dao Thu, dressed as a telegraph boy, was accompanying D'Arboussier to his auto, while the stripped messenger lounged about in Adelbert's room until dusk when, wearing an old suit of Adelbert's, he left under the sharp scrutiny of the concierge—but with three thousand francs in his pocket.

It was not until he left that Adelbert, whose thoughts were all of Dao Thu, suddenly remembered the message. It was a cablegram from his father, saying "Grandfather very ill. He wants to see you. Come immediately." It held a draft for a thousand dollars.

Adelbert liked his grandfather. He had always seemed to him a nice old man, perhaps a bit too anxious to be accommodating to the world, shrewd but honest. His father sometimes criticized him as an Uncle Tom, but he, too, had a good deal of respect for him. Now when it came to returning to America for the old man's funeral, Adelbert had not the slightest idea of doing such a thing. It was useless ancestor worship and he'd have none of it. Moreover, he felt he had to see Dao Thu again, that until he did so he would not re-order his life—as he was firmly determined to do.

It was a week before he received a letter from D'Arboussier, at Marseilles, urgently inviting him to attend a meeting of persons interested in the future of Africa. Without hesitation, Adelbert packed his belongings and took the train South. He rode slowly down the valley of the Rhone. Unable to get near the buffet at Dijon because of the crowd, he was ravenously hungry by the time he finally was served a meal in the Wagon-restaurant between Avignon and Marseilles. Yet, he found it a rewarding journey as his train pounded past vineyards and ancient churches, leaving in his mind memories of dissident popes, Roman ruins and Frederick Barbarossa.

He climbed to a castle of Provence, encircling the knife edge of a ridge, above the blue and isle-dotted sea. He threaded narrow, tortuous streets, clean and filled with workers, children, stray cats and dogs. He passed along high walls with great square towers, narrowly slitted, enclosing courts with pleasaunces where a thousand years ago gay princes and their ladies must have laughed at the world—where now are these smiles of yesteryear?

The vast castle grounds, once flowered and turfed, were now covered with dark cypress and lime. The enemy without was no longer the barbarians from the north, but sullen toilers in fields of the plain below these walls, peasants full of envy and resentment, frowning today, as their descendants did through the centuries, on unearned wealth and unmerited leisure. He wound down little, half-hidden curving paths to the square below where the bus halted on the way from Hyeres to Toulon.

At last, in the late afternoon, he came to the hills of Marseilles and, registering at a little hotel, strolled down the Cours de Belsunce to the Cannebiere. He particularly noted the large numbers of colored folk, African and Asiatic laborers, sailors and artisans. It was a fitting place for a meeting such as he had come to attend.

He saw her the moment he entered the small parlor—not because she was near the door or seated prominently in front of the room, but because unconsciously he was looking and thinking of no one else. He crossed to her slowly and she arose and, putting her hands lightly on his shoulders, kissed him on the lips. Then she sat down as D'Arboussier came and sat beside them.

"We have had enormous difficulties," he said. "The police are searching all France for Dao Thu—determined she shall not reach Viet-Nam and help foil the plans they have concocted for their puppet emperor. But there they are mistaken. Their plans are already foiled; the only man who might have rescued them is dead. Dao therefore is not needed just now in Viet-Nam. But she is needed in Africa and perhaps the shortest way to Viet-Nam and to Indonesia and China is through Africa—in two senses of that phrase." He beckoned and the dozens or more others in the room gathered around more closely.

Adelbert observed them carefully. Houphouet-Boigny of the Ivory Coast, the obvious leader, was black, Negroid, with high forehead and intelligent eyes; Felix-Tchicaya, of the Middle Congo, was dark, with a handsome face; the eyes of Kenate, of the Sudan, blazed, while Coulibaly, an Ivory Coast leader, was sombre. Diori, of the Niger, was a mulatto; Lisette of the Chad was black and keen-faced—he had long served as clerk in Eboué's office; Victor of the Ivory Coast, was hard-faced and serious; while Malange, also of the Congo, had an ugly, non-committal face. Franchiai was a handsome mulatto. There were others, but before Adelbert could examine them farther a map was spread over which all bent. It was a map of French Africa.

Adelbert was startled to realize that seething French Africa constituted a major component of the black world; it ranged alongside the seven millions of the Anglo-Egyptian Sudan; the nine millions of the Belgian Congo, speaking the same tongues, allied to the same Bantu races; British West Africa, the greatest center of African nationalism, where Nkrumah was building an independent black nation. Beyond these and in their sphere of influence lay Ethiopia and Uganda, with native ruling dynasties; and Kenya, where the white land thieves ruled and where Jomo Kenyatta was leading revolution. And still beyond, lay the hell of the Rhodesias and South Africa, with twelve or more millions who had more to fight for than any other people on earth.

"And you aim to raise Africa against all its mighty oppressors?" asked Adelbert.

"Not at all," several replied. "We aim to make Africans support and work for themselves as the Chinese are beginning to do. United, conscious and determined to do this, none can make them do aught else. We want to make the workers of France, and eventually the workers of the world, realize that here in Africa—and today—are forged the chains of *their* continued bondage, the bondage of poverty, of land theft, of monopoly of raw materials, of machine regimentation, of chained thought and dominated education, of slave labor cheaper than the cheapest.

"Here it is that the Englishman, determined to regrasp his lost dominion; France, set to recapture the taste and fashion of the world; America, determined to outdo the universe in power and control—right here in Africa—and today—the great exploitation to restore the pre-war imperialism of the European white world has begun, and right here and now in its beginnings it must be met and thwarted—or the Dark Age descends on civilization."

"We have already begun," added D'Arboussier, "and we want your help. Dao, the most gifted organizer in the world today must go to Africa to get home if she ever reaches home or," he paused significantly, "or ever wishes to. For her to enter French colonial Africa, she must marry a colonial official. And you, Adelbert Mansart, have been commissioned as a French colonial civil servant, provided you accept and surrender your American citizenship."

Adelbert did not need to pause for consideration. With barely conscious impulse he arose and crossed over to Dao's side. "We accept," he said for both.

Why should he hesitate? What was there to hesitate about? He knew from his own experience, from everything he had been reading for years, from what Americans had bluntly said in his hearing. To a large part of white America the colored world was dirt—useful, but not human.

To most Americans a free and equal China was simply inconceivable. The Chinese were and always had been good, humble workers who could be kicked and cuffed and who would never be anything else. If, therefore, there had come a revolutionary change in their government it must be the result of some kind of conspiracy or accident, of betrayal by Americans of Americans business, or perhaps of a political blunder which would soon be remedied. They therefore awaited—with impatience but with certainty—for the collapse of Chinese Communism just as they had waited for years for the collapse of Soviet Communism. The longer this collapse was deferred, the more angry they were at the traitors in America who had cut them off from so rich a source of profit.

Toward Africa their attitude was even clearer. There was not the slightest chance in the world that Africans would ever really govern themselves or work for their own benefit. They were fated to be serfs of white men. The ridiculous pretense of the black folk of the Gold Coast, Nigeria, the Congo to set up independent governments, the absurd shadow of revolt smoldering in South Africa, the horrible crimes of resistance of the Mau Mau in Kenya—all this proved what the future of Africa would be unless America took firm control.

The dangerous task of escape from France to colonial Africa confronted Dao and Adelbert. Alone he could go freely, by way of Algiers or Morocco, to Bamako and Timbuctoo, across the ancient trails of the vast desert. But Dao? A woman, a confessed murderer on whose head lay a fortune in reward? Adelbert raised the question of funds; there seemed no difficulty there. When he offered his thousand dollars, Dao looked at him strangely then laid on the table a fortune in jewels and gold and silver ornaments.

"These are yours," she said to D'Arboussier. "If I go to Africa, it will be in complete poverty. Is it not so with you?" she asked, turning to Adelbert.

He arose slowly and said with his old air of detachment, "I start with nothing too."

Two nights later, two men and a slender boy with only a small knapsack sauntered slowly down the Cannebiere toward the old port and stood looking at the ruins which were once the shame of Marseilles. Two policemen strolled after them, but when they reached them the men turned and started back; the boy had disappeared. An hour later, in the Place D'Afrique a man and boy raised themselves cautiously from the rubble and stepped onto the quai where a low-slung sailboat was idling, apparently deserted. They turned toward it, when a policeman appeared.

"Madam Dao Thu I believe," he said with a bow, and his hand was at his belt. Adelbert's hand flew to his automatic but she seized it and tossed it to the ground. Then she stepped forward and said, "Yes."

Adelbert saw at a glance that the policeman was Asiatic. Dao began to speak. She spoke in a low and clear tone, never raising her voice, but it quivered with earnestness. Her words seemed to pour out in a stream, sometimes stern, changing to scorn and denunciation; at times almost hissing hate and contempt, then appealing to hope and greatness. They were words that recalled cruelty, hurt and death. He saw the man stiffen, recoil, raise a hand in protest and hurt, then shiver and wilt. At last, with head bowed, he turned silently and walked away.

Suddenly a platoon of French soldiers surrounded the two. A sergeant stepped forward and raised his hand, when a whistling bullet struck him dead. The soldiers hesitated, confused, as a voice cried in the gathering gloom: "There, over there! They're escaping!"

Far down the quai a couple appeared running swiftly toward a great ship looming in the darkness. The soldiers whirled and ran, spraying shot all over and around the two dim figures who suddenly stumbled, fell and lay still in a crimson pool.

Unnoticed and alone for the moment, Adelbert and his bride walked swiftly to the little boat rocking gently in a darkened cove. They quickly stepped aboard and the boat, raising its crimson lateen sail, glided into the night toward Africa.

Who it was that made the supreme sacrifice for them, back there on the shores of France, they never knew.

With shining eyes, they sailed toward the black South.

She sat with her hand in his.

"Just where are we going, my master?" she asked. He gazed into her eyes, then looking to the South, said:

"First over the sea to Algiers, where I become a French official. Then across the Sahara, 1,500 miles to Timbuktoo; then 500 miles down the Niger and west to Mossi, where we become African. Then to Ghana."

"Ghana? I never heard of Ghana!"

"Your great grandfathers knew it. It awaits us. Our children shall love it."

They sang:

The Congo came rolling from Heaven to Hell
Embracing the jungle and thundering a knell
The roar of its waters, the kiss of its breath
Told God of its birth pains, told Man of his death.

CHAPTER XIX

The Sanctuary of Marriage

Awaiting the Great Commencement, when Manuel would be free to come to her, Jean Du Bignon worked a year as a factory hand in Atlanta. She knew well that she could not accomplish much in so short a time and with so narrow an opportunity. But as the year passed, Manuel's plan suffered a change, not important as it seemed at first, but in the end almost fatal.

It had been the plan of the new Southern leaders to keep down agitation on the race question by making Negro schools as near equal to white as possible. For this object they would favor Federal aid to common schools and give the Land-Grant colleges a more equitable share of current funds. But the Negro organization, the NAACP, had gone into court and was not only breaking down segregation in residence, travel and voting, but also in education. They had already forced entrance of Negro students into white Southern graduate and professional schools.

All this was being implemented slowly, and was also widely resisted. But in the end law was law—and what would happen if the cases on segregation in the common schools were decided by the Supreme Court in favor of the Negroes? Moreover, just at this time Limes, the candidate selected to succeed Mansart, riding home too fast in his new Packard car, killed a tall young cotton wood tree and himself. Why not postpone Mansart's retirement until his eightieth birthday in 1956? To his amazement, this was proposed at the Christmas meeting of the Board.

Mansart objected; he had made his plans. They insisted—well, to please the Board would he stay a couple of years, say until Commencement 1953? He consented reluctantly. They then voted that upon retirement he be given a pension of half pay. Characteristically, he gave little attention to this decision. His salary had long been $5,000—his pension would be $2,500.

Mansart's teachers were genuinely glad that he was to stay at least two more years. Even those who had hoped by this change to find advantage were relieved to be certain at least of what they had. All talked of the coming revolution in Negro education. A few hailed the expected decision of the Supreme Court—"which cannot go against us"—as the long-last end of the Emancipation which Lincoln began in 1863.

But most of the teachers were silent. What they were thinking, Mansart knew well—they were thinking of the 70,000 Negro teachers, most of whom might lose their jobs. They were thinking of who would teach the next generation of black children, and what and how; and they were wondering how many of these children, discouraged and rejected in school, would run the streets and land in jail. They were questioning where young black graduates of the future would find work, and why they should study and graduate—but Mansart interrupted their thoughts. He smiled and said:

"I know! This indeed is not the completion of Emancipation. It is but the beginning of another phase—and only the beginning. By force and cheating, separate Negro schools will persist for a generation in many areas. If I had the power, I would postpone this disappearance of the separate Negro school. It was a noble institution with an heroic history. It could rebuild a people and a history.

"This I had planned—but not since I girdled the globe, not since I conceived of One World instead of increasing congeries of new peoples and nations, infinitely dividing and subdividing until nationalism becomes a virulent cancer that threatens to kill humanity. I realize that unity in variety is the true end of this world and also I can see that the world is ripe or ripening for such union.

"I once deemed this impossible for at least 250 years, particularly in the United States, so bitterly did whites hate blacks and blacks distrust whites. But this may no longer be true. American whites have found something they hate and fear more than Negroes—they call it Communism.

"It is really fear of lessening income, power and prestige, fear of having to share power with the mob, which once they thought was black but which now they learn may turn out to be yellow, brown or even white. Fighting this chimera, they must stop fighting us. What then must we do? If we are fools, we'll join in Red-baiting and witch-hunting and hasten to make money out of the hides of our own people as well as from whites. But if we are wise, we will know that the world needs us and is waiting to welcome our memories and experience and hopes; not all of them eagerly, indeed, some bitterly, but needing us just the same.

"So that this is really a great step toward freedom!" Mansart concluded.

"How many steps are there, and how long?" one of the group asked, a visiting high school principal.

"Patience, patience——"

"Patience? I don't think we Negroes have been exactly fretful. It's 90 years since the 13th Amendment——"

"Well, suppose it's 100—that's also progress."

"Is it? I wonder! At this rate—of a century to a step—we're not exactly bursting into freedom. And remember, even this is not freedom—it's only a step. All this dumping of a black child here or a few black children there into schools with little white devils and vindictive white teachers—can't you see the price these little victims will pay? They'll drop out of school—or be dropped out—by the thousands and roam the streets and go to hell!

"We've yet a vast desert to cross, President Mansart. Despite all the yelling about 'white primary,' most eligible American Negroes still can't vote; we still ride 'Jim Crow' cars; we are still, in most cities, refused accommodations by hotels, motels, restaurants; we still have difficulty getting a decent place to live; we're still refused better paid jobs and a chance for promotion. This is open, clear, brutal and flagrant discrimination. But back and around and above all that is the intangible, the inhuman attitude of most Americans—the repulsion, the hatred, the sneering, the exclusion on every plane, in every action, the insult open and implied—all this and more. Tell me, Sir, at the rate of a century a step, when will black America be free? My guess is somewhere between 2,500 A.D. and *Never!*"

"Son, despite some exaggeration, granted all you say. Nevertheless, admitting that civilization moves slowly, will not a decision of the Supreme Court to stop segregation by race in American public schools be something to rejoice over?"

"True. So is the decrease of lynching and of burning human beings alive—something, but not everything. In fact, between you and me, not much!"

Mansart looked at the young principal. "Listen, son, you'd better not talk that way or you'll find yourself without a job and in jail!"

"But I am already in jail. I can't talk; I can't think; I can't hope for promotion; I don't dare marry or have children. Jail? What the hell do you mean, jail?—I beg pardon, sir, I was carried away! But I'm glad we had this talk. Well, good-bye. I must get back to my schoolwork."

Mansart watched him leave and said, "The worst thing about a young man like that is not that what he thinks is not absolutely true, but that he passionately believes his ideas will be true forever, immune to change. Our greater task now begins—the education of our children not as a group separate from the world but as an integral part of it.

"We must organize to see that our children are in school; that schools have good teachers, good quarters, high ideals and the necessary facilities for teaching. We must discover and expose every infraction of equality and justice for any child at any time. We must provide in home and group what the public school omits or distorts. This will be no easy job, my friends. It will take time and money, and many, a great many will lose their jobs. Our day of tribulation does not end—it dawns anew."

"Shall we turn to Communism, Mr. President?"

"We must certainly turn to finding out what Communism really means and what it does not mean; what it does and what it cannot do; and what Capitalism can't do or won't. Meantime we must fight crime, conspiracy, lying and theft even if crime, conspiracy, lying and theft call themselves 'Free Enterprise.' And we must seek the right of all to work and live decently even if this is called 'Communism!' "

The teachers drifted out. Said one: "Sounds to me like the old man is leaving just in time."

George Walker, who had come in earlier and had seated himself in the back of the room, smiled understandingly. He was an old friend of the President though he had not seen him for fifteen years. Walker was a well-formed, handsome man, light yellow of skin and with a genial easy-going manner. He was frank, sometimes painfully frank, unwilling that anyone should think him afraid of the truth, no matter how unpalatable to himself or to others. Mansart had known him when, as a student he had led a student strike against white chauvinism at a great Negro college, and won and lost—won by driving out the sycophantic white president; lost because the world condemned his boldness and refused him work. It was a bitter day, and it shook much of Walker's faith. He had crusaded like a knight of old, unselfishly, with no thought of gain. His reward was punishment for doing right. Thereafter he became cold and cynical of righteous causes. For several years he taught in small, mean schools which existed by begging gifts from the rich.

Then, following the Depression, he helped put the FEPC in action in the South. Mansart met him then calmly sitting down with white Southern employers whom he was able to persuade—because he had no faith in their honesty—that hiring Negroes honestly would pay larger dividends than cheating them as they always had cheated them.

And now, after fifteen years, he came again to visit his old friend and teacher. He was gray and older, but his eye still had that cynical twinkle and that stubborn daring to look truth straight in the eye.

"How are you, Mr. President? Well, you've got a fine plant here, and a body of students worth looking at, worth teaching. What are you teaching them? That honesty is the best policy? They won't believe you because they respect you and they damned well know what the white people of Georgia—helped by your own colored people—are doing to ruin you. No, no, don't protest. I know they won't do all they want to—but they'll do plenty. And you can't help yourself and what's worse, you can't even teach your boys and girls the plain truth. That's the tragedy of colored youth today, I know. It's not just being poor; it's not just being kicked and insulted; it's coming to realize that this is a world where goodness and truth just don't exist. Or, if they do, you can never prove it."

Mansart interrupted: "I do not believe you, George—I know better. I have met good men. I have seen the right triumph and truth prevail."

"Sure you have, or you think you have, which is the same thing. For me, my friend, the Negro problem has been the killing of all my faith, all my ideals. Listen, Mansart, I don't talk like this often. But I am a lonesome man, hopeless, often in physical, always in mental pain. Everything I've done; everything I have hoped for, everything in which I believe, has been utterly ruined or so near ruined that in my life I'm sure I will never see any reasonable residue retrieved. Way back in college I learned that when you see dishonesty and wrong, shut your mouth and run away—because I did not, I was ruined almost before my life began.

"I tried to tell the truth to colored students and lost my job. I went into the trade union movement and at once learned that the less I said about admitting Negroes and striving for their rights, the more secure my job. I learned this thoroughly, but like a fool I couldn't quite believe it; so when I got a job as reporter on a great metropolitan newspaper, I thought I saw freedom at last. *Freedom of the Press!* At last I could know the truth and write it for people also yearning to know it. Imagine such hooey in the 'free democracy' of America? I held the job two years. I began to think I was doing good work—I knew I was capable of it. But the owners knew I was talking too much about Negro rights and against the new white prosperity of the South. So out I went. I had to live. I had a wife whom I loved more than God; I had a baby, crippled at birth, the last blow of a grinning, maligned providence. What did I do? I went into a nest of grafting union leaders. I was the mouthpiece of the illiterate thief who led them. I helped his plans, did his dirt and wrote his words. Of course, I lashed out at 'Communists.' That was my ticket of admission to rent, food and physicians; to a home for my devoted wife. Well, what more? What's the use of talk in this gagged world? I'm going now. Soon I'll die, I hope. Don't forget me, Mansart, and keep your students' hopes high, even if you have to lie to do it, as of course you will—and do."

"Walker, I am sorry for you. You are twisted, distorted——"

"Mansart, I'm much more sorry for myself than you are for me. In a decent world—but, goodbye!"

Jean was startled by the new turn of affairs. First, there was the extra year of waiting. Then Manuel had mentioned, quite casually, his retirement "on half pay." Suddenly she realized just what a salary of $2,500 meant today. In the past as they were working together they were getting $9,500 in regular salaries and numerous expenses which made living easy. Now, with soaring prices, they would have to live on a quarter of that.

She remembered that in the past, trustees and teachers had often alluded to what Mansart's well-to-do children would be only too glad to furnish him for his old age. But what would his family say, not only to this meager income for two instead of one, but at the marriage under any circumstances? She had never forgotten Douglass' sneer when she refused his own offer of marriage. Would he be willing to contribute to alleviate his father's poverty and assure him comfort, books, travel? And could *she* take anything from him even if it was offered? What would Revels say, he who had defended her in court so silently and unemotionally? And even Sojourner?

Moreover, Jean's own plans had run into difficulties. The work in the mills was hard; not only physically exhausting but even more, spiritually deadening—the sameness and boredom, the doing of senseless things over and over again, hour after hour and day after day. There was little time for talk and propaganda. All of the factory hands were overstrained; for this was the Spring rush when after the winter lay-offs there was the mad rush to furnish Milady patterns which she had put off deciding on and then leisurely chosen for the Summer. The factory was open day and night; the tasks lengthened and the race was breathless. Throughout the nation there were 500,000 more children at work than a decade before; one child in eleven was at work instead of one in 23. This was another gift of war.

She also worked in the union office, but did so after hours, on weekends and on holidays. The double work proved too much, and finally drove her exhausted to bed for a month. She could not return to the mill. She undertook full employment in the office at pay which scarcely supported her. Of all this she wrote nothing to Manuel. She put off the meetings which they had planned in Atlanta. She had to give him an excuse which she hated to voice:

"My boss, the Secretary and his very cooperative wife know that I am colored, and agree that Negroes and whites must in time be integrated in the union. But few of my fellow workers even suspect my 'race,' and its chance discovery might ruin the strike which we plan for next Spring."

This strike had long been a matter of anxious exploration. The union members had for the most part never been in a strike. They were in awe of the powerful and rich employers. They were not satisfied with their wages and working conditions, but they were better than less or nothing. They feared a strike. They believed that Negroes stood all too ready to displace them.

But their leaders knew that so long as they took what was offered, the longer their wages would be low—and would soon get lower and the work harder. Now was the time to fight. So at last the strike was determined on. It would be declared in the late winter, the slack season, and would threaten the season of wild rush to fill the Spring trade orders.

Jean realized something more. This situation was not so simple as she had assumed. It was not a privately owned industry dealing with a group of laborers. Into the situation entered the State as controller of police and imposer of taxes. This State was also so tightly controlled by Business that what the community wanted in profit the State tried to furnish. Industry, not local but national, which could seek the cheapest location, became a factor. To induce it to come South a community could offer lower taxes or none; it could give it police protection for driving out labor organizers, and it could guarantee low wages by breaking strikes. Also, it could confine skilled wages to white labor even if white labor saw the wisdom of admitting Negroes to the union. Race prejudice was set and enforced by the community and not simply by the unions.

Moreover, the community, by confining black labor to menial work, secured servants and common labor at rates which enabled even the poorest whites to exploit Negroes. Thus bribery, special legislation, and mob law could displace the economy of a whole nation, while the labor unions were helpless. All this Jean learned too late. The strike began.

So the strike came, lasted, flared into violence followed by swift retaliation; then was crushed and lost—and more than lost. Jean was aghast. Much as she had heard and read of strikes she had never before seen one, much less taken part in one, guided, advised, suffered. She had not seen a mass of people, hungry, angry, in despair. She had not seen dying children, cursing women and bloodstained men fronting stolid, leering police and armed soldiers. Pompous employers swore at her with filthy charges. And especially the press—the voluble, all-knowing daily papers said almost nothing about the strike. The nation, the state, even the main population outside the city got no news of this struggle. Jean finally staggered aboard a midnight train and rode to Detroit, simply because that happened to be the train's destination.

It was in a cheap boarding house a week later that, reading the morning paper, she saw the advertisement. One of the smaller colleges of the many colleges of Ohio wanted a teacher of the social sciences for the Summer. She applied. The Dean was impressed by her graduation from Radcliffe and the doctorate from Chicago; but uncertain because of her recent work for a labor union and her former teaching in a college for Negroes. Correspondence with President Mansart, however, would be sure to furnish a recommendation. Jean wrote to him and explained.

After the first interview the Dean was still uncertain. "The woman says she is only 53, but she looks old and frail; her hair is turning grey; she is feeble, in fact. Yet there is something about her that intrigues me."

"She has personality," her assistant answered. "Could we not try her for the summer semester? It's so hard to get anyone to teach the social sciences now, and this woman has had experience, even if it was in one of those Negro colleges in the South."

"All right," said the Dean. But she still had her doubts.

The work progressed quite well for four of the six weeks. But the pace was swift and the work grueling. The summer students were for the most part grim and verging on middle age—there was none of the resiliency of youth. One day in the classroom Jean Du Bignon sat facing her class. A little uncertain and with her mind wandering, she looked at them, and they did not look at all familiar to her until she saw a brown face at the back of the class. She did not look at him but she was conscious of him all the time and being conscious, her words became more connected and her thoughts clearer.

She said: "You know, we sociologists—and I hope I do not have to apologize for the name—for a long time were a little ashamed of our statistical methods, our 'probabilities,' our frank or perhaps not so frank, acknowledgement of chance when we wanted certainty—that good old certainty of the 19th century when we knew everything or could know it—given a little more time for measurement and examination of matters measurable.

"Today this attitude seems changing. We are depending on statistics and probabilities not only for the deeds of human beings, but also for the physical world—the world of atoms, the world of biology and of psychology. We have come down from our high horse of measured certainty to the business of collecting with infinite pain the facts, and coming to possibilities and probabilities as to the real conclusions of science. In fact," said Jean almost laughing, "we have opened the doors to our old friends, Chance and Free Will."

A voice came out of the back of the room. "And God?"

"Well, at any rate," said Jean reflectively, "and gods. There may be a considerable number of minds contributing to change the course of history and social development."

"Would you say," asked someone else, "about ten such gods—or minds—or ten million?"

"Something in between these extremes, I would say. Not everyone really makes decisive choices. Such choices are not made every day. But from adult and disciplined and sane people come numbers of such important decisions; and in the aggregate they may constitute an historically decisive social force."

"And," asked a girl, "would you make the number of sane people large or moderate?"

Jean's eyes became vague and she almost forgot the class. She looked first through the window and then seemingly through the walls and out over the earth. "Sanity," she said, "after all, is a comparative thing. What I am about to say may seem a little insane to you, but what insanity is to a few or to a time or to a place may in the larger world be the reality of a greater sanity."

And then, losing sense of time and place, she began to talk rapidly.

"There is not only the energy within the atom; there is not only the vast mystery of the cosmic rays from the outer world. This world must reach into a world beyond—with its flames and leaders. I seem to see a white flame lighting up the North, with Hitler and Bismarck, Wagner and Freud, a flame that blazes furiously then droops and dies; behind comes the flaming tri-color of the boastful West, with Napoleon and Mussolini in front and Washington and Churchill in the rear.

"And then, rising in the East to light up the sky, the red flame of Lenin and Pushkin, Buddha and Sun Yat-sen, and the dazzling Black Flame of the South—the Black Flame of Tarharqua and Askia, Toussaint and Lobengula. That flame of the North, with its thin paleness, will fail; and Spengler has told us how the flame of the West is declining. But that of the East, as we can see, is growing, growing. Oh, few of you know as I know what the Black Flame of the South will bring.

"Away down there in the Antarctic, at the end of the world, we have been building an ice palace. Nothing the world has seen is of such size. The inches of the pyramids have been yards in this massive and gigantic building; the Empire State Building is a mere pilaster. The building already looms so that at the end of the globe the earth soon will lurch, and swinging outward into the barriers of the stars lay open a universe with no assumptions of Space nor hypotheses of Time.

"And then between the pillars of the universe, looming from highest Heaven to lowest Hell, will appear again the Black Flame."

Her head sank upon the desk and the students stared, and then moved uneasily.

"I think the old girl has gone crazy," said one.

"Either that or she has seen a vision," said another. "Do you think we ought to let the Dean know?"

"My god, is she dead?" cried the brown boy, leaping up.

Jean opened her eyes slowly. She somehow felt more rested than she had for a long time past, longer than she could remember. She looked out on a green and lovely yard, the window framing hollyhocks and sunflowers, roses and geraniums; vines climbed over an old stone wall and trees here and there rustled in the gentle breeze. A startling thought flitted through Jean's mind—she might be dead and forever at rest. Then quickly she drew her dreams back and looked about the room: white and blue, with only a few pieces of furniture. One picture hung on the wall—what was it? She half rose and a nurse appeared.

"I think you will enjoy a bit of lunch," she said as she set down the tray. Jean's questions elicited the information that she had been quite ill for a couple of weeks. There were periods of coma when she had to be fed intravenously. But the illness had taken a turn for the better and now she was on the mend.

"And your friends will want to see you."

Of course, thought Jean, the Dean will have her dismissal ready with properly polite excuses. She would understand and quickly assent. But then, what would she do now? Where could——

The door opened and through it came the wife of Judge Revels Mansart. Jean had not seen her often but she recognized her at once. She wanted to speak—but

Mrs. Mansart pressed her back and said, "Now, now! No talking, no effort. First you must get well!"

"But I must explain——"

"There is nothing to explain. I know you have been worrying about the future—your life and work. There is no need. Our son's life was insured for $25,000. We paid the premium—about which he never would have given a second thought. He is dead and my husband and I have more than enough for our needs. Therefore we have transferred to his father, Manuel, the whole of this sum. So you have nothing to worry about because in addition to his, our home will always be yours."

She paused, and Jean slipped her hand in hers.

"We have you whom my son loved," Mrs. Mansart continued. "And our father, whom you love. He was afraid to offer you poverty and you were afraid to take it. You're both foolish. You both belong to us now, and you are both together at last."

She opened the door and Manuel Mansart entered. His face was lined, but his eyes laughed with the pleasure of seeing Jean again. He took her hand in his and caressed it.

In a few weeks Jean left the hospital and the Bishop came up from Texas and married them. They flew west, planning a long rest in the midst of the strange beauties of California and the Pacific. It was a new and wonderful experience to be together again, to talk and tell and to touch each other's flesh, gently, lovingly and uninhibited.

The world—the cruel and puzzling world—became strangely responsive and soft. People seemed more gentle and considerate. It was a good world and they loved it, and especially they loved each other with deep and abiding affection.

They came to a valley among mighty mountains. It was a glorious morning. The sky was glass—the wind a whisper. Like solemn sentinels on either side stood enormous trees, brown as dried blood and tall as heaven—trees that were living when Christ was born. Beyond and above them loomed a domed mass of piled granite, already old when Homer sang—even perhaps when the morning stars sang together and the sons of God shouted for joy. And far below and between, surged and sinuously swayed the silver, swinging mist of living waters, plunging, singing, roaring, curling in the golden sunshine.

Later, they lingered in San Francisco, dwelling high in the Hopkins Hotel, whence they could scan the Golden Gate. Together they re-lived the past and dwelt fondly on each incident, each triumph and failure. They found new persons in each other, new thoughts and novel desires. California was beautiful—they talked of spending the rest of their lives here in this paradise, yet knew even as they talked that life was stirring too strongly within them and that work called too loudly for them to contemplate complete rest—even though Mansart was 78 and Jean 54.

It was the decision of the Supreme Court on race segregation in public schools that aroused them. Mansart gave voice to their ideas.

"So, the Supreme Court has spoken and with one voice. They are wise. They know that if, for another century, we Negroes taught our children—in our own bettering schools, with our own trained teachers—we would never be Americans but another nation with a new culture. But if beginning now, gradually, all American children, black and white, European, Slavic and Asiatic are increasingly taught as one—in one tradition and one ideal—there will emerge one race, one nation, one world. It must have been a hard choice to make—they had to surrender 'superiority' and accept eventual miscegenation. Social equality would displace the divine right of white folk. Otherwise, there loomed a world so split with hatred that it spelled suicide.

"Am I glad? I should be, but I am not. I dreamed too long of a great American Negro race. Now I can only see a great Human race. It may be best. I should indeed rejoice———"

From then on began a restless probing and inquiry. What could they do in this crisis? They both had so much experience; they both were still strong.

Jean said, "Once I conceived a great measurement. I arranged to count the deeds of a segregated group in ten states or more; year in and year out for decades; to centralize the classifying and interpreting of these facts in one place, under the direction of experts whom the best judgment of nation and world could furnish and which therefore must include our own dark scholars. This plan failed. Today white men, without benefit of the judgment and experience of blacks, are telling the world what black folk think and are. I wish—I still wish———"

Mansart looked up from his newspaper and scowled.

"Jean, dear," he said, "what's wrong with the world? What's happening to America? I never dreamed we could act this way. Spies, stool-pigeons, professional liars hired by government; theft, waste, gambling, crime. I cannot understand. I'm all at sea!"

They decided it would be best, for a few months at least, to rent a cottage near the ocean, and just rest and plan. They were not surprised to run into the usual difficulty colored folk encounter in securing even temporary shelter in a good community. At last, they obtained a short lease on a cottage in the San Mateo area; it belonged to a retired professor who was glad to get the extra income to cover the cost of repairs. He himself arranged board and lodging with a neighboring merchant not far away. It proved a pleasant arrangement; the professor became a regular caller, and several neighbors accepted the newcomers when they learned they were persons of culture and would not stay long enough to depress real estate values.

They continued their intensive reading and talking. The neighbors became interested in this dark man and his pale wife. Most of them said little, but they listened all the more. Mansart, at rest and relaxed, found himself talking more and more freely than had been his usual habit.

He said one day: "I've been thinking seriously. I'm puzzled—and terribly troubled. I have lived long. I've circled the world. Yet, when I look on this my native land, I am forced to ask: what have we to fear more than ourselves. We seem as men stupid to the point of backwardness. Our schools are growing worse, not better; our children are wild. There is more unhappiness than happiness in our land. People are becoming dishonest, they steal and gamble. We are far poorer than we boast because we buy clothes, jewels and furs instead of food, and cars and washing machines instead of books. We live on debts, not savings. We don't argue—we threaten and accuse. We don't read, we don't think; most of our leisure hours are spent in staring at poor pictures and worse advertisements of things we can well do without. We seldom see the moon rise or the sun set!"

A caller who had stopped by and heard Mansart, insisted: "Your people are freer!"

"Freer for what? For good or evil? For mending or spending, for waste or crime, for blackmail——?"

"Perhaps you'd prefer Russia?"

"No, I prefer America, but not this America—rather the America that might be——"

Jean managed gently to halt his outpouring. When the neighbor left, she said, "My dear husband, you must not speak so frankly—at least not to strangers. It isn't safe these days."

"Safe? What do you mean? I was just talking to someone we know. What earthly harm——?"

Jean shook her head, and beckoned him in to dinner.

One day Jean brought three books which Manuel examined inquiringly. They often read books together, Jean doing the reading aloud, then both discussing the contents.

"Jessie Fauset?" he asked, "I somehow remember the name, but——"

"It's so characteristic of our problem," said Jean. "Here are three books. They are literature. They interpret human life deftly; but the life of a small group—not the loud rich but of silent colored Philadelphia—the carefully bred and forward faring guild of caterers, the churchmen and upper servants; treating of their joys, sorrows and development.

"But this picture did not interest white Philadelphia or white America. They forgot to notice this segment of American life. As always, they never knew it even existed. Consequently black America also neglected what white America neglected. Only three or four of these exquisite studies appeared and then Jessie Fauset stopped writing at the height of her literary possibilities.

"It was a shame, a deep loss. I saw her once only in passing—a small, rather plump girl, beautiful and comely, a brilliant brown, and sparkling of eye and soul. How an eighteenth century Britain would have lionized her or a France of Baudelaire's day! But an America of the raging twenties did not even read her few delicate poems. So, my dear, this day we'll read out of this author's *There Is Confusion!*"

As time passed, on pleasant afternoons neighbors frequently dropped in at the Mansarts' at tea time to sit and chat on the wide porch overlooking the sea. They had, in fact, instituted afternoon tea as a regular custom.

One day, a neighbor, the retired professor, was there, and Jean was pouring tea when a middle-aged woman who taught in one of the city high schools came by to borrow books on Negro history—a subject in which the public libraries were weak. The neighborhood grocer, who had brought her there in his station wagon along with the week's groceries, also dropped in, and a stranger, who said he was a landscape painter and who had stopped to admire the roses, then at their top brilliance, was also invited in. Another neighbor, a writer, whom they knew slightly, stopped in at about the same time to borrow a match for his browning Meerschaum.

The talk, at first desultory and casual, soon became animated. The old professor launched into his favorite theme.

"We Americans are stupid and afraid. We're scared stiff, and why?"

The teacher broke in with what seemed to her the most logical answer: "Bad schools and growing worse; poor teachers and too few of any kind."

"I never heard of so much lying and stealing as goes on today, or so much suspicion of each other," interpolated the grocer. "Don't know what to believe, if anything——"

The professor continued. "Does anyone really believe that Communism is an international conspiracy and that Russia is planning to destroy us?"

Mansart mused. "I am more and more convinced that Americans are being forced to think and act against their own real beliefs by a small group of powerful men who control most of our wealth and media of communications."

"Now we're getting somewhere," said the old professor.

"Listen, there are 127 men who hold 289 directorships in 66 billion-dollar corporations which control 75 per cent of all corporate assets in the United States. These men are not elected to office and power by any democratic process. They are selected by interested parties or select themselves by their individual initiative. This oligarchy is becoming smaller in number and more powerful in its grip on industry in America and in the world. The small business man is disappearing and the artisan is pricing himself out of the market. What to do? Suppose now that the wealth and legal control of industry was by law taken from this 127 and given to the state. Suppose intelligent democracy controlled the state and that high ideals for the good of all people activated the voters and that the men they elected to control of the state were honest and self-sacrificing—how's that for Socialism without revolution?"

A chorus of voices rushed to challenge this thesis, question piling upon question.

"Would the 127 assent to being stripped of power and without desperate fighting?"

"How would the 127 be recompensed for this theft of their property?"

"Where is this 'intelligent democracy'?"

"How can we get 'honest civil servants of high ideals'?"

The old professor did not answer—he smiled and slipped away.

The writer sneered: "We don't even dare discuss the situation for fear of being bludgeoned with poverty if not with prison."

"Only real democracy can cure this," said the teacher. "but democracy is what we haven't got—and we're losing even what we had."

Jean said, "We're bribing the Negroes with civil rights and hushing union labor with high wages in return for war and voting rights."

The painter picked a rose as he left. "The only answer is revolution!" was his parting remark.

"No," said the teacher. "The answer is lawyers. We are ruled by lawyers; lawyers make our laws, apply the laws. They nominate lawyers for judges; judges interpret the laws which the lawyers have made. We are a world of lawyers, run by lawyers, for lawyers. Which explains why we are so lawless—with injustice the rule rather than the exception. Small wonder revolution always aims at the courts, the judges and the lawyers."

Laughing, they bid each other and their hosts good night and slowly departed.

Next day they were astounded to learn that the old professor had been arrested, though the charge against him was not clear.

A few days later a quiet and well-dressed stranger called at the cottage and showed his badge. He was an agent of the FBI.

"I was wondering," he asked Mansart politely, "if you would be willing to cooperate with the Government?"

"Why certainly," answered Mansart, "in what way?"

The agent brought out a memorandum book and took a seat.

"You had a meeting here lately?"

"A meeting? No, there's been no meeting——"

Jean interrupted. "He probably means the friends who come to tea."

"Very well. Will you give me their names and——"

Mansart arose angrily. "I certainly will not!"

"Then you refuse to cooperate?"

"I refuse to be a stool pigeon! Good day!"

As Jean feared, it was not long before Manuel Mansart was subpoenaed to testify before a Congressional committee which began sitting in the Pacific area. Mansart was surprised but not averse to going. He could not imagine any information he had which would be of interest to these men. And he never dreamed, as Jean surmised, that he would be accused of subversion and that the committee wanted confession and information. Jean spoke over the long-distance phone to Douglass' son-in-law, Dr. Steinway, in Los Angeles. She also wired to Revels, in New York.

The appearance before the Committee was brief and unbelievably vicious. Mansart was from his very entrance treated as a convicted criminal.

"Were you ever in Russia?"

"Who paid your way?"

"Were you ever in China?"

"Are you a Communist?"

"What Communists do you know?"

"Was your wife ever accused of Communism?"

"Was she dismissed from your school for subversion?"

"When did you join the Party?"

Finally a witness appeared—none other than the painter who had stopped to admire the roses and been invited into the Mansarts' home.

"Do you know this Negro, Mansart?"

"I attended a meeting once at his house. These were the persons present." He handed the chairman a list. "I heard the United States attacked and revolution advocated."

"Is Mansart a Communist Party member?"

"I have been told on high authority that he is."

Then to Mansart again.

"Tell the truth or you'll be prosecuted for conspiracy!"

"What?"

There was a brief pause and whispering. Dr. Steinway entered and approached one of the Congressmen who shook hands with him cordially. The proceedings were abruptly dismissed.

The retired professor went to jail. The teacher lost her job. The writer became a carpenter, but the painter got a good position in Washington. The local merchant kept still and stopped visiting and conversing.

Mansart was not recalled to the witness stand. He was furious at his treatment and wanted to get in touch with a lawyer, but Revels arrived next day. He had just come from Washington where he had seen the Attorney General. The proceedings against Manuel Mansart had been dismissed.

"And now, father," said Revels, "let's face it. These are abnormal times. The world is shell-shocked. The nation is insane with fear—fear not of Communism but of itself, of what it will do and can do, and of what it owns. Never mind 'why'—that is the truth!"

"For most of us there is but one thing to do and that is—nothing. Just keep still until the nation recovers from this attack of hysteria and comes back to normalcy. No, this may not be heroic but it is damned good sense.

"Now, I want you and Jean to come back with me to New York. It is not as beautiful there as here, but it is safer. Come and live with me and my wife. We need company. We'll talk, listen, drink and eat. We'll have a few friends in now and then. We'll go to the theater and movies and drive in the suburbs."

"In other words," said Jean, "we'll be clams."

"Precisely! And believe me, it's clams or death here today! And I prefer to live!"

Both Mansart and Jean said, "I wish we were as sure as you are!"

CHAPTER XX

Death

After this excitement, the beast in Manuel's stomach, which had slept with only slight snarling over the decades, suddenly began to speak with bite and sting. "Acid indigestion," said the local physician, to which diagnosis another somewhat hesitantly agreed. But Dr. Steinway, before he left and after a careful examination, said definitely, "Cancer. The fools should have told you, sir, five years ago!"

"No," said Manuel. "I was the fool that at forty I did not become a physician."

He knew now that he had but months to live, and after the first cold fright felt a certain satisfaction in being so certain of the date and nature of the end that was approaching.

They finished out the term of their lease on the cottage, but with no more visitors, no more teas and talks. At last, they flew back east over forest, mountains, desert and river. They gazed on the Grand Canyon—that gash in the earth excavated by giant hands down to the red blood and yellow entrails of earth, leaving pale flesh above and thin black skin. They saw mountain and valley, great rivers and great cities. They saw New York.

Once in New York, they organized a simple life which included reading and music, occasional rides in the parks and along the great highways which branched out to the suburban centers fifty and a hundred miles away. Jean read widely, especially books and periodicals from abroad. Manuel sat long hours listening to her and thinking of death as the pall of age began falling upon him.

One evening Jean laid down the book she was reading, and looking out over the lights of Harlem, said, "What is happening in the world seems quite clear—socialism is succeeding and bids fair to include the whole civilized world in a future not very distant. From the day when it was ridiculed as unworkable, through the bloody days when wide, concerted efforts were made to overthrow it by force, we come now to a day when it is working successfully in the Soviet Union and its neighboring states, and in vast China.

"Other great states, like India, are being drawn into the socialistic current, while Scandinavia still pursues her 'Middle Way.' Britain began socialization but is held back by her skilled labor which shares with aristocratic capitalists, exploitation of white common labor at home and dark colonial labor overseas. Its Labor Party is split and the Socialist half is fighting fiercely for control.

"This success of socialism in the world drives Big Business in the United States toward all-out fascism. It thinks to stop socialism by an immense array of military force; by the atom bomb; by encouraging revolt beyond the 'iron curtain'; by repression of thought and expression at home, lest the nation know the truth. This is succeeding today. But tomorrow it will fail. Americans are not complete fools nor will they remain perpetual cowards.

"Today we are misled by the mirage of a false prosperity—false because it is based on the income of high taxation hidden by high wages; false because the millions who toil in factory and office are being used in a frightful waste of material and effort to prepare for a war which will destroy civilization. It is a prosperity expanded by almost unlimited debt and wide-open gambling on everything from the stock market to horse races, open to all who conform by silence, lies or corruption. On, on and up, dazzling a dizzy world until the crazy bubble bursts!"

Revels, who was present, looked at Jean long. Then he said, slowly, "I am not sure how far you are right. Socialism has spread remarkably. Will it continue? Will it triumph in Britain and France? Which way will Germany go? Then, how and when will the United States act? Can capitalism reform and survive here and elsewhere throughout the world? I really do not know."

Jean smiled. "I'm afraid it cannot. I am afraid it spawns the seeds of its own destruction."

Mansart interrupted. "One thing I know. Today, more than ever, war is utterly evil and completely indefensible in terms of human morals or decency or civilization. Nothing on earth is so completely useless, so inexcusably vile. War no longer brings victory to either side. It is planned and deliberate murder of human beings, the complete destruction of the earth's treasures. The purpose is calculated evil on the widest possible scale with every refinement of suffering, maiming and destruction. There is today no imaginable hurt or devastation which war tries to avoid or does not envision as its legitimate end.

"Once men of courage led their followers to war. Today statesmen and generals far in the rear of the war fronts push into hell the youth of the world, utterly ignorant of reasons or ends. Men with the barest education, devoid of culture, without the experience or compassion of human thought and feeling, completely unmoved by pain and suffering, rule over the lives of thousands of youth absolutely and despotically with no appeal, no redress. Lying, cheating, stealing, corruption and disease follow armies as night follows day.

"The most brutal and brazen invasion calls itself defensive war. This does not make it any the less offensive, ruthless and founded on greed, spying and lying. Rape is the legitimate sport of war today, and one of the chief occupations of armies is arranging for prostitution and control of sexual disease.

"Down with war! Never again war! War is the bottomless depth to which human beings have fallen in this 20th century of the miscalled Prince of Peace!"

During his stay at the home of his son, Revels, Mansart had time to examine Harlem more carefully than before. Formerly it had always been a hasty scrutiny, a quick judgment based more on what he had read and thought and what others said than on his own observations. Now, for the first time, he had the opportunity to walk slowly along the Harlem streets, taking in its sights and sounds, its teeming restlessness and explosive energy. He would take the bus from Edgecombe Avenue down to 135th Street. Then he would walk west to glimpse the gray buildings and ivy-covered walls of City College; south along Eighth Avenue to 125th Street, across and north on Seventh, east on some cross street to Lenox; north and west, south and east, until weary, he would at last take a cab home. Invariably he would reach home discouraged and brooding and enter into long discussions with his family.

Harlem was a city within a city—a crossroads through which ran an endless stream of strangers, surging and whirling about a nucleus which itself changed more slowly. The physical city was slowing falling into ruins, and the rents extracted over the decades could never keep up with the decay. Houses and streets alike were literally crumbling into rubble, dying out. Yet, from this progressive decay, a stream of humanity was emerging, migrating to north and west, surmounting the Heights of Washington and flowing down nearer to the Hudson's East bank. Some of the dark and well-to-do folk had even reached Riverside Drive. Eastward the flood had entered the Bronx, some eddies heading north toward New Rochelle and Westchester.

Another stream of the better-to-do class spilled over into sections of Brooklyn, and even reached into upper Long Island, creeping ever further on. This expansion represented not only an explosion of over-concentrated population, but the dividing of the Negro community into classes—the richer leaving Harlem and their place being taken by newcomers from the South. A few, who formed a powerful nucleus of the better-off, remained to exploit the mass of the poor, to corral their votes and wield the power generated by their sheer numbers. Liquor stores, pool rooms, joints of various sorts, owned by whites and Negroes, abounded. Two kinds of churches—old and opulent churches with fine buildings, but also congeries of little churches in stores and homes, centers of religious orgies, graft and every type of social effort. It was difficult, almost impossible to judge Harlem. Any sweeping characterization or generalized description was bound to be partially wrong. Here was a human ganglion, neglected, exploited, oppressed, brutalized, hated and loved. It was slowly and inexorably grinding out a fatal vintage but no one could measure its potency. Here and there, amid its ruins and rubble, arose new housing projects, an earnest of its future, yet already so packed with humanity that one wondered what they would mean in ten years.

One of Manuel Mansart's greatest pleasures was a morning ride with Jean in his son's beautiful Cadillac. Jean was an expert and careful driver, and they usually sought out the suburbs to the north or out on Long Island, or over the bridge or ferry to New Jersey. Gliding along at moderate speed, they were intensely interested in the world, its people, its piled mass of masonry, its markets, piers, fields and flowers. It was a happy period for both Manuel and Jean. They talked of things past and things to come and of how good life had been to them both.

On a morning in early September, 1954, they had driven north and paused in Van Cortlandt Park to view the wide sweep of landscape to the west. A car drove alongside with three passengers; an old man, and a young, fashionably dressed woman who alighted, and with a wave of farewell the car and its driver, a middle-aged man whirled about and drove away. Manuel glanced sharply at the old man as he stood bareheaded, his fine face lifted to the sky. He appeared extremely frail, almost ghostly as the breeze made a halo of his white hair.

A wave of memory swept across Mansart; and when the white bearded rabbi turned to walk away, removing his skull cap, suddenly Manuel remembered. He saw again, as though it was yesterday, the darkened bookshop in Berlin, the cautious clerk and the old proprietor in the rear.

"Dr. Blumenschweig!" he cried, as he hurried to step down from his car.

Jean stared, and the young Jewish woman, turning toward them, seemed to look annoyed. But the old man turned and peered intently through his glasses; then, letting go the arm of the young woman, he tottered forward with outstretched arms, crying, "Oh, oh, dear old friend, my very dear old friend."

They clasped each other in their arms, the rabbi murmured the lament from Jeremiah, "Oh, that my head were waters and mine eyes a fountain of tears, that I might weep day and night for the slain of the daughter of my people."

Barely holding back his tears, he continued. "Little did I know, little did I dream of what was going to happen to my people when I saw you, my friend, there in Berlin, in 1936. I knew we would suffer, perhaps even deserved to suffer; but I do not think that I could have lived if in my wildest imagination I had known that six million of the best of the Jewish faith were going to be murdered in less than a decade by that maniac.

"Well, it is over and now again we take up our burden and look forward.

"Many times I have sought to get in touch with you for I have some things to say about your folk which I wished to communicate to you above all people. I was not able to find you all these years and now the God of Abraham has sent you to me!"

He turned to introduce the young woman. "This is my son's wife, Rebecca, and my daughter, this is Manuel Mansart. We met once many years ago in my bookstore in Berlin."

The woman bowed coldly and glanced doubtfully at Jean. She seemed to resent her father-in-law's show of emotion which appeared to her un-American, and his conduct in demonstratively embracing a Negro in public. She herself tried to avoid colored people when possible. And this woman, was she colored, and if not, what was she doing with a colored man? It was obvious that the young woman did not approve of the situation.

The Rabbi, noticing nothing, or ignoring Rebecca's annoyance, said, "Can we sit down a moment? I have a word to say before we meet next Friday."

"Next Friday?"

"Yes, have you not received your invitation?"

They entered Manuel's car and seated themselves in the rear seat, while Rebecca strolled off toward the gate.

"I did receive an invitation," said Manuel, "but I hardly glanced at it and did not plan to accept."

"Well, my friend, you must be sure to accept and come. Listen, I have travelled widely since we met. In 1939, I escaped to Israel. Thence, as secret emissary, I travelled through the Middle East, especially Arabia, and then Africa. I lived among the black Falashas in Ethiopia and the Jews of North Africa and the Sudan. I learned much, very much.

"Manuel, Africa is arising. The rape of Ethiopia is a thing of the past. Ethiopia has stretched forth her hands unto God and He has clasped them—in Kenya and Uganda, in the vast Sudan, Egyptian, British and French; in the Congo and Tanganyika, in the Rhodesias, in the tortured Portuguese colonies, and even the bedevilled Union of South Africa, everywhere, everywhere, but especially on the British West Coast, where great Nigeria and Ghana are destined to redeem Africa.

"But, my friend, it should not be a surprise to you that along with mighty Africa's awakening, the jackals are also astir. That is the significance of the Knighthood of the Garter just bestowed on the Emperor of Ethiopia. Never in the history of Europe, since the Renaissance, has a colored man been so honored by Nordic bandits, the only exception being the Emperor of Japan who had won a war against Russia. No Indian, no Chinaman, no East Asiatic, not even a white colonial from Canada, Australia or New Zealand has dared aspire to this highest of British honors. Why does it happen now? Think, Manuel, think. Why now?

"I will tell you why—because Africa is beginning to rise in her might with all the festering memories of the British slave-trade, of centuries of American slavery and European exploitation, of a frightful burden of rape, murder, theft and insult. The end of white supremacy nears, and the beginning of a black world looms. That is why Britain is hastening to placate the colored world. And not Britain alone, but America, her eager heir to empire.

"One of my missions to America is this: I learned while in Africa of a project begun in the United States to seize Negro leadership in Africa and America so as to control and guide the blacks. Manuel, you belong, do you not, to the so-called Negro College Fund?"

"No, my friend. That is composed of heads of private Negro schools. I was head of a state school and so was not eligible."

"This organization is going to have a special meeting this month in the Rainbow Room on top of Rockefeller Center. Many prominent Negroes are invited and you are included."

"But, you see, I am retired—and there are other reasons why I cannot attend."

"There are none, absolutely none, strong enough to keep you away. My son is an official of the National Association of Manufacturers, real promoters of this movement. You see, much American capital is in the Union of South Africa, in the Rhodesias, in the Belgian Congo and in North Africa. The owners of this capital are impatiently waiting to enter West Africa if they can be sure that the coming rulers will play along with them. They are ready to offer not simply the old 'employment' at starvation wages, but real partnership on high levels, even with a degree of social recognition, which they count upon to intoxicate black men. They have, therefore, drawn into collaboration certain social leaders who are prominent in this curiously jumbled modern world.

"Your invitation, for example, came from a certain Zegue de Laurinberg. Her family were barons in Czarist Russia, pretty much down at the heels before the Revolution. She was enlisted in Churchill's spy ring and became an effective agent of Reilly. After the Second World War, she paraded as a countess in Paris, then came to America where she became a princess and ran a beauty parlor on upper Fifth Avenue exclusively for the super rich. Recently she married a Southern millionaire and graduated into society and into Big Business in one step.

"It is her scheme to bring together on a brilliant social occasion, though it is not to be too much advertised publicly, a gathering of African rulers, West Indian leaders and prominent American Negro leaders—from the subsidized Negro press; from insurance and banking which is dependent on white finance; and also from among the colored college presidents. It is this meeting which is to take place next Friday at midnight, immediately after the meeting of the Negro College Fund adjourns—what?"

He turned as the car with his son and son's wife drove up. She had met it as it entered the park to pick up the rabbi, and she had evidently warned her husband of the situation. He greeted Mansart briefly and nodded to Jean. He was evidently in a great hurry, but the rabbi was not, and the latter's stern glance reduced his son to listening.

"Benjamin, you know that President Manuel Mansart has been invited next Friday."

"Yes, papa, I know, and hope to see him——"

"Yes, Benjamin, you'll see him. You'll drive him there with me. Now, President Mansart, we'll call for you Friday. Goodbye and may the God of Abraham, Isaac and Jacob bless you and your seed forever!"

When they reached home, Jean quickly scanned the mail and among yesterday's letters they found the invitation which had been carelessly laid aside. Along with the letters, newspapers and magazines addressed to Jean had come a manuscript which she put aside unopened. Manuel noticed that she made a wry face.

"What now?" he asked. "What is this—a manuscript? Whose?"

"Well, now that it's over, I might as well tell you. You see, while in California it occurred to me that I might try to write that semi-biography of mine which had so long been in the back of my head. The life of a person, black but in appearance white, or white but inwardly black, ought to make a good novel. Well, I tried, working on it for months. Finally it was in a shape where I felt I could send it off. It has now been refused by five publishers and for curiously similar reasons. As far as I can see now, there is nothing further to do.

"Soon after we came to New York, I had a personal talk with this last publisher. It was, he said, a good novel, just as all the other publishers had assured me—only the climax. Whom would my white-black girl marry and live with happily the rest of her life? She must not marry a white man—that would condone 'miscegenation.' She could not marry a colored man, for she was too white. Yet, she must marry or where is the purpose of the novel? It was all too silly and the matter was clinched when I said, 'But I have married a Negro and we're very happy.' The editor gave me a look of disgust and did not even shake hands when I left. So that is that, and here is the script.

"There was one incident that I developed in the story that none of the publishers liked but which I hate to give up. Do you remember the oil marriage that was making the headlines just before we left the West Coast?"

"Oh yes, the millionairesss of seventy who married the widowed millionaire and threw a fabulous party?"

"Yes. Well, I put it in my script; now, that party was fabulous but it was also uniquely American. Listen, this is almost word for word as it appeared in the press:

> *Champagne will gush like the oil that's paying for it tonight at Hollywood's biggest blowout of the year, the $30,000 Mocambo party being tossed by newlyweds. The bridegroom is a widower and has grown children. He has oil interests in the San Joaquin Valley and Texas. The bride is 74 and the daughter of an oil king who at his death left her over $17,000,000. The couple have taken over the entire nightclub for the evening, with 300 guests, including film stars and politicians, invited to the glittering white-tie affair.*
>
> *As a starter, there will be 80 pounds of caviar, costing $2,200. The club will be decorated with about $6,000 worth of gardenias, which will garland even the cages of the Mocambo's famed parakeets. A horshoe of blooms will form an arbor over the entrance to the cocktail lounge. Available to guests will be 20 brands of Scotch whiskey and 25 types of Bourbon. But champagne will be the featured beverage. It will spout from a fountain decorated with a wedding bell and doves of ice.*
>
> *The hostess will wear a $5,000 creation of white embroidered French lace with full skirt in the new ankle length, and a canary yellow taffeta cummerbund and full length coat of the same material. All this will be enhanced by about $500,000 worth of jewelry.*

"I'm not particularly envious or catty," Jean said. "But this sort of thing makes me sick—positively ill. The woman who gave this party never did a stitch of work—her wealth and power was literally handed to her on a silver platter. The wealth of her father and husband came from oil that God made. The price paid for this orgy would send fifty students through my college. Just remember, when you contemplate this party, that five million American families live on less than $1,000 a year. Yet, here is a woman who has $30,000 to waste in one night on her second wedding."

"Oh, come now. I would like to have had a good spoonful of that caviar," said the Judge, who had entered, "and a sip—just a sip—"

"Really, this is no joke," said Jean reproachfully.

The Judge answered, "No wonder, dear Jean, your book was refused. Don't you understand that talk like that is not allowed today?"

"But this talk was printed. It appeared in a newspaper."

"Sure; but not as weighted and interpreted by you."

"By me? But why me?"

"Elementary," said the Judge. "You are probably on 'The List.' The men who own the publishing business have decreed that your word must not reach the public. Do you realize that only half as many books are published in this country today as were issued half a century ago? And that bookstores are becoming practically extinct?"

"What are we coming to?" asked Mansart.

"It's crazy," said Jean, "to stop or try to stop or limit talking or writing, especially in a day like this. There are questions so fundamental that not to talk about them is—to die."

"We're dying," said Mansart. "Listen to this invitation:

> 'Her Highness, the Princess, Zegue de Laurinberg, is pleased to request the presence of President Manual Mansart at midnight September twenty, 1954, in the Rainbow Room of the Rockefeller Center, to hear a rescript on the future of Africa and the Black Race. There will be in attendance African rulers, West Indian officials and leaders of the Negroes of the United States.
>
> 'Our Steward at the Waldorf-Astoria will await his acceptance.'

"This," said Manuel, "sounds like cheap propaganda in the guise of melodrama. I hate to waste my time."

"Wait," said the Judge. "This is propaganda and it is certainly theatrical. But it has power behind it. It means something. It has impressed thoughtful Jews. You cannot remain ignorant of its efforts. My advice is to attend. To my mind, this is the idea of white American business aimed to dazzle Africans; and their ideas have been dramatized by what czarist Russian exiles still regard as the airs of High Society. I doubt if it impresses Africans as much as it will influence American Negroes—who are ready to jump wherever white society beckons. How far will that influence sift down to the fifteen million of the black rank and file? But you must attend—you most certainly must attend."

On the appointed night, the automobile with the old rabbi called promptly. The rabbi said as they rode along:

"I was most eager to have you attend this meeting to which you have been invited by this so-called princess. It was originally planned to bring to New York the leaders of the African peoples to indoctrinate them against subversive movements and extend American influence among them. My son told me of the plan and I asked if you were to be invited. He said no, and intimated that you had gone radical. Against his own judgment and on my insistence, he secured an invitation.

"Lately, the nature of the meeting has been changed to make it more social than political. And this society woman who has been an underground political figure and has recently married some Southern millionaire—Baldwin, I believe is the name—has been put in charge."

"Will many Africans be present?"

"Not as many as they hoped, but a few. West Africa will be represented by Azikiwe, of Nigeria."

They arrived and were ushered in with ceremony. It was an impressive hall, lofty, and richly decorated. Opposite the entrance was a huge mirror in an elaborate gilt frame, covering nearly the whole wall. On a low platform, in the center of this mirrored wall stood a highly ornamented gilt armchair, like a low throne.

There were about fifty persons present, nearly all showing various degrees of color, and many in foreign dress. There were a number of women. All were standing about in groups conversing.

Mansart learned the identity of several of the guests. Two were African Prime Ministers, one from the Egyptian Sudan and one from West Africa. There were two African rulers. One of them, the Kabaka of the Buganda, wearing a red fez and ceremonial robes, was returning to Uganda after a forced exile in England. There were also the young King of the Bamangwato and his English wife, whose return to South Africa was still barred. Nkrumah of the Gold Coast was not there, but Azikiwe of Nigeria, who would probably one day be prime minister, represented West Africa. From South Africa came only a Zulu student, with credentials from the South African Negro Congress. From the West Indies had come white-haired Bustamente, the Jamaica leader; Adams, the reactionary Prime Minister of Barbados, and a number of trade union officials and members of colonial legislatures. From the United States, there were two colored Congressmen, a Federal Judge, three insurance executives, two bishops and four college presidents; six members of state legislatures, five municipal judges and five city councillors. They made an impressive throng, lending color and dignity to the gathering.

After a shrill blast on a silver trumpet, a richly uniformed bodyguard and several ladies-in-waiting elaborately gowned entered and arranged themselves on either side of the dais. The princess entered unattended. She was a tall and impressive woman. Her rather broad face was white and smooth and on it skilled artists had limned a beauty almost fantastic; with touch of light and line of shade, a heightening of color and depth of shadow, arched eyebrows and long black lashes. At rest her face was singularly beautiful, but when its surface bent there seemed to flash through some faint hint of evil and of age. Her hair above rose sculptured and cemented into firm and lovely dark crimson curls and rolls, dyed and polished and unmoved by wind or emotion.

From her long, slender neck and low cleft bosom to her bare arms her flesh was flawless marble. To her long, crimson-pointed hands, she was braceleted and ringed with a fortune in precious metal and blazing gems. Her bosom, with the contrivance of wire and elastic, was built out almost too full for her long, lithe limbs which undulated beneath billowing fabric whose embroidery must have kept a hundred skilled costumers working a hundred days until now their delicate folds concealed and at the same time revealed the perfection of her form. Her feet were shod in slippers of beaten gold and writhing silver.

There was a studied harmony and simplicity in all her magnificence, and the total impression, when with a studied languor she extended her bejeweled hand to the guests, was beauty and opulence.

As she entered, there was a murmur of subdued applause. Some of the Africans raised their hands and bowed low; the West Indians bowed slightly and many of the women curtsied. The foreigners exchanged remarks in low tones. A group of the American Negroes talked in almost audible whispers from the sides of their months.

"Listen, who's back of this baby?"

"Search me—may be a phoney!"

"Phoneys don't hire these diggings or put on all this side."

"They might—with the right sugar daddy."

"Take it from me—there's money back of this gal and you can't lose playing along. I think I know the folks in Washington and New York behind all this—here she comes—boy, she sure sends me!"

Behind the princess, as she glided easily to her throne, she drew a train of billowing velvet which with one sinuous motion she draped about her, as half bowing in gracious condescension, she subsided into her gilded armchair. She spoke slowly and distinctly in a deep and lovely contralto voice, waving the fiery tip of an ivory cigarette holder. She welcomed by name and station the royal and chief African delegates as they gravely responded. The rest she addressed in general words; then, pointing to the great mirror behind her, she said:

"I am not here alone, your highnesses, excellencies, gentlemen and ladies; nor am I your host. Some of the sixty men who own America and are the real rulers of one world are behind me, sitting back of this great mirror and seeing you clearly although you do not see them. They are modest men, in accord with American tradition among business leaders, but as you and I well know, they are the ones who act and do. They are the ones who have invited you here and you have been selected with thought and calculation."

The old Rabbi leaned toward Mansart and whispered:

"If you think the battle for socialism is won in East Europe you reckon without your hostess. The landlords of Poland and the shoddy aristocracy of Hungary and the Balkans, buttressed by religious reaction and American investment, will fight many years to regain dominion over their millions of serfs."

The Princess, with a perceptible change in attitude and tone and a slight tensing of her voice, continued crisply. "You will do well to heed my words. A world crisis is upon us and it is high time that those whom you represent and others not here, understand perfectly what those who are and intend ever to be masters of the world, have ordained. You see, gentlemen, that I mince no words and conceal nothing.

"For five hundred years the British, French and German empires, and lately the United States, have ruled Europe, Asia, Africa, the Seas and all America. That rule has been temporarily disturbed in some areas. It will be restored and perpetuated—of that there is no shadow of doubt in our minds and none really in yours. We are masters, because masters we were born and masters we will remain by the will of almighty God!"

She was now sitting straight and arrogant—the embodiment of wealth and power. "You may have been swayed by current world gossip that American business is led by fools and criminals. Very good. Let us hasten to admit that the rulers of the greatest industrial realm the world ever saw or is likely to see, are human. If you were to look behind this mirror," she continued cynically, "you might find perhaps several sorts of men—gamblers who have taken chances and won; freebooters who, laws unto themselves, have robbed some people but used their loot for the good of all men; heirs who inherited fortunes for which they did not need to work, born as they were to the purple; merchants who, trading honestly or dishonestly, piled up untold riches; artisans and engineers who used rare skills to amass and pyramid wealth. All these men are owners of wealth and power—whether they are dreamers for the future or indulgent in drink and women, liberal or reactionary; men who read and think or men who do not whether they are good or bad.

"The point I bring you is this—they are the powerful of the earth. They rule. What I want you to do in the time that you are with us is to think of your own future under them. Will you join with the white European race to help crush and beat back the crazy Chinese and Russian Communists, help bring that world back to its normal procedures; or will you join this rebellion against established authority—this revolt against civilization?"

She paused and looked about. There was a dead silence. Azikiwe raised his outstretched arms in African courtesy, but was silent. The Kabaka, in his red fez and ceremonial gown, said in impeccable Oxford English:

"We have heard, Highness, and we will consider your words."

Bustamente of Jamaica growled inarticulately but said nothing.

Then an American Negro, a business man evidently chosen for the task, stepped forward and began to speak. "Your Highness, we want to thank you for this advice. I know the power of the white race and what it has done to help my people. I assure you that we Negroes are loyal Americans. We hate communism and despise Communists. We ask of the white world only such recognition as we deserve and treatment as equals only for such of us as are equal. We want the right to vote and hold office when we qualify. We believe in property and private profit. We want the right to work and save and we do not believe in labor trying to compel capital to pay wages it cannot afford. We want the right to spend our wealth without discrimination, to live where we can afford and to secure public accommodations when we can pay the price. We will always be glad to defend the nation which made us citizens and which is gradually—"

He suddenly paused and looked around—there was vague, elusive unease in the air. It was not a noise or an interruption, but was it neither applause nor approval. It was something that denoted that subtle disagreement, which Negroes know so well how to suggest. It was then that Manuel Mansart spoke—without premeditation, without design. The other speaker did not protest—he merely stopped speaking and stepped back.

Manuel said, "Madame, permit me. For many years I hesitated, uncertain as to just what my part in this world was to be, what it should be. But now I know. Now—rather suddenly—I know. We human beings are not all equal—but none are born rulers or predestined slaves. Up from the masses of all kinds of men can and will rise the gifted and the good. And no man—no men—no force—can stop this rise. The uplift of mankind is limited neither by color, race nor descent. We do not rise by stepping on each other but with each other, helping each other, and in time the overwhelming mass of men will achieve understanding and wealth enough for all their needs, all their yearnings, for every wish, every desire. Mankind, all of mankind will be strong and healthy, free of the corrupting power of greed and envy.

"Every industrial merger you make, every integration of monopoly power, every new penetration and enlargement of market, or seizure of new sources of raw materials, is just a step to the social ownership and conduct of industry by all for all. I therefore greet that land which first enacted equality of races—Russia. I'll never fight her. I hate, I detest the pretensions of the white race. They shall not continue to rule—their end is near, Socialism is not creeping, it is marching, and in its triumphant march I see the end of all war.

"We black folk will make a great mistake if we continue to ape white folk, whose wealth and power is based on taking from workers most of what the workers earn, and using it to amass untold power and luxury for parasites who have no right to it. Socialism is the effort to render the worker owner of what he creates, and it is this which the Soviet Union, China and the other Communist nations are trying—despite enormous difficulties and opposition—to accomplish. They are educating, healing, strengthening, encouraging the masses of the people so that this tremendous task may be done better. If those who deride and hinder and slander this effort can do better, let them try. Let them not spend their power in war and preparations for war to overthrow what these striving new nations, in blood and sweat attempt.

"Today, we Americans, black and white, whether we work by hand or brain, suffer from recurrent unemployment with its toll of insecurity. We fear sickness and disease, and gamble to escape it. We fear old age and steal to avert its sufferings. We need rest and recognition but cannot afford it. Education is so bad and so costly that many of our children sink to crime. Prices are so high, most of us cannot live decently—yet are forced to waste the little we have.

"Black Brothers, let us never sell our high heritage for a mess of such White Folks' pottage!"

A dead silence had descended as Mansart began to speak. When he concluded, all eyes turned to the Princess. At first she showed indifference, patience, then surprise and at last anger as she realized the tenor of what Mansart was saying—this was not the speech planned. She glanced about uncertainly until gradually realizing that Mansart's speech was shattering what had been so carefully planned—and at such great cost—she stamped her foot and arose waving her cigarette holder imperiously. But before she could utter a word, there came a sudden blast of trumpets and the curtains at the side of the long hall were quickly drawn, disclosing a large room, gaily decorated with an orchestra and flowers and an enormous table in the center laden sumptuously with foods of all kinds, temptingly displayed. Tables at the side offered a great variety of drinks. White-liveried servants stood ready to wait on the guests and from other rooms beyond appeared fifty or more white men and women to welcome the dark guests. All were guided to seats, carefully mixed by race and color, and a lively buzz of conversation soon ensued.

Hardly anyone noticed, as the curtains to the dining room opened, that two tall footmen, moving unobtrusively, had quickly taken Mansart's arms, one on each side and led him away from the food and guests and music, into the entrance hall. The Jewish Rabbi quietly followed as an attendant quickly brought their coats and hats, and an elevator stood ready with open door. Swiftly they glided down to the main floor thirty-two stories below.

As they crossed the plaza the rabbi said, "Out of five thousand years of glorious history, the barbarians of Western Europe have enslaved the world for the past 500 years. But their day of infamy begins to end in Asia—from Finland to Calcutta—in Africa—from Israel to Good Hope—in America—from Arctic to Antarctic. Men—all men—reassume the power which is theirs by right and by might."

The Cadillac was standing ready on Fifth Avenue, but Benjamin, the son, was not in it. Mansart hailed a cab. The rabbi turned, his head uncovered and his white hair blowing in the frosty night so that he loomed ghostly in the glow of the lights. He placed his hands on Mansart's shoulders and blessed him:

"Yevorechecho Adonoi veyishmerecho;
Yoer Adonoi ponov eilecho vichuneko;
Yiso Adonoi ponov eilecho veyosem lecho sholom."

Months passed. Manuel Mansart continued in outward health and seeming enjoyment of the world. He celebrated his 78th birthday. But Jean knew that his end was near. The physicians whom she unobtrusively called in were puzzled.

"I thought it was cancer. But the pain has disappeared and the other symptoms are not there. I just don't know what it is; nevertheless, he is not going to live long."

"We physicians know so little. We are especially ignorant about old age, because we have no time to study it."

"God! If we just had the hospitals and funds some nations have—"

"But we haven't," said Manuel, opening his eyes, "and after all what difference? It is only a matter of a few years, more or less. Jean and I have had a full life—full and fruitful. I know I am leaving her and this world soon—and forever. But while we live we will always have our memories—our memories and dreams."

Jean looked at him long and intensely, and whispered, "Have you no hope—I mean—afterward—?"

He smiled gravely and answered, "None." He continued, "We continually assume that if a thing seems desirable, it must for that reason be true. And if a man does not believe that what he would like to have so is so, then somehow he is held to blame. Most human beings would like to live again—prolong and either correcting or fulfilling this so imperfect existence. Naturally, some wouldn't—they are satisfied with one try, and ready to call quits after that.

"If a man faces the facts and says honestly, 'I don't know, and see absolutely no proof that we will live again'—should such a soul be derided or accused or read out of the Congregation of the Righteous—while hypocrites, liars and fools crowd into that comfortable refuge?

"Would it not be wiser and better to say, 'I do not know' or 'I do not hope?' No matter what Paul preaches, I know Hope is not Truth. In any case, I will not lie. If others believe in immortality, I respect their right to that belief. But what I fear and hate are the fanatics who would send me to hell for not consenting to lie." Then he added, "God is no playwright. His lives end dimly, and without drama; they pile no climax on tragedy nor triumph on defeat. They end quietly or helplessly—they just end."

The days passed slowly and pleasantly for Manuel Mansart despite unpleasant occurrences in the nation and the world. Jean drove him one morning to the Brooklyn Botanical Gardens to look at the blossoms. She sensed that he was gradually growing weaker, and that he knew it. As they rode back across the East River, he sang in low voice, with the silhouette of Manhattan looming before him:

"Swing low, sweet chariot, comin' for to carry me home—"

When they reached their apartment house he had to be helped more than usually into the elevator and to their door. Settled in his armchair, with a blanket across his lap, he whispered to Jean:

"Call all my scattered children from the Seven Seas, every one. Douglass, my first-born, is in Chicago with his wife; call him and his daughter and child from California with her husband. Revels is here but his son Philip settled in Hawaii with its golden rain. Be sure to summon him and Marian—Harry Bridges will spare them. Sojourner and her Bishop will hasten to me gladly from Africa. I want to see Jackie and Ann again and Marian's brother and sister with their mother. Then there are two young people in Atlanta named Baldwin, and young Moore in Arkansas—perhaps they will come. I still hope Douglass' boy will return from Europe. I want you to cable him. It will be good to have my brood stand around me when I die, which I hope will not be long now. And you, dear faithful Jean, are always with me. I want us to say goodbye together in this old and evil and incredibly beautiful Earth."

When word reached them his family started by train and plane, by cab and car, over road and river and sea to be at the bedside of Manuel Mansart. They gathered, one by one, or in couples, or in family groups—all a little apprehensive, a little uneasy. After the first greetings, the older folk talked about family problems, their children's careers, current developments, the state of business, the season's weather, styles and clothes. Gradually as the days passed, all seemed to separate into age groups and one lowering night the younger members of the family group climbed to the roof and sat there in the drizzly night, huddled under umbrellas and raincoats, staring west across the city to glimpse the dim Palisades on the New Jersey side of the Hudson. Someone began to speak—it was too dark at first to discern who it was but the voice spoke clearly.

"We're here to watch the ending of a life. It was a good life but it was ineffective. It's up to us to carry it on and make it work for the future—the future of our colored people here in America; yes, and the future of mankind, too.

"Our professional men and civil servants, our white collar workers are paralyzed into silence and inactivity. They practice their profession, work hard, make good money and keep still. They buy cars and refrigerators; rent better apartments, often even buy and build if their bank credit is good. But when all is said and done, what does it all add up to? The most and the best you can say of the Negro is, 'He's rising from nether to upper Hell.'"

By now, everyone recognized that it was Phillip's voice speaking. "We have all been disappointed in various ways and degrees. Small business, even when carried on by intelligent Negroes with some capital, is impossible—it is at the mercy of white banks and chain stores and Big Business. Directly or indirectly, it must live on exploitation of the poor, with practically no freedom of thought, or action. Jackie and Ann, down in Mississippi, cannot exist as small farmers—they are manipulated by the white market, pawns of petty white politicians, under perpetual threat of the mob. Even my brother-in-law here, in New York, installed in a Rockefeller Center office, prospective vice-president of a huge corporation, looks forward only to being a cog in the vast wheel of an international oil trust with no real voice in its aims or operation."

Ann's rich cultured voice, full of anguish, interrupted.

"Oh, I am ashamed, ashamed of my people. We have lost all clarity of vision, of purpose. We have forgotten our purple history, of endless resistance to white terror, of suffering which made us strong, of struggle which made us wise; we despise our own great and rush pellmell to embrace white America. Why?"

A low bass voice in the rear barely audible took up the strain from *Elijah*—"*Then did Elijah the Prophet burst forth like a fire; his words appeared like flaming torches*"—but Ann, flinging off her head-covering, lifting her face to the rain, continued.

"What is this America to which we all crawl? The East no longer stands for literature, philanthropy, a heritage of culture. It is a naked and brazen financial and industrial dictatorship. Our free West? The old glory of pioneer California has disappeared; Grafters rule labor in the Northwest where Joe Hill never died, and in the South, bestial backwardness reigns supreme as it did a century and more ago. Was America born for this—or to soften, strain out, select, blend the finest of Europe, Asia, and Africa, even those long buried in poverty and ignorance. Perhaps it will yet do this. But here and now, the German-Americans no longer even remember their rich heritage. The Scandinavians forget their folklore. So many Italians have lost sight of the glory that was Rome and remember only what the slums of Naples and the degradation of Sicily taught. Why, the boast of our tallest Jewish statesman is that at thirty-five he had successfully gambled in stocks—with stacked cards—for the right to wield as his own a million dollars of property he never earned.

"The Irish, forgetting the Gaelic revival, Fianna Fail, and the Irish theater, are still running from one of the loveliest spots of earth. What have we Negroes and the Indians to compare even with this? The Indians are spiritually dead in this nation, but with neither literature nor history. The Negroes are seemingly mesmerized. Where is the outburst of literature which we began a generation ago—the poetry and music, the dance and drama? In the last decade we have not produced a poem or a novel, a history or play of stature—nothing but gamblers, prizefighters and jazz."

"But Ann, you are being unjust. Will publishers publish or critics review, or booksellers handle anything but Negro's lauding of white philanthropy? Can Sterling Brown or Rayford Logan get a book in print even if it is a classic?"

"Right—and why? Because Negroes themselves do not buy books—they prefer Cadillacs, spring hats, and balls. Their publishing houses spend millions a year on religious trash and on picture magazines that ignore the mass of our workers while glorifying the pushers and social climbers. Negro Yearbooks disappear. Remember when the greatest composer in Europe sat at the feet of our Burleigh to learn from him the inner meaning of Negro sorrow songs? Now we sell musical trash to any idiot rich enough to buy, while one of our laureate poets, bursting with talent, clowns on Broadway to make morons laugh at simple distress!

"We go to Europe aping white Americans in bad manners, loud voices, and extravagant expenditure. On the one matter in which Europeans sympathize and want to help—our own status in the United States—we are dumb or reticent or deliberately lie to cover up for the bestialities of our oppressors.

"It is the paradox of our age that we—the largest group of Negroes with sufficient education and cultural status within our grasp sufficient to place us among civilized peoples—are actually falling behind our motherland, Africa. Ethiopia and the Sudan surpass us in political organization. Ghana and Nigeria, which began by seeking education in our colleges, are now forging ahead of us in grasp of modern cultural problems and in ability to meet Europe and Asia face to face as equals. Even Liberia, our foster child, can sit and vote in the United Nations—where we have not even the right of petition."

One could sense the general acceptance of Ann's views and outlook, and others joined in the discussion, eager to develop it further.

"Read our Negro newspapers and magazines—compare them with Tim Fortune's *Age* before Booker Washington bought its silence. Or, compare them with the *Crisis* at its proud, unabashed, unchallenged zenith."

"Dead dreams of Douglass, Chesnutt, and Dunbar—where are Tanner's spiritual children? What can Barthe find to do?"

"Oh, that my head were waters, and mine eyes a fountain of tears that I might weep day and night for the slain of the daughter of my people."

A man's voice broke in.

"Once we could hear Shakespeare in Harlem. Once Williams and Walker built a clean and dignified comedy. Now we fill our lungs with cigarette cancer and our bellies with 70 percent rot-gut whiskey. And our time goes into gambling, into newspaper, television, church, and whorehouse, aping our white friends."

Sojourner, who had listened quietly, now spoke. "Remember, dear kin, we are a nation of sixteen millions. We almost equal in number Canada, Ethiopia, Iran. We are twice the size of Portugal, Australia, Austria, Ceylon, Bulgaria, Greece, Hungary. Over half the nations in the United Nations are smaller in population than we. Yet we are voiceless and dumb, unnoticed, unable to say a word to the world. In the great movements—for peace, for health, for the abolition of illiteracy, and the greatest enemy of man, poverty—our organizations are silent."

Someone asked: "Do you belittle what the NAACP has done and what the Urban League has attempted?"

Another answered: "No, never. But a social organization outlives its usefulness unless it grows with the time and renews itself with a developing world. For fifty years the NAACP has fought to secure for black Americans civil rights long deemed inherent to white folk; and for the right to vote inseparable from democracy. The victories achieved on these lines have been unparalleled in modern group history. But today, it is clear that legal rights and the suffrage are not enough for modern democracy. With these must go economic justice and universal education. The NAACP has tried to turn to this broader field of effort, but has not yet succeeded. The Urban League did begin with an effort to secure economic justice for Negroes; but from the first, it was compelled by white industry to curtail and distort its broader aims. It is today bound helplessly in ropes of its own weaving.

Philip broke in again: "Today we carry almost no weight politically. Our Congressmen are for the most part nonentities. Our dozen or so legislators champion no great causes. Our judges almost all hew to the standard line; it's safe that way. What does it benefit us that we have a representative in the Labor Bureau or that a political figure in high public office in New York or Chicago happens to be black? Do you remember what a black city councilman in New York once meant to the world?—his reward was jail."

A voice almost hissed: "Listen, Sojourner. We've been patient three hundred years. I'm damned tired of patience. Yes, any kind of patience—even the patience of Manuel Mansart, bless him. I want to fight."

Death did not come swiftly to Manuel Mansart. He was too used to life. In the apartment below, he lay in a semi-coma until he woke to watch the sun as it rose over Hell-Gate Bridge.

It was one of New York's most beautiful Fall days. Manuel, at his own whispered request, was wheeled out on the terrace facing East. The morning sun poured over him, while far below pulsed and roared the powerful rhythms of black Harlem, at work and play, in song and sorrow, never silent, never still. Manuel was wan and alarmingly frail but he gazed long and intently at his gathered brood, who had been called to his side—the judge and his calm wife, always gentle, always poised; the prosperous always well-dressed Douglass Mansart with his heavyset and over-dressed wife. The California physician stood there always so sure of himself, with his well-groomed wife and brown and beautiful new baby, whose great black eyes gazed solemnly at her great-grandfather. Manuel beckoned for the child to be brought closer.

He kissed her gently and in a barely audible voice asked, "Can you tell me, dear little one, what the world will be which you will see before you die?"

The baby smiled.

Suddenly the body of Manuel Mansart stiffened. He shuddered in a convulsion. Sweat glistened on his forehead and tears slid from the corners of his eyes. For a moment he writhed as though in agony, then in an unexpectedly strong though hoarse voice, he shrieked, "I have come from Hell—I saw bombs filling the skies—I heard the scream of Death. Moscow was aflame, London was ashes, Paris was a clot of blood, New York sank into the sea. The world was sorrow, hate and fear—no hope, no song, no laughter. Save me, my children. Save the world!"

They hurriedly wheeled him indoors, lifted him into his bed and covered him with blankets. He could still glimpse the Jersey Palisades in the setting sun. Jean held him while the physician gave him an injection of morphine. His body relaxed, his eyes opened wide and he stared at the faces congregated about his bed. At last he whispered, "Was it true? What I saw—was it true?"

Douglass said, "Perhaps, father. But you mustn't fret."

Revels said, "It could be. It could be."

Jean, her arm still pillowing Mansart's head, said, "Never!"

Mansart slept. He slept a long hour during which the Bishop arrived and a cablegram came with roses from Adelbert. There was silence as the physician, who had been feeling Mansart's pulse, said, "The end is near."

Mansart opened his eyes and whispered, "It was a nightmare. I know it now. I am back from a far journey. I saw China's millions lifting the soil of the nation in their hands to dam the rivers which long had eaten their land. I saw the golden domes of Moscow shining on Russia's millions, yesterday unlettered, now reading the wisdom of the world. I saw birds singing in Korea, Viet-Nam, Indonesia and Malaya. I saw India and Pakistan united, free; in Paris, Ho Chi Minh celebrated peace on earth; while in New York—"

He paused as if exhausted and lay back in Jean's arms. Behind, the group clustered around Mansart's bed. Sojourner had taken her violin from its case. She raised her bow and from her violin leapt a dissonant flame of protest, flaring to anguished heights, then swooning and softening to sheer breathless melody. It was as though a storm of stars had struck across the moonbeams and dropped on the full glory of the sun!

The Bishop stepped forward and clasped his hands. His voice faltered between the strains of melody:

"I shall not want—He leadeth me beside the still waters—Yea, though I walk through the Valley of the Shadow of Death—in the presence of my enemies—Goodness and mercy shall follow me—"

Gently Jean closed the lifeless eyes.

And so died Manuel Mansart, in the seventy-eighth year of his life—and of the emancipation of the Negro in America, the ninety-first.

Over his dead body lay a pall of crimson roses, such as few kings have ever slept beneath.

Afterword

The Black Flame, Then and Now
Mark A. Sanders, Emory University

> Our great ethical question today is, therefore, how may we justly distribute the world's goods to satisfy the necessary wants of the mass of men.
> —W. E. B. Du Bois, *Dark Water*

I
Cold War Culture and the Unmaking of an Icon

Looking back on Du Bois's long, illustrious career, it is easy to forget how marginal a figure he was by his final decade. When on February 23, 1951, he walked into Small's Paradise in Harlem to celebrate his eighty-third birthday, he was already persona non grata in New York and was well on his way to becoming a national pariah. Essex House, the original downtown venue for the birthday party, had canceled the group's reservation, while Arthur Spingarn, Mordecai Johnson, Ralph Bunche, Margaret Mead, and other noted guests sent their regrets[1]—all in the wake of an indictment of Du Bois by the Justice Department for "failure to register as an agent of a foreign principal"[2] (in effect, for allegedly aiding and abetting the Soviet Union). Du Bois's indictment and trial were watershed events in this last phase of his career; together they were both the beginning and the end, the crucial break that inaugurated Du Bois's more rapid movement farther to the left, culminating in self-imposed exile. Prior to the events of 1951, Du Bois had been very active in the post-World War II peace movement. In 1950, he had been appointed chairperson of the Peace Information Center, a group promoting peace and protesting American aggression in Asia; that same year Du Bois ran for a U.S. Senate seat in New York on the American

Labor Party ticket; and the year before that, he had attended the Conference for Peace at the Waldorf-Astoria in New York and the World Peace Meeting in Paris—both events roundly condemned in the American press as pro-Soviet, anti-American agitation. Indeed, by 1951 Du Bois's pro-peace/anti-imperialism and pro-labor/anti-capital positions were direct affronts to the Cold War foreign and domestic policy, and he and many others interpreted the indictment as naked intimidation: clearly his views and activities would be costly for him and his supporters.

Though the case against Du Bois was thrown out of court, the federal government continued its harassment, tampering with his mail, questioning neighbors about his activities, and more.[3] From 1952 to 1957 the State Department refused to issue Du Bois a passport, resulting in an internal exile of sorts. Black colleges that had previously welcomed him declined to invite him to lecture, black presses bowed to government pressure and stopped publishing his columns, and no "mainstream" publishers would accept his manuscripts. In fact, by 1955, when he began looking for a publisher for his trilogy, only the "fringe" Left publisher Masses & Mainstream, Incorporated would consider it. "It says much of the nature of dominant society in the United States in the 1950s," Herbert Aptheker later lamented, "that such an effort from such a man was not even considered for publication by any 'reputable' publisher."[4] Although one thousand people gathered to celebrate Du Bois's ninetieth birthday,[5] from the moment of the indictment forward, Du Bois never again had the same access to "mainstream" audiences (either black or white) that he had prior to World War II.

Yet it was precisely as pariah, precisely in the context of the post-World War II culture of fear—its attack on dissent and civil liberties, its reduction of political debate to Manichaean oppositions, and its will to conformity—that Du Bois wrote some of his most important works. *The World and Africa* (1947), *The Autobiography of W. E. B. Du Bois* (1968), his incendiary columns in the *Chicago Defender* and the *National Guardian*, and his epic trilogy *The Black Flame*—all of these works consistently railed against imperialism abroad and against racial oppression at home, demanding a critical assessment of capitalism and its exploitation of labor.

If, in fact, "the nature of dominant society" was powerful enough to force the foremost black intellectual of the twentieth century to the margins of public debate, what in particular was so powerful in that culture of conformity, and why, well after the era, have critics continued to ignore Du Bois's final novel, and indeed Du Bois's entire final decade?

The answers may lie in the overlapping effects of literary criticism and magazine culture in shaping the literary taste of the 1950s; closely related too, shifting trends in African American literature, the emergence of the civil rights movement and its own discourse, and of course Du Bois's own artistic and political evolution all combine to explain perhaps more fully the trilogy's invisibility then *and* now.

To start, the early Cold War period witnessed the birth of a new era in the academy, one that was particularly hostile to the literary traditions and approaches to art that informed Du Bois's own creative writing. Emerging from

World War II as a global superpower, the United States called for a cultural pedigree to legitimize its newfound might, and the academy responded with the creation of New Criticism, the American literary canon, and the field of American Studies; although all three had antecedents older than 1945, it was the postwar moment that elevated these relatively fledgling and disparate academic pursuits to hegemonic status. New Criticism provided a critical approach, separating text from context and locating meaning strictly in the realm of the aesthetic. Naturally, New Criticism went in search of texts to reflect its critical practices, formulating a canon less invested in polemic than in the fine arts as such. Using the "American Renaissance" as its foundation—Emerson, Thoreau, Melville, Whitman, et al.—New Criticism constructed a canon of high modernism in the twentieth century that located conflict largely at the site of artifice: formal fragmentation, interiority, self-referentiality, linguistic density, and so on. Meanwhile American Studies legitimized the myths of the West and of manifest destiny, American exceptionalism, self-reliance, and rugged individualism, and so defined America in romantic, largely uncritical terms. Perhaps the best example of the new American literary hero was William Faulkner, who turned the anguish of the white southern burden inward; such devices as nonlinearity, stream of consciousness, and poly-vocal montage delivered the landscape of the southern white psyche as the locale for social critique.

Apropos for the times, just two months before Du Bois's indictment, Faulkner stood before a Stockholm audience to accept the Nobel Prize for literature, proclaiming the transcendence of the "human spirit" even in the face of nuclear annihilation. Not only was the event a personal victory for the southerner, it was a ringing endorsement of American high modernism. From this point forward, American high modernism would not have to compete with other literary traditions; it would be the only tradition of note or record so far as the academy and refined literary tastes were concerned. Committed to a vision of American triumph, New Criticism, high modernism, and American Studies remapped the literary landscape, ushering in a set of Cold War-friendly literary texts and approaches and effectively erasing from the historical record traditions that insisted upon connections between text and the material world—the very traditions of which *The Black Flame* was an integral part.

More specifically, Du Bois and *The Black Flame* find their artistic and philosophical context in the plethora of literatures and philosophical approaches circulating at the turn of the twentieth century through the 1930s. From Du Bois's point of view, pragmatism, nativism, pluralism, realism, naturalism, social realism, and muckraking, combined, constitute, at the risk of oversimplification, a larger tradition of art as propaganda, art as protest, and art as social movement. This tradition shared space with a tradition of fine arts and high modernism, (art for art's sake if you will), borrowing freely across a quasi-fictional divide; but for Du Bois, art in the propaganda tradition was of better use, particularly literature grounded in American pragmatism. Beginning with William James (whose salvific influence Du Bois cites in all three autobiographies), pragmatism replaced ahistorical absolutes with meaning that was rooted in subjectivity, contingency, and interpretation. The arts expressed individual, subjective experiences of the world, and through continual interpretation would yield the communal values defining the society. And as per John Dewey, it is through the aesthetic—that is, through subjective experience re-presented by art—that the individual communicates with the group, and that different groups communicate with one another. Both approaches helped to shape the nativist/pluralist movement that championed literature as a means of interethnic communication and communion—all in the service of democratic renewal. In turn, pragmatism, nativism, and pluralism informed Charles Johnson's approach to art in *Opportunity*, Du Bois's approach to literature in *The Crisis*, and Alain Locke's approach to framing the Harlem Renaissance. So, too, periodicals and so-called little magazines such as *The Nation*, *The Seven Arts*, *The New Republic*, *The Liberator*, *The Masses*, *American Mercury*, and early editions of *The Dial* promoted art in service to social change.[6]

In this context, realists and naturalists such as Jack London, Frank Norris, Theodore Dreiser, and Upton Sinclair depicted economic deprivation and harsh working conditions—descriptions free of the idealization of romance or the predictability of melodrama. Sinclair in particular demonstrated the ability of muckraking to change public opinion and thus to effect change; Waldo Frank's nativism envisioned an ethnically democratic America that would usher in a new era of true egalitarianism; and John Steinbeck's social realism documented the plight of Depression-era farmers. Perhaps more hyperbolic than factual, Van Wyck Brooks went so far as to claim the entire era for the art-as-propaganda crowd. Commenting on the modernist era, Brooks insisted that "Every writer I came to know called himself a radical, committed to some programme for changing and improving the world. . . . They had, or wished to have, the feeling of common cause, the sense of a community of writers building a new culture."[7]

Not only did the protest/propaganda tradition coexist beside high modernism, it had the nerve to castigate high modernism for its commitment to authority, hierarchy, and the status quo. By the time that Du Bois began writing *The Black Flame* in 1949,[8] the tables had already begun to turn; by 1957, his literary context was gone.

These titanic shifts in American literary taste were by no means lost on the younger black writers of the fifties. In fact, if the tradition of art for art's sake was first established in African American literature during the Harlem Renaissance of the 1920s, it reached its apex in the 1950s with noted writers garnering far greater acclaim than their Harlem Renaissance progenitors. In literary and cultural circles beyond the academy, Ralph Ellison, James Baldwin, Gwendolyn Brooks, and even a post-*Native Son* Richard Wright enjoyed broad critical acclaim as they depicted African American life and the evils of racism within a fine arts, high modernist tradition.

For example, where Ellison had spent much of the thirties working in socialist and communist circles—a "fellow traveler" writing for the *Partisan Review*, *New Masses*, and the like—he later made a conscious choice to pursue his writing in what he regarded as a broader artistic and philosophical arena, one that also aligned more or less with emerging literary and geopolitical trends: "The collapse of the Left indicated for Ellison an inevitable rapprochement with the *Partisan Review* crowd," Lawrence Jackson recounts, "in part because of the growing prominence of the New Critical approaches to literature, which continued to push for a separation between art and politics. . . . As he increasingly embraced the Aristotelian logic espoused by Kenneth Burke, and further left behind his Communist associations, Ellison too, accommodated the separation. His ideas about politics were also mellowing."[9] Ultimately Ellison wanted to "stand as an independent artist and not the icon of a social movement."[10]

Similarly, Brooks's *Annie Allen* (1949), for which she won the Pulitzer Prize, and her only novel, *Maud Martha* (1953), placed Brooks squarely within a fine arts tradition, taking, like Ellison, full advantage of the high modernist innovations in form, language, and philosophical approach. Perhaps most conspicuously, Baldwin made a name for himself early in his career with an unequivocal rejection of the protest tradition. "Everybody's Protest Novel" and "Many Thousands Gone" together helped to move Baldwin out of *Native Son*'s long shadow and to place him firmly in the competing camp.[11] And after the stunning success of *Native Son* (1940), Wright also moved away from the protest/propaganda tradition. Chafing under the prescriptions of John Reed Club-style "proletariat literature," Wright gravitated toward greater experimentation in the use of existentialism. While he continued to criticize racism, Wright's fiction of the fifties did so in the more acceptable literary mode.

Not only was Du Bois out of sync with the newly dominant fine arts tradition, but his approach to the historical novel was at odds, too, with popular trends. Where Du Bois regarded the historical novel as a means of telling the truth about the past, by the fifties the historical novel had become a popular means of *escape* from some of the harsher historical realities, particularly concerning race and the American South. *Huckleberry Finn* (1884) notwithstanding, the historical novel was by and large a subgenre of romanticism, a means of idealizing a particularly painful or unresolved past. For example, southern literature had been dominated by the plantation tradition since the end of the Civil War, a tradition that depicted an idealized past in which contented slaves worked happily under the stewardship of benevolent masters. Works such as Joel Chandler Harris's *Uncle Remus: His Songs and Sayings* (1880) or Thomas Nelson Page's *In Ole Virginia* (1887) gave northern and southern readers alike a past free of the regional and racial strife that marked the late nineteenth century, while Margaret Mitchell's *Gone With the Wind* (1936) carried the plantation tradition well into the twentieth century. Even within African American literature of the fifties, the historical novel did not do the political work that Du Bois hoped it would. Frank Yerby, the one black writer who outsold all of his more famous contemporaries combined, wrote historical romances strictly as light entertainment. Though his work turned to more serious concerns later in his career, his fiction of the fifties is representative of the dominant trend.

Finally, just as Du Bois was at odds with virtually all of the literary trends of the fifties, so he stood at a distance from one of its defining social movements: civil rights. He regarded the *Brown v. Board of Education* Supreme Court decision with skepticism, doubting the efficacy of sending black children to white schools and instead emphasizing the need for greater resources in black schools. So, too, the Montgomery bus boycott was "something of a puzzle."[12] While he entertained the possibility that Martin Luther King Jr. was a latter-day Gandhi, in the end Du Bois found the civil rights movement insufficient because of its lack of a material critique or an economic agenda; in short, integration into a bankrupt economic system was misguided at best. In a larger sense, Cold War culture, mainstream literary tastes, the new African American literary paradigm, the budding civil rights movement—the zeitgeist, in effect—had no room for Du Bois and his ideas. At best he was an anachronism, at worst a real threat.

II

Art, Propaganda, and *The Black Flame*

If the 1950s were for Du Bois a study in movement to the left, Du Bois's final decade may serve as a coda for his entire career as an activist-intellectual. From his earliest days at Fisk and at Harvard, Du Bois had "something to say to the world,"[13] a contribution to make in answering that "great ethical question, . . . how may we justly distribute the world's goods to satisfy the necessary wants of the mass of men."[14] His gender-exclusive language notwithstanding, such a commitment launched Du Bois on a lifelong quest for ever-better theories and methods for effecting positive change; scholarship, teaching, writing for public forums, speech making, protests, organizing, travel, voracious reading—all these served Du Bois's ever-evolving search for "the broadest measure of justice [for] all human beings."[15] Over his ninety-five years, Du Bois transformed from being a liberal democratic scholar convinced of the power of learning and persuasion to eradicate racial oppression, to being a card-carrying Communist who called for "the overthrow of capitalist monopoly."[16] Early Du Bois, most often represented through *The Souls of Black Folk* (1903), firmly believed that "race prejudice was based on widespread ignorance,"[17] and that in response the "Talented Tenth" of both races—"a few white men and a few black men of broad culture, catholic tolerance, and trained ability, joining their hands . . ."[18]—could ameliorate racial strife and thus allow the republic to live up to its founding ideals. But by 1911, the year that he published his first novel, Du Bois had joined the Socialist Party, and although he resigned the next year, his engagement with Marxism, with dialectic materialism, and with what he saw as a global struggle between capital and labor lasted the rest of his life. Indeed, later in life he looked back on his earlier writings—principally, *The Suppression of the African Slave Trade in the United States* (1896), *The Philadelphia Negro* (1899), *The Souls of Black Folk*, and *John Brown* (1909)—and lamented the naive belief that, alone, "carefully gathered scientific proof that neither color nor race determined the limits of a man's capacity or desert"[19] could reverse centuries of racial oppression. "I was not at the time sufficiently Freudian," he confessed of his early phase, "to understand how little human action is based on reason; nor did I know Karl Marx well enough to appreciate the economic foundations of human history."[20]

Intensified European colonization of Africa, the Sam Hose lynching of 1897, the larger context of two thousand blacks lynched during Du Bois's years at Wilberforce and at Atlanta University[21] and the Atlanta race riot of 1906 all drove home for Du Bois the limits of liberalism and reasoned debate. By the end of World War I, and despite his call to "close ranks," Du Bois understood the first global war as an extension of the Berlin Conference of 1885; global warfare was simply a more barbarous form of competition for the markets and resources that African colonies would provide.[22] So, too, Du Bois came to regard "broad culture" and its bourgeois participants as coconspirators with imperialism, firmly invested in the privileges derived from colonial exploitation.

Du Bois's increased alienation from liberalism resulted in the scholarly and political contributions for which he is most famous: the first Pan-African congresses (beginning in 1919), the linking of domestic racial oppression and imperialism, the paradigm-shifting scholarship of *Black Reconstruction in America* (1935),[23] the establishment of *Crisis* as a leading voice of black protest. Equally important, Du Bois's theory of art and of art's connection to progressive politics played an enormous role in the American and African American culture of the first half of the twentieth century, even though, as we have seen, the theory and its approach fell out of critical discourse soon after World War II.

In his famous 1926 *Crisis* essay "Criteria of Negro Art," Du Bois articulated his vision of art in what amounted to a recommendation to the budding generation of Harlem Renaissance writers to resist market-driven black portraiture and to create "beauty" as he saw it. According to Du Bois, creating beauty necessarily involves telling the "Truth"—creating accurate portraiture free of the racist caricature of the minstrel stage, popular literature, advertising, and film; truth is also grounded in historical accuracy. Furthermore, truth is necessarily tied to "right" and "justice" because for Du Bois accurate representation and the accurate historical record invariably lay claim to universal human needs, aspirations, and progressive political change:

> ... it is the bounded duty of black America to begin this great work of the creation of beauty, of the preservation of beauty, of the realization of beauty, and we must use in this work all the methods that men have used before. And what have been the tools of the artist in times gone by? First of all, he has used the truth—not for the sake of truth ..., but as one upon whom truth eternally thrusts itself as the highest handmaid of imagination, as the one great vehicle of universal understanding. Again artists have used goodness—goodness in all aspects of justice, honor, and right—not for sake of ethical sanction but as the one true method of gaining sympathy and human interest.
> The apostle of beauty thus becomes the apostle of truth and right.[24]

As mentioned earlier, Du Bois's theory of art is rooted in pragmatist philosophy, and thus he values literature as a means of fostering "universal understanding," as a means of building communities, fomenting values, and, more immediately, transmitting vital information. Furthermore, this conflation of the aesthetic and the ethical was for Du Bois yet another form of political expression; or as Arnold Rampersad puts it, "His turn to art . . . was not relief from the hurly-burly of political action but was an aspect of political action itself."[25] Promoting literature through *The Crisis*, *Phylon*, or *The Moon Illustrated Weekly*, creating the Krigwa Players Little Negro Theatre, and of course writing his own poetry and fiction all functioned as a part of the "greater fight," "an upward look—a pushing onward."[26]

Thus in the etymological sense of propaganda, art serves to propagate or to spread ideas, here of black people and their claims to human rights. Ultimately, for Du Bois, the artist as propagandist is a servant to society in providing "beauty" that by definition destroys lies and therefore pursues "right" and "justice"; furthermore, beauty functions in the aesthetic sense, beauty that serves to *propagate* a people, that helps to sustain their psychic and emotional lives.

In his very first novel, *The Quest of the Silver Fleece* (1911), Du Bois announces his aim to execute this theory of art: "He who would tell a tale must look toward three ideals: to tell it well, to tell it beautifully, and to tell the truth."[27] Throughout his novels, Du Bois pursues beauty and truth largely through the themes of education, of the individual quest for greater understanding, and of collective communal resistance to racist exploitation, and through female characters possessing "the gift of clarity of vision."[28] These themes tend to operate in a realist/naturalist mode prone to didacticism in which the narrator as instructor often imparts knowledge to the audience.

For example, the theme of education in *The Quest of the Silver Fleece* and in his second novel, *Dark Princess* (1928), is borne primarily by the protagonists as they attempt to acquire formal education that will allow them to advance professionally. Yet they must confront the limitations of formal education for the black subject in a racist society, and thus embark on a quest for greater understanding and solutions, a quest that provides supplemental education through experience. As a result of their toils and sacrifices, both Bles and Matthew Towns achieve "heroic redemption through suffering," and serve as the "embodiment of a redemptive consciousness."[29] Arriving at a higher plane of awareness, they are better able to provide greater aid to their communities in a collective struggle.

As Claudia Tate points out, Du Bois's protagonists are invariably helped by a black female character who "is the intellectual and spiritual superior to her mate."[30] In *The Quest of the Silver Fleece*, Zora "is a heroine who is dark-skinned, unpedigreed, and sympathetic"—a first in the African American novel, according to David L. Lewis.[31] And it is through Zora's example that Bles grows to realize his mission in life. In *Dark Princess*, Kautilya pushes Towns toward his redemption as she, too, searches for a means to resist the European imperialism threatening her people.

These novels pursue thematic and character development while delivering a materialist critique of the world of both characters and reader. For example, *The*

Quest of the Silver Fleece counters the plantation tradition's depiction of the agrarian South with a withering exposé of greed, exploitation, and corruption as southern planters and northern financiers scramble to extract the last bit of surplus capital from black labor. Indeed, Du Bois's documentary approach to sharecropping and to the Cresswell-Taylor maneuvers to corner the cotton market "struck many readers knowledgeable about market transactions as vividly modern and realistic."[32] According to Arnold Rampersad, *The Quest of the Silver Fleece* is in fact "the first black novel to present and analyze economics in a significant manner."[33] *Dark Princess*, too, devotes at least a third of the narrative to muckraking. "The Chicago Politician" subordinates Towns's development to the detailed depiction of ward politics, suggesting muckraking as an end in itself, not just as a literary device for thematic development.

It follows, of course, that these dominant themes obtain in *The Black Flame*, but now on an epic scale, and now featuring history itself as the medium of beauty, truth, and instruction. Elsewhere, Du Bois commented that he did not have access to mass media such as film and radio because of lack of capital.[34] He therefore relied on less expensive forms of communication and entertainment—demonstrations, community theater, and pageantry, for example—in order to bring his message to the masses. In this sense, *The Black Flame* is a low-budget mass-media broadcast, delivering an essential yet neglected history to the people who need it most. Du Bois had tried to do the same before through *Black Reconstruction in America*, but that book's academic approach to history guaranteed that it would have a relatively small audience. This time around, Du Bois tried to answer the "great ethical question" with an epic history in fiction, following chronologically right on the heels of *Black Reconstruction*. In fact, *The Black Flame* can best be read as a fictionalized sequel to *Black Reconstruction*,[35] as Du Bois himself suggests in his postscript: "I am trying by method of historical fiction to complete the cycle of history which has for a half century engaged my thought, research and fiction."[36]

Previously, *Black Reconstruction* had destroyed the Dunning-Dixon school that depicted Reconstruction as a "tragedy" visited upon southern whites. Instead, Du Bois presented the era as an "extraordinary experiment in democracy,"[37] one in which blacks stood as agents and actors in a great American drama, just as Manuel Mansart and his family play central roles in African American, American, and global history from 1876 to 1954. Indeed, *The Ordeal of Mansart* (1957) opens by striking the dominant chords played throughout *Black Reconstruction*: education, participatory democracy, land reform, the liberation of labor and the possibility of interracial labor solidarity, the year 1876 as shibboleth, and South Carolina as center stage.

Relative to education, Du Bois in *Black Reconstruction* asserted that the creation of public schools and the establishment of black colleges and universities were among the greatest contributions to democracy that Reconstruction could make. The concept of free schools lasted throughout the twentieth century, laying the foundation for poor and working-class blacks and whites to participate in the political process more fully. But more immediately, education afforded the freedman preparation for political competition and supplied teachers to staff and to sustain new black institutions of higher learning. "Had it not been for the Negro school and college," Du Bois concluded, "the Negro would, to all intents and purposes, have been driven back to slavery."[38] So, too, Reconstruction inaugurated true participatory democracy, with blacks participating in the political process as voters and as elected officials—an essential exercise not simply for the principle of equal representation, but for the more practical issue of economic competition. By participating in the political process, blacks could hope to protect and support their economic interests. Here, for a Marxist scholar, the issue of labor is also enormously important. Du Bois viewed Reconstruction as the emancipation of black labor, as well as the opportunity for white labor to resist the exploitation of concentrated capital. Equally important, the gesture toward land reform—the reapportionment of plantation land to freedmen—also held out new democratic possibilities, affording blacks a modicum of economic independence. The year 1876, the last year of Reconstruction and the opening of *The Ordeal of Mansart*, looms as the watershed moment in which northern capital and southern white supremacy broker a deal to end the experiment. As both the end of the experiment and the beginning of modern black life in America, 1876 looms as the defining moment in American and African American history. Finally, South Carolina as center stage for the drama—it is the opening of both *Black Reconstruction* and *The Black Flame*—is symbolic of the promise and the failure of the American democratic experiment. As a state more than fifty percent black (suggesting the possibility of real black political power), as one of the first states to implement land reform under General W. T. Sherman's Special Field Order Number 15, as one of the first states to establish public schools, and as one of the most violent states in resisting "radical" Reconstruction, South Carolina encapsulated Du Bois's major concerns for the era, and thus serves as the starting point for the Mansart odyssey.

In terms of Du Bois's theory of art, history here serves as the central medium of "beauty" and "truth." The family name itself, "Man's Art,"[39] strongly suggests the protagonist working on the metaphoric level from the outset, locating the ideal of beauty within the drama's historical context. Perhaps more than simply a creation of bourgeois refinement used by white elites to control blacks, as one reviewer read it, "Mansart" suggests a protagonist in a quest for art in Du Boisian theoretical terms—in a quest for beauty that naturally serves justice and black progress.

Certainly in a more mechanical sense, "Mansart" functions as a means of documentation that will allow Du Bois to move geographically and thematically as he bends his fiction toward the interpretation of historical events. So, too, Mansart's growing awareness of his surroundings serves as a metaphor for the expanding black political consciousness, one that will eventually make links between domestic racial oppression and the global struggle between capital and labor. Further, Mansart's quest, like Du Bois's own, will look for lasting solutions, for a path that leads to an appraisal of global economic systems and to an encounter with Marxist theory and praxis.

Thus *The Ordeal of Mansart* (1957) begins by making the black experience of the demise of Reconstruction symbolic. Borrowing from the picaresque convention of mistaken poverty, Manuel Mansart begins a life of poverty and hardship occasioned by his father's murder—the symbolic death of Reconstruction. Now Manuel, a metaphor for the race, is cut off from his birthright, the Constitution, and is thrown out into the world to survive according to his own devices, and to grow toward a consciousness that will redeem both his family and black people as a whole.

With Mansart's trajectory established, his journey proceeds through three fairly discrete stages. First, his youth and early adulthood entail description of his early years and formal education. This first section culminates with the completion of his formal education at Atlanta University, in 1898. Significantly, Mansart gives a speech on the Spanish American War, extolling Antonio Maceo's heroics to free the island *and* praising "the philanthropy of America the Emancipator."[40] Even though his professor has pointed out that North American slave interests had tried to annex the country and that Spain had surrendered before the U.S. declared war, Manuel "modified his essay but did not change it much."[41] Perhaps as a nod to Ellison's battle royal scene in *Invisible Man* (1952), Du Bois ends this first section referring to a speech that illustrates Manuel's limited understanding of race and oppression.

The second stage entails Manuel's early professional career, beginning with his first job as principal in Jerusalem and ending with the Atlanta race riots. As a Booker T. Washington devotee, Manuel believes in compromise and tries to work under the current system, which channels insufficient funds to black schools and trains black students largely for manual labor. But the 1906 riot exposes black vulnerability that is the result of disenfranchisement, plunging Mansart into a crisis of faith in Washington's gradualism: "Mansart now faced for the first time and inexorably the life problem with which he was destined to struggle three-score years and ten and yet never answer to his own satisfaction or that of anyone else: how shall Integrity face Oppression?"[42]

The final stage begins with Manuel trying to move away from the Washington approach and ends as he takes the position of supervisor, but supposedly with a more aggressive attitude to gain more resources for black schools and thus to improve their quality. Faced with the choice of taking this job or taking a better-paying one in the "free" North, Manuel interprets the meaning of "the black flame." "I was freed and yet did not understand until this riot," he tells his children, "this horror of hate and death which swept over us. Now I stand up. I am that Black Flame in which my grandmother believed and on whose blood-stained body she swore."[43] Choosing to stay in the South and to struggle for blacks, he ironically echoes Washington (again like Ellison's protagonist): "Therefore I will burn right here in Atlanta where I have let my buckets down."[44]

Thus the first volume of *The Black Flame* ends suggesting growth toward consciousness, yet signaling the long journey still ahead of Mansart and black America. Du Bois also uses Mansart's linear development as a means for moving freely across historical topics, documenting a daunting list of events between 1876 and 1916. Moving from the Tuskegee Machine to the rise and fall of Populism to Atlanta city politics, for example, Du Bois's narrative voice—almost as though he were presenting fictionalized essays—often subsumes his characters, delivering pertinent information directly to the reader. Quite often, in fact, the exigencies of character and plot development clash with Du Bois's documentary imperative, creating an animating tension across all three volumes.

The second volume of *The Black Flame, Mansart Builds a School* (1959), concerns itself with formal and experiential education as well, and like the first volume it offers Mansart's limited growth as a cautionary tale. Mansart conceives of his new school as a means for blacks to control agricultural production in the South and thus supply white-controlled manufacturing with cotton and other raw materials. In this way, blacks would be better able to secure wealth and some level of political power. As Du Bois widens the protagonist's apperceptive aperture, we see Mansart take interest in the first Pan-African Congress of 1919, pay particular attention to the Bolshevik revolution, and even admit at one point to having read *The Communist Manifesto* with great interest. Still, as he searches for solutions in what he regards as approaches beyond the Washington model, Mansart closes the volume again questioning the effect of the contributions that he has tried to make. Although he has an economic plan, it lacks global context and it fails to examine how capital operates. Walking alone at night, Mansart again reflects on the meaning of the black flame and thus the effect of his efforts. His highest level of political awareness (and thus peace) awaits him in the final volume.

The second volume also allows Mansart's children to bear more metaphoric weight. As second-generation middle-class blacks of the twenties and thirties, they represent the children of New Negroes; as such, their experiences serve to illustrate, among other things, the limitations of class privileges in a color-caste society—limitations that prove fatal for at least one son. And true to his attention to female characters, Du Bois depicts the difficulty of navigating the Scylla and Charybdis of race and gender through the characters of Sojourner and Jean Du Bignon. Both must confront the strictures of gender roles while pursuing their own individuality and creativity.

Finally, as the third volume, *Worlds of Color* (1961), elevates the drama—and Mansart's awareness—to a global plane, Mansart's world tour allows for the connection between domestic and international political conditions so elemental to Du Bois's worldview. Like the young Du Bois, Mansart still "simplifies the Negro Problem as one of education and ethics,"[45] and thus his tour of Europe and Asia helps him to consider the relationship between capital and labor, between Europe and the "world of color."

In fact, Mansart's pointed questioning of John Essex and his unearned wealth—"The black workers who served your grandfather got paid once; their descendants are being paid not for what their fathers did but for what they do now. Why this difference between the pay of the European and the African?"[46]—signals a level of awareness impossible in the first two volumes.

Equally important, Jean Du Bignon's role as guide and caretaker for Mansart reiterates this Du Boisian pattern of women providing instruction for male protagonists. It is Du Bignon who first observes that socialism will inevitably take over the world and provide peace. Faced with the two visions on his deathbed,

Mansart chooses the utopian example that he saw in Russia, in China, and in Vietnam's struggle for independence.

Twenty years before the completion of the trilogy, Du Bois ended *Black Reconstruction in America* on a similar note: "A clear vision of a world without inordinate individual wealth of capital with profit and of income based on work alone," he prophesied, "is the path out, not only for America but for all men."[47] Perhaps carrying forward not so much Marxist dogma, but rather the idealism at the heart of Marxist praxis, Mansart's "redemptive consciousness" makes symbolic Du Bois's parting hope.

Combined, the three volumes of the trilogy offer in three stages for Mansart (and for black America) the possibility of "redemptive consciousness." In the first volume, Mansart must grapple with the limitations of Washingtonianism, its failures to claim political rights for blacks, and its firm investment the southern political economy. In the second volume, Mansart develops a slightly broader perspective and so must confront the limitations of liberalism. Though he understands that blacks must control a greater portion of the political economy, he remains unable to envision an alternative and more just social model. The final volume offers Mansart's last stage, the one in which Mansart gains a fuller materialist perspective on capital and labor, and thus grows toward a utopian vision of global socialism.

As Mansart moves along this bildungsroman trajectory, this notion of growth toward "redemptive consciousness" operates on at least two levels. In one sense, Mansart symbolizes the race's potential to grow intellectually, spiritually, and politically; but beyond Mansart as symbol, the sheer documentary force of the trilogy speaks directly to the edification of the reader. Ultimately readers must interpret the history of their time, and so arrive at a level of political awareness that will aid black communities. In short, Du Bois hopes that "the world of color" will advance global socialism at least in part through the wisdom of his trilogy.

Of course, Du Bois's hope has not come to fruition, which perhaps partially explains the ongoing neglect of the trilogy—partially, but not entirely. To be sure, too, in Du Bois's later writings an encroaching authoritarianism marred his worldview—his defense of Stalin's purges is but one glaring example. But current neglect of late-phase Du Bois is more deeply rooted in contemporary American culture and its ties to the fifties. It is not simply that Du Bois was at odds with the major cultural and political trends of his moment; more to the point, his final phase continues to expose the limitations in the present of cultural and political formations largely shaped in the fifties. Civil rights-style integration into the body politic as such, the hegemony of the autonomous artist and the tradition of art for art's sake, and narrowed liberal versus conservative political and cultural debate all strain for answers to the still-pregnant questions that late-phase Du Bois and *The Black Flame* pose. As Du Bois's withering criticism of "omnivorous turbo-capitalism"[48] and its perpetual search for cheap labor continues to resonate in an age of globalization and free trade, we ignore the trilogy and its implications to our own detriment.

NOTES

1. W.E.B. Du Bois, *The Autobiography of W.E.B. Du Bois: A Soliloquy of Viewing My Life from the Last Decade of Its Century* (New York: International Publishers, 1968), p. 368, and David Levering Lewis, *W.E.B. Du Bois: The Fight for Equality and the American Century, 1919–1963* (New York: Holt, 2000), p. 549.
2. Lewis, *W. E. B. Du Bois: The Fight for Equality in the American Century*, p. 547.
3. Du Bois, *The Autobiography of W. E. B. Du Bois*, p. 349.
4. Herbert Aptheker, "Introduction," in W. E. B. Du Bois, *The Black Flame: A Trilogy*, book 1, *The Ordeal of Mansart* (Millwood, N.Y.: Kraus-Thomson Organization, 1976), p. 6.
5. Lewis, *W. E. B. Du Bois: The Fight for Equality in the American Century*, p. 558.
6. George Hutchinson, *The Harlem Renaissance in Black and White* (Cambridge, Mass.: Harvard University Press, 1995), pp. 29–61, 78–93, and 250–277.
7. Van Wyck Brooks, *Van Wyck Brooks: An Autobiography* (New York: Dutton, 1965), pp. 271–272.
8. Lewis, *W. E. B. Du Bois: The Fight for Equality in the American Century*, p. 545.
9. Lawrence Jackson, *Ralph Ellison: Emergence of Genius* (New York: Wiley, 2002), p. 355.
10. Jackson, *Ralph Ellison*, p. 327.
11. Important to note, too, Baldwin and Ellison in particular came under attack from the literary and political Left—Robert Bone, Irving Howe, *Masses and Mainstream* editors, and the rest—for not writing in a protest tradition. Unfortunately, the Left adopted the same formula as the New Critical Right, insisting that there could be only one tradition. In response, both Ellison and Baldwin declared the right and responsibility of artists to develop their craft and to produce the best art piece possible. Indeed, if Hughes first articulated the position of the African American autonomous artist in "The Negro Artist and the Racial Mountain," the Ellison-Howe debate enshrined the position as the dominant pose of the modern African American writer. See Ralph Ellison's "The World and the Jug," in *Shadow and Act* (New York: Random House, 1964), pp. 107–143.
12. Lewis, *W. E. B. Du Bois: The Fight for Equality in the American Century*, p. 557.
13. W. E. B. Du Bois, *Dusk of Dawn: An Essay toward an Autobiography of a Race Concept* (New York: Harcourt, Brace and World, 1940), p. 39.
14. W. E. B. Du Bois, *Dark Water: Voices from within the Veil* (New York: Harcourt, Brace and Howe, 1920), p. 99.
15. Du Bois, *Dark Water*, p. 142.
16. W. E. B. Du Bois, "The Present Leadership of American Negroes," in *W. E. B. Du Bois: A Reader*, edited by David Levering Lewis (New York: Holt, 1995), p. 357.
17. Du Bois, *The Autobiography of W. E. B. Du Bois*, p. 228.
18. W. E. B. Du Bois, *The Souls of Black Folk* (New York: Penguin Books, 1989), pp. 71–72.
19. Du Bois, *The Autobiography of W. E. B. Du Bois*, p. 228.
20. Du Bois, *The Autobiography of W. E. B. Du Bois*, p. 228.
21. Du Bois, *Dusk of Dawn*, p. 29.
22. Du Bois, *Dark Water*, p. 49.
23. Lewis, *W. E. B. Du Bois: The Fight for Equality in the American Century*, p. 367.
24. W. E. B. Du Bois, "Criteria of Negro Art," in *W. E. B. Du Bois: A Reader*, edited by David Levering Lewis (New York: Holt, 1995), pp. 513–514.
25. Arnold Rampersad, "W. E. B. Du Bois as a Man of Literature," in *Critical Essays on W. E. B. Du Bois*, edited by William L. Andrews (Boston: G. K. Hall, 1985), p. 62.
26. Du Bois, "Criteria of Negro Art," p. 509.
27. W. E. B. Du Bois, *The Quest of the Silver Fleece* (Chicago: A. C. McClurg, 1911), p. 11.
28. Nellie McKay, "W. E. B. Du Bois: The Black Women in His Writings—Selected Fictional and Autobiographical Portraits," in *Critical Essays on W. E. B. Du Bois*, edited by William L. Andrews (Boston: G. K. Hall, 1985), p. 249.
29. Herman Beavers, "Romancing the Body Politic: Du Bois's Propaganda of the Dark World," in *Modern Critical Views: W. E. B. Du Bois*, edited by Harold Bloom (Philadelphia: Chelsea House, 2001), p. 219.

30. Claudia Tate, "Introduction," in W. E. B. Du Bois, *Dark Princess* (Jackson: University Press of Mississippi, 1995), p. viii.
31. David Levering Lewis, *W. E. B. Du Bois: Biography of a Race, 1868–1919* (New York: Holt, 1993), p. 450.
32. Lewis, *W. E. B. Du Bois: The Fight for Equality in the American Century*, p. 448.
33. Rampersad, "W. E. B. Du Bois as a Man of Literature," p. 60.
34. Du Bois, *Dusk of Dawn*, p. 274.
35. Sidney Finkelstein, "W. E. B. Du Bois' Trilogy: A Literary Triumph," in *Critical Essays on W. E. B. Du Bois*, edited by William L. Andrews (Boston: G. K. Hall, 1985), p. 196.
36. W. E. B. Du Bois, *The Ordeal of Mansart* (New York: Mainstream, 1957), p. 316.
37. W. E. B. Du Bois, *Black Reconstruction in America* (New York: Atheneum, 1992), p. 8.
38. Du Bois, *Black Reconstruction in America*, p. 667.
39. Truman Nelson, "Du Bois' Epic of the Negro," *National Guardian*, July 17, 1961, p. 8.
40. Du Bois, *The Ordeal of Mansart*, p. 195.
41. Du Bois, *The Ordeal of Mansart*, p. 195.
42. Du Bois, *The Ordeal of Mansart*, p. 275.
43. Du Bois, *The Ordeal of Mansart*, p. 313.
44. Du Bois, *The Ordeal of Mansart*, p. 314.
45. W. E. B. Du Bois, *Worlds of Color* (New York: Mainstream, 1961), p. 18.
46. Du Bois, *Worlds of Color*, p. 30.
47. Du Bois, *Black Reconstruction in America*, pp. 706–707.
48. Lewis, *W. E. B. Du Bois: The Fight for Equality in the American Century*, p. 570.

William Edward Burghardt Du Bois: A Chronology

Compiled by Henry Louis Gates, Jr. and Terri Hume Oliver

1868	Born William Edward Burghardt Du Bois, 23 February, in Great Barrington, Massachusetts—the only child of Alfred Du Bois and Mary Silvina Burghardt. Mother and child move to family farm owned by Othello Burghardt, Mary Silvina's father, in South Egremont Plain.
1872	Othello Burghardt dies 19 September and family moves back to Great Barrington, where Mary Sylvina finds work as a domestic servant.
1879	Moves with mother to rooms on Railroad Street. Mother suffers stroke, which partially paralyzes her; she continues to work despite her disability.
1883–1885	Writes occasionally for *Springfield Republican*, the most influential newspaper in the region. Reports on local events for the *New York Globe*, a black weekly, and its successor, the *Freeman*.
1884	Graduates from Great Barrington High School. Works as time-keeper on a construction site.
1885	Mother dies 23 March at age 54. A scholarship is arranged by local Congregational churches so Du Bois can attend Fisk University in Nashville. Enters Fisk with sophomore standing. Contracts typhoid and is seriously ill in October; after recovering, resumes studies and becomes editor of the school newspaper, the *Fisk Herald*.
1886–1887	Teaches at a black school near Alexandria, Tennessee, for two summers. Begins singing with the Mozart Society at Fisk.
1888	Receives BA from Fisk. Enters Harvard College as a junior after receiving a Price-Greenleaf grant.
1890	Awarded second prize in Boylston oratorical competition. Receives BA *cum laude* in philosophy on 25 June. Delivers commencement oration on Jefferson Davis, which receives national press attention. Enters Harvard Graduate School in social science.

1891	Awarded MA in history from Harvard. Begins work on doctorate. Presents paper on the suppression of the African slave trade at meeting of American Historical Association in Washington, D.C.
1892	Awarded a Slater Fund grant to study in Germany at Friedrich Wilhelm University in Berlin.
1893	Grant is extended for an additional year.
1894	Denied doctoral degree at Friedrich Wilhelm University due to residency requirements. Denied further aid from Slater Fund; returns to Great Barrington. Receives teaching chair in classics at Wilberforce University in Xenia, Ohio.
1895	Awarded a PhD in history; he is the first black to receive a PhD from Harvard.
1896	Marries Nina Gomer, a student at Wilberforce. His doctoral thesis, *The Suppression of the African Slave-Trade to United States of America, 1638–1870*, is published as the first volume of Harvard's Historical Monograph Series. Hired by the University of Pennsylvania to conduct a sociological study on the black population of Philadelphia's Seventh Ward.
1897	Joins Alexander Crummell and other black intellectuals to found the American Negro Academy, an association dedicated to black scholarly achievement. Appointed professor of history and economics at Atlanta University. Begins editing a series of sociological studies on black life, the *Atlanta University Studies* (1898–1914). First child, Burghardt Comer Du Bois, is born in Great Barrington on 2 October.
1899	*The Philadelphia Negro* is published by the University of Pennsylvania. Burghardt Gomer Du Bois dies on 24 May in Atlanta and is buried in Great Barrington. Publishes articles in *Atlantic Monthly* and *The Independent*.
1900	In July attends first Pan-African Congress in London and is elected secretary. In an address to the congress, he declares that "the problem of the twentieth century is the problem of the color line." Enters an exhibit at Paris Exposition and wins grand prize for his display on black economic development. Daughter Nina Yolande born 21 October in Great Barrington.
1901	Publishes "The Freedman's Bureau" in *Atlantic Monthly*.
1902	Booker T. Washington offers Du Bois a teaching position at Tuskegee Institute, but Du Bois declines.
1903	*The Souls of Black Folk* is published in April. Publishes the essay "The Talented Tenth" in *The Negro Problem*.
1904	Resigns from Washington's Committee of Twelve for the Advancement of the Negro Race due to ideological differences. Publishes "Credo" in *The Independent*.
1905	Holds the first conference of the Niagara Movement and is named general secretary. Founds and edits *The Moon Illustrated Weekly*.

1906	Second meeting of the Niagara Movement. *The Moon* ceases publication. The Atlanta riots, in which white mobs target blacks, occur in September; Du Bois responds by writing his most famous poem, *A Litany of Atlanta*. After the riots Du Bois's wife and daughter move to Great Barrington.
1907	Niagara Movement in disarray due to debt and dissension. Founds and edits *Horizon*, a monthly paper that folds in 1910.
1908	Fourth conference of Niagara Movement; few attend.
1909	The National Negro Committee, an organization dominated by white liberals, is formed (it will later be renamed the National Association for the Advancement of Colored People [NAACP]); Du Bois joins. The fifth and last Niagara Conference is held. *John Brown*, a biography, is published.
1910	Appointed director of publications and research for the NAACP; becomes the only black member of the board of directors. Moves to New York City to found and edit *The Crisis*, the official publication of the NAACP.
1911	Attends Universal Races Conference in London. Publishes his first novel, *The Quest of the Silver Fleece*. Joins the Socialist Party.
1912	Endorses Woodrow Wilson in *The Crisis*. Resigns from Socialist Party.
1913	Writes and presents *The Star of Ethiopia*, a pageant staged to commemorate the fiftieth anniversary of emancipation.
1914	Supports women's suffrage in *The Crisis*. Supports the Allied effort in World War I despite declaring that imperialist rivalries are a cause of the war.
1915	Booker T. Washington dies on 14 November. *The Negro* is published. Protests D. W. Griffith's racist film *The Birth of a Nation*.
1917	Undergoes kidney operations early in the year. Supports the establishment of separate training camps for black officers as the only way to insure black participation in combat.
1918	In his July editorial for *The Crisis*, he publishes "Close Ranks," urging cooperation with white citizens. The War Department offers Du Bois a commission as a captain in the army in an effort to address racial issues, but the offer is withdrawn after controversy. Goes to Europe in December to evaluate the conditions of black troops for the NAACP.
1919	Organizes the first Pan-African Conference in Paris, and is elected executive secretary. Returns to the U.S. in April and writes the editorial "Returning Soldiers," which the U.S. postmaster Albert Burleson tries to suppress; the issue sells 106,000 copies, the most ever for *The Crisis*.
1920	Founds and edits *The Brownies' Book*, a monthly magazine for children. Publishes *Darkwater: Voices from within the Veil*, a collection of essays.

1921	The second Pan-African Conference is held in London, Brussels, and Paris. Du Bois signs group protest against Henry Ford's support of the anti-Semitic forgery, *Protocols of the Elders of Zion*.
1922	Works for passage of the Dyer Anti-Lynching Bill, which is blocked by Senate.
1923	Writes "Back to Africa," an article attacking Garvey for encouraging racial division. Organizes the third Pan-African Conference in London, Paris, and Lisbon; declines to attend Paris session due to disproval of French assimilationists. Receives the Spingarn Medal from the NAACP. Travels to Liberia to represent the United States at the Liberian presidential inauguration.
1924	Publishes *The Gift of Black Folk: The Negroes in the Making of America*.
1925	Contributes "The Negro Mind Reaches Out" to Alain Locke's *The New Negro: An Interpretation*, one of the most influential works of the Harlem Renaissance.
1926	Founds the Krigwa Players, a Harlem theater group. Travels to the Soviet Union to examine life after the Bolshevik Revolution. Praises Soviet achievements in *The Crisis*.
1927	The fourth and last Pan-African Conference is held in New York City.
1928	Daughter Yolande weds the poet Countee Cullen in Harlem; the marriage ends within a year. Du Bois's novel, *Dark Princess, A Romance*, is published.
1929	*The Crisis* faces financial collapse.
1930	Awarded honorary Doctor of Laws degree from Howard University.
1932	Du Bois's daughter Yolande and her second husband, Arnett Williams, have a daughter, Du Bois Williams.
1933	Losing faith in the possibilities of integration, Du Bois begins to publicly examine his position on segregation. Accepts a one-year visiting professorship at Atlanta University. Relinquishes the editorship of *The Crisis* but retains general control of the magazine.
1934	Writes editorials encouraging voluntary segregation and criticizing the integrationist policies of the NAACP. Resigns as editor of *The Crisis* and from the NAACP. Accepts the chairmanship in sociology at Atlanta University. Named the editor in chief of the *Encyclopedia of the Negro*, which is never completed or published.
1935	Publishes the revolutionary historical study, *Black Reconstruction*.
1936	Spends five months in Germany on a grant to study industrial education. Travels through Poland, the Soviet Union, Manchuria, China, and Japan.
1938	Receives honorary Doctor of Laws degree from Atlanta University and honorary Doctor of Letters degree from Fisk.
1939	*Black Folk, Then and Now*, a revised edition of *The Negro* is published.

1940	Publishes his first autobiography, *Dusk of Dawn*. Founds and edits *Phylon*, a quarterly magazine examining black issues. Awarded honorary Doctorate of Humane Letters at Wilberforce.
1941–1942	Proposes and then coordinates the study of southern blacks for black land-grant colleges.
1943	Organizes the First Conference of Negro Land-Grant Colleges at Atlanta University. Informed by Atlanta University that he must retire by 1944, he attempts to have the policy reversed.
1944	Named first black member of the National Institute of Arts and Letters. Despite his protests, he is retired by Atlanta University. Although hesitant to work with Walter White, he rejoins the NAACP as director of special research and moves back to New York. Publishes the essay "My Evolving Program for Negro Freedom" in Rayford Logan's collection *What the Negro Wants*.
1945	Writes a weekly column for the *Chicago Defender*. Serves as consultant, with Mary McLeod Bethune and Walter White, at the San Francisco conference that drafts the United Nations charter; criticizes the charter for failing to oppose colonialism. In October he presides at the Fifth Pan-African Conference in Manchester, England. Nina Du Bois suffers a stroke, which paralyzes her left side. Publishes the first volume of *Encyclopedia of the Negro: Preparatory Volume* with coauthor Guy B. Johnson. Publishes an anti-imperialist analysis of the postwar era, *Color and Democracy: Colonies and Peace*. Resigns from the American Association of University Professors in protest of conferences held in segregated hotels.
1946	Invites leaders of twenty organizations to New York to draft a petition to the United Nations on behalf of African Americans; the appeal becomes an NAACP project.
1947	Edits and writes the introduction to *An Appeal to the World*, a collection of essays sponsored by the NAACP to enlist international support for the fight against racial discrimination in America. At the United Nations, the appeal is supported by the Soviet Union but opposed by the United States. Publishes *The World and Africa*.
1948	Fired from the NAACP after his memorandum critical of Walter White and the NAACP board of directors appears in the *New York Times*. Supports Henry Wallace, the Progressive Party candidate for president. Takes unpaid position as vice chairman (with Paul Robeson) of the Council of African Affairs, an organization listed as "subversive" by the U.S. attorney general. Begins writing for the *National Guardian*.
1949	Helps sponsor and addresses the Cultural and Scientific Conference for World Peace in New York City. Attends the First World Congress of the Defenders of Peace in Paris. Travels to the All-Union Conference of Peace Proponents in Moscow.
1950	Nina Gomer Du Bois dies in Baltimore in July; she is buried in Great Barrington. Elected chairman of the Peace Information

Center, an organization dedicated to the international peace movement and the banning of nuclear weapons. Organization disbands under pressure from the Department of Justice. Du Bois is nominated by the American Labor Party for U.S. senator from New York. Receives 4 percent of the vote statewide, 15 percent in Harlem.

1951 Secretly marries Shirley Graham, aged 45, a writer, teacher, and civil rights activist, on Valentine's Day. Indicted earlier that month as an "unregistered foreign agent" under the McCormick Act: Du Bois, along with four other officers of the Peace Information Center, is alleged to be agents of foreign interests. He suffers the indignity of being handcuffed, searched, and fingerprinted before being released on bail in Washington, D.C. National lecture tours and a fundraising campaign for his defense expenses raise over $35,000. The five-day trial in Washington ends in acquittal.

1952 Publishes *In Battle for Peace*, an account of the trial. The State Department refuses Du Bois a passport on grounds that his foreign travel is not in the national interest. Later, the State Department demands a statement declaring that he is not a Communist Party member; Du Bois refuses. Advocacy of leftwing political positions widens the distance between Du Bois and the black mainstream.

1953 Prints a eulogy for Stalin in *National Guardian*. Reads 23rd Psalm at the funeral of Julius and Ethel Rosenberg, executed as Soviet spies. Awarded International Peace Prize by the World Peace Council.

1954 Surprised by the Supreme Court decision in *Brown v. Topeka Board of Education*, which outlaws public school segregation, Du Bois declares "I have seen the impossible happen."

1955 Refused a U.S. passport to attend the World Youth Festival in Warsaw, Poland.

1956 Supports Reverend Martin Luther King Jr. during the Montgomery bus boycott. Refused a passport in order to lecture in the People's Republic of China.

1957 Publishes *The Ordeal of Mansart*, the first volume of the *Black Flame*, a trilogy of historical novels chronicling black life from Reconstruction to the mid-twentieth century. A bust of Du Bois is unveiled at the Schomburg Collection of the New York Public Library. Refused a passport to attend independence ceremonies in Ghana. His great-grandson Arthur Edward McFarlane II is born.

1958 A celebration for Du Bois's ninetieth birthday is held at the Roosevelt Hotel in New York City; 2,000 people attend. Begins writing *The Autobiography of W. E. B. Du Bois*, drawing largely from earlier work. A Supreme Court ruling allows Du Bois to obtain a passport. His subsequent world tour includes England, France, Belgium, Holland, Czechoslovakia, East Germany, and

	the Soviet Union. He receives an honorary doctorate from Humbolt University in East Berlin, known as Friedrich Wilhelm University when Du Bois attended in 1892–1894.
1959	Meets with Nikita Khrushchev. In Beijing, makes broadcast to Africa over Radio Beijing and meets with Mao Zedong and Zhou Enlai. Awarded the International Lenin Prize. Publishes the second volume of the *Black Flame* trilogy, *Mansart Builds a School*.
1960	Participates in the celebration of Ghana's establishment as a republic. Travels to Nigeria for the inauguration of its first African governor-general.
1961	Du Bois's daughter Yolande dies of a heart attack in March. *Worlds of Color*, the final book in the *Black Flame* trilogy, is published. Du Bois accepts the invitation of Kwame Nkrumah to move to Ghana and direct a revival of the *Encyclopedia Africana* project. Before leaving for Africa, Du Bois applies for membership in the Communist Party.
1962	Travels to China. His autobiography is published in the Soviet Union.
1963	Becomes a citizen of Ghana. Turns ninety-five in February. Dies in Accra, Ghana, on 27 August, on the eve of the civil rights march on Washington. W. E. B. Du Bois is buried in a state funeral in Accra on the 29th.
1968	*The Autobiography of W. E. B. Du Bois* is published in the United States.
1992	Honored by the United States Postal Service with a 29-cent commemorative stamp as part of the Black Heritage Series, and again in 1998, with a 32-cent commemorative stamp.
1999	Du Bois's efforts to produce alternately an encyclopedia of the Negro and of Africa and Africans are realized when *Encarta Africana* is published by Microsoft, and *Africana: The Encyclopedia of the African and African American Experience*, edited by Kwame Anthony Appiah and Henry Louis Gates Jr. is published by Basic Civitas Books. In 2005 a second much-expanded edition of *Africana* is published by Oxford University Press.

Selected Bibliography

WORKS OF W. E. B. DU BOIS

The Suppression of the African Slave-Trade to the United States of America, 1638–1870. New York: Longmans, Green, 1896.
Atlanta University Publications on the Study of Negro Problems. Publications of the Atlanta University Conferences, ed. Du Bois (1898–1913).
The Philadelphia Negro: A Social Study. Boston: Ginn and Company, 1899.
The Souls of Black Folk: Essays and Sketches. Chicago: A. C. McClurg, 1911.
John Brown. Philadelphia: George W. Jacobs, 1909.
The Quest of the Silver Fleece: A Novel. Chicago: A. C. McClurg, 1911.
The Negro. New York: Harcourt, Brace, 1928.
Darkwater: Voices from within the Veil. New York: Harcourt, Brace and Howe, 1920.
The Gift of Black Folk: Negroes in the Making of America. Boston: Stratford, 1924.
Dark Princess: A Romance. New York: Harcourt, Brace, 1928.
Africa—Its Place in Modern History. Girard, Kansas: Haldeman-Julius, 1930.
Africa, Its Geography, People, and Products. Girard, Kansas: Haldeman-Julius, 1930.
Black Reconstruction: An Essay toward a History of the Part Which Black Folk Played in the Attempt to Reconstruct Democracy in America, 1860–1880. New York: Harcourt, Brace, 1935.
Black Folk Then and Now: An Essay in the History and Sociology of the Negro Race. New York: Henry Holt, 1939.
Dusk of Dawn: An Essay toward an Autobiography of a Race Concept. New York: Harcourt, Brace, 1940.
Color and Democracy: Colonies and Peace. New York: Harcourt, Brace, 1945.
Du Bois, W. E. B., and Guy B. Johnson. *Encyclopedia of the Negro, Preparatory Volume with Reference Lists and Reports*. New York: Phelps-Stokes Fund, 1946.
The World and Africa: An Inquiry into the Part Which Africa Has Played in World History. New York: Masses & Mainstream, 1947.
I Take My Stand for Peace. New York: Masses & Mainstream, 1951.
The Ordeal of Mansart. New York: Mainstream, 1957.
In Battle for Peace: The Story of My 83rd Birthday. With Comment by Shirley Graham. New York: Masses & Mainstream, 1952.
Fourty-Two Years of the USSR [sic]. Chicago: Baan Books, 1959.
Worlds of Color. New York: Mainstream, 1961.

An ABC of Color: Selections from over a Half Century of the Writings of W. E. B. Du Bois. Berlin: Seven Seas, 1963.

The Autobiography of W. E. B. Du Bois: A Soliloquy on Viewing My Life from the Last Decade of Its First Century, ed. Herbert Aptheker. New York: International Publishers, 1968.

COLLECTIONS

Aptheker, Herbert, ed. *Creative Writings by W. E. B. Du Bois: A Pageant, Poems, Short Stories, and Playlets*. New York: Kraus-Thomson Organization, 1985.

Aptheker, Herbert, ed. *The Complete Published Works of W. E. B. Du Bois*. 35 vols. Millwood, NY: Kraus-Thomson, 1973.

Aptheker, Herbert, ed. *The Correspondence of W. E. B. Du Bois*. 3 vols. Amherst: University of Massachusetts Press, 1973–1978.

Aptheker, Herbert, ed. *Writings by W. E. B. Du Bois in periodicals Edited by Others*. 4 vols. Millwood, NY: Kraus-Thomson, 1982.

Foner, Philip S., ed. *W. E. B. Du Bois Speaks: Speeches and Addresses 1890–1919*. New York: Pathfinder, 1970.

Huggins, Nathan I., ed. *W. E. B. Du Bois: Writings*. New York: Library of America, 1986.

Lewis, David Levering, ed. *W. E. B. Du Bois: A Reader*. New York: Henry Holt, 1985.

Sundquist, Eric J., ed. *The Oxford W. E. B. Du Bois Reader*. New York: Oxford University Press, 1996.

BIBLIOGRAPHIES

Aphtheker, Herbert. *Annotated Bibliography of the Published Writings of W. E. B. Du Bois*. Millwood, NY: Kraus-Thomson, 1973.

McDonnell, Robert W., and Paul C. Partington. *W. E. B. Du Bois: A Bibliography of Writings About Him*. Whittier, CA: Paul C. Partington Book Publisher, 1989.

Partington, Paul C. *W. E. B. Du Bois: A Bibliography of His Published Writings*. Whittier, CA: Paul C. Partington Book Publisher, 1977.

BIOGRAPHIES

Broderick, Francis L. *W. E. B. Du Bois: A Negro Leader in Time of Crisis*. Stanford: Stanford University Press, 1959.

Du Bois, Shirley Graham. *His Day is Marching On: A Memoir of W. E. B. Du Bois*. Philadelphia: Lippincott, 1971.

Lewis, David Levering. *W. E. B. Du Bois: The Fight for Equality and the American Century, 1919–1963*. New York: Henry Holt, 2000.

Marable, Manning. *W. E. B. Du Bois: Black Radical Democrat*. Boston: Twayne, 1986.

Rudwick, Elliot M. *W. E. B. Du Bois: Propagandist of the Negro Protest*. 1960; reprint. New York: Atheneum, 1968.

CRITICAL WORKS

Appiah, Anthony. "The Uncompleted Argument: Du Bois and the Illusion of Race." *Critical Inquiry* 12 (Autumn 1985): 21–37.

Aptheker, Herbert. *The Literary Legacy of W. E. B. Du Bois*. Whit Plains, NY: Kraus International, 1989.

Ashton, Susanna. "Du Bois's 'Horizon': Documenting Movements of the Color Line." *MELUS* 26.4 (2001): 3–23.

Baker, Houston A., Jr. "The Black Man of Culture: W. E. B. Du bois and *The Souls of Black Folk*." In *Long Black Song*. Charlottesville: University of Virginia Press, 1972.

Balfour, Lawrie. "Representative Women: Slavery, Citizenship, and Feminist Theory in Du Bois's 'Damnation of Women.'" *Hypatia: A Journal of Feminist Philosophy* 20.3 (2005): 127–148.

Bauerlein, Mark. "Booker T. Washington and W. E. B. Du Bois: The Origins of a Bitter Intellectual Battle." *Journal of Blacks in Higher Education* 46 (Winter 2004–2005): 106–114.

Bell, Bernard, Emily Grosholz, and James Stewart, eds. *W. E. B. Du Bois on Race and Culture: Philosophy, Politics, and Poetics*. New York: Routledge, Chapman, and Hall, 1996.

Bhabha, Homi K. "The Black Savant and the *Dark Princess*." *ESQ: A Journal of the American Renaissance* 50.1–3 (2004): 137–155.

Blight, David W. "W. E. B. Du Bois and the Struggle for American Historical Memory." In *History and Memory in African-American Culture*, ed. Genevieve Fabre and Robert O'Meally. New York: Oxford University Press, 1994.

Bremen, Brian A. "Du Bois, Emerson, and the 'Fate' of Black Folk." *American Literary Realism* 24 (Spring 1992): 80–88.

Bruce, Dickson D., Jr. "W. E. B. Du Bois and the Idea of Double Consciousness." *American Literature: A Journal of Literary History, Criticism, and Bibliography* 64.2 (June 1992): 299–309.

Byerman, Keith. *Seizing the Word: History, Art, and the Self in the Work of W. E. B. Du Bois*. Athens: University of Georgia Press, 1994.

Castronovo, Russ. "Beauty along the Color Line: Lynching, Aesthetics and the Crisis." *PMLA: Publications of the Modern Language Association of America* 36.2 (2006): 1443–1159.

Crouch, Stanley, and Playthell Benjamin. *Reconsidering the Souls of Black Folk: Thoughts on the Groundbreaking Classic Work of W. E. B. Du Bois*. Philadelphia: Running Press, 2002.

Early, Gerald, ed. *Lure and Loathing: Essays on Race, Identity, and the Ambivalence of Assimilation*. New York: Allen Lane, 1993.

Fisher, Rebecka Rutledge. "Cultural Artifacts and the Narrative of History: W. E. B. Du Bois and the Exhibiting of Culture at the 1900 Paris Exposition Universelle." *MFS: Modern Fiction Studies* 51.4 (2005): 741–774.

Fontenot, Chester J., Mary Alice Morgan, and Sarah Gardner, eds. *W. E. B. Du Bois and Race*. Macon, Georgia: Mercer University Press, 2001.

Frederickson, George. "The Double Life of W. E. B. Du Bois." *New York Review of Books* 48.2 (February 8, 2001): 34–36.

Frederickson, George. *The Black Image in the White Mind: The Debate on Afro-American Character and Destiny, 1817–1914*. New York: Harper and Row, 1971.

Gabiddon, Shaun L. "W. E. B. Du Bois: Pioneering American Criminologist." *Journal of Black Studies* 31.5 (2001): 581–599.

Gooding-Williams, Robert. "Du Bois's Counter-Sublime." *The Massachusetts Review: A Quarterly of Literature, the Arts and Public Affairs* 35.2 (Summer 1994): 202–224.

Herring, Scott. "Du Bois and the Minstrels." *MELUS* 22 (Summer 1997): 3–18.

Hubbard, Dolan, ed. *The Souls of Black Folk One Hundred Years Later*. Columbia, Missouri: University of Missouri Press, 2003.

Jones, Gavin. "'Whose Line Is It Anyway?' W. E. B. Du Bois and the Language of the Color-Line." In *Race Consciousness: African-American Studies for the New Century*, ed. Judith Jackson Fossett and Jeffrey A. Tucker. New York: New York University Press, 1997.

Judy, Ronald A. T., ed. "Sociology Hesitant: Thinking with W. E. B. Du Bois." Special Issue: *Boundary 2: An International Journal of Literature and Culture* 27.3 (2000).

Juguo, Zhang. *W. E. B. Du Bois and the Quest for the Abolition of the Color Line*. New York: Routledge, 2001.

Kirschke, Amy. "Du Bois, *The Crisis*, and Images of Africa and the Diaspora." In *African Diasporas in the New and Old Worlds: Consciousness and Imagination*, ed. Geneviève Fabre and Benesch Klaus. Amsterdam: Rodopi, 2004. 239–262.

Lemke, Sieglinde. "Transatlantic Relations: The German Du Bois." In *German? American? Literature? New Directions in German-American Studies*, ed. Winfried Fluck and Werner Sollors. New York: Peter Lang, 2002. 207–215.

McCaskill, Barbara, and Caroline Gebhard, eds. and introd. *Post-Bellum, Pre-Harlem: African American Literature and Culture*. New York: New York University Press, 2006.

McKay, Nellie. "W. E. B. Du Bois: The Black Women in His Writings—Selected Fictional and Autobiographical Portraits." In *Critical Essays on W. E. B. Du Bois*, ed. William L. Andrews. Boston: G. K. Hall, 1985.

Meier, August. "The Paradox of W. E. B. Du Bois." In *Negro Thought in America, 1880–1915; Radical Ideologies in the Age of Booker T. Washington*. Ann Arbor: University of Michigan Press, 1963.

Miller, Monica. "W. E. B. Du Bois and the Dandy as Diasporic Race Man." *Callaloo* 26.3 (2003): 738–765.

Mizrunchi, Susan. "Neighbors, Strangers, Corpses: Death and Sympathy in the Early Writings of W. E. B. Du Bois." In *Centuries' Ends, Narrative Means*, ed. Robert Newman. Stanford, CA: Stanford University Press, 1996.

Moses, Wilson Jeremiah. *Creative Conflict in African American Thought: Frederick Douglass, Alexander Crummell, Booker T. Washington, W. E. B. Du Bois, and Marcus Garvey*. Cambridge, England: Cambridge University Press, 2004.

Pauley, Garth E. "W. E. B. Du Bois on Woman Suffrage: A Critical Analysis of His *Crisis* Writings." *Journal of Black Studies* 30.3 (2000): 383–410.

Peterson, Dale. "Notes from the Underworld: Dostoyevsky, Du Bois, and the Discovery of the Ethnic Soul." *Massachusetts Review* 35 (Summer 1994): 225–247.

Posnock, Ross. "The Distinction of Du Bois: Aesthetics, Pragmatism, Politics." *American Literary History* 7 (Fall 1995): 500–524.
Rampersad, Arnold. *The Art and Imagination of W. E. B. Du Bois*. Cambridge, MA: Harvard University Press, 1976.
Rampersad, Arnold, and Deborah E. McDowell, eds. *Slavery and the Literary Imagination: Du Bois's* The Souls of Black Folk. Baltimore: Johns Hopkins University Press, 1989.
Rothberg, Michael. "W. E. B. Du Bois in Warsaw: Holocaust Memory and the Color Line, 1949–1952." *Yale Journal of Criticism* 14.1 (2001): 169–189.
Schneider, Ryan. "Sex and the Race Man: Imagining Interracial Relationships in W. E. B. Du Bois's *Darkwater*." *Arizona Quarterly: A Journal of American Literature, Culture, and Theory* 59.2 (2003): 59–80.
Schrager, Cynthia D. "Both Sides of the Veil: Race, Science, and Mysticism in W. E. B. Du Bois." *American Quarterly* 48 (December 1996): 551–587.
Siemerling, Winfried. "W. E. B. Du Bois, Hegel, and the Staging of Alterity." *Callaloo* 24.1 (2001): 325–333.
Smith, Shawn Michelle. *Photography on the Color Line: W. E. B. Du Bois, Race, and Visual Culture*. Durham: Duke University Press, 2004.
Sundquist, Eric J. "Swing Low: *The Souls of Black Folk*." In *To Wake the Nations*. Cambridge, MA: Harvard University Press, 1993.
Temperley, Howard, Michael B. Katz, and Thomas J. Sugrue. "W. E. B. Du Bois, Race, and the City." *The Times Literary Supplement*. No. 4996 (1999).
"The Study of African American Problems: W. E. B. Du Bois's Agenda, Then and Now." *Annals of the American Academy of Political and Social Science* 568 (March 2000): 1–313.
Warren, Kenneth W. "Troubled Black Humanity in *The Souls of Black Folk* and *The Autobiography of an Ex-Colored Man*." In *The Cambridge Companion to American Realism and Naturalism: Howells to London*, ed. Donald Pizer. Cambridge: Cambridge University Press, 1995.
West, Cornel. "W. E. B. Du Bois: The Jamesian Organic Intellectual." In *The American Evasion of Philosophy: A Genealogy of Pragmatism*. Madison: University of Wisconsin Press, 1989.
Williamson, Joel. *The Crucible of Race: Black-White Relations in the American South Since Emancipation*. New York: Oxford University Press, 1984.
Wolters, Raymond. *Du Bois and His Rivals*. Columbia, Missouri: University of Missouri Press, 2002.
Zamir, Shamoon. *Dark Voices: W. E. B. Du Bois and American Thought, 1888–1903*. Chicago: University of Chicago Press, 1995.
Zamir, Shamoon. "'The Sorrow Songs'/'Song of Myself': Du Bois, the Crisis of Leadership, and Prophetic Imagination." In *The Black Columbiad: Defining Moments in African American Literature and Culture*. Cambridge, MA: Harvard University Press, 1994.
Zwarg, Christina. "Du Bois on Trauma: Psychoanalysis and the Would-Be Black Savant." *Cultural Critique* 51 (2002): 1–39.

The manufacturer's authorised representative in the EU for product safety is Oxford University Press España S.A. of El Parque Empresarial San Fernando de Henares, Avenida de Castilla, 2 - 28830 Madrid (www.oup.es/en or product.safety@oup.com). OUP España S.A. also acts as importer into Spain of products made by the manufacturer.
Printed and bound by CPI Group (UK) Ltd, Croydon, CR0 4YY

20/03/2026
02075336-0015